HISTORY AND SILENCE

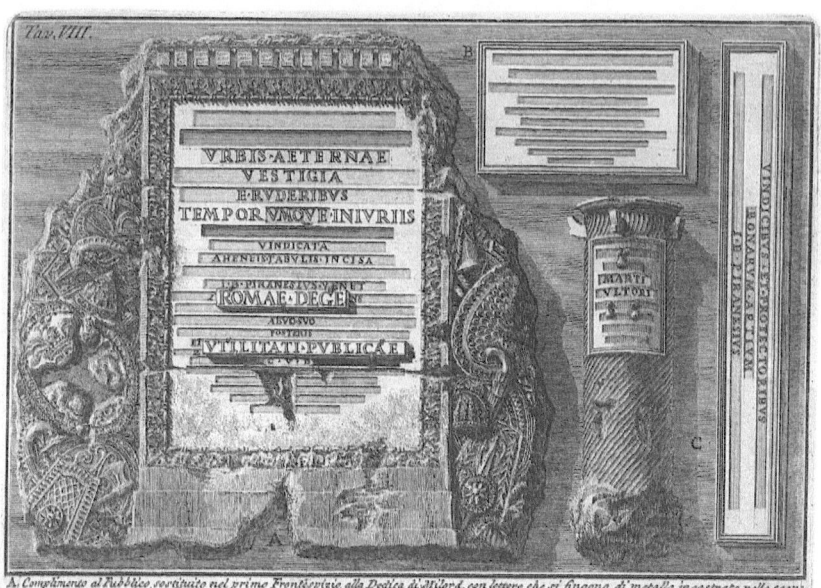

HISTORY AND SILENCE

PURGE AND REHABILITATION

OF MEMORY IN LATE ANTIQUITY

Charles W. Hedrick Jr.

UNIVERSITY OF TEXAS PRESS, AUSTIN

Copyright © 2000 by the University of Texas Press
All rights reserved
Printed in the United States of America
First edition, 2000

Requests for permission to reproduce material from this work should be sent to Permissions, University of Texas Press, P.O. Box 7819, Austin, TX 78713-7819.

∞ The paper used in this book meets the minimum requirements of ANSI/NISO Z39.48-1992 (R1997) (Permanence of Paper).

LIBRARY OF CONGRESS
CATALOGING-IN-PUBLICATION DATA

Hedrick, Charles W., 1956–
History and silence : purge and rehabilitation of memory in late antiquity / by Charles W. Hedrick.
 p.   cm.
Includes bibliographical references and index.
ISBN 978-0-292-71873-9
 1. Inscriptions, Latin—Italy—Rome. 2. Palimpsests—Italy—Rome. 3. Flavianus, Virius Nicomachus, ca. 334–394. 4. Forum of Trajan (Rome, Italy) 5. Memory—Social aspects—Italy—Rome—History. 6. Monuments—Italy—Rome—Conservation and restoration—History. 7. Elite (Social sciences)—Italy—Rome—Historiography. 8. Rome—Politics and government—284–476—Historiography. I. Title.
CN535.H43   2000
937—dc21   99-29835

FRONTIS: Giovanni Battista Piranesi, *Lettere di giustificazione* (1757)

FOR MY FATHER

CONTENTS

List of Illustrations   ix

Preface   xi

Acknowledgments   xxv

CHAPTER 1   A PALIMPSEST   1

CHAPTER 2   *CURSUS* AND CAREER   6

CHAPTER 3   UNSPEAKABLE PAGANISM?   37

CHAPTER 4   REMEMBERING TO FORGET
The *Damnatio Memoriae*   89

CHAPTER 5   SILENCE, TRUTH, AND DEATH
The Commemorative Function of History   131

CHAPTER 6   REHABILITATING THE TEXT
Proofreading and the Past   171

CHAPTER 7   SILENCE AND AUTHORITY
Politics and Rehabilitation   214

APPENDIX   CONCERNING THE TEXT OF *CIL* 6.1783   247

Notes   259

List of Abbreviations   297

Secondary Works Cited   301

General Index   321

Index of Passages Cited   331

LIST OF ILLUSTRATIONS

FRONTIS. Giovanni Battista Piranesi, *Lettere di giustificazione* (1757) tav. 8.
1. *CIL* 6.1783.
2. Simulation and dissimulation.
3. Plan of the imperial fora.

PREFACE

IN 1757 GIOVANNI BATTISTA PIRANESI published the final edition of his collection of etchings of the ruins of ancient Rome, *Le antichità Romane*. The frontispiece to that edition shows a palimpsested inscription: the original letters have been erased and over them a new text, announcing the book to the reader, has been carved. Piranesi explains this unusual illustration and its prominent position at the beginning of the book in great detail in another of his works, a polemic entitled the *Lettere di giustificazione*.[1] An Irish nobleman, James Caulfield, Lord Charlemont, had promised a substantial subvention for the publication of the book, but at the last moment had reneged on his guarantee. The work was already complete, and Piranesi had commemorated Charlemont's name and patronage in inscriptions strategically placed in the various etchings throughout the volume. When Charlemont declined to provide the promised funding, Piranesi went through the engravings of the book, eradicating his onetime patron's name almost everywhere.

The inscription on the frontispiece of *Le antichità Romane* had at first borne a text dedicating the entire work to Charlemont. Piranesi reproduces the unblemished original in his *Lettere di giustificazione*. In eliminating the dedication, Piranesi might have tried to make his modifications unnoticeable: for example, he might have made an entirely new plate; he might have utterly erased the text of the old inscription and incised a new one on the *tabula rasa*. Instead, inspired—as he himself says—by Caracalla's famous erasure of his detested brother Geta's name from the arch of Septimius Severus, Piranesi created on the face of the inscription an obvious erasure, superimposing over it a new inscription. Piranesi is not here attempting to forget the wrong done him by Charlemont, to "put it into the past." To the contrary. Imitating the ancient custom of the Romans, he has created his own *damnatio memoriae* for Charlemont. His purpose is not to anesthetize the public's knowledge of the man, but to make a grand and eloquent gesture of dishonoring: to place a black mark over his name that will last as long as the inscription—or book—will endure. Here Piranesi shows that he has a solid grasp of the basic political principles and goals that "under-write" the ancient Roman *damnatio memoriae*.

The ancient *damnatio memoriae* was a set of more or less formal and traditional strategies for attacking the memory of a dead public enemy. These were in use throughout the period of the republic and empire, from the fifth century B.C. through the sixth century A.D. In broadest outline techniques of the *damnatio memoriae* included the eradication of visual representations of the person, a ban of the name, and a prohibition of the observance of the funeral and mourning. Roman authors of all periods describe the *damnatio memoriae* as an attempt to eradicate memory. Despite such pretensions (as I argue in Chapter 4), the procedure was not invoked with that intent and could not have had that effect. Certainly it may be possible (as some contemporary totalitarian regimes have come close to proving) to obliterate tradition itself, by destroying all trace of the existence of a person or thing. The procedures of the *damnatio memoriae*, however, worked to produce traces of their own operation—ostentatious erasures and noticeable omissions—which confound their apparent purpose. To use a phrase from the Theodosian Code (15.14.9), the *damnatio memoriae* was an "interdict of silence," not one of thought. As such it should be understood as a productive gesture, not as an abstract annihilation. The Roman *damnatio memoriae* worked like Piranesi's: to *dishonor* memory, not to destroy it.

The key to the argument is a consideration of the semantic character of the silences and erasures that are produced by the *damnatio memoriae*. To be sure, such things pretend to be the opposite of signs, the negation of representation—just as the *damnatio memoriae* purports to be the destruction of memory, and not its dishonoring. Nevertheless, it must be recognized that silences and erasures are themselves signs. So much is shown by the mere act of noticing them: what is recognized is always, by virtue of the operation of perception itself, a thing that refers and connotes. The *damnatio memoriae* does not work to negate the evidence of the past, but to produce new signs of it. The silences and erasures are themselves significant, and they tell against the professed purpose of the purge. So, paradoxically, the *damnatio memoriae* works to confirm memory even as it dishonors it.

But Piranesi is also sensitive to other, larger connotations of the *damnatio memoriae*. On the lower part of the inscription, two phrases are shown as engraved on strips of metal, attached over the erasures on the inscription with clamps: *Romae dege-* and *utilitati publicae*. These phrases occur in the original dedication to Charlemont. Piranesi means us to understand that he has cannibalized that dedication for innocuous phrases that can be used in the new dedication. The reuse of these phrases once more calls to mind the earlier inscription and its text.

At the same time, Piranesi is playing here on the relationship between the ancient Roman monumental inscription and the new medium he has used to represent it: the etching. The fragments attached to the stone are shown as strips of metal in order to evoke the plate from which the drawing of the original stone dedication was printed. As the text of the new frontispiece makes explicit, the inscription we see is not actually the stone it appears to be, but the etching of a stone, *aeneis tabulis incisa*. So Piranesi juxtaposes two media that give access to the immortality of historical recollection: the traditional monument, which safeguards memory through its unique and stubborn permanence; and Piranesi's etchings, which now replace and represent the ruinous, fragmentary monuments of Rome. These illustrations can hold out the promise of eternal fame not because any particular book can last as long as a stone inscription, but because the medium of print allows their endless multiplication. Piranesi's etchings are now guaranteeing the survival of the cracked stones of old Rome. And Charlemont, Piranesi suggests, has been excised from both media.

As Piranesi makes so clear in the text of the inscription by which he condemns the memory of his onetime patron, the same logic that underlies the *damnatio memoriae* and rehablilitation also supports the traditional practice of history. This same connection is made in the inscription of rehabilitation. The gestural, dishonoring function of the erasure applied by contemporary political power is only one, structural aspect of defacement. There is also a related, diachronic overtone to the eradication of monuments. The greatest defacer of monuments, the chief destroyer of memory, is time. It is the traditional duty of the historian to oppose this tyrant. So, in the inscription he has carved over his self-imposed erasure, Piranesi says that he has "vindicated the traces of the eternal city from the rubble and the injuries of time" (*urbis aeternae vestigia e ruderibus temporumque iniuriis vindicata*), and the ruinous state of the inscription seconds his sentiment. Time may be the destroyer of the present, but it is also the creator of the past. The damage that it leaves in its wake is the essential indicator of the historicity and authenticity of the document.

The defacement inflicted on an inscription by the *damnatio memoriae* is analogous to the more generalized damage inflicted on everything by time. By virtue of his art and the power of the press Piranesi has the power to put a halt to this deterioration, to give or withhold immortality. Charlemont's shame will be forever recalled in the frontispiece to Piranesi's book, in the marks of the erasure to which Piranesi has condemned him. Many die and vanish in forgetfulness, leaving nothing behind to mark their passing except perhaps some vestige of their erasure from this life—a ruin or a tombstone. Some, though, will survive if their story is told and handed down to posterity. From this point of view, the story of the past can be conceived as a writing over an erasure: history is a rehabilitation.

This book of mine, like Piranesi's, takes its beginning from an inscription. Like Piranesi's, my inscription is a palimpsest, quite literally a text carved over an erasure. That text (*CIL* 6.1783) was carved on a statue base and was dedicated in A.D. 431 at the forum of Trajan in Rome. In that year, a member of one of the most prominent families of the city of Rome, by name Virius Nicomachus Flavianus the younger, achieved one of the supreme offices of the western Roman empire: he was appointed praetorian prefect at the court of Valentinian III. The inscription was erected because of his influence and prestige in that year, in honor of his father, Virius Nicomachus Flavianus the elder, who had died some thirty-seven years earlier, in A.D. 394.

In 394 a usurper named Eugenius led a revolt against the power of the emperor, Theodosius the Great. The causes of this usurpation were, as we might expect, complex. Christians of the period such as Ambrose and Augustine, however, represented the rebellion in exclusively religious terms, as a pagan revolt against Christianity. For them, the chief ideologue of this pagan reaction was one of Eugenius' lieutenants: Virius Nicomachus Flavianus the elder. The younger Flavian was also involved in the usurpation. In 394 he was appointed to the prestigious position of urban prefect (roughly, "mayor") of the city of Rome. Later that year Theodosius defeated the rebels at the battle of the Frigidus. Flavian the elder committed suicide. For his crimes, he and the other leading figures of the rebellion were placed under an "interdict of silence": that is, they suffered a *damnatio memoriae*—a purge, a "condemnation of memory." Evidence of the historical existence of the traitor was destroyed or mutilated; mention of him was regarded as a criminal act. The erasure over which the inscription of 431 is carved may be owing to that decree. Flavian the younger was also disgraced. Although he was not forced to commit suicide, he did have to return the money that his family had received from Eugenius and disavow the prestige of having served as urban prefect. At this time he was also pressured by the emperor to convert to Christianity, and acquiesced.

The period between the condemnation of Flavian the elder in 394 and his rehabilitation in 431 is extraordinarily important in the history of the Roman senatorial class. By the 380's and 390's the conversion of the elite to Christianity had been under way for the better part of a century. Still there remained many prominent and influential individuals who continued to adhere to the old paganism: people like Praetextatus and his wife Paulina, Symmachus, and the elder Flavian. In the aftermath of the usurpation of 394, however, Theodosius insisted that the surviving pagan elite convert. By 431 the Christianization of the senatorial class was essentially complete. These powerful new Christians, however, were products of a prestigious culture, which only recently had been pagan. They were not prepared to disavow their past entirely. At the same time, in their present situation the past could not be accepted without qualification: certain things had to be forgotten.

This forty-year period is vitally important not only for this history of the Roman elite, but also for the general intellectual and cultural history of Europe. The Christianization of the ancient world is one of the major stories in Western history, and the conversion of the Roman senatorial class is only one small part of that story. Nevertheless, the Roman elite can claim its own peculiar importance even within this larger context. As Peter Brown noted some years ago in his classic essay on the subject, it is through the elite that the traditions of old Rome and its high culture survived to be transmitted and transformed from the old pagan world into the new Christian order.[2] Its preservation of tradition in a time of transformation, the juxtaposition of the discontinuity of conversion with the continuity of historical memory, makes the history of the Roman elite interesting and important.

The elder Flavian was a pivotal figure in these developments. In the years immediately following 394, he came to be regarded by some Christians as an irreconcilable and militant foe of Christianity, a blood-fouled addict of sacrifice, an enthusiastic devotee of the unholy arts of prognostication, the moving spirit behind the "last pagan resistance to Christianity": in short, in retrospect he came to exemplify the despised old order in its death throes. For a long time after his condemnation he was unnamed in any source—though as the issue shows, he was not forgotten. Suddenly, in the 430's, he appears as a prominent character in two texts: Macrobius' *Saturnalia* and the inscription of rehabilitation. The rehabilitation alludes to Flavian's life and character in the years before his disgrace. The *Saturnalia* also looks back to these years, to the Rome of the 380's and 390's, the Rome of the last pagan senators.

Macrobius' *Saturnalia* should be regarded as the single most important document of the late antique Roman senatorial class. The text has received a great deal of attention from scholars in recent years. The book is addressed from father to son as a compendium of information that will be useful in life. The information is couched in a series of dialogues, set at the winter festival of the Saturnalia, probably in 383, just before the death of Praetextatus, who is one of the leading characters of the book. The other central figures in the dialogue are, like Praetextatus, eminent Roman political and literary figures and pagans. The best known of these are Symmachus and Flavian the elder. If tedium is an index of harmlessness, then most of the topics of discussion are utterly innocuous: the *Saturnalia* is well known for its interminable discussions of the literary qualities and erudition of Vergil. In some places, however, topics with more troublesome connotations are raised. For example: the nature of augury; the practice of sacrifice; the character of various gods, including the popular pagan deity of late antiquity, the syncretic Sol Invictus.

Above all, the setting and characters of the dialogue are puzzling. Why should the Christian elite of the 430's look especially to their notoriously pagan ancestors of the end of the fourth century for guidance? How are we to understand this representation of the pagan past? What is the significance of a Praetextatus, or a Symmachus, or a Flavian in the Rome of the 430's? Alan Cameron, who has done as much as anyone to improve our understanding of the *Saturnalia*, has represented the dialogue as a completely assimilated view of the end of the fourth century, as a hindsight interpretation in which the leading figures of that period have been absolutely domesticated, a revisionist history that offers nothing to offend their Christian heirs in the 430's.[3] The argument is persuasive in certain respects. After all, one of the chief functions of history (and, for that matter, memory) is assimilation, the choosing out and preservation of what is acceptable in the past for the purposes of the present: from this perspective history can be regarded as a kind of appropriation. But such an interpretation is one-sided. The past may as easily serve to confound as confirm the assimilative purposes of the present. The nonsensical event, the pointless gesture, the inconvenient detail all persist to disturb the dreams of historians in measure with the efforts they spend to reconcile them. In 431 the best and most complete form of assimilation for paganism and for dead pagans such as Flavian and Praetextatus would have been to forget them entirely. As the *damnatio memoriae* of the elder Flavian shows, this strategy of dealing with the past is always available to the present. But, as Flavian's subsequent rehabilitation also gives evidence, utter forgetfulness is not necessarily within our power. What we work to forget sometimes comes back, like the "return of the repressed." In fact, it is important to keep in mind that the very instrument of discontinuity by which the elder Flavian had been eradicated from the past, the *damnatio memoriae,* is itself a highly traditional procedure. Appeal to this method of forgetting is not only evidence for a rupture between the present and the traditions of the past; it is also evidence for a profound continuity of practice, which reaches back deep into the history of pagan Rome.

The *Saturnalia* shows that the past of the Roman elite is not only something to be forgotten or modified according to the needs of the new Christian world; it is also something that resists such appropriation, insists on being recalled. So we should not only ask, with Cameron, in what ways the *Saturnalia* idealizes the pagan past; we should at the same time question why that past is recalled at all. If idealization reconciles past and present, the fact of recollection itself is what unsettles the relation. Idealization would be unnecessary if only it were possible to truly and absolutely forget, to escape the burden of history. So while it is true that the *Saturnalia* is evidence for the assimilation of the past to the circumstances of a new world, it also must be considered as evidence for resistance to those cultural changes. Macrobius' text works to reconcile pagan past and Christian present, but at the same time it reflects the stubborn persistence of that inconvenient past.

In recent years there has sometimes been a tendency to treat the past, as known through memory, tradition, and history, as a mere by-product of present concerns: as present society changes, it remakes the past according to its new needs and demands. There is some truth to this attitude. Still it is important not to overlook the constitutive functions of the past in making the present. The present produces its past, but at the same time it is a product of its past. The processes of remembering and forgetting are not completely subordinate reflections of present social being and transformation. They are the very instruments by which a society makes itself.

In the modern world, present circumstances are conceived in terms of a projected future. What we are depends on where we are going, not where we have been. To the extent that the power of the past is acknowledged at all, it is seen as a burden, as an impediment to progress and self-realization, as something to be overcome. By contrast, traditional societies (and Rome of the fifth century A.D. is by modern standards a very traditional society) look much more to the past for the determination of who and what they are:

hence the ancient prestige of the genre of history.[4] The transformation of the Roman senatorial class in the early fifth century is not just reflected in its changing attitudes toward the past; it is actually accomplished through the modification of tradition. The *Saturnalia* is in part the manifestation of a preexisting problem that the Roman elite faced in the mid-fifth century: the reconciliation of its pagan past and its Christian present. At the same time, though, it is an act of self-definition that inscribes and perpetuates those contradictions as a part of the character of the elite. The protreptic proem to the work, for example, is addressed to the author's son: the young man is expected to internalize the conflicted memory of his class.

The problem of the interaction of present and past through the mediation of remembering and forgetting is central to any appreciation of the character and function of Macrobius' *Saturnalia*. The only comparable text is the inscription rehabilitating the elder Flavian—and, unlike the *Saturnalia,* it has received very little serious attention since its publication by De Rossi in 1849. This inscription raises the same problems as Macrobius, and more, but in a much more provocative fashion. The text presents itself as a rehabilitation, and its central and clearly stated goal is to restore the memory and honor of the elder Flavian from the disgrace that had befallen him, to reverse the posthumous *damnatio memoriae* imposed on him and his family. The function of the rehabilitation is very like that of a history; in fact, the text explicitly compares the two. So the inscription immediately poses the most basic and profound historiographical problems: What is the motivation for recollection and speech? What is the relationship between the figuration of silence (as produced by the *damnatio memoriae* or, in a larger way, by time) and realistic discourse (e.g., the rehabilitation or, more generally, historical representation)? Between representation and memory? Between remembering and forgetting?

Such problems are crucial for the history of the period, when the elite is struggling to remake itself and deciding what of its past should be remembered and what left to oblivion. If the inscription rehabilitating Flavian is concerned with the elementary problems involved in the practice of history, it is because the relationship of the Roman elite to its past had become problematic by the 430's. By talking about history and rehabilitation and the correction of texts, the rehabilitation suggests ways by which present and past—which are conceived as being more or less at odds—can be reconciled; it then proceeds to do precisely that in the case of the elder Flavian.

There is more at issue in the rehabilitation of the elder Flavian than just the commemoration of one individual and the restoration of the honor of his particular family. Because of his posthumous notoriety and his imagined role in drawing the end to an era, Flavian has a wider significance. He represents his generation and its culture as manifested in a repertoire of ideologically connected activities: not only its religious attitudes but its political activities, its reputation for literary and historical erudition, its interest in the traditions of old Rome, even its habit of proofreading and autographing manuscripts—in short, all of the facets of cultural life that are emphasized in the dialogues of the *Saturnalia*.

The ideological coherence of literary activity with the broader political, cultural, and religious attitudes of pagans in late antiquity has lately become controversial. Some thirty years ago the opinion of Herbert Bloch dominated the field, and it was common to imagine that the elite pagan culture of the late fourth century was unified; notably, Bloch felt that the literary output of the period was produced as part of a general program of pagan polemic.[5] Since the 1970's, largely as a result of some vigorous polemics by Alan Cameron, it has become equally common to maintain that political activity and literary production and religious allegiance have nothing to do with one another in late antique pagan circles.[6] Cameron's arguments have been influential, and increasingly modern scholars have come to treat the culture as fragmented, one area of behavior sealed off from the next. In particular, it is the trend today to isolate the paganism of the late Roman senatorial class, to view it as a zone of behavior quarantined from politics and literary culture.

The historiography of late antiquity here is marching counter to trends in the field at large. In broad institutional terms, the writing and teaching of history has moved from a predominantly political approach, to a social approach in the 1970's, to the cultural history of the 1980's and 1990's, which insists on the significance and political complicity (in a very broad sense) of a very wide array of cultural phenomena.[7] Cameron certainly has registered many telling points, and I would not propose a crude or uncritical return to Bloch's position. Nevertheless, the idea that the various cultural activities of the late antique senatorial class have nothing to do with one another seems at first glance highly unlikely and, from a contemporary general historical perspective, perverse. Furthermore, leaving aside such general considerations, the argument is unsustainable from an empirical point of view. As I will show, in the particular case of the inscription rehabilitating Flavian, all of these areas—with the highly significant exception of religion—are explicitly linked in such a way as to leave no doubt of the fact of their mutual coherence. The prestige of these activities is emphasized and perpetuated by these texts. The apparent absence of religion altogether from the rehabilitation is notable, and marks a radical ideological change from the late fourth century. At the same time, this silence shows how the techniques of remembering and forgetting are used simultaneously to create and bridge the gap between the 430's and the 390's.[8]

The inscription recording Flavian's rehabilitation, then, raises very basic historiographical problems. At the same time it suggests the implication of these problems in the profound social and cultural transformation of the late antique Roman senatorial class. The period and events with which the inscription deals are crucial for an understanding of the end of the ancient world and the beginning of the Middle Ages, and their interpretation is vigorously contested. Given the complexity of my theme and the variety of scholarly interpretation and controversy that has accumulated around every aspect of the material, it may be helpful if I summarize here how the evidence is presented and the way in which the argument develops in the body of this book.

I begin (Chapter 1) with a presentation of the text of the rehabilitation, a translation, and a history of the text's discovery and editing. Parts of the text are quite difficult to read, and the decipherment of some sections is problematic. Due attention must be given to the material aspects of the text for their own sake, for here the physical character of the text mirrors its content; as will become apparent (especially in Chapter 7) the connotations of medium and content complement and sometimes even undermine each other.

I continue with my general exposition of the background to the rehabilitation in Chapter 2. There I focus on the political careers provided in the inscription for the individuals mentioned: the elder Flavian, Flavian the younger, and Appius Nicomachus Dexter. The list of offices provided as part of the rehabilitation constitutes one of the chief sources for the biographies of these men and for the political events that led up to and issued from Flavian's disgrace and rehabilitation. When Flavian was condemned, his career was eradicated; so too were certain parts of his son's career. As the text of the rehabilitation makes clear, the careers as reported in this inscription are by this act restored. So these lists are not just representations of offices held, but edited and modified re-representations. They consequently have to be scrutinized not just as evidence for "what really happened" in the careers of Flavian and his son, but also as as evidence for the nature of the rehabilitation.

The four central chapters of the book (3 through 6) deal with the historiographical issues raised by the inscription and with their relation to the cultural, social, and political problems that the Roman elite faced in 431. The text is explicitly a rehabilitation, and it deals with that function and with the *damnatio memoriae* in literal and relatively unambiguous language. On the other hand, it also describes its activity metaphorically: first as an act of formal, literary historical commemoration, then again as if it were a correction made to a corrupt manuscript. In all of these ideas there is at once a sense of obligation and duty to Flavian, and a sense of being at odds with him. While he must be recalled, this memory of him must simultaneously be sanitized. These attitudes take us to the central theme of the present book: the ambivalence of the Roman senatorial class toward their own past in the 430's. These men are unable or unwilling to disavow their ancestors, but they are also unwilling or unable to return to paganism. Their solution is to make a conscious effort to remember selectively and to forget selectively—and this solution is epitomized in the very action of the rehabilitation of the elder Flavian.

The text of the rehabilitation makes no discernible reference to Flavian's religious beliefs (though there is a subtle allusion to Flavian's paganism in the material circumstances of the erection of the monument: see Chapter 7). In Chapter 3 I rehearse the evidence for paganism among the late antique elite of the city of Rome and for Flavian's religious beliefs, and I discuss the significance of the absence of any allusion to the subject in the rehabilitation. Whether or not Eugenius' usurpation was motivated by religion, whether or not Flavian really was a pagan activist, after his death Christian authors made sure that he was remembered in this light. Here, then, I open the question of the survival and destruction of paganism in the medieval world, and begin to discuss the productive relationship between remembering and forgetting.

In Chapter 4 I provide a description and an analysis of the ancient *damnatio memoriae,* relating them to the particular case of the elder Flavian. The ancient Romans never attempted to utterly eradicate all trace of an individual. The *damnatio memoriae* left signs to mark its implementation: silences, significant omissions, gaps and erasures. Such signs pose as the negation of representation; at the same time, however, they call attention to what they conceal, and undermine their own express purpose. So there is a tension implicit in the *damnatio memoriae,* between its apparent purpose, which is to destroy memory, and the effects of its implementation, which work in a backhanded way to confirm memory.

The inscription of rehabilitation begins with an allusion to Roman historiography, and, as the text later emphasizes, Flavian himself was an historian. In Chapter 5 I explore the logic of this equation of political rehabilitation and the practice of history. At the same time, I try to situate this idea within the larger tradition of Roman history-writing that it invokes, taking Tacitus as an example both because of his eloquence as an exemplar of the tradition and because of his appropriateness to the special context of Flavian's inscription of rehabilitation. The notion that history's function is chiefly commemorative, that the historian's duty is to vindicate the evanescent past by lending it a voice and giving it representation, is not restricted to ancient Rome. It is typical of traditional historiography generally, and it remains vigorous in modern historiography as well. As Tacitus says in the last line of his *Agricola,* "Forgetfulness has buried many of the ancients, as though they had neither reputation nor quality. Agricola will outlive death as his story is told and handed down to posterity" (*Agr.* 46). Everyone ends in death, but through history some may survive. So the representation of the past can be conceived as a writing inscribed over the erasures of time.

The themes of rehabilitation and historiography are continued by yet another metaphor. The inscription suggests that Flavian's restoration and the writing of the past are both like the correction (*emendatio*) of manuscripts. Many wealthy Romans of the late fourth and fifth centuries A.D. are known to have corrected manuscripts: their names are known from subscriptions, autographs written at the ends of various manuscripts, which attest that they have read (*legi*) and corrected (*emendavi*) the book. These autographs were preserved in the medieval manuscript tradition, copied along with the book in which they were entered. Flavian the younger and Nicomachus Dexter, both of whom appear in the text of the rehabilitation, are also known from a famous set of subscriptions to the text of the Augustan historian Livy. Flavian the elder was a historian as well, a fact that is emphasized in his rehabilitation. So, to elaborate the comparisons being made: the rehabilitation of a dead historian is like the composition of a history as it is like the correction of the manuscript of a historian.

In Chapter 6 I work through the implications of this metaphor, trying especially to draw out the broader cultural implications of the techniques of the correction of manuscripts (*emendatio*) for the late antique Roman elite, as they can be reconstructed from the inscription rehabilitating Flavian and from other sources. The topic is controversial. Many years ago Herbert Bloch suggested that the correction of manuscripts was part of a large political project of historical conservation undertaken by certain pagan Roman senators in late antiquity. Recently Alan Cameron has argued energetically that the process is culturally unimportant, merely a mechanical, reflexive by-product of the act of reading.[9] Bloch's position is extreme and does not do justice to the full range of known subscriptions, and I would not defend his specific conclusions. At a very general level, however, his position is preferable to that of Cameron. The correction of manuscripts in this period is more than just an ideologically neutral, mechanical procedure.

The leading qualities of this text are ambivalence and ambiguity: the mixed feelings of the new Christian elite when confronted with the pagan past of their class. To understand this text it is necessary to look at the multiple interpretations to which it is susceptible, and not read them out. Traditionally, historians and critics have taken *the* meaning of a text to be what its author intended. In the rehabilitation, the traditional appeals to authorship and authorial motivation as a control on meaning are not very helpful, because the text seems to be saying contradictory things. The problem is further complicated because the text is obsessed with its own motivation and authority—or, rather, with their dissimulation. In Chapter 7 I look carefully both at the construction of the narrator and at motivation in the rehabilitation. The rehabilitation presents the emperors as its nominal authors, as is customary. On closer examination, the situation is more complicated. Not only is the author of the text uncertain, but the representation of the author in the text is ambiguous. The narrator of the rehabilitation attempts to disclaim his authority. He manages this feat in the same way that historians and philologists have traditionally done: by presenting the substance of the text as a re-creation, a restoration, rather than as an original composition.

Others were involved in the erection of the inscription. Texts are more than collections of abstract words; they are also documents, artifacts that communicate in other ways as well. The rehabilitation is not just a text: it is an inscription, carved on a statue base, which has been once erased. The whole stood on display in a prominent position at the heart of the late antique city. In sum, it is a monument, and as such its documentary, material qualities are too insistent to ignore. These qualities are chiefly associated with the physical uniqueness and permanence of the object, and above all with the damage it suffers through time. In Chapter 7 I discuss the ways in which the monumental medium reflects the meaning of the text—and contradicts it. The procedures of the *damnatio memoriae* and its reversal, the rehabilitation, developed along with Roman "epigraphical culture"; the meaning of these practices is deeply implicated in the symbolism of the monumental inscription. So, for example, the text is a palimpsest, and the connotations of that physical fact echo certain points that are made in the text of the inscription. Likewise the circumstances of the dedication of the inscription, the time and place at which it was erected, even the casual damage it has suffered since its erection, confirm the concerns of the text, even while signaling certain omissions within it.

To couple "high theory" and historiography with a close philological and historical examination of a documentary text so pedestrian and obscure is an unusual project. The fruitfulness of the approach can be seen in the results it yields. Keeping in mind the mixed audience I hope the book will attract, I have tried to write in a way that will be accessible to everyone, keeping the theoretical discussion as clear as possible and free of jargon, marking off technical philological and historical discussions clearly so that they can be skipped or skimmed easily, and translating all Latin.

I finished most of the writing of this book at the beginning of 1998, and I have included only a few references to works I encountered later.

ACKNOWLEDGMENTS

THE BEST THING ABOUT PUBLISHING a book is that it provides an opportunity to acknowledge publicly the debts that have been incurred in writing it. I first began working on the inscription rehabilitating Virius Nicomachus Flavianus more than a decade ago in a seminar on Roman epigraphy with R. E. A. Palmer at the University of Pennsylvania. He is responsible for much of what I know about epigraphy, and he deserves a share of the credit for whatever is good in this book. He should also be vindicated from responsibility for anything that is not up to his standards.

I spend a great deal of time in this book disagreeing with Alan Cameron. I would regret our disagreements if they had not been so pleasurable and educational for me. Here I would like to thank him for his help. He read the manuscript and gave me supportive criticisms that saved me from many errors. He also let me see a manuscript draft of his forthcoming book, *The Last Pagans of Rome*. He is witty, erudite, engagingly polemical, and intellectually generous: an exemplary scholar.

My thanks to Josh Ober, Adrienne Mayor, Ian Morris, and Cathy St. John for encouragement and all sorts of aid and comfort when I needed it. Jenny Lynn criticized the manuscript, helped me proofread it, and gave emotional support. My parents and sisters have sustained me, as always. My son Chaz has been inspirational. My daughter Meg arrived just in time to be acknowledged.

In the summer of 1991 I received a travel grant from the American Philosophical Society, which made it possible for me to spend the summer in Rome, editing the inscription and familiarizing myself with Roman topography "on the ground." Various scholars, above all Silvio Panciera, helped me locate the inscription and get extended access to it.

In the fall of 1994 I gave a series of lectures for the Program in the Ancient World at Princeton University. In one of these I summarized my interpretation of this late antique Roman inscription. Then and later I received much helpful advice from various members of the community of scholars there: Ted Champlin, Jim Luce, Christian Wildberg, and Froma Zeitlin were especially helpful.

I have given outlines of some of the arguments in this book to various audiences around the country. Their reactions have helped refine and modify my views. I single out comments made at lectures at the University of Texas, Austin, and at Stanford University as being particularly helpful.

Many have read the manuscript in part or in whole and have criticized it, sometimes gently, sometimes ferociously. I am appreciative of their time and expertise, and I have always given their suggestions serious consideration—even when I have not adopted them. My gratitude to T. D. Barnes, Peter Brown, Hal Drake, Peter Euben, David Hoy, Bob Kaster, Peter Kenez, Adrienne Mayor, Ron Mellor, Ian Morris, Josh Ober, Jim O'Donnell, and Hayden White.

Countless others have listened to me rant about Flavian and his rehabilitation. Some have responded with interest and to my profit, among them: Harry Berger, Norman Brown, Lowell Edmunds, Arch Getty, David Halperin, David Konstan, Jack Peradotto, and James Packer.

I owe thanks to my colleagues in Classics at UC Santa Cruz as well, as friendly and stimulating a group as I could hope to work with: Karen Bassi, Mary Kay Gamel, John Lynch, Gary Miles, and Dan Selden.

This work was assisted by a grant from the University of California.

In the course of writing this book it has become increasingly clear to me that it is for my father: a token of love and admiration.

HISTORY AND SILENCE

ILLUS. I. *CIL* 6.1783. Courtesy of Silvio Panciera.

CHAPTER 1

A PALIMPSEST

IN A.D. 431 A STATUE was erected in the Forum of Trajan in honor of an eminent Roman of the past, Virius Nicomachus Flavianus. The base of the statue has survived: it is about a meter and a half tall and three-quarters of a meter wide, and although the back of the base has been cut away, more than half a meter of its depth is preserved. An inscription is carved on the front of the base, recessed within a frame. (For the history of the inscription, with detailed description and comments on the text, known as *CIL* 6.1783, see the Appendix.) The field of this text measures about a meter high by more than half a meter wide; it shows signs of an earlier erasure. The lettering is very worn and is now in places barely legible; it has formal affinities with bookhands of the period. The inscription contains lists of the offices held by Flavian and his son and an imperial letter, written to the Roman senate in the names of the emperors of the western and eastern halves of the empire, Valentinian III and Theodosius II. The prose style is typical of bureaucratic texts of the later Roman empire: effusive and convoluted. In its practices of orthography and abbreviation the letter is comparable to contemporary juristic texts. (See Illus. 1.)

By this imperial letter Flavian was formally rehabilitated from a disgrace that he had incurred some forty years before, in the reign of Theodosius I. Flavian had suffered a *damnatio memoriae:* the record of his existence had been purged, statues and inscriptions destroyed; his family had not even been permitted to mourn him. The letter does not specify the reasons for his disgrace, but Flavian was prominent enough that we are well informed from other sources. He had been a leading figure in the usurpation of Eugenius in 394, a rebellion against imperial power that some ancient authors and modern scholars have preferred to see strictly in religious terms as the abortive "last revolt of paganism against Christianity."[1] The translation and text follow; the translation below and on page 4, the text on pages 3 and 5.

> To Nicomachus Flavianus, consular of Sicily, vicar of Africa, quaestor at the court of the blessed Theodosius, twice praetorian prefect of Italy, Illyricum, and Africa, because of his worth and prestige in the senate and as a judge. The statue was restored in honor of his son, Nicomachus Flavianus, consular of Campania, proconsul of Asia, frequently urban prefect, incumbent praetorian prefect of Italy, Illyricum, and Africa.
>
> The emperors Flavius Theodosius and Flavius Placidus Valentinianus, ever August, greet their senate:
>
> To defend against the pitfalls of mankind's lot the dignity of men renowned and eminent in the state[2] when corrupted to some extent by interpolations[3] and to recall the recollection of a deceased man to eternal fame may be regarded as a correction, so to speak,[4] of his fate, which is considered as a preliminary judgment and the greatest supplement (?) of a man's worth.[5] Senators, on this noble and auspicious occasion you join us by recognizing at last that, whatever we accomplish in restoration of the glorious [?] and the most reverend remembrance we all cherish of the elder Flavian, we do honor to our blessed grandfather if we recall to the monuments and inscriptions of his worth the man whom our grandfather desired to survive for us and be spared for you—many of you remember his words before you—so that you may realize that whatever Flavian suffered from underhanded insinuations was far from the wish of that prince. It was the kindness that the emperor showered upon him and tendered even to his *Annals*[6] (he wanted his quaestor and prefect to dedicate them to him) which excited the jealousy of scoundrels. Now if we have given sufficient evidence of our filial devotion, hear another reason: that we are fortified by your feelings for Flavian and by the judgments of all the provinces, for whose benefit the funds of the state still quite wealthy were either preserved or even increased, and produced such esteem with us as well, that what we do today, we know, has been in your hearts and minds and far from any interruption of intervening forgetfulness. For this very reason, senators, above all do you protect his memory no less than you do our persons, so that not undeservedly do we thank your forbearance lest we seem to have undertaken any part of the rehabilitation prompted rather than of our own accord, when furthermore even the very honor of

Nicomacho Flaviano, cons(ulari) Sīcil(iae), vicār(io) Afrīc(ae), quāest(ori) aulae
divi Theodosi, praef(ecto) prāet(orio) Ītal(iae) Illyr(ici) et Afric(ae) iterum,
virtutis auctoritatisq(ue) senatoriae et iudiciariae ergo
reddita in honorem filii Nicomachi Flaviani, cōns(ularis) Cāmp(aniae),
5 procōns(ulis) Asiae, prāef(ecti) urbi sa⟨e⟩pius, nunc prāef(ecti) prāet(orio)
Italiae Illyrici et Africae.
Imperatores Caess(ares) Fl(avius) Theodosius et Fl(avius) Placidus Valentinianus
semper Augg(usti) senatui suo salutem.
clarorum adq(ue) inlustrium in r̄ep(ublica) virorum adversum casus condicionis
10 humanae interpolatum aliquatenus adserere honorem et memoriam
defuncti in lucem aet[ernam] revocare emendatio quaedam eius sortis
videtur, quae praeiudic̣[ium sum]mumq(ue) [supple]mentụm virtutum
    exsistimatur.
bono nobiscum, p̄(atres) c̄(onscripti), [faustoq(ue) o]min⟨e⟩ ịṇṭelligitis profecto
    quidquid in resti-
tutionem pr[.]ṇ[..]inis inlustris et sanctissimae aput omnes recor-
15 dationis Flaviani seniọ[ri]s adimus, divi avi nostri venerationem esse,
si eum quem vivere nobis servariq(ue) vobis — quae verba aput vos fuisse
pleriq(ue) meministis — optavit, sic in monumenta virtutum suarum titulosq(ue)
    revo-
cemus ut quidquid in istum caeca insimulatione commissum est, procul ab eius
principis voto fuisse iudicetis; cuius in eum effusa benevolentia et usq(ue) ad an-
20 nalium quos consecrari sibi a quaestore et praefecto suo voluit, provecta
excitavit livorem inproborum. nunc si aput vos abunde causas piaetatis
adstruximus, accipite aliud: quod de vestris in illum sensib(us) et provinciar(um)
omnium iudiciis muniamur, quib(us) per illum locupletioris adhuc rei p̄(ublicae)
bona vel adservata vel etiam aucta tantum et aput nos reverentiae contule-
25 runt ut quod hodie facimus in pectorib(us) et sensib(us) vestris absq(ue) interpellatione ulla mediae oblivionis fuisse noverimus. ex quo quidem ipso non min[us]
memoriae illius quam nobis, p̄(atres) c̄(onscripti), supra omnia praestitis, ut non
    inmerit[o]
patientiae vestrae gratias agamus, ne quid erga restitutionem honoris eius
admoniti potius quam sponte fecisse videamur. cum alioqui ipse etiam de institu-
30 tione illius probatus saepe nobis parentibusq(ue) nostris Flaviani filiụ[s]

the son of Flavian, which has often been found true both by us and by our relatives in accordance with his father's rearing, is half complete even when crowned by the praetorian prefecture which he daily increases by his prudence and industry, and may be thought to have been betrayed if he is not absolved at last of the debt of duty owed the dead by his whole house and family.

Accordingly, rejoice with us, senators, in an excellent work of our reign, as you review it with us, and approve the restoration of the remembrance of the prestige of that senator both to you and to the country: in his company your senatorial dignity has been increased and through his descendants you continue to thrive in our esteem.

I, Appius Nicomachus Dexter, senator and former urban prefect, supervised the erection of the statue to the best of grandparents.

On the Left Side:

Dedicated on the Ides of September, in the consulship of the eminent Bassus and Antiochus.

honor semiplenus etiam sub praefecturae praetorianae apice, quem provide̞[ntia]
et industria sua cottidie auget, delatus exsistimetur nisi integer tandem et
    abs[olutus]
[r]eligiosi muneris debito totius domus eius familiaeq(ue) sit. gaudete ergo
    nob[iscum]
p̄(atres) c̄(onscripti), optimo imperii nostri opere, ut nobiscum recognoscitis et
    redditam vobis e[t]
35 *patriae senatoris eius memoriam et dignitatem probate, cuius consorti̞[o]*
clariores fuistis et in posteris eius eadem aput nos reverentia vigetis.
Appius Nicomachus Dexter, v̄(ir) c̄(larissimus), ex pr̄aef(ecto) ur̄b(i), avo optim[o]
statuendam curavi.

In Latere Sinistro:

dedicata id[ibus] Sept(em)b(ribus)
[Bas]so et Antiocho, v̄v̄(iris) c̄c̄(larissimis), conss(ulibus)

CHAPTER 2

CURSUS AND CAREER

THE INSCRIPTION of rehabilitation begins, as almost all Roman honorific inscriptions do, with a formulaic prescript which provides a dedicatory statement, reasons for the dedication, and an account of the career of the person honored, in Latin a *cursus honorum*. In this chapter I will use the word *cursus* (pl. *cursus*) to describe such a specific, selective account. I will use the English word "career" to refer to the general sum of honors and offices actually held, so far as they can be known. The *cursus* is a selective statement in a particular historical context. The "career" is compiled by looking at the total of all *cursus;* it is more complete, but it is also divorced from the historical context.

This rehabilitation honors two individuals. Its preamble includes the *cursus* of both Flavian and his son. A third member of the family, Appius Nicomachus Dexter, is mentioned after the end of the imperial letter. Consideration of these *cursus* will be useful for the general historical and political background they provide. In addition, however, the display of these *cursus* is central to the function of the rehabilitation, and poses important problems of internal consistency, of omission and inclusion—all particular manifestations of the more general difficulties created by the *damnatio memoriae* and subsequent rehabilitation of the elder Flavian.

The interpretation of these *cursus* is complicated. The inscription has been revised: so much is stated in its preamble. Consequently the *cursus* provide not so much an account of the lives of Flavian the elder and Flavian the younger as a restoration of an earlier account of those lives. In considering the careers every detail becomes subject to doubt. Are the various *cursus* of these individuals complete and accurate? Do they provide lists of all offices actually held, or only a list of the offices regarded as legitimate after the rehabilitation? Was the rehabilitation thoroughgoing, or are certain aspects of the careers still suppressed?

In this chapter I will provide a general account of the careers of the elder Flavian, his son, and Dexter, and I will survey the controversies they have provoked. While I hope this account is clear and even interesting, I have not been concerned to simplify and solve the difficulties in these careers or to iron out the scholarly controversies; to the contrary, I have attempted to emphasize them to the extent possible. In evaluating the rehabilitation, it is not so important to resolve ambiguities and omissions as it is to identify them and understand their motivation. Here it is the problem that is important, not the solution.

The *cursus* that are presented in the rehabilitation insist on their own literary character in unusually emphatic ways. This literary character is made obvious because they are represented as revisions. They are not imagined as accounts of the "real lives" of Flavian and his son; instead, they are conceived as altered, corrected citations of other texts. Consequently, they resist treatment as straightforward descriptions of reality, and they insistently raise fascinating questions of addition, omission, and implication; issues of representation and rhetoric.

THE IDEA OF THE *CURSUS*

The *cursus honorum* is severely economical and formulaic: a list, an ordered juxtaposition of details. As a rule, the *cursus* will be organized either in ascending or descending order: it will proceed chronologically, from less important to more important offices, or in the reverse order.[1] The offices of both the elder Flavian and his son are listed in ascending order.

Most studies of this inscription have concentrated on the two *cursus* and have neglected the imperial letter. Since 1970 there have been no fewer than six studies of chronological problems in the *cursus* of the elder Flavian, and virtually nothing on any other aspect of the inscription.[2] This pattern is significant. Roman epigraphers have always given particular attention to the *cursus,* and for very practical reasons.[3] The *cursus honorum* is a common feature of Roman inscriptions; in fact, many inscriptions consist of little but a *cursus*. These provide a wealth of information about general administration, specific magistracies, and individual biography.[4] Their content and organization is formulaic and regular, so they invite systematic comparison with those found in other inscriptions: it is not only possible but reasonable, for instance, to speak of "the typical *cursus*" of a senator or equestrian under Augustus, or in the late empire. Furthermore, the careers of important individuals will frequently be attested on more than one inscription, providing the opportunity to compare and verify, to evaluate the development of the career, or to consider the emphasis given particular offices in certain contexts.

Another reason for the fixation of epigraphers on the *cursus* is doubtless the dominance of the "Symean" approach to Roman epigraphy and history in the latter half of the twentieth century.[5] In *The Roman Revolution* and elsewhere Ronald Syme argued that it is a universal principle that elites exist within societies, dominating and supporting them: "In all ages, whatever the form and name of government, be it monarchy, republic or democracy, an oligarchy lurks behind the facade."[6] The history of Rome (and, for that matter, of any other society) consequently can be regarded as the story of the various formations of such oligarchies and their struggles for power: "The composition of the oligarchy of government therefore emerges as the dominant theme of political history. . . . [I]t is something real and tangible, whatever may be the name or theory of the constitution."[7] The description of the "composition of the oligarchy of government," Syme thought, should proceed through prosopographical research, that is, through the study of the names and careers of various individuals, their affiliations and marriage connections, the rise and fall of their fortunes, as manifested by the offices they hold: "The noble houses of Rome and the principal allies of the various political leaders enter into their own at last."[8] Syme's approach to history might have been designed to make best use of the extensive available evidence for the careers of various elite individuals provided by Roman inscriptions. It has certainly been profoundly influential for the study of all periods of Roman history and has provided a large and pointed historical program that gives a justification and encouragement to the traditional prosopographical research of epigraphers.

There is a more profound reason, however, for the prestige of the *cursus* among Roman historians and epigraphers: they seem to be more objective, truer than other kinds of accounts. The Romans themselves were finicky about the precision of the *cursus*.[9] In addition, accounts of Roman careers may exist in many copies or versions, and by comparing them it may seem possible to verify the truth of the facts of a given career. The impression of truth, though, is to a large extent produced in subtler ways, by the rhetorical form of the *cursus*. The organizational principle of the list, metonymy, or juxtaposition is the trope of realistic, mimetic presentation in Western literature.[10] There could hardly be a narrative more severe than the *cursus:* it is a bare list of offices. The citation of a position or honor seems straightforward and referential, either true or false, with no apparent in-between of interpretation. It appears to refer immediately to something concrete and real, to something outside of language. So the very baldness of the *cursus* is considered a virtue and a guarantee of objectivity.

A list of offices seems to admit of factual and objective evaluation to the extent that it seems *not* to be rhetorical. By contrast, other, more "literary" texts may be castigated as biased, unreliable, "anecdotal in the worst way."[11] We might, for example, compare the careers of Flavian and his son with the imperial letter of rehabilitation that follows them. These careers appear to say only and precisely what they mean: "Flavian held the following offices." Each word and phrase apparently corresponds to something particular and real, knowable and verifiable. The statements of the *cursus* are either true or false, and the decision between these alternatives is clear-cut. The imperial letter, by contrast, seems very abstract, allusive, rhetorical: its relationship to some extratextual reality appears to be much more problematic than that of the careers.

Yet the accounts that inscriptions provide of the career of any particular person will frequently be inconsistent with one another. Now some office may be included or left out, now even the name of the person may be differently cited.[12] In general, however, epigraphers treat these inconsistencies as a problem to be solved: the traditional procedure of epigraphy and prosopography is to disassemble each *cursus* into its basic factual elements—magistracies and so forth—and then reassemble those elements as part of a larger, systematic narrative, which takes account of all of the available evidence for the career of an individual. This approach evaluates each career strictly from the perspective of its content; as a simple, factual record. What is significant is not the individual case, a given inscription's particular attestation of a *cursus,* but the career as whole, taken as the totality of evidence for it. So in practice most scholars give their attention to factual questions, such as whether and when a particular office was held or not, rather than examining the significance of the particular *cursus* in its context. As a consequence, they sometimes oversimplify very complex issues of representation. The point can be illustrated from the scholarship on the careers of Flavian and his son, which I will summarize in this chapter. Although it is clear that the *cursus* of Flavian and his son are problematic, most ignore the problems they pose in the particular context of the rehabilitation.[13]

This predisposition of epigraphers and prosopographers is consistent with the methods of other modern disciplines, such as history or textual criticism: sources are collected and collated, inconsistencies among them are identified and resolved. A demonstrable benefit is to be had by comparing and compiling the huge body of evidence for the careers of individuals and the magistracies of the ancient Roman world. Still the significance of the particular witnesses should not be entirely dissolved into the more general compilations of prosopography. If the prosopographical project is imagined as ultimately producing a kind of vocabulary and grammatical structure of the Roman career in general, then the individual *cursus* might be seen as a particular utterance in that "language." As such, it is not merely a repository of factual information, but a meaningful statement, a judgment, an interpretation. The organizing principle of any *cursus,* the thing that the various offices listed have in common, is an individual. At the most basic level, the *cursus* should be regarded as a particular comment on the status or particular circumstances of the person to whom the offices are attributed at a particular place and time, by those particular people who have dedicated the text. So, like the rehabilitated *cursus* of Flavian and his son, any particular *cursus* must be regarded as an "edition" of a life, rather than as a "transcription." It is an interpretive historical composition, in the sense that it is a list of certain offices, selected according to some criteria of relevance, organized in a certain order, manufactured for a certain occasion.

REHABILITATION AND THE *CURSUS*

The *cursus* of Flavian and his son are presented in the context of a particular action. The elder Flavian is being rehabilitated; his *cursus* was composed to be seen as a revised text. It is not an account of his life; it is an account of an account of his life. Consequently the *cursus* here must be regarded not as a simple "presentation" of Flavian's career, but as a "re-presentation" of his career, or even as an explicit "re-edition" of his career. This issue is raised immediately in the preamble of the inscription and is then restated at length in the imperial letter. Flavian's career has suffered from the vicissitudes of history: at first it was complete, then it was removed, finally it was restored (*reddita, restitutio,* etc.). The notions of restoration and rehabilitation, like the idea of representation, suggest an equivalence: the person or thing is to be "brought back," and the restoration is to "stand for" them. At the same time, these ideas suggest a difference. A restoration is a rendering of what has been missing, but it can never be identical with the thing it replaces. Any restoration, no matter how accurate, is never the same as the original; it is always a remaking of the original. Just so, a representation stands for something else, suggesting an equivalence without actually being the same as the thing it evokes. Thus the accuracy of the account of Flavian's career is conceived as problematic by the text.

The imperial letter alludes in several places to Flavian's *cursus* and monuments. It describes them as restorations, re-editions, as opposed to straightforward "representations." So, for example, the letter claims to "recall (the elder Flavian) to the monuments and inscriptions of his worth" (*in monumenta virtutum suarum titulosque revocemus,* line 17). The statue base on which the letter is inscribed is itself one of the "monuments of Flavian's worth," and it has been restored: the *cursus* and the imperial letter have been carved over an erasure, over the traces of another text. This earlier text was presumably, but not necessarily, an earlier dedication honoring Flavian: statue bases were frequently reused in antiquity. This uncertainty is not troubling: whatever its origin, in this context the erasure reinforces the idea and point of the rehabilitation. Likewise, the *cursus* at the head of the imperial letter would have to count among the inscriptions that are now restored to Flavian. So the material circumstances of the imperial letter, the *cursus* that precedes it and the statue base on which it is inscribed, reiterate and confirm what the text says. On the other hand, the statements of the imperial letter, like the erasure of the earlier text on the statue base, help to mark the *cursus* and monument as restorations, that is, as modified representations of some other, earlier *cursus* and monument.

There are also a few less overt references to Flavian's career in the imperial letter. At two places the *honor* of the elder Flavian is mentioned (*adserere honorem,* line 10; *restitutionem honoris,* line 28). Among the meanings of *honor* is "magistracy."[14] Part of the "honor restored" to Flavian is the credit for the offices he held.

The imperial letter also refers to the career of Flavian the younger. One of the reasons for the restoration of the elder Flavian is to vindicate the son, whose honor is "half complete" (*honor semiplenus,* line 31). The rehabilitation is not intended to bring new honor to the younger Flavian, but to bring to fulfillment something that already exists. Restorations, after all, are not supposed to be new constructions, but repairs, or supplements, to the old.

The statue is labeled as "restored": *reddita* (line 4). The general meaning here is obvious. The precise interpretation of this word (as of the general structure of the preamble), though, is surprisingly difficult.[15] The chief difficulty comes from the fact that two individuals and their *cursus* are mentioned in the dedication: Flavian the father and Flavian the son. The logic of the connection between the two is by no means obvious. The *cursus* of the elder Flavian is in the dative, as is normal in dedications. The *cursus* of the younger Flavian is in the genitive, depending presumably on *in honorem*.

The word *reddita* must refer to the dedication itself, the *statua*. Reference to the thing dedicated is frequently omitted from honorific inscriptions, because the object itself is there to be seen. It is tempting to understand the phrase following, *in honorem,* with *reddita*: "the statue has been restored to honor" (cf. the imperial letter, lines 10–11, 28, 34–35). Given the genitives following, however, it is necessary to separate them: the statue is "restored, in honor of Flavian the younger."

It is possible to regard the preamble as a dedication to both father and son. According to the imperial letter, the elder Flavian is restored "because the honor of his son is half complete" (lines 29–31). The statue base was rededicated in large part because of the prestige of the younger Flavian. This interpretation, however, does not account for the difference in expression in the dedications to the two. Why is one expressed by simple datives, the other by *in honorem* and a genitive, and what is the significance of this difference? For example, the inscription might simply have been dedicated "to Flavian the father and to Flavian the son" (*Flaviano patri et Flaviano filio*). There are many such dedications.

The best solution is to regard the preamble as describing two separate dedications. The first would be the statue and accompanying *cursus* of the elder Flavian. The name and offices mentioned here are expressed, as they often are on statue bases, in the dative. This dedication would end with line 3. Grammatically it can stand satisfactorily as an autonomous dedication. The second would be the dedication of the *restoration* of this statue in honor of the younger Flavian, which is unambiguously expressed as *reddita in honorem*. This dedication begins with line 4 and also can stand on its own as a dedication. The two careers, however, seem to be unrelated grammatically. The solution to the problem is to understand the statue, the base, *and* the inscribed *cursus* of the elder Flavian as described by *reddita*. All of these, including the account of Flavian's career, are restored "in honor of Flavian the son." The dedication to Flavian the elder, then, is bracketed by the dedication to his son. To express this relationship by punctuation in the text, we might imagine quotation marks around the datives of the career of the elder Flavian.

So the *cursus* at the head of the rehabilitation are marked as "restored" in a variety of ways. The elder Flavian's career is explicitly labeled as such in the preamble and imperial letter. It is bracketed within another dedication and within an erasure. When these *cursus* are compared with other witnesses for the lives of Flavian and his son, it becomes obvious that certain details have been omitted from the careers. These careers allude to things unsaid in other subtle ways as well: by the use of vague and ambiguous words, through erasure, and ultimately by the status of the document as a rehabilitation. These *cursus* should arouse suspicion—not only because they prove incomplete on examination, but because they are composed in such a way as to create the perception that they may say less (or more) than the precise truth.

THE *CURSUS* OF THE ELDER FLAVIAN

The political career of the elder Flavian may be reconstructed from a variety of sources.[16] His good friend and posthumous in-law, the orator Symmachus, addressed numerous letters to him and his sons.[17] Some of his activities attracted the attention of Ammianus Marcellinus. He was also one of the leading characters in the *Saturnalia* of Macrobius. Several constitutions, collected in the Theodosian Code, are addressed to him.[18] The most systematic evidence for his career, though, is provided by the *cursus honorum* that head the three extant inscriptions erected in his honor.

Other than the rehabilitation from the Forum of Trajan, the most important witness for the career of the elder Flavian is a statue base, found on the Caelian hill in Rome, dedicated by the son of the orator Symmachus (*CIL* 6.1782 = *ILS* 2947):

> *Virio Nicomacho Flaviano, v(iro) c(larissimo),*
> *quaest(ori), praet(ori), pontif(ici) maiori,*
> *consulari Siciliae,*
> *vicario Africae,*
> 5 *quaestori intra palatium,*
> *praef(ecto) praet(orio) iterum, co(n)s(uli) ord(inario),*
> *historico disertissimo,*
> *Q(uintus) Fab(ius) Memmius Symmachus, v(ir) c(larissimus),*
> *prosocero optimo.*

To the noble Virius Nicomachus Flavianus, quaestor, praetor, *pontifex maior,* consular of Sicily, vicar of Africa, quaestor at the imperial palace, praetorian prefect twice, ordinary consul, most eloquent historian. The noble Quintus Fabius Memmius Symmachus (erected this statue) for his excellent grandfather-in-law.

This inscription must be considered in connection with another statue base, also found in Rome on the Caelian and dedicated by Q. Fabius Memmius Symmachus (*CIL* 6.1699 + 39103 = *ILS* 2946):

Eusebii.
Q(uinto) Aur(elio) Symmacho, v(iro) c(larissimo)
quaest(ori), praet(ori), pontifici
maiori, correctori
5 *Lucaniae et Brittiorum,*
comiti ordinis tertii,
procons(uli) Africae, praef(ecto) urb(i),
co(n)s(uli) ordinario,
oratori disertissimo,
10 *Q(uintus) Fab(ius) Memm(ius) Symmachus,*
v(ir) c(larissimus), patri optimo.

[This is a statue] of Eusebius (which was the *signum*, or "nickname," of Symmachus).[19] To the noble Quintus Aurelius Symmachus, quaestor, praetor, *pontifex maior,* corrector of Lucania and Brittii, imperial companion of the third rank, proconsul of Africa, urban prefect, ordinary consul, most eloquent orator. The noble Quintus Fabius Memmius Symmachus erected this statue for his excellent father.

Both bases were found on the Caelian hill, where the orator Symmachus is known to have kept a residence (Symm. *Epp.* 3.12, 88; 7.18, 19):[20] these statues were surely installed in the family's home. Both bases were dedicated by a son of Symmachus, who was also grandson-in-law of the elder Flavian. They are parallel in language and format, and were evidently erected as a matching pair.[21] If so, they are contemporary. The date of the dedication of the inscriptions is not specified. The latest office mentioned in either inscription is the elder Flavian's illegitimate term as consul in 394. Because Flavian suffered a *damnatio memoriae* it should have been illegal to erect an inscription in his honor between his death in 394 and his rehabilitation in 431, never mind one mentioning his consulship. Consequently some scholars once dated the two honorific inscriptions from the Caelian to precisely the year of Flavian's consulship, after he had received the office from the pretender Eugenius but before the suppression of the revolt by Theodosius.[22] However, since Q. Fabius Symmachus refers to Flavian as his "grandfather-in-law," the dedication must certainly be dated after his marriage to Flavian's granddaughter, which was surely celebrated in 401 (Symm. *Epp.* 4.14; 9.93, 104–107).²³ As the bases are a pair, it would be entirely appropriate if they were erected at least in part to commemorate the marriage alliance between the two houses. The famous "diptych of the Symmachi and Nicomachi"(see Chapter 3 below) was likely made for this same occasion.

I would favor a slightly later date for the dedication of these statue bases. The elder Flavian was dead when the statue on the Caelian was dedicated to him. The statue of Symmachus might also be a *post mortem* dedication. Symmachus died around 402. So this pair of statues might have been set up around 402/403, soon after the death of Symmachus and while the marriage alliance was still relatively fresh.

The third account of Flavian's career is provided by a statue base erected by the people of Lepcis Magna in honor of Flavian in 377 or 378 (*IRT* 475):

Flavianii v(iri) c(larissimi).
Nicomacho Flaviano agentis
tunc vicem praefectorum prae-
torio per Africanas provincias
5 *pubescente Romani nominis glo-*
ria et vigente fortuna
dominorum principumq(ue) nostrorum
Valentis Gratiani et Valentiniani
perpetuorum semper Auggg(ustorum) et ubiq(ue)
10 *vincentium Lepcimagnensis*
fidelis et innocens ordo cum po-
pulo prestantissimo patrono
votis omnibus conlocavit.

[This is a statue] of the noble Flavianius (evidently the *signum,* or nickname, of the elder Flavian).²⁴ To Nicomachus Flavianus, then acting²⁵ in place of the praetorian prefect in the provinces of Africa, in the youth of the glory of the Roman name and the prime of the fortune of our lords and emperors Valens, Gratian, and Valentian, always and ever August, everywhere victorious. The faithful and blameless senate of Lepcis Magna with the people erected (this statue) to its most eminent patron with the prayers of all.

Flavian is honored by the population of Lepcis Magna for his outstanding administration as an official acting *vicem praefectorum praetorio,* that is, as *vicarius* (see below for discussion of the magistracy). This inscription has been carved on the reverse side of an earlier statue base (*IRT* 562), a dedication to a certain Flavius Archontius Nilus, who had been governor of Tripolitania around 355/360. This dedication had been erected "in the forum for the eternal memory of posterity" (lines 15–17), yet it was reused to honor Flavian within about twenty years. Flavian served as *vicarius* of Africa from 376 until 378, when he helped clear the town of Lepcis Magna of any charge of wrongdoing in connection with the corruption of the general Romanus (Amm. 28.6.28). The town surely honors him out of gratitude for those services. There is no sign that the inscription suffered any damage or erasure as a result of Flavian's later disgrace.

It is clear from the statue base found on the Caelian and from the literary sources that the rehabilitation does not provide Flavian's entire name: one element, Virius, is omitted. This name is also omitted from the dedication from Lepcis Magna. In late antiquity the traditional rules of Roman nomenclature (the use of the so-called *tria nomina,* i.e. *praenomen, nomen,* and *cognomen*) were increasingly disregarded; in particular the gentilitial *nomen* is supplanted by the *cognomen,* and the practice of nomenclature in the rehabilitation may merely reflect this change.[26] Such omissions and variations are frequent in late antiquity. Changes made to the name of a person in various documents should be regarded as meaningful, even if it may be difficult to know what to make of them in any given situation.[27]

The name Virius was in origin a family name, or gentilitial.[28] Little is known about the family, or *gens,* of the Virii. The name is Italian. Attested among many of the peoples of Italy, it is most commonly found in Campania.[29] The family first became noticeable in Roman politics during the second century A.D., and by the third century two of its members had achieved the consulship. The family fades from view around the time of Flavian and his son.[30]

Flavian's immediate family belonged to the senatorial class of the city of Rome.[31] Of his recent ancestors, only his father is known, a certain Virius Volusius Venustus, who came from Canusium (Macrob. *Sat.* 1.5.13).[32] Venustus evidently did not enjoy any special distinction in his official career. It may also be, as Seeck suggests, that there is some connection between Flavian's family and the wealthy and famous family of the Anicii: the names "Nicomachus" and "Flavianus" are both to be found in this family.[33]

In the years following the death of the elder Flavian, the name "Nicomachus" seems to have usurped the function of the traditional gentilitial. Flavian shared only the name Virius with his father. By the time of the rehabilitation, however, Flavian, his son, and Dexter are all identified as Nicomachi, not as Virii. The shift in nomenclature seems to have occurred already some years earlier. At the beginning of the fifth century the famous diptych is identified as belonging to the family "of the Nicomachi," *Nicomachorum*.[34] It is interesting that the family, in the sensitive period soon after 394, came to adopt a name that derives from the elder Flavian.

Flavian's career, even in the edited form reported in the rehabilitation, is extraordinarily distinguished. For most Roman senators in late antiquity the culmination of the life of public service would have been the urban prefecture. Few were selected (or would have wanted) to serve at the imperial court, never mind the imperial court of the east, and fewer still achieved a position so high as that of praetorian prefect.[35] The *cursus* may seem straightforward at first glance: Flavian was "consular of Sicily, vicar of Africa, quaestor at the court of the blessed Theodosius, twice praetorian prefect of Italy, Illyricum, and Africa" (lines 1–2). As we look more carefully, however, it will become apparent that there are significant omissions and, despite the telegraphic style of the *cursus,* ambiguities.

No specifics of Flavian's youth are known. He was probably born about A.D. 330.[36] Like other families of the senatorial class in the late empire, Flavian's family was probably obliged to undertake certain minor offices on his behalf during his youth, if not during his infancy. The dedication from the Caelian hill mentions two such offices, neither of which can be dated: the quaestorship and praetorship.[37] The rehabilitation does not mention these two positions, but this silence is unlikely to have been prompted by Flavian's condemnation. They may have been omitted here for the sake of brevity; or, again, the offices are routine enough that they may not have been considered worthy of inclusion in such a public document (as opposed to a dedication in the family home on the Caelian). There is no mention of them in the inscription from Lepcis Magna either.

Another of Flavian's offices, mentioned in the statue base from the Caelian and ignored in the rehabilitation, was that of *pontifex maior.* Again, one must ask whether the omission has any special significance. De Rossi thought not: he suggested that the office was not listed in the rehabilitation because in 431 pagan priesthoods were no longer mentioned in public inscriptions. Few of the pagan priesthoods survived at this late date.[38] This argument should be given due weight. The fact that paganism had largely vanished from the Roman senatorial class by this time, however, does not mean that the omission of the priesthood would have been insignificant or unnoticeable. Members of Flavian's family would have remembered that he had been one of the *pontifices,* and if that fact slipped their minds they had the inscription in the house on the Caelian to remind them. Anyone familiar with the recent history of the Roman senatorial class will have regarded Flavian as a pagan (see Chapter 3 below). Furthermore, as I will argue (Chapter 7), there is a subtle allusion to the *pontifices* and their religious concerns in the circumstances of the dedication. So the omission may be significant.

In late antiquity the first important step in a senatorial career was the governorship of a province.[39] The preamble of the rehabilitation and the dedication from the Caelian hill both note Flavian's term as governor of Sicily, a post he held in 364/365 (Symm. *Ep.* 2.27.44).[40] His father had held the same post sometime earlier, before 362 (Symm. *Ep.* 4.71),[41] and the family possessed estates in the vicinity of Enna (Symm. *Epp.* 2.30; 6.57.66 and the subscription to Livy, bk. 7), so it is unlikely to be mere chance that Flavian first served here.[42] If the fulsome praise that Symmachus gave Flavian at the time is more than a rhetorical exercise, his excellent administration of Sicily augured future promotions and honors (*Ep.* 11.44). Perhaps Symmachus' praise should be regarded with some suspicion, though, for there is no record that Flavian held any position during the following twelve years.

The next public office mentioned in the rehabilitation is *vicarius* of the imperial diocese of Africa, a position Flavian held in 377 (*CTh* 16.6.2; cf. *CJ* 1.6.1).[43] This vicar was a kind of traveling judge, charged with the supervision of the civil administration of his provinces. In particular he was expected to judge appeals *vice sacra,* in place of the emperor—hence the description of him in the dedication from Lepcis Magna as acting "on behalf of the praetorian prefects" (*vicem praefectorum praetorio*).[44] Flavian was both renowned and notorious for his conduct in this office.

For some years a renegade general named Romanus had abused the province of Africa (Amm. 28.6).[45] In 363 he had allowed the territory of Roman Tripolis to be devastated by marauding nomads, the Austoriani. Lepcis Magna, a large city of that district, had suffered quite heavily from the incursions. The senate of the city complained to the emperor (at that time Valentinian I), alleging the acquiescence of Romanus, but its testimony was discredited owing to the intrigues of the general. When Flavian took office, he and the proconsul Hesperius, "men whose fairness and prestige were most just" (Amm. 28.6.28), captured and interrogated under torture a certain Caecilius, who was an advisor of Romanus. They secured a confession from him and delivered their findings to the emperor, thus vindicating the city of Lepcis Magna and incriminating Romanus. It turned out that among his many crimes Romanus had been guilty of misappropriating army funds. As a result of their report, Romanus was removed from his post.

Flavian's reputation for his accomplishments as *vicarius* in Africa survived him by many years. Sometime soon after he held the position, the grateful citizens of Lepcis Magna erected the statue in his honor, their "most outstanding patron." In his history, issued some twenty years after Flavian's term in Africa, Ammianus gives him high praise (Amm. 28.6). Even thirty years later, in 414, there are indications that his service was remembered in North Africa and the imperial court. In that year, after a period of absence from politics, Flavian's son was appointed as an extraordinary envoy to the province of Africa. His chief tasks were to collect any complaints of the provincials and, like his father, to investigate the distribution of the army payroll. The appointment of the son was likely influenced by the enduring reputation of the father in the province.

Some fifty years later, the rehabilitation alludes to this office. Already in the *cursus* it is stated that the statue is restored "because of his worth and prestige as a senator and judge" (line 4). This phrase, which appears in the middle of the *cursus*, might refer either to the elder Flavian or to his son. The imperial letter provides some clarification. The elder Flavian is rehabilitated because "we are fortified by your feelings for Flavian and by the judgments of all the provinces, for whose benefit the funds of the state still quite wealthy were either preserved or even increased" (lines 22–24). The reference to Flavian's judicial excellence (*iudiciariae*, line 3) may allude to Flavian's function as *vicarius*.[46] The interesting use of the word *iudicium*, "judgment," to describe the gratitude of the provinces that he judged (*provinciarum omnium iudiciis*, lines 22–23) is probably a reference to the same office. The phrase describing the "preservation and increase of the state's funds" may describe his role in uncovering the fiscal malfeasance of Romanus.

Flavian's time in Africa was not entirely free from controversy. Although his disposal of Romanus was renowned, his dealings with the Donatists were notorious. The Donatist heresy had arisen in North Africa in the aftermath of Diocletian's "Great Persecution" (303–313) because of a dispute over the actions of certain clergy, including the bishop of Carthage.[47] They were condemned by Rome and the emperor. According to Augustine, when they interceded for certain criminals with Flavian, he "behaved like a man of their persuasion" (August. *Ep.* 87.8).[48] Whether Flavian's judgments were prompted by sincere favoritism or by the simple indifference of a non-Christian, his partiality seems to have been so pronounced that it prompted the emperor Gratian to dispatch the enactment of 17 October 377, ordering him to exercise more severity toward heretics (*CTh* 16.6.2; cf.*CJ* 1.6.1). Flavian's embroilment with the Donatists may have temporarily damaged his reputation at the imperial court. He evidently did not serve again under Gratian.

There is little undisputed about the rest of Flavian's career. He is next known to have served as *quaestor sacri palatii*, an office mentioned on both the rehabilitation and the dedication from the Caelian hill. The phrases used in those inscriptions to describe this office, *quaestor aulae divi Theodosi* and *quaestor intra Palatium*, are unparalleled.[49] Flavian seems to have obtained the position through the influence of a friend, Flavius Rufinus (Symm. *Ep.* 3.90).[50] The quaestor was the chief legal advisor to the emperor; he would have drafted many of the constitutions in the Theodosian Code, for instance. The tenants of the post were often recruited from the ranks of lawyers and rhetoricians. In this period the emperor more commonly chose his quaestors from the provincial aristocracy than from the senatorial class of old Rome.[51]

The date of Flavian's tenure of the quaestorship must be determined with reference to Flavian's first term as praetorian prefect—another thorny problem. There is no direct evidence for the date of Flavian's quaestorship. Two dates are currently argued for the inception of his first term as praetorian prefect: 383 and 389. Flavian almost certainly would have served as quaestor before he was appointed praetorian prefect for the first time: this sequence of offices was normal, perhaps even invariable, in the late empire, and the order of offices listed in his *cursus* confirms this expectation. There was probably little or no interval between the two offices. It was normal for officials to move directly from the quaestorship to the praetorian prefecture, and Symmachus seems to confirm that the transition was immediate in Flavian's case.[52]

The praetorian prefects were the most important administrative officials in the late empire. They served directly under the emperor and were responsible for the management of the prefectures, large areas of the empire. Like the *vicarii* they had some responsibility for the administration of justice in their provinces: so, earlier in his career, Flavian served as *vicarius* with appellate jurisdiction; that is, he was acting in lieu of the praetorian prefect.[53] The references in the letter of rehabilitation to Flavian's virtues as a judge (discussed above with reference to his term as *vicarius* in North Africa) might allude not only to his term as *vicarius* in North Africa but also to his terms as praetorian prefect. The inscription from the Caelian claims that Flavian was "praetorian prefect twice." The rehabilitation from the Forum of Trajan specifies his provinces: he was "prefect of Italy, Illyricum, and Africa twice."

There is evidence that Flavian was praetorian prefect in 383. Two extracts from a law addressed to Flavian during his term as praetorian prefect are cited in the Theodosian Code; these are dated to 27 February 383 (*CTh* 7.18.8 and 9.29.2).[54] This date has been supported by appeal to certain letters of Symmachus. In several letters, Symmachus couples Flavian's term as praetorian prefect with his son's voyage to Asia to take up his proconsulship—a voyage that certainly took place in 383.[55]

If Flavian first held the praetorian prefecture in 383, then he was quaestor in 382/383.[56] If this date is correct, then he could only have served in Constantinople: the rehabilitation describes Flavian specifically as quaestor of Theodosius, and the emperor Gratian controlled the western empire until his death at the hands of the pretender Magnus Maximus in 383. In 382/383 Theodosius' realm was restricted to the eastern empire.[57] Flavian's appointment as quaestor would then precede by a little his son's selection as proconsul of Asia. So the appointment of the younger Flavian as proconsul of Asia may be related to his father's prominence at the eastern imperial court at about this time.[58]

There is also good evidence that Flavian served as praetorian prefect in 389/390 (*CTh* 9.40.13, 16.2.18, 16.3.1, 13.5.19). Those who believe that Flavian was already praetorian prefect in 383 take 389 as the beginning of his second term in that office. However, a letter of Symmachus to Rufinus mentions Flavian's promotion from quaestor to praetorian prefect, and thanks Rufinus for helping Flavian (*Ep.* 3.90). This Rufinus was *magister officiorum* at the imperial court in Milan in 389;[59] moreover, he does not appear in Symmachus' correspondence until that year. So Flavian may have first become praetorian prefect in 389 or 390, and the evidence for his earlier tenure of prefecture must somehow be explained away. Theodosius, who controlled the western empire and even kept his court there in 389 and 390, would be responsible for Flavian's initial appointment to the post.

If Flavian first held the praetorian prefecture in 389, then he might have been appointed as quaestor in 388.[60] If this date is correct, then Flavian need not have traveled to Constantinople; he might well have served at the imperial court in Italy, which Theodosius now controlled as a result of his wars with Magnus Maximus.[61] Recently some additional support for this date has been mustered. Tony Honoré notes that Symmachus, in one of his letters to Flavian (*Ep.* 2.13.1), praises a law for its clarity and unselfishness.[62] This law is reported in the Theodosian Code (4.4.2) and dated to 23 January 389. As quaestor, one of Flavian's responsibilities would have been to draft such imperial constitutions. If Flavian was quaestor in 388/389, he might well have drafted this particular law. Honoré makes the attractive suggestion that Symmachus' praise of the letter is a friendly gesture, intended to be interpreted as a compliment to the author of the law, his correspondent Flavian.

Recently Malcolm Errington has proposed yet another solution to these problems. Following the evidence of Symmachus, he accepts a date of around 388 or 389 for the quaestorship, but suggests that this office precedes Flavian's second (rather than first) term as praetorian prefect. So Flavian would have been appointed praetorian prefect for the first time in 383, then quaestor in 388, then praetorian prefect for the second time in 389. This sequence of offices would be unparalleled. As Errington remarks, however, the quaestorship at this time would under no circumstances have been a "normal career stage" for a man of Flavian's background. The office was usually recruited from the provincial aristocracy.[63]

In 391 Theodosius returned to the east, leaving the adolescent Valentinian II as emperor of the western empire. Flavian was perhaps reappointed by the young emperor and his *magister militum,* Arbogast, as praetorian prefect in that year. The evidence for Flavian's position in 391 is arguable: it depends on redating some imperial constitutions addressed to Flavian from 383 to 391.[64]

There are no doubts about Flavian's service as praetorian prefect during the last two years of his life. The pretender Eugenius appointed Flavian praetorian prefect in 392, and Flavian held this position until his death in 394 (Symm. *Epp.* 2.32, 33, 33A, 41, 42, 66, 75, 87). There are some doubts, however, as to whether or not his position in these two years should be regarded as a separate term from the service beginning in 390, and whether or not this position was regarded as legitimate even after the rehabilitation.[65]

Flavian may have held the praetorian prefecture for as many as six years. It is not a simple task to reconcile this picture with the representation of two terms that we find in his various *cursus*. Several solutions have been put forward. Seeck originally proposed that Flavian's first prefecture should be dated to 383; he suggested that the period in which Flavian held the prefecture continuously, 390–394, should be imagined as a single term. So Flavian would have held the position twice, and the various accounts of his career would be historically accurate.[66] Somewhat later, Seeck revised this argument. Again he suggested that Flavian held the prefecture for the first time in 383, with the second prefecture beginning in 390. He suggested now, however, that the second term ended in 392, when Flavian joined Eugenius and Arbogast. So Flavian would have actually held the prefecture three times, the last of which was illegitimate and consequently omitted from his *cursus*.[67] Finally, Seeck abandoned the prefecture of 383 altogether. According to Seeck's final interpretation, Flavian held the prefecture for the first time from 389 to 392; he was appointed for the second time by Eugenius in 392.[68] On this interpretation, Flavian would have held the prefecture twice: the first time, he would have been appointed by Theodosius; the second time by Eugenius. Both terms would have been reported in the inscriptions from the Caelian hill and the Forum of Trajan.[69]

There is another difficulty with the praetorian prefectures of Flavian: What were his provinces of authority? The rehabilitation specifies his areas of administration as Italy, Illyricum, and Africa. If Flavian served as praetorian prefect of Theodosius in 383 he cannot have administered all of these areas: in 383 the emperor whom he served, Theodosius, controlled only the eastern part of Illyricum. Consequently Flavian, if he was prefect at all in this year, can have been prefect only of eastern Illyricum.[70] From 389 to 392, as praetorian prefect in the western empire, Flavian may well have been charged with Italy, Illyricum, and Africa (*CTh* 9.40.13, 11.39.11 + 16.7.4–5, 1.1.2 + 3.1.6, 10.10.20; Symm. *Epp.* 2.13, 18, 20). Once he joined Eugenius and Arbogast, however, his authority would have been rapidly diminished by the counterattacks of the emperor of the eastern empire. Illyricum was quickly lost to Theodosius. By 393, Africa had also been taken. At his death in 394, Flavian can have been praetorian prefect of Italy only.[71] So by no reckoning can he have been "praetorian prefect of Italy, Illyricum, and Africa twice," as the rehabilitation claims. At most, he administered all of these provinces during only one of his terms—and perhaps only during *part* of one of his terms (if 390–394 is counted as a single term). The rehabilitation, however, should not be regarded as lying; rather, it is imprecise. Flavian did in fact administer either Illyricum or Italy at least twice (depending on the chronology preferred for his prefectures); if the word *iterum* is construed only with one or the other of these two provinces, then the *cursus* is in some sense accurate (though misleading).

Flavian also held that most prestigious office, the ordinary consulship. The consulship carried with it no duties at this late date. The elite continued to covet it, however, because of the status attached to it: the ordinary consuls gave their names to the year.[72] Flavian received this position in 394, from the pretender Eugenius. Later, his term as consul was certainly regarded as invalid (*CTh* 15.14.9; cf. *CTh* 15.14.11 and below). Already in 394, Theodosius named as his own consuls his sons, Arcadius and Honorius. Flavian's consulship is mentioned in several contemporary Christian inscriptions, but in no official state documents (*ICUR* suppl. 1855 [= *ILCV* 1482]; n.s. 2.4503 [= *ILCV* 4321], 6460 [= *ILCV* 3822]; 3.8648; 5.13361, 13364, 13368; 7.19975).[73] There is no overt reference to Flavian's consulship in the rehabilitation. It is remarkable to find the consulship listed in the dedication from the Caelian hill, even though it was erected in a private home.

One of the most perplexing problems that arises from the comparison of the *cursus* of the rehabilitation with that of the dedication from the Caelian hill is not owing to a discrepancy, but to a correspondence.[74] The inscription from the Caelian claims the illegitimate consulship of Flavian, although it is not mentioned by the rehabilitation. The consulship was illegitimate because Flavian received it from the pretender, Eugenius. Flavian also received his final term as praetorian prefect from Eugenius, and he held that office in the same year as the consulship. If the consulship was regarded as illegitimate because it was received from the usurper, then so too must have been the term as praetorian prefect. The inscription from the Caelian does not hesitate to claim the illegitimate consulship, so why would it hesitate to claim the illegitimate term as praetorian prefect? The rehabilitation does not claim the illegitimate consulship; presumably it would not have claimed an illegitimate prefecture either. If Flavian's final term as praetorian prefect was illegitimate, two possibilities spring to mind: either Flavian actually held the office three times, and the dedication from the Caelian (inconsistently with its practice of claiming illegitimate offices) has excluded the illegitimate term; or he actually held the office twice, and the rehabilitation (inconsistently with its practice of excluding illegitimate offices) has included the illegitimate term in its count. Beyond these two possibilities, it might be argued that even though Flavian's term as consul was not recognized as legitimate, the term as praetorian prefect was acknowledged.[75] If so, then Flavian would have held the praetorian prefecture twice, both times legally, and consequently the correspondence between the two *cursus* would not need to be explained.

Comparison of the *cursus* of the rehabilitation with other evidence for Flavian's career—particularly with the *cursus* from the Caelian hill—is disquieting. Still, none of these documents actually falsifies the information provided by the rehabilitation. They do suggest, however, that some offices have been omitted, passed over in silence. The rehabilitation does not mention Flavian's minor offices, the quaestorship and praetorship, nor does it mention his pagan priesthood, the pontificate. The description of Flavian's terms as praetorian prefect is ambiguous, and the claim that he was prefect twice may or may not tell less than the entire story. Flavian's illegitimate stint as ordinary consul is not mentioned—nor could it possibly be, since Theodosius had assigned the year to other consuls (see Chapter 4 below)—though it is claimed in private contexts.

THE *CURSUS* OF FLAVIAN THE YOUNGER

Flavian's son was compromised by the usurpation of Arbogast. He had received many of his earlier offices through the influence of his father, and in 394 he continued to follow his father's lead. As with his father, our best evidence for his political career comes from various inscriptions. The evidence from the rehabilitation may be supplemented by a statue base erected to him by the city of Naples (*ILS* 8985).[76] Since this statue base describes the younger Flavian as "urban prefect twice" it should be dated to after his second legitimate term in that office (his third term absolutely), perhaps ca. 408.[77] Since the inscription does not mention his term as praetorian prefect, it must have been erected before 431:

[V]ir[tutu]m o[mnium ac tot meri]torum viro, censurae
culmine et moderatione
praecipuo, provido semper
et strenuo, indulgenti
5   bono benigno iustissimo,
Nicomacho Flaviano v(iro) c(larissimo)
consulari Campaniae,
proconsuli Asiae, praefecto
urbi iterum, patrono
10 originali, statuam censuit
ordo ab his semper defensus
ac populus.

To a man of all virtues and so many deserts, a man distinguished in respect of loftiness of judgment and moderation, always prudent and prompt, an obliging, good, kind, and very just man, Nicomachus Flavianus, consular of Campania, proconsul of Asia, twice prefect of the city, patron by birth; the senate, always championed by his family, and the people decreed the statue.

Another witness for the younger Flavian's career is a fragment of a statue base from the Forum of Caesar, dedicated by him to Arcadius:[78]

> D(omino) n(ostro) Arca[dio]
> [p]erpetuo A[ug(usto)]
> [Ni]comachus Flavian[us]
> praef(ectus) urbi iterum v[ice]
> 5 sacra iudicans

To our lord Arcadius, ever August, Nicomachus Flavianus, urban prefect with appellate jurisdiction twice in the place of the emperor (made this dedication).

The text presented here differs slightly from that of the original publication, by Paribeni. From the photograph of the stone, it is clear that there is not enough space available to restore Virius as the first word of the younger Flavian's name (as Paribeni does). Furthermore, this element is not attested as a part of the younger Flavian's name,[79] nor is it used to describe even his father in the rehabilitation of 431. The name by which the family was known seems to have changed in the early fifth century: the old gentilitial was dropped in favor of one of the elder Flavian's *cognomina,* Nicomachus (see above). I have also printed the first C of Nicomachus (unlike Paribeni, who bracketed it): the lower-right edge of the letter is clearly visible from the photograph.

This inscription must date to the reign of Arcadius, between 395 and 408. It cannot have been erected any earlier than 399–400, the year of the younger Flavian's second actual term (but first valid term) as urban prefect. As will be seen below, however, it is also possible that the inscription may have been dedicated later, during his third actual term (but second legitimate term) as urban prefect.

The younger Flavian's career, like that of his father, is distinguished: "consular of Campania, proconsul of Asia, frequently urban prefect, incumbent praetorian prefect of Italy, Illyricum, and Africa" (lines 4–6). To be singled out for service as governor of an eastern province, and one so wealthy as Asia, was an extraordinary honor for a Roman senator in late antiquity. The urban prefecture was the culmination of a distinguished career, and few senators achieved it. The younger Flavian held the post "rather frequently": three times, twice legally, more often than all but one of his contemporaries. Finally, late in life, after twenty years away from public office, he was recalled to serve as praetorian prefect. Again the presentation of the career here seems straightforward, but the simplicity is only apparent.

To judge from his career, the younger Flavian must have been born in about 358.[80] It is uncertain when he held his first attested office, *consularis Campaniae*, governor of Campania. In view of its relative unimportance and its position in his *cursus*, this must have been one of his earliest offices. He surely held this position sometime before he went to Asia as proconsul in 383.[81] The location of this first governorship is significant: the younger Flavian surely received this position by reason of his family's connections with Campania. The name of the family itself, Virius, may suggest a connection with the area: it is an Italian name, found most commonly in Campania (see above), and other Virii are attested in the fourth century holding this office.[82] The elder Flavian had a villa near Neapolis, in the neighborhood of Symmachus' villa (Symm. *Epp.* 2.60.1–2).[83] The younger Flavian was also likely connected to the local aristocracy of Campania by marriage. He was married for the first time early in life. On the presumption that Appius Nicomachus Dexter is his son, it is likely that he married the daughter of a certain Appius Claudius Tarronius Dexter, a man of some importance in Naples.[84] The statue base from Naples acknowledges the traditional connections of the family with Campania by describing Flavian the younger as *patronus originalis*, a phrase which indicates that the members of his family are traditional protectors and benefactors of the city.[85] The inscription further notes that the town council has always been championed by him and his family, *ab his semper defensus*. This first marriage was dissolved by 383 (Symm. *Ep.* 2.22.2); later, probably between 392 and 394, he would marry the daughter of Symmachus.[86]

Flavian the younger held the prestigious office of proconsul of Asia in 383. There is no question about the date of his term in this office: an imperial constitution of 10 May 383 is addressed to him in this capacity (*CTh* 12.6.18).[87] His term in Asia may or may not coincide with his father's stint as quaestor in the eastern imperial court. If it does, the appointment of father and son to important posts in the eastern empire would be related: Flavian the younger would have received his position owing to the influence of his father at the imperial court in that year.[88] The younger Flavian did not distinguish himself as proconsul: he was dismissed from the office for having a local town councilman flogged, in defiance of imperial law (Libanius, *Or.* 28.4).[89] Symmachus would compare the son's disgrace in that year to the one later suffered by the elder Flavian (*Ep.* 3.69).

For several years afterward, Flavian the younger held no magistracies. Then, in 394, he was appointed urban prefect by Eugenius. This position is not mentioned in any of his public *cursus* because it was not regarded as legitimate; the evidence for it is provided in the correspondence of Symmachus. In a letter written during Flavian the younger's later term as urban prefect under Honorius, Symmachus mentions the earlier term that Flavian had received "from the usurper" (*beneficium tyranni*), noting the stigma attached to it.⁹⁰

Flavian the younger survived the usurpation of Eugenius and the year of his father's consulship, but not without some disgrace. He was the son of Eugenius' praetorian prefect and consul, and he had participated in the revolt himself by accepting the urban prefecture. His connections with Eugenius and Flavian would haunt him for several years. In the immediate aftermath, the emperor was relatively lenient, allowing him to keep his inheritance, forcing him only to repay the salary that his father had drawn in the service of Eugenius (Aug. *Civ. Dei* 5.26.1; Symm. *Epp.* 4.4, 6, 19, 51; 5.47; 6.12).⁹¹ His recovery from the disaster of 394 did not take long: it is one of the best-documented episodes in this story. Flavian the younger himself aided the recovery by converting to Christianity (Aug. *Civ. Dei* 5.26). Theodosius himself restored his inheritance (Symm. *Ep.* 4.19), and Symmachus worked tirelessly writing letters on his behalf (Symm. *Epp.* 4.2, 5; 5.5, 6; 6.10, 30, 36, 52, 56, 59, 63).⁹² Finally, on the recommendation of the eminent general Stilicho (Symm. *Epp.* 4.6; 6.10, 36), the emperor sent a letter (Symm. *Epp.* 6.30, 36; 7.95) inviting him to the inauguration of Flavius Mallius Theodorus as consul (Symm. *Epp.* 5.6; 6.10, 30, 35, 36; 9.47). Symmachus sent along letters of introduction and advice (Symm. *Epp.* 4.6, 39; 5.6; 7.47, 95, 102; 9.47). Flavian the younger returned to Rome an urban prefect, his honor restored by the emperor (Symm. *Epp.* 4.4; 7.93, 96, 104; 8.29). So in 399 he holds the urban prefecture—but this time legally. He would hold the office through the end of 400 (Symm. *Ep.* 7.104 [cf. 4.4; 7.50, 93, 96; 8.29]; *CTh* 14.10.3, 13.5.29, 3.31.1, 11.30.61, 15.2.9. Cf. *AE* 1934, 147 [quoted above]).⁹³

The date of the younger Flavian's second legitimate term as urban prefect (and third term overall) is far less secure. Seeck argued that the third term as prefect must date between 402 and 412.⁹⁴ During his prefecture Flavian the younger had built a structure known as the *secretarium senatus*, which burned down and was rebuilt in 412; therefore, Seeck believed that he must have served before 412.⁹⁵ Furthermore it is significant that there is no reference to this third prefecture in the letters of Symmachus: the prefecture must date after the death of Symmachus in 402. And it may be possible to date the prefecture more precisely. A law cited in the Justinian Code is addressed to Flavian as "praetorian prefect." If the title here were emended to read "urban prefect," the third term would be dated to exactly 408.[96]

The various summary references to the younger Flavian's terms as urban prefect are all highly unusual in some way; either inaccurate, misleading, or vague. The younger Flavian is known to have corrected books 6–8 of Livy, signing his name in a subscription at the end of each book (see Chapter 6 below). In these subscriptions he describes himself as *praef. urb. ter*—urban prefect three times. Here, then, the younger Flavian does not hesitate to claim all of his terms as urban prefect, including the invalidated term, which he held under the usurper Eugenius in 394.

The younger Flavian's dedication to Arcadius seems at first glance more innocuous. The precise date of this inscription depends on the interpretation of the reference to the younger Flavian as *praefectus urbi iterum vice sacra iudicans*, "urban prefect twice with appellate jurisdiction in the place of the emperor." J. J. O'Donnell, understanding the word "twice" to refer to the office of urban prefect, argued that if the inscription dates to the younger Flavian's third term as urban prefect, then the word "twice" would refer to his two legitimate terms in the office only; if the inscription dates to his second term as urban prefect, then the word "twice" would include his first, illegal term.[97] O'Donnell did not realize that the phrase *iterum vice sacra iudicans* is used here in a peculiar and idiosyncratic way: the word "twice" does not modify the entire phrase, but rather only the appellate jurisdiction (*vice sacra iudicans*). The "appellate jurisdiction" modifies two offices: the urban prefecture and another, which is not specified. Before becoming urban prefect a man would regularly hold the position of governor (proconsul) of some province; this position also carried with it appellate jurisdiction. When an urban prefect claims to "hold appellate jurisdiction for the second time," it may regularly be presumed that the first tenure of that power is an earlier term as proconsul, even if that term is not mentioned on the inscription.[98] So instead of claiming to have been urban prefect twice, the younger Flavian would rather be representing himself as having had appellate jurisdiction twice. By 399 he had held two legitimate offices with this power: as proconsul of Asia in 383 and as urban prefect in 399–400. He does not mention his term as proconsul on this inscription because he does not need to. This inscription, then, should certainly be dated to the year of the younger Flavian's first valid term as urban prefect, 399–400.

The interpretation of this formula put forward by Chastagnol and Cameron is conclusive; even so, it must be pointed out that its use in this context allows for a certain ambiguity. O'Donnell's interpretation of the phrase as referring to the younger Flavian's terms as urban prefect is not an unnatural one. In 399 the younger Flavian was urban prefect for the second time within five years: despite the fact that the first had been invalidated, this was still an extraordinary achievement, unparalleled in the recent past. Any Roman viewer of the dedication would surely have been aware of this accomplishment. Any reference to his urban prefecture (never mind one so unclear as this)—in fact, the mere fact of his holding the urban prefecture—would have called the earlier term to the minds of contemporary Romans, as it does for modern scholars.

This formula is convenient for someone in the younger Flavian's position. By using it, he is able to safely allude to his invalid term as urban prefect. Even within the limits of the formula, he might have been clearer had he wished to exclude any possibility of misunderstanding. For example, he might have mentioned his proconsulship, and moved the word *iterum* to the end of the phrase, away from the reference to his urban prefecture. By omitting any reference to his position as proconsul of Asia, he has left the inscription open to O'Donnell's interpretation—and he has done so without doing anything improper.

The description of the younger Flavian's terms as urban prefect in the rehabilitation is notorious. Rather than claiming that he was urban prefect twice, or even three times, the inscription says that he was urban prefect "rather often," *saepius*. The use of this word in this way in an epigraphical career is extremely rare, and the reading of the word itself is problematic (see Appendix). Silvio Panciera has recently published an inscription in which the emperor Maxentius is certainly described as "having held the consulship rather often (*saepius*)."[99] This inscription was probably erected in the third of Maxentius' four terms as consul. There was no question about the legal status of any of his consulships: all were officially recognized. Panciera also draws attention to an important third-century A.D. inscription from Ephesus, in which L. Egnatius Victor Lollianus is described as "proconsul frequently" (ἀνθύπατος πολλάκις: *AE* 1902, 244). Lollianus had served as proconsul of Asia for three consecutive years, and this unusual distinction is explicitly noted in other inscriptions.[100] Again, there is no question about the legitimacy of any of his terms of office.

The term *saepius* is vague. In the inscriptions honoring Maxentius and Lollianus it seems to suggest that the honorands had held office more than was normal; consequently the word in those texts has positive connotations, and suggests a special distinction.¹⁰¹ Panciera would argue that the word must have the same connotations in the inscription rehabilitating the elder Flavian: here the intention is to "emphasize the extraordinary honor of the younger Flavian's three terms as urban prefect which he had held many years before, in different circumstances."¹⁰²

I cannot agree with Panciera that the force of *saepius* in the inscription rehabilitating the elder Flavian is positive, as in the inscriptions honoring Maxentius and Lollianus. One of the younger Flavian's terms as urban prefect had been discounted; the context is different, and so are the overtones of the word. Panciera believes that the "distance of the event (i.e. the usurpation of Eugenius) and the intervening rehabilitation of the elder Flavian and of the family" warrants his interpretation.¹⁰³ He ignores, however, the fact that this unusual phrase occurs at the head of the letter of rehabilitation itself, and that this letter no more authorizes the younger Flavian to take credit for his illegal term as urban prefect than it authorizes his father to be granted credit for his illegal term as consul. The traditional interpretation—that the adverb is used to leave vague the precise number of times he had held the prefecture—is preferable here.¹⁰⁴

At the same time, it would be a mistake to regard the use of this word as a simple means of avoiding an unpleasant and uncomfortable subject, that is, the younger Flavian's first, illegitimate term as urban prefect. The word, because of its very oddity and vagueness, stands out like a neon light in the formulaic, precise environment of the *cursus*. It does not merely leave vague the number of times that the younger Flavian held the urban prefecture. Instead of concealing the illegitimate term, it draws attention to it, giving the younger Flavian credit for his term without doing so overtly and explicitly.

In the years immediately following his last term as urban prefect (if this office is indeed to be dated to 408), the younger Flavian vanished from political life. Then, in 414, he participated in an extraordinary commission to Africa (*CTh* 7.4.33). After the death of the African usurper, Heraclianus, the emperor Honorius feared that the provincials might feel neglected. To placate them, he dispatched two representatives: a certain Caecilianus, an expert on African affairs,¹⁰⁵ and the younger Flavian. Their chief tasks were to collect any complaints and to investigate the distribution of the army payroll. The appointment of the son shows that the imperial court (and the province) still remembered the exemplary conduct of the father during his own term as *vicarius* in Africa. It is curious that there is no reference to this African mission in any of the younger Flavian's careers. It is especially odd that it is omitted from the *cursus* of the rehabilitation, since the imperial letter there alludes in several places to the elder Flavian's services in Africa, and even alleges them as a major reason for the restoration of his honor and reputation.

After the mission to Africa in 414, nothing is known of the younger Flavian's activities for some twenty years. The career recounted on the rehabilitation suggests that he held no political office during this period. Then, in 431 under Valentinian III and his mother, Galla Placidia, he abruptly emerges to hold the highest political position possible for a senator in the west, the praetorian prefecture.[106] At the same time, his father is rehabilitated. This sudden leap to prominence after a long period of apparent inactivity is extraordinary, and it begs some explanation.

The rehabilitation of the elder Flavian is linked to the prominence of Flavian the younger in this year. The *cursus* states that the younger Flavian is "currently praetorian prefect" (line 5) and that "the statue of the father is restored in honor of the son" (line 4). The imperial letter also makes it clear that Flavian is restored at least in part for the sake of his son (lines 29–33), whose honor is only "half complete, even though crowned by the praetorian prefecture" (line 31)—that is, unless his father's good name is restored.

The younger Flavian's sudden return to the imperial court and high office is striking, but no compelling explanation for it has been proposed. Why should Flavian the younger, in particular, be chosen for this honor at this time? Some suppose that the son's promotion and the father's rehabilitation in this year were special favors, granted at the wish of the generalissimo Aëtius; others suggest that Galla Placidia herself was behind these events. At this time Aëtius and Placidia were struggling for dominance in the imperial court. Aëtius was attempting to consolidate his importance and power; Placidia wished to be rid of Aëtius. Both needed support. The dignities granted to Flavian the younger and his father in 431 may have been an attempt by one or the other to gain the help of the Roman senatorial class in the battle.[107] The inscription itself is typically equivocal about the motivation for the rehabilitation of the father and the advancement of the son.

NICOMACHUS DEXTER

The dedicator of the statue, Appius Nicomachus Dexter (lines 37–38) is the grandson of the elder Flavian and almost certainly the son of Flavian the younger. Some have supposed that he was the son of a certain Clementianus, on the basis of the subscriptions to Livy, books 3–5.[108] In these subscriptions, Dexter claims to have corrected his text from the copy of his *parens* Clementianus (for the subscriptions, see Chapter 6 below). The word *parens*, however, does not mean "parent," but "relative"—and in late antiquity it need not mean even this much.¹⁰⁹ So, for example, in line 30 of the imperial letter of rehabilitation, the word *parentes* does not refer to the "parents" of Valentinian III, Galla Placidia and Constantius III, but to his imperial "relatives," Theodosius and Honorius. In fact, the use of the word *parens* in the subscriptions serves to prove that Clementianus was *not* Dexter's "parent." If he were, he would surely have been described as *pater,* "father." Flavian the younger married a daughter of the orator Symmachus in 392 or 393 (Symm. *Epp.* 2.88, 4.51, 6.1–81). Because of his name, though, it is unlikely that Appius Nicomachus Dexter was the offspring of that union. As Seeck suggested, Dexter must be the son of Flavian the younger by an earlier marriage, probably to the daughter of a certain Appius Claudius Tarronius Dexter.¹¹⁰

Only one position held by Dexter is mentioned in the inscription from the Forum of Trajan: the urban prefecture. This position is not mentioned elsewhere. Dexter must have held the post sometime before he had his grandfather's statue and inscription restored in 431, but beyond that specification the date is uncertain.

MEANING AND OMISSION

I began this chapter with a little polemic about the tendency of epigraphers to focus on the career as a whole—that is, on the systematic compilation of all evidence for a career, at the expense of an appreciation of the significance of the various particular attestations of the *cursus.* Some might protest here at the end of the chapter that I have done much the same. Certainly I have attempted to pull together all of the evidence for the careers of the individuals mentioned in the inscription. The establishment of the most accurate and comprehensive account of the careers, however, has been only an incidental goal of this chapter. I have composed this account as a means of coming to grips with the particular meanings of the rehabilitated careers of Flavian and his son. The particularity of a given *cursus* can be understood only in relation to some more general standard. It is not enough to look at the offices that are included in a *cursus;* it is necessary to look also at what has been left out. To put it in an oracular style, the meaning of a text resides not in what it says, but in what it does not say.¹¹¹

No narrative ever could or would say everything about something. Even the most accurate and factual accounts, such as a typical Roman *cursus honorum,* must always be selective. Even if it were possible to say everything, it would not be desirable. A true and all-inclusive account of a thing would mean nothing. Meaning is produced precisely by the selection of significant detail, the identification and inclusion of what is relevant; or, to put it in a negative way, by the exclusion of what is irrelevant. It might be argued that selection and exclusion are merely two faces of the same coin—and so they are; nevertheless, each becomes intelligible only in light of the other. Confronted with a text, there is a tendency to focus exclusively on what is included in it, expressly stated: what is there. To understand the criteria by which this material is selected, even to realize that the material has been selected at all, it is necessary to have some sense of what has been kept out of it as well.

In the case of the *cursus* of Flavian and his son, it is impossible to ignore the problem of exclusion. The idea is central to the procedures of the *damnatio memoriae* and rehabilitation. The fact that these penalties and their exclusions are imposed by the state is absolutely irrelevant. When Errington, for example, says that the omission of Flavian's consulship is "beside the point in view of the explicit cancellation of *dignitates*,"[112] he is begging the problem. He would presumably elaborate that the state is the guarantor of the legitimacy of offices; if it does not recognize such an event, then it must be treated as a nonevent, as though it never happened. Cancellation of an office by the state, however, even the cancellation of an illegitimate office, is merely another form of exclusion, but now a political one: here, instead of the author determining the criteria of inclusion, the state does so. The very notion of "cancellation" acknowledges that these offices have been held, even as it insists on their omission. The sense that these careers are somehow not complete, that something is missing, is the problem that the rehabilitation is meant to address, and no reading of the text that ignores this point can be adequate. The most obvious omissions from the *cursus* of the rehabilitation are references to offices held by either Flavian or his son under the usurper Eugenius in 394. So there is no mention of Flavian's term as consul; the number of terms as praetorian prefect credited to him may be smaller than the number of times he actually held the office; his areas of jurisdiction while praetorian prefect may be imprecisely described. The most notorious ambiguity in the text of the rehabilitation surely occurs in the younger Flavian's *cursus*: the use of the vague word *saepius*, "often," to describe the number of times he held the urban prefecture. The ambiguity of this term may allow him to take credit for his illegitimate term as urban prefect in 394. More significantly, however, this is a word that draws attention to itself, that suggests something is not being said explicitly.

The same problem crops up in the evaluation of any career. A rehabilitation is a rare thing; the careers described in most inscriptions are presented as nothing more than straightforward accounts of offices held. And yet, these careers are more often than not incomplete, omitting this or that office. The reasons for these omissions are seldom clear.[113] Some omissions of this sort occur in the text of the rehabilitation. For example, there is no reference here to any minor magistracies, such as the quaestorship or the praetorship. These details are provided by the statue base from the Caelian hill. Such minor offices are frequently left off late antique honorific inscriptions, and it is unlikely that their absence from the statue base from the Forum of Trajan has anything to do with the *damnatio memoriae* or the rehabilitation. Nevertheless, it is through the omission or inclusion of details such as these that careers convey their meaning; and their omission here should certainly be closely considered, even if it is only possible to conclude in the end that such offices were regarded as trivial, or that they had become associated with family privilege rather than public accomplishment (hence their mention within the home, but not in the Forum), or that they were omitted through carelessness, or that we cannot know the reason for their exclusion.

Even where the reason for the omission of an office is innocuous, the implications of its absence may be serious. For example, De Rossi is surely right that, by the middle of the fifth century A.D., pagan priesthoods—if any such continued to be held—were not mentioned in public inscriptions, and this argument may suffice to explain why there is no mention of Flavian's service as *pontifex maior* in the rehabilitation. This omission is probably significant and related to the rehabilitation, and there may be a more subtle acknowledgment of this priesthood elsewhere in the inscription (Chapters 3 and 7 below). Still, there is a difference between the notice of an omission and its motivation: the one does not depend on the other. Even if the reasons for leaving the term as *pontifex* out of this *cursus* were innocuous, its absence still might be noticed. In the *Saturnalia,* for example, Macrobius describes Flavian as learned in the mysteries of the augural law (a specialty of the *pontifices*) and religion (Chapter 3 below). The statue base that stood in Flavian's family home mentioned the priesthood. Anyone familiar with texts such as these might easily be aware of the omission of his priesthood from the rehabilitation.

The argument can be applied at a much more general level. No Roman career is an account of an individual's life: it is a highly selective set of extracts, limited almost exclusively to political office. The nature of the *cursus* says something profound about the ideology of the Roman elite. What mattered above all to them was political activity. This Roman obsession can be found in other kinds of texts: histories, for example (see Chapter 5 below). The *cursus* is only the most distilled expression of that sentiment. To appreciate the ideological character of these *cursus,* though, it is necessary to keep in mind all of the things about a person's life that might have been said, but were not. Only in such a light do these *cursus* come to appear as the highly selective documents they are. The inscription from the Forum of Trajan, because it is a rehabilitation, insists on such evaluation. The problem of exclusion here, however, is not unique, only explicit.

CHAPTER 3

UNSPEAKABLE PAGANISM?

MODERN SCHOLARS know Flavian best for his religious activities. If the generalist knows of him at all, it is as the intransigent (or reactionary) champion of Roman paganism against the new religion of the empire, Christianity. From De Rossi's initial publication on, it has always been remarked that there is no apparent reference to paganism in the rehabilitation. There is no mention of his pagan priesthood in the *cursus* at the head of the inscription, nor can any allusion to paganism be deciphered in the text of the imperial letter. Certainly there is some "religious" vocabulary. The letter speaks of the "restoration of the 'reverend recollection' of Flavian" (*sanctissimae recordationis*, lines 14–15), and claims that that restoration is an "homage" (*veneratio*, line 15) to Theodosius. The emperor Theodosius hoped that Flavian would "dedicate" (*consecrari*, line 20) his histories to him and speaks of his own piety (*piaetas*, line 21). The current emperor, Valentinian III, speaks of his feelings toward Flavian as "reverence" (*reverentia*, lines 24 and 36) and alludes to certain traditional rites, absolving the family of Flavian of "the debt of duty owed the dead" (*religiosi muneris debito*, line 33). However, it would be foolish to put any weight on such vocabulary. With the exception of the reference to the "debt of duty owed the dead," the context of the letter does not dictate any strictly religious sense.

The meaning of the absence of reference to religion in this document is not immediately clear. Some have argued that the omission is innocuous: by 431 public documents no longer mentioned pagan religious activities, but restricted themselves to political offices and deeds. On this interpretation the silence of the rehabilitation is merely a product of the monumental medium.[1] Others might maintain that although Christianity had decisively triumphed by the time of Flavian's rehabilitation, religion remained a sensitive subject, and while many may have been comfortable with the rehabilitation of Flavian the statesman and historian, it was not possible to honor or even mention Flavian the pagan. Or it might be argued that while Christianity dominated life in the imperial court, even in the mid-fifth century many in the Roman senatorial class continued to adhere to paganism. The emperor might allow the elite to rehabilitate Flavian, but only to a point. So the silence might be understood as a repression of this aspect of Flavian's life by the Christian imperial court.[2]

To the extent that scholars discuss this problem at all, they implicitly acknowledge that Flavian's religious activities remained notorious at the time of his rehabilitation, and that their omission from the document requires some explanation. The discussion is only about the implications of the omission, not about the fact of it. Before attempting to come to terms with the meaning of this silence, however, it is necessary to establish that there is a silence here at all. Is something deliberately not being said, or is there actually nothing that is not being said? Is Flavian's paganism a significant fact, which the rehabilitation suppresses for some reason? Or is his paganism simply forgotten or irrelevant in the context of this letter, one of an infinite number of things not mentioned because they are not remembered or do not matter? For example, it might be argued that Flavian's disgrace had less to do with religion than with politics; that his role as "champion of the pagan cause" has been greatly exaggerated by modern scholarship; that there is no reference to his paganism in this inscription because religion was irrelevant to his original condemnation and so is not worth mentioning in the rehabilitation. Another position might be that paganism was "ancient history" by 431; that the religious affiliations of prominent men of Flavian's generation had become largely irrelevant (if perhaps still of some cultural importance as an object of nostalgia and romanticism); that no matter what the function of religion in Flavian's activities in the usurpation of 394, it had long been forgotten by 431.

Any attempt to identify a silence—or the absence of it—in this document will have to set the problem in two separate but related contexts. First there is the problem of the elder Flavian's activities in 394 and his subsequent condemnation. What was the character of Flavian's religious views? Did he use the usurpation of Eugenius as an occasion to promote paganism against Christianity? Was he regarded by others as having done so? Were his religious views conceived as part of the justification for his *damnatio memoriae?* At the same time, there is a historiographical dimension to the problem. What was the attitude toward the usurpation of Eugenius from the distance of 431? Was it remembered at all? The fact of the rehabilitation shows that Flavian was remembered, at least by some. How did they regard him? How had the religious attitudes of the Roman elite changed by 431?

This second context is if anything more difficult to evaluate than the first, but it is also more important. The question of what the Christian Roman elite remembered and forgot of its pagan past is central for an understanding of the more general transformation of the Roman world from paganism to Christianity. What was there in the past that could be integrated into Christianity? What resisted such assimilation? How did the elite deal with those elements of its past which could not be mentioned or even were not to be remembered?

There will be some relationship between "what really happened" in the 380's and 390's—whatever that might be—and its assessment in the 430's. Nevertheless, it is important to keep in mind that the two need not coincide; indeed, since the "facts" were undeniably modified by the *damnatio memoriae* and rehabilitation, they very likely do not coincide. The same is doubtless true of contemporary accounts of Flavian and the usurpation of Eugenius. A Christian source like Ambrose or Augustine is certainly prompted by something that "really happened"; still, it would be rash to imagine without confirmation that they are necessarily sympathetic or faithful to the event or to the intent and motivation of Flavian. The judgment pronounced by Theodosius on Flavian is by its nature a brief for the prosecution, not a case for the defense. Fortunately, in evaluating the rehabilitation, the irrecoverable truth about Flavian's psyche is less important than what his contemporaries and succeeding generations said about him. Even if religion played no part in Eugenius' usurpation in 394, if people in 431 thought of that event as "the last pagan resistance to Christianity" and conceived of Flavian as its chief engineer, then it would be necessary to think of religion, though nowhere mentioned, as a major subtext of the rehabilitation.

THE USURPATION OF EUGENIUS

Since late antiquity the usurpation of Eugenius has been understood as emblematic of a larger conflict between paganism and Christianity. Some Christians of the day, those to whom we owe the principal accounts of the usurpation, saw it as an apocalyptic duel between themselves and the old state religion. Modern scholarly opinion has until very recently followed them. Gibbon, remarkably enough, gave a largely political account of the event in his *Decline and Fall;* indeed, in his edition of the work, Bury reproached him for having underemphasized the importance of religion.[3] Other historians have understood the usurpation as a rebellion motivated by pagan sentiment, and it has been given a unique significance in the religious history of the west. Herbert Bloch argued in two influential articles that the usurpation of Eugenius is to be considered "the last pagan revival in the west," the "last resistance of paganism to Christianity," the end of an era or perhaps even an age.[4]

As the story has traditionally been told, the usurpation of Eugenius is the culmination of a religious conflict that had been brewing for almost a century. The growth of the prominence of Christianity among the administrators of the Roman empire of the fourth century A.D., from "the great persecution" under Diocletian and his fellow tetrarchs (303–311), to the conversion of Constantine and his "edict of toleration" (313), to the short-lived revival of paganism under the emperor Julian (361–363), is one of the major themes of ancient history, perhaps even of European history. This complex story has accumulated an immense bibliography.[5] Briefly, the growth and dissemination of Christianity, particularly among the lower economic echelons of Roman society, began long before it was officially recognized by the state. Then, over the course of the third century, the government of the Roman empire itself was increasingly and swiftly "Christianized" as "crypto-Christians" were incorporated into the administration of the state.[6] With the reign of Constantine at the beginning of the fourth century, emperors themselves espoused Christianity, and avowed Christians began to serve openly in positions of power and influence.[7] Yet, even though the explicitly political importance of the new religion grew, the old pagan state religion of Rome survived. The economic, social, and intellectual forces underlying paganism were too powerful and deeply entrenched to be casually legislated out of existence (although some emperors tried to do so). By 341 the emperor Constans was attempting to enforce a decree abolishing pagan sacrifices (*CTh* 16.10.2). Again in 356, Constantius II tried to abolish sacrifices and close pagan temples (*CTh* 16.10.6). Neither of these measures was successful.[8] Nevertheless, paganism was certainly waning in the fourth century. Julian's repudiation of Christianity in favor of a revived and revised paganism was merely an interlude. His paganism did not outlive him. Christian opposition was by this time well established, and the Neoplatonic philosophy that motivated his adherence to paganism was perhaps too intellectual, too elitist, to have much widespread religious appeal.[9]

After Julian's brief reign, Roman emperors once more sanctioned Christianity, and the Roman empire became again a government of two religions. Paganism and Christianity now coexisted more or less uneasily until the reign of the child emperor Gratian, when imperial tolerance for the old gods came to an abrupt end.[10] In 382 Gratian moved against the traditional state religion, confiscating the endowments that supported the priestly colleges of Rome, including that of the Vestals. At the same time, he had removed from the Roman senate house the altar of Victory, which had for many years been the occasion of disputes between the pagan senatorial class of Rome and the Christian emperors.[11] Gratian also became the first emperor to refuse to accept the traditional imperial title of *pontifex maximus,* head of the old state religion, chief of the pagan state priests.[12]

Those most obviously offended by Gratian's measures were among the Roman senatorial elite. They reacted with circumspect outrage, dispatching an embassy to the emperor in protest. The emperor refused to receive it. In 383, however, Gratian was executed by his own mutinous troops. Most of the western empire fell into the hands of the Spaniard Magnus Maximus, who established a court in Trier; many of the Roman senatorial class, including the orator Symmachus, supported him.[13] Italy alone remained in the hands of the imperial dynasty. There Gratian was succeeded by another child emperor, the twelve-year-old Valentinian II. He was apparently less hostile toward paganism (or at least toward certain pagan senators of Rome) than his predecessor: in 384 he appointed perhaps the most famous pagan of the day, Vettius Agorius Praetextatus, as praetorian prefect of Italy. Not only was Praetextatus a well-known and unabashed devotee of pagan cult, but his career had been advanced some years before by the apostate emperor Julian. During his term of office, Praetextatus restored a pagan building, the *Porticus deorum consentium*—the last major pagan dedication undertaken by a state official in Rome (*ILS* 4003).[14]

That same year, the emperor chose the orator Symmachus to be urban prefect. As urban prefect, he reported directly and regularly to the emperor. Symmachus used one of his official reports (*relationes*) as an opportunity to argue for the restoration of the altar of Victory. This text came to be regarded as the characteristic statement of devotion to paganism in its declining years.[15] The historical prosperity of the Roman empire, Symmachus suggested (like others before and after him), was owing in part to the favor of the gods; to neglect the sanctioned, traditional religious observances was to risk that favor and, consequently, the prosperity of the state: "We seek the restoration of the cult to its previous condition, which has long been beneficial to the state" (*repetimus igitur religionum statum qui rei publicae diu profuit*) (*Rel.* 3.3).[16] Symmachus refrained from attacking Christianity; rather, he urged mutual religious tolerance. In his famous phrase, "It is not possible to arrive at so great a truth by one road" (*uno itinere non potest perveniri ad tam grande secretum*) (*Rel.* 3.10). The letter was persuasive, and might have been successful but for the opposition of the powerful bishop of Milan. Ambrose sent a letter to the emperor in which he threatened to excommunicate him if he gave in (Ambrose *Ep.* 18), and the request was denied.

In 384 the western half of the Roman empire was in shambles, divided by civil war and with a child for an emperor. Finally, the senior Augustus of the east, Theodosius the Great, intervened. He marched west to Gaul, where in 388 he defeated the usurper Magnus Maximus. He then returned to Italy, where he undertook to arrange the government of the west.[17] In 389, the Roman senate approached him again, requesting the restoration of the altar of Victory (Ambrose *Ep.* 57.4). Once more they were refused. Theodosius remained in Italy until 391. In that year he dispatched the young Augustus of the west, Valentinian II, then age twenty-one, to the court at Vienne in the keeping of his pagan, Gothic generalissimo (*magister militum*), Arbogast. He himself returned to Constantinople. The senate thought this might be a good time to ask once again for the restoration of the altar of Victory. Valentinian refused (Ambrose *Ep.* 57.5).

Valentinian II resented Arbogast's supervision, and Arbogast seems to have been hardly more pleased with his youthful charge. In May of 392, Valentinian was found dangling from a noose in the palace, either a suicide or a victim of murder (Rufinus *HE* 11.31). As a Goth, Arbogast could not hope to become emperor himself. Nevertheless, in Valentinian's timely demise Arbogast saw an opportunity to elevate his own man to the throne. He chose a Christian cipher named Eugenius, a palace functionary and former professor of rhetoric, to be the new emperor of the west.[18] He then appealed to the emperor of the east, Theodosius, to accept Eugenius, swearing his innocence in the recent demise of Valentinian. Theodosius temporized. Reading the emperor's hesitation rightly, Arbogast began to consolidate his newly acquired realm in preparation for the inevitable military reaction from Constantinople. Realizing that support would be needed if he and Eugenius were to successfully oppose Theodosius, Arbogast evidently courted and received the backing of the senatorial class of Rome, choosing as his right-hand man one of its most prominent representatives, Virius Nicomachus Flavianus. In 392 Flavian joined Arbogast as praetorian prefect of Italy. Later, in 394, he served as ordinary consul. That same year Flavian's son, Flavian the younger, was appointed urban prefect.

In the early years of his reign, Theodosius had displayed tolerance toward paganism.[19] He had, however, recently antagonized the pagan senators of Rome by issuing legislation of unprecedented severity against the old state religion.[20] On 24 February 391, he forbade all public sacrifice and visitation of temples (*CTh* 16.10.10), and on 8 November of the following year he extended his ban to the private cults of the Lares, Genius, and Penates (*CTh* 16.10.12). Eugenius too was doubtless a Christian (cf. Ambrose *Ep.* 57); nevertheless, under his rule these measures were reversed, either with his assent or, as some have suggested, by Flavian and Arbogast in spite of him. The new regime reversed the decisions of the old quietly, perhaps so as not to give unnecessary offense too soon to the powerful western church. The endowments of the Vestals and the priestly colleges were returned; the money, however, was not given directly to the colleges, but passed to leading senators who were to dispense it as they saw fit (Ambrose *Ep.* 57). The altar of Victory was also restored to the old Senate house "at the request of Flavian and Arbogast" (Paulinus *Vit. Ambr.* 26).

Not only did Arbogast and Flavian allow the senatorial class to resume pagan worship, but sacrifice and haruspicy, the old science of prediction from the entrails of the victims, played a significant role in their preparations for the showdown with Theodosius. The contemporary historian of the church, Rufinus, provides a vivid account of Flavian's leadership in these activities. He says that Theodosius prepared for battle by going to churches and praying to the Christian god,

> but the pagans, who continuously breathe life into their mistakes with new mistakes, renewed their sacrifices, stained Rome with the gore of their cursed victims, examined the entrails of cattle, and from the premonitory knowledge contained in the entrails announced the certain victory of Eugenius. Flavian, who was then prefect, performed these superstitious rites, and he did so with utter conviction; because of his assured statements (for he had a great reputation for wisdom) they took it for certain that Eugenius would win.
>
> *at pagani, qui errores suos novis semper erroribus animant, innovare sacrificia, et Romam funestis victimis cruentare, inspicere exta pecudum, et ex fibrarum praescientia securam Eugenio victoriam nuntiare, superstitiosus haec agente,*

> *et cum omni animositate, Flaviano tunc praefecto, cuius assertionibus (magna enim erat eius in sapientia praerogativa) Eugenium fore pro certo praesumpserant.* (Rufinus *HE* 11.33)

Flavian may have made other predictions as well. According to Augustine (*Civ. Dei* 18.53–54) an oracle was circulating which said that Christianity would come to an end after a year of years, that is, after as many years had passed as the year has days. If we date the Crucifixion to A.D. 29 and add 365 years to it, then 394, the year of Eugenius' usurpation and Flavian's consulship, would be the term of Christianity and the beginning of this pagan millennium.[21] If this oracle is to be associated with the revolt of Eugenius, as seems plausible, then at least some of the rebels saw themselves as participating in more than a limited political revolt; the usurpation is given grand connotations and becomes a kind of cosmic confrontation between religious systems.

It is uncertain how much support there was for the usurpation of Eugenius among the Roman senatorial class. The elder Flavian and Arbogast are the only names explicitly associated with a "pagan revival." Flavian the younger, who served as urban prefect in 394, was also a pagan at the time of the revolt. Some believe that an inscription from Ostia provides evidence for a more widespread resurgence of interest in pagan cult among the Roman senatorial class. Recording the restoration of a local temple of "the unconquered Hercules," *Hercules Invictus* (*AE* 1941.66), it is dated to 393 or the beginning of 394, the consulship of Theodosius, Arcadius, and Eugenius:[22]

> For our lords Theodosius, Arcadius, and Eugenius, pious, fortunate, over all the world victorious, ever reverend, the noble Numerius Proiectus, prefect of the grain supply, restored the temple of Hercules.

> *[Domini]s n[ostris Th]eodosio Arca[di]o et Eu[genio]/[pi]is felicibus [toto] orbe victoribus semper [Auggg(ustis)]/[..] Numerius Proiect[us] v(ir) c(larissimus) pra]ef(ectus) ann(onae) cellam Hercu[lis restituit].*

The superintendent of the grain supply (*praefectus annonae*) was active in Rome's port, Ostia; nevertheless, he was an official of the city of Rome and reported to the urban prefect, who in 394 was Flavian the younger.[23] This superintendent, Numerius Proiectus, is not well known, though.[24] Symmachus refers to a certain Proiectus as a friend (*familiaris*) (*Ep.* 3.6.4), and it is tempting to identify the two. In any event, because Proiectus was a subordinate of Flavian the younger, Bloch argued that he should be regarded as a follower of the pagan cause and a member of the circle of the elder Flavian. Proiectus' restoration of the pagan temple of Hercules, then, might be understood in the context of the elder Flavian's religious activities.

By 394 the temple of Hercules in Ostia was very ancient, dating back about five hundred years to the time of Sulla. This particular Hercules was an oracular god. A relief, dedicated in republican times by a *haruspex,* a seer who prophesied from the entrails of animals, has been recovered, showing Hercules distributing oracles by a kind of lottery. Hercules is known to have been an oracular god elsewhere, particularly at Tibur, where oracles of the god are known to have been distributed by allotment.[25] Hercules also was singled out as a special patron of the pagan cause at the battle of Eugenius and Theodosius at the river Frigidus. Furthermore, prescience played an important role in the usurpation of Eugenius: as we have seen, an oracle may have been circulating at this time which foretold the impending demise of Christianity, and Flavian was notorious for his interest in the art of prediction.

The court of Eugenius took up residence in Milan, the traditional home of the western emperors and the seat of Ambrose's bishopric. Ambrose, who had so long served as a Christian watchdog and as the conscience of emperors, was forced to flee. When the news came that Theodosius was marching on Italy, Eugenius, Arbogast, and Flavian marched out of Milan to meet him. As they left they are reported to have promised that once they had defeated Theodosius they would return to Milan, turn Ambrose's cathedral into a stable, and draft the local clergy into the army (Paulinus *Vit. Ambr.* 31), and Ambrose describes their army as "pagan"(*exercitus infidelium*) (Ambrose *De obitu Theodosii* 10). They took up position at the river Frigidus, a natural pass into Italy, and awaited the army of Theodosius there.[26] Flavian set up statues of Jupiter hoisting thunderbolts of pure gold on the bluffs overlooking the river valley where the battle would occur, and consecrated them "by unknown rites" (Aug. *Civ. Dei* 5.26). Standards featuring the hero Hercules may also have been prepared, to be carried before the army as it went into battle (Theodoret 5.24.4; cf. 17).

The method of invoking the gods here is itself profoundly significant from both a religious and a historical point of view. The notion of consecrating an image (in this case, the statues of Jupiter) in order to make a divine spirit enter it and give it power has a long history in Greco-Roman religion. The erection of such consecrated images at boundaries to ward off invasion or other threats is also common in the ancient world.[27] The invocation of Hercules' protection by fixing his image to the standards of the army also has a long pre-Christian history; and yet, at the time of the battle, the most famous and recent precedent was *Christian*. Before the battle of the Milvian bridge in 312, Constantine had a vision of the cross with the words *in hoc signo vincas*—"Under This Symbol Conquer." Inspired by the god (*instinctu divinitatis,* as he would later claim on his triumphal arch), he had some sign of Christ—the cross or perhaps the Chi-Rho—placed on the shields and standards of his army.[28]

The tandem of Jupiter and Hercules as protectors and emblems is also provocative. These two gods were associated with the rulers of the empire, most particularly with the tetrarchy initiated by Diocletian in 293. Diocletian was responsible for the institution of what would become a permanent administrative division of the Roman empire into east and west. To rule these two realms, he co-opted a second ruler. In the iconography of the tetrarchy, these two emperors (Augusti) were associated with particular divinities: Jupiter and Hercules. So the selection of these two gods by Flavian and Arbogast may well have had political overtones.[29]

Moreover, these two gods associated with the tetrarchy carried anti-Christian connotations. Since the time of Constantine's "edict of tolerance" in 313, Diocletian and his colleagues were recalled as the "great persecutors" of Christians. At the end of the third century, Christians were to be found at all levels of the army and imperial administration. The Great Persecution was intended to stop and even reverse this "infiltration." So a violent purge was ordered by Diocletian in 303; it was implemented with remarkable energy by Galerius.[30] The rebels' selection of the two gods linked to the Great Persecution cannot have gone unnoticed by Theodosius and his historians.

The battle of the Frigidus began poorly for Theodosius: the terrain worked against him, and his army was outflanked and then surrounded by the forces of Eugenius. By the end of the first day's fighting he had lost more than ten thousand men. On the morning of the second day, however, he went up on the bluffs overlooking the battlefield where both armies could see him, opposite the statues of Jupiter, and knelt in prayer. As if in answer to his prayer a wind sprang up, blowing dirt and debris in the faces of the pagan soldiers, blinding them and throwing them into confusion. A Christian miracle had apparently helped Theodosius win the battle against Eugenius while the powerless statues of Jupiter impassively watched their defenders go down to defeat. Arbogast survived the battle, but ultimately could not escape and so had to kill himself. Eugenius was dragged before Theodosius and executed. Flavian, irreconcilable with the cause of the victors, preferred the death of Cato and committed suicide.

MODERN CRITICISM OF RELIGIOUS CONFLICT

This interpretation of the usurpation of Eugenius at least has the virtue of summarizing the available sources. Since the 1970's, however, it has been subject to much criticism. Revisionist thought on the relationship between paganism and Christianity in this period takes its beginning from Alan Cameron's famous 1966 essay on Macrobius, in which he argued that the composition of the *Saturnalia* dated to the 430's rather than to the 390's as had previously been supposed. By redating the *Saturnalia,* Cameron removed the major piece of evidence for pagan sentiment, organization, and cultural politics in the 390's to a later generation. So, as he says, it is necessary to regard it as a piece of nostalgia or antiquarianism, rather than as a political and religious manifesto.[31] Cameron's argument invited a skeptical re-evaluation of all the evidence for the traditional historical reconstruction of a combative pagan "party" in the late fourth century.[32]

One result of this revisionism has been to replace the traditional historical model of religious conflict in late antiquity with one in which the accommodation and assimilation of paganism is emphasized.[33] There is ample evidence for religious combativeness in this period; documented hostilities, however, for the most part originate from Christians rather than from pagans. Paganism was by its very nature agglutinative, inclusive: there is no inherent reason why the god of the Christians should not have been worshiped along with Zeus and Mars. From a pagan perspective Christianity might be regarded as just another oriental cult, like that of Mithra or the Magna Mater—and many such flourished side by side in late antique Rome. So the leading characteristic of paganism could be considered its religious tolerance. Christians, on the other hand, regarded their god as preemptive: one could not be a Christian and worship other gods. The dichotomy of pagan versus Christian is a characteristically Christian opposition, as it is the distinguishing characteristic of Christianity to make exclusionary religious distinctions.[34]

Proceeding from this premise, some scholars have begun to rethink the political and religious history of the fourth century. Their strategy has been to treat all evidence of hostility or conflict as emanating from Christians. So, for example, the legislation against sacrifice, which dates to the reigns of Constans and Constantius II (341–356), is held to be irrelevant to the pagan senatorial class: it "did not give rise to a uniform pagan political reaction in the middle of the century, nor does it indicate conflict between pagans and Christians."[35] The militance of the pagan reaction under Julian is also seen as a product of Christianity: Julian had spent his childhood as a Christian and must have learned intolerance from them. In any event, Julian is seen as idiosyncratic, an exceptional figure, whose attitudes were not shared by any larger group.[36]

The story of the "last resistance of paganism" in the 380's and 390's would seem at first glance to resist such explanation. Gratian's confiscation of the endowments of the old Roman priestly colleges certainly did offend the Roman senatorial class, as did his removal of the altar of Victory from the senate house. These policies led to the well-documented protest from some Roman senators epitomized in Symmachus' famous third *Relatio*. Theodosius' legislation against public and private pagan cult in the early 390's must also have had some effect on the wealthy pagans of Rome.[37]

Cameron has argued that even here religion is not a common ground for conflict. Certainly for Christians religion was the preeminent issue in all matters. The sermons, poems, and laws of the fourth century against those who had not embraced the true faith take up volumes. There is, however, little evidence—Cameron would say none—for a pagan response on specifically religious grounds: "reaction of any sort is conspicuous by its absence. Apathy, rather, born of aristocratic complacency."[38] Cameron would argue that the evidence is not there, not because the later Christian tradition has suppressed it, or because the pagans, outnumbered and under attack, settled on a prudent policy of reconciliation, but because the elite of this period were preoccupied not with the present but with the past: "On all sides we find this preoccupation with what was past, rather than a realistic attempt to grapple with the present. Perhaps Christianity would just go away one day."[39] So, from the Christian perspective, there was a conflict with paganism. From the point of view of a pagan Roman senator, there was disinterest and a sense of frustration because the Christians did not seem to understand his concern with traditional culture.

The account of Flavian's actions in the 390's might seem to provide unambiguous testimony of the religious overtones at least of the war between the forces of Eugenius and Theodosius. Nevertheless there are gaps and inconsistencies in the account of the revolt that are vulnerable to criticism. The usurpation of Arbogast and Eugenius was prompted in part (some would say entirely) by dissatisfaction with the dynastic succession in the west. The senatorial class of the west may well have bristled at the interference of the emperor of the east, Theodosius, and may have mistrusted his choice for emperor of the west, the arrogant and incompetent adolescent Valentinian II.[40] In addition, the leadership of the usurpation was not uniformly pagan: Flavian was a pagan, but he joined the revolt late. Arbogast, given his early prominence in the court of Theodosius and Valentinian II, very likely was a professed Christian, even though his name is consistently coupled with that of Flavian later on as an enemy of Christianity in reports concerning the actions of the usurpers. The emperor Eugenius was a Christian. Also there is little evidence to suggest any larger social support for a "religious rebellion" in 394. Few other Roman senators are known to have supported Eugenius. There are no signs of a renaissance of pagan ritual in that year: the dedication to Hercules from Ostia is a thin reed to rely on. So Flavian comes to appear to be a "single rather foolish figure prophesying victory for a usurper who never had a chance."[41] Certainly the sources for the usurpation, which would include Ambrose and Augustine among others, explicitly speak against these criticisms. All of these writings, however, are by Christians; no statement from the rebels has survived. Since Christians are considered to be intolerant and obsessed with religious difference, it has proved easy to dismiss these sources as an "angry, overblown, propagandizing reaction."[42]

It is difficult to say how influential or controversial these arguments are among specialists in late antiquity at this point. I have not found any detailed responses in print. Many scholars, however, continue to treat the 380's and 390's as a period of "pagan revolt," the climax of which is the usurpation of Eugenius in 394. There have been some who would minimize the religious aspect of even this rebellion,[43] but most scholars, even those who follow Cameron's interpretation, regard it as motivated at least in part by religious sentiment.[44]

Cameron and those who have followed him have undeniably scored some telling points against the traditional interpretation of Bloch; in the end, however, they are too concerned to refute Bloch, and their position comes to be determined by what they are trying to contradict. Instead of pointing out the limitations of Bloch's arguments, accepting what is good (and there is some good in Bloch's construction of the culture of the period), discarding what is bad, and proposing something new, they produce a mirror image of Bloch's picture of the period. Cameron is aware that his arguments produce this impression: "it may well seem that much of what I have been saying is pretty negative. But it was not at all my purpose simply to debunk the circle of Symmachus." He goes on to say that he has rather been arguing that there is no pagan reaction; that the pagan elite of the period are characterized by apathy.[45] Elsewhere, in his article "The Latin Revival of the Fourth Century," he proposes to show that the revival of letters in this period is not "just one aspect of the pagan religious revival," but was "a much wider and more complex phenomenon than usually supposed."[46] In the end, though, after a long and negative discussion, he finds little of importance in the role of literary activity within the period, no broader cultural ramifications to the behavior: "Ultimately, then, the revival was important because it was the literary tastes of the fourth century that were passed on to the Middle Ages."[47] This is tantamount to claiming that the secular literature of the period is important only as a bridge from one period to the next. When others use Cameron's arguments, they make comparable assertions: "we should not think of a general 'pagan revival' in this period centred round a clearly demarcated 'circle of Symmachus,' as formerly proposed, but rather of a range of attitudes existing among the pagan upper class, from commitment to pagan cult and Roman tradition down to a simple fondness for the status quo."[48] In other words, religious ideology among pagans during this period had no noticeable significance as a producer of social solidarity.

I do not wish to minimize the gains that have come with this re-evaluation of the usurpation of 394. It has been shown, for example, that in its origins the motivation for the usurpation was to some extent political. In this it has proved a useful antidote to explanations that focus too exclusively on religious conflict as the explanation for the revolt of Eugenius—or, indeed, as *the* explanation for the history of the fourth century. More important, these criticisms have led to a more nuanced and articulated understanding of religious identity in this period. There was a range of pagan sentiment in the late fourth century, as there was a range of Christian feeling; the dividing line between the two was sharply drawn by some, as it was rather hazy for others: there was surely some overlap.[49] Some advocates of this revised interpretation, however, have reacted too strongly against the traditional position represented by Bloch, and have attempted to read religious conflict completely out of the political and social events of this period. Such a position is intrinsically unlikely, and it should be rejected.[50] Religious assimilation and conflict are not mutually exclusive, but are two faces of the same coin. Both are a reaction to a social tension, a religious differentiation, and it is necessary to read each in light of the other, not to choose one over the other.

It is pointlessly reductionist to insist on political causes for the revolt of Eugenius to the exclusion of other factors, including religion. Wars, ancient and modern, typically have had religious (and other) overtones. Religion and war and politics and literature should not be treated as a quarantined areas; they always impinge on each other and on other spheres of economic and social and political and intellectual behavior. Cultural behavior of all kinds is coherent—and that is precisely one of the larger points I have to make in this book. In addition, it is wrong to portray Flavian as an eccentric and isolated figure. To the extent that he was a leader and commanded the allegiance of his followers, his very position demonstrates that he was not isolated. Whether or not Ambrose is to be trusted when he describes the army as "pagan," they did follow Flavian through his sacrifices and belligerence; they did fight under the shadow of the statues of Zeus, and perhaps beneath the standard of Hercules.

The ideological role of religion in the usurpation of Eugenius is further supported by the settlement imposed by Theodosius. In the aftermath of the usurpation, Theodosius took steps to eradicate paganism from the Roman senate, encouraging the mass conversion of the elite (cf. notably Augustine *Civ. Dei* 5.26, Prudentius *Contra Symmachum* 1.506–607, and the discussion below). For critics, however, it is the nature of the evidence itself that is at issue. The sources are all Christian, and Christians are regarded as untrustworthy and biased. So it is profitless to attempt to resolve the question of the religious overtones of Eugenius' usurpation by appeal to the consistency or inherent likelihood of the received accounts. It may be possible to show the plausibility of religious conflict during this period, and hence better understand the sources for the usurpation, by looking in a more general way at the social context of religion and the extent of pagan allegiance among the Roman elite during this period. This issue is of more importance than the connotations of a single battle anyway (we will return to the battle below). Nevertheless, some more general points need to be made about the presumptions of these criticisms.

The major problem at issue here is the nature of paganism in late antiquity or, more precisely, the question of the subjectivity of the pagan. Scholars, it is argued, should attempt to recover the self-consciousness of the pagan, rather than merely repeat the hostile caricatures provided by Christians. The very word "pagan" is held to be inadequate and inappropriate for use in modern scholarship; it is a slur, a term that "came into common use (only among Christians) at this period: a bit of sarcasm used behind the victim's back, or occasionally, for the fun of it, to his face."[51] The alternative "polytheism," derived from the usage of anthropology, has been proposed.[52] I fail to see the benefit of changing the vocabulary here.[53] The shift to an opposition of monotheism versus polytheism, with the larger comparative perspective it implies, may yield new insights, but it will also lose some of the old specificity of the historical opposition of religions in late antiquity. Furthermore, whether it is imagined that this vocabulary reproduces historical pagan sentiment more faithfully, or that it reflects a neutral and objective modern analytic agnosticism, it should be clear that it is no freer of bias than the old pagan/Christian dichotomy.

This entire discussion seems to me to be founded on a misapprehension of the nature of social identity. It begins from the presumption that any group can be something outside of its relation to other groups; that it is meaningful or useful or possible to treat a religious category, be it "paganism" or "polytheism," as something innate, as the product of an autonomous self-consciousness. Social identity, like individual identity, must be treated in systematic rather than essential terms. It is the product of a set of relationships, not of an intrinsic self-awareness.[54] For example, American black ethnic identity is a product of a particular set of interactions within American society; it is not an innate quality. If it were innate, then we would expect to find a "black character" which transcends place and time. Of course this is not the case, and the contemporary American idea of "blackness" makes no sense whatsoever in social contexts where "whiteness" is not at issue (e.g. precolonial sub-Saharan Africa). The same would be true of the category "Indian" in contemporary America. To take another crucial modern example, Western Jewish identity should be understood as the product of a history of relations with the society of Christian Europe. None of these identities is natural, even though they are frequently buttressed with an appeal to "scientific" categories such as race; they are the product of a set of social and cultural relationships. Although these categories are fabricated, political creations, products of an environment, they have their own reality and force; no account of American or European society that ignored racial categories could be satisfactory.[55] Just so, "paganism" (as everyone agrees) comes into existence in late antiquity, precisely with the rise of Christianity to a position of political dominance. It is a creation of the dialectical opposition of two groups, but it is nonetheless socially real, and any account of the period must consider it. Millar seems to be moving toward an appreciation of this systematic character of religious identity when he observes that "by the fourth century the challenge of Christianity had long since forced those who observed the cults of the gods into explicit philosophical reflection on their system of belief and practice—which we may therefore appropriately call paganism."[56] Religious identity, like any identity, is constituted through struggle, which is manifested in the dynamic processes of assimilation and resistance. These processes are not products of a preexisting conflict of identity; they are the forces through which identity is constituted. So the name "pagan" and the diatribes of the Christians are not to be discarded as "biased" and "propagandizing"; they are highly relevant to a knowledge of the character of this group in late antiquity, a substantial part of what it meant to be "not a Christian."

The idea that subjectivity is intrinsic to the consciousness of the individual, that it exists outside and independent of social interactions, has long been a staple of liberal humanism. If subjectivity itself is a product of politics and society, some would say, meaningful criticism and resistance are impossible. The fact that resistance and even the self-consciousness of subordinate groups are themselves products and manifestations of their oppression does not make them any the less "real" as social phenomena. One reasonable response is not to insist on their innate and autonomous character, but to reverse the perspective and show the reciprocity of the relationship. Black identity may be a construct of white society in America, but it is also necessary for the very existence of white society; European Christians have traditionally known what they themselves are in part through the construction of the idea of "the Jew." So in the combative or cooperative interactions of Christians and pagans in late antiquity we can see not only the creation of the religious category "pagan," but also the emergence of Christianity. Paganism in this period is nothing outside of an implied reference and opposition to Christianity; but Christian identity during this period (and for long after) is also established by the exclusion of paganism. Pagans, like witches and magicians and later "infidels" of other kinds, were a necessary "alterity," an exclusion that functioned to help Christians know themselves. To shore up Christian identity, paganism had to be kept in mind, so that it could be constantly anathematized and forgotten (see Chapter 4 below); and this paradox is one of the reasons for the survival of the literature, history, and institutions of pagan Rome after the final triumph of the Christian church.[57]

I do not mean to oversimplify the nature of late antique paganism. Paganism cannot be reduced to nothing more than its opposition to Christianity. There are other sets of systematic relations operating simultaneously. The most important of these is the relation of paganism to its past, that is, the identity of memory. The character of this historical identity, again, is not innate but constructed, the product of a developing dialectic between present situation and past "facts," as both are perceived at any given time. In late antiquity there was a tension between the dominant historical traditions of paganism and its subordinate position in the new Christian world. The conflict and mutual dependence of these two conflicting senses of self—one a product of the relation to the past, the other of the relation to the present—is at the heart of the problem of paganism in this period; it is both the product and the wellspring of assimilation and conflict. The resolution of this problem is not to be found in the decisive triumph of Christianity, but in the survival of Roman secular traditions within Christianity.

THE CHRISTIANIZATION OF THE ROMAN ELITE

Many causes have been alleged for the conversion of the Roman world to Christianity, ranging from the economic to the existential.[58] In the case of Flavian's social milieu, the immediate causes are political: most Roman senators had a cultural and political and even an economic investment in the continuation of the traditions of the Roman state, as they were embodied in those things which lasted, such as literature, institutions, and history. Like most elites they tended to be culturally conservative, and they remained attached to paganism long after the rest of society had converted to Christianity. The emperors, on the other hand, tended to be culturally more innovative, and had been since the foundation of the principate. When Constantine espoused Christianity, the senatorial class did not uniformly follow suit. Some did, but many remained pagan. So a split developed between the pagan Roman senate and the Christian imperial court. Conversion of the senatorial class was slow but ultimately inescapable, because the emperor had the superior force on his side.[59] Once Christianity had become the imperial religion, the conversion of the elite began. Many senators converted voluntarily. Others were forced to convert by the increasingly numerous and intolerant Christians and by a series of imperial decrees from Constantine, Constantius II, Gratian, and Theodosius. This explanation has not been uncommon. Contemporary Christians such as Ambrose and Prudentius argued it, and it has been taken up by many modern scholars.[60]

For scholars of Bloch's generation, it was generally assumed that the Roman senate was predominantly pagan until the end of the fourth century when, in the wake of the "last revival of paganism," they were forced by Theodosius to convert. So 394 is a watershed, and the general conversion of the senate is dated to the generation of Flavian's son, roughly the first third of the fifth century. Even Peter Brown, who argued against Bloch's model of radical religious conflict and in favor of a model of gradual religious assimilation, accepted this chronology.[61] More recent prosopographical studies seemed to confirm this scenario. In 1971 Werner Eck argued that the Roman elite were uniformly pagan at the beginning of the fourth century.[62] In his 1975 dissertation, R. von Haehling carried the analysis down to the end of the century,[63] basing his discussion on a tabulation of certain senior imperial officers (e.g. praetorian prefect, urban prefect, proconsuls of Africa, Asia, and

Achaea, etc.). His results seemed to demonstrate conclusively that the majority of the Roman senate remained pagan at least until the time of Gratian.

In a recent series of studies, T. D. Barnes has criticized this representation of the religious affiliations of the Roman elite.[64] He has numerous points to make against von Haehling, regarding both the accuracy of his data and his procedures of categorization and interpretation. Barnes' most important point, however, is a methodological one: in coming to his conclusions, von Haehling counted offices held rather than holders of offices.[65] Since a given individual might typically hold more than one office or hold a given office more than one time, this method of counting may easily inflate the influence of one group or the other. By counting the individuals who held offices rather than the offices held, Barnes shows that von Haehling's statistics seriously underrepresent the presence of Christians in the senior offices of the empire from the time of Constantine on and, by extension, contribute to a minimization of the extent of Christianity within the Roman elite in these years. He concludes that already in the reign of Constantine, as Eusebius says (*VC* 11.44), the emperor appointed by preference Christians to high office. In fact, from the time of Constantine on, under every emperor except Constans (337–350) a majority of those appointed to high office were Christian.

The percentage of Christian officeholders need not be representative of the extent of Christianity among the elite as a whole. Nevertheless Barnes' figures do show that the Christianization of the Roman elite was well under way from the early fourth century, long before most had imagined. It is significant, too, that the first Christian consul, Ovinius Gallicanus (317),[66] was a member of an established senatorial family, not a provincial parvenu. From the 320's on, a significant proportion of the Roman senate must have been Christian.[67] This conclusion has large implications for the interpretation of elite religious conflict later in the fourth century. Under Julian, under Gratian, in 394 during the usurpation of Eugenius, the Roman senatorial class was not a monolithic pagan bloc, as has been traditionally thought. A substantial number of senators in these years were Christian, and had been so already for several generations. So in the later fourth century the religious constituency of Julian and Praetextatus and Flavian was certainly not the senatorial class as a whole and perhaps not even a majority of that group.

The conversion of the senate to Christianity was far from completed under Constantine. Many senators, probably even the majority, remained pagan: throughout the fourth century a substantial minority of officeholders was always pagan, and under Constans there was a reversion to the preference of pagans in higher magistracies. Julian's revival of paganism in the early 360's, of course, also suggests that at this late date there was still significant support for paganism among the elite.

Barnes has proven that the Christianization of the Roman elite began much earlier than most had imagined. The usurpation of Eugenius, however, remains a watershed in the history of this process, even if its significance is not as epochal as had been thought previously. After the battle of the Frigidus, pressure was brought on prominent pagans to convert to Christianity. As Augustine remarks, Theodosius "wanted them to become Christian because of this event" (*Civ. Dei* 5.26). Prudentius describes this conversion of the senatorial class, naming several prominent individuals, in a famous passage of his poem "Against Symmachus" (*Contra Symmachum* 1.506–607).[68] The younger Flavian may serve as an example. After the pagan revolt, he suffered a period of disgrace. Because of the efforts of Symmachus this period was shorter than it might otherwise have been, and within five years he had managed to "rehabilitate" himself. As part of the campaign to restore his political fortunes, he converted to Christianity (Augustine *Civ. Dei* 5.26.1).

After 395, it should be presumed, the majority of the Roman senatorial class had professed allegiance to the Christian faith.[69] Nevertheless it is clear that a substantial pagan sentiment lingered on for many years, either because the Christianized elite retained their loyalty to traditional institutions and practices, including those of paganism, or because some recalcitrant individuals refused to convert.

Even in Honorius' time prodigies continued to be observed, interpreted, and expiated, as in the great panic that ensued in Rome over the "omen of the wolves," which Claudian attempted to soothe.[70] A decade after the usurpation of Eugenius, in 407 or 408, a decree was issued by Honorius to the western empire, ordering that "if any images stand even now in the temples and shrines . . . they shall be torn from their foundations. . . . The buildings themselves of the temples which are situated in cities or towns shall be vindicated to public use. Altars shall be destroyed in all places." The fact of the decree implies that there is still some survival of pagan sympathy. As the emperors themselves note in the decree, "This regulation has often been decreed by repeated sanctions" (*CTh* 16.10.19). During the first siege of Rome by Alaric in 408/409, the prefect of the city, Gabinius Barbarus Pompeianus, attempted to revive pagan worship in an effort to win back the favor of the old gods and lift the siege of the invaders.[71] Rumor had it that the Christian Pope, Innocentius, was frightened by the invasion and gave his permission for Pompeianus' pagan celebrations in December of 408 and the early winter months of 409 (Sozomen 9.6.3). The pagan interlude was brief. By February 409 Pompeianus was dead, killed in a riot over the food supply.

Pompeianus' return to pagan ritual illustrates both the continuing vitality of the idea that the fortunes of Rome were tied to the proper worship of the old gods and that the idea survives in the early fifth century, even among the Roman elite. The most famous evidence for the survival of this idea in the fifth century is Augustine's *City of God*. Augustine was inspired to write the book in part by the sack of Rome in 410. Rumors were circulating that the city had fallen because of its neglect of the old pagan gods who had raised it high. Augustine desired to refute such notions (see *Epp.* 135–138).[72]

The conversion of the senatorial class and the survival of paganism in the early fifth century can also be confirmed in detail in the cases of particular Roman families, such as the Anicii, the Caeionii, and the Rufii Festi.[73] From the history of such families it is apparent that the elite did not convert utterly as a result of the military defeat of Eugenius and the subsequent settlement imposed by Theodosius. The process of Christianization, continuing from the early fourth century, was more drawn out. The conservatism of certain individuals, their allegiance to the paganism of their ancestors in the face of very real political disincentives, is often remarkable. In one extreme case, a prominent senator, Rufius Antonius Agrypnius Volusianus, did not abandon paganism for Christianity until just before his death in 437 (*Vit. S. Melaniae* 50–55).[74] After about 440 no further pagans are attested among the elite of the city of Rome.

The conversion of the Roman senatorial class, then, occurs over the course of more than a century, from the time of Constantine through the time of the rehabilitation of Flavian. As Brown argues, it is the gradualness of this religious and social transformation of the elite that accounts for the continuities of secular and even pagan traditions from the old world of Rome into the new Christian order. The shift from pagan to Christian was not immediate and universal, but slow and haphazard, leading to "a blurring of the sharp division between pagan past and a Christian present."[75] Because this transition was amorphous and protracted, it made a more substantial survival of the old traditions and customs possible. The preservation of this tradition accounts for the special historical importance of the story of the conversion of this group. For example, the senatorial class had always been concerned to read the texts of classical authors who deal with overtly pagan material, such as Livy and Vergil (see Chapter 6 below). This interest continues in the fourth and fifth centuries despite the Christianization of the elite and, indeed, is taken up by many Christians. Certain pagan religious observances survived down to this time as well, even within the city of Rome itself, including various festivals, such as the Lupercalia and the Isidis Navigium.[76]

There is an apparent contradiction between the ideals of Christianity and the survival of pagan history and literature and religion. In his important recent book, R. A. Markus has shown that Christians dealt with this contradiction in part by treating such survivals as strictly cultural rather than as religious phenomena, thus disarming to some extent their subversive character.[77] There is substantial merit in this argument; however, it would be a mistake to imagine that the Roman secular tradition was ever completely domesticated in that manner. For Christians, the evocation of pagan Rome always summoned up with it a whiff of brimstone. The scandalousness of pagan observances had a useful and instructive role to play in the never-ceasing construction and consolidation of the Christian community. To take one example, the pagan festival of the Lupercalia continued to be celebrated in Rome down to the end of the fifth century, long after the social base of paganism had vanished. The long-suffering bishop of Rome, Gelasius I, attacked the celebration as a work of the devil (*diabolica figmenta*) (Gelasius *Ep. adversus Andromachum*). A Christian, Andromachus, responded that the celebration was only the appearance (*imago*) of a pagan festival, and he repeated the old argument that the continuance of such observances was necessary for the health of the community.[78] This ambivalence regarding the continuance of Roman secular tradition will be a hallmark of Christianity through the Middle Ages and beyond.[79]

MILITANT PAGANISM

Perhaps the most famous conversion of the period occurred in the 350's, when the teacher and orator Marius Victorinus publicly declared his faith in Christianity.[80] According to Augustine (*Conf.* 8.2), Victorinus was initially leery of making his new religious beliefs known, for fear of alienating his powerful pagan friends. When finally he did make his conversion known, it made a profound impression on the city of Rome. Victorinus did not suffer for his faith at this time, though several years later in 362 he, like other Christians, was required by Julian to desist from teaching rhetoric (Aug. *Conf.* 8.5). The relative percentages of Christians and pagans within the senatorial class during this period are unknown, though Victorinus was certainly far from the first convert among the elite of Rome: his conversion was hardly the epochal event in Roman social circles that some have taken it to be.[81] More important, Augustine suggests that at this time at least some pagan senators were hostile toward Christianity and its converts, a point that is central to much of his other writing, especially the first books of the *City of God*.[82]

Many senators in the later fourth century are known both from literary sources and from inscriptions to have practiced pagan cult.[83] In addition there are some more ambiguous iconographic sources for the pagan affinities of the senatorial class. For example, a large number of coin-shaped tokens called contorniates have survived from this period. These tokens, which seem to date from about 350 to 410, may have been manufactured as New Year's gifts or perhaps for distribution at public events, such as the circus. They typically bear portrayals of famous Roman political and literary figures, scenes from myth and legend, or aspects of contemporary religious rites—including rites of eastern orgiastic religions.[84] There are also the famous ivory diptychs, on which are represented religious themes, both pagan and Christian. The interpretation of such images is difficult: there is syncretism between paganism and Christianity in this period, and Christians are known to have possessed such objects and even to have had them made.[85] One might also ask to what extent pagans were exclusively pagan and did not simultaneously profess some faith in the Christian god as well.

Few pagans can clearly be shown to have been actively adversarial toward Christianity. The emperor Julian worked against Christians. In the 380's and 390's, however, Flavian is the only unambiguous example of a militant pagan senator. He and his son are the only Roman senators known to have been involved in the usurpation of Eugenius; no others are named. So O'Donnell emphasized Flavian's isolation and concluded that, to the extent that Flavian himself was motivated to participate in the revolt from religious conviction, he acted without the support of others.[86] There is, however, reason to believe that we are not well informed about other participants in the revolt. The emperor did not allow any survivors of the revolt to take credit for offices they had received from the usurper; so the younger Flavian was deprived of the credit for his term as urban prefect.

Aside from Flavian, the most prominent pagan senator of the period is Vettius Agorius Praetextatus. Even in his case, however, there is little evidence for overt religious hostility. He did hold high office under Julian (Amm. 22.7.6), and forty years later Macrobius made him the leading character in the *Saturnalia*. Many of his activities were un-Christian, though few should be regarded as necessarily combative.[87] When he did come into contact with Christians, as in his settlement of the disruptions caused by the supporters of Damasus and Ursinus in their contest for the papacy during his term as urban prefect (367–368), he behaved with moderation and circumspection—much as Flavian did with respect to the Donatist controversy while he was in Africa. Praetextatus' attitude toward Christianity here might be characterized as a kind of benign contempt, exemplified by a comment he is supposed to have made to Pope Damasus at the time: he too, he said, would convert to Christianity if he could be bishop of Rome (Jerome *Contra Ioan. Hieros* 8).

The ongoing controversy about the altar of Victory provides confirmation that pagan senators did not always acquiesce to the intolerance of Christians. Most other evidence for Christian and pagan interactions within the Roman senatorial class, however, suggests that many pagans were accommodating toward their Christian peers. There are, for example, many cases of "mixed marriages" among the elite, in which the women in particular might be Christians even though their husbands remained pagan.[88]

One of the key pieces of evidence for a militant pagan reaction against Christianity in the later fourth century is the so-called "poem against the pagans" (*Carmen contra paganos*). This anonymous and inelegant poem has been preserved in a single copy, bound in with a text of Prudentius (*Cod. Par. lat.* 8084). The manuscript of Prudentius dates to late antiquity and is written in the "rustic capitals" of the period. As the subscription to it shows, the text of Prudentius is a copy (and a very early one) of a text by this author that had been corrected by a descendant of Praetextatus, Vettius Agorius Basilius Mavortius, consul in 527. The text of the *Carmen* was written later, in an uncial hand. It is unknown how it came to be appended to the text of Prudentius. The text was discovered in the seventeenth century, but the first scholarly editions of it date to the 1860's.[89]

The *Carmen* is a polemic against those who are "devoted" to the old gods, in particular against a certain unnamed individual who attempted to restore pagan rituals at Rome. Most scholarship about the *Carmen* has focused on the identity of the anonymous pagan. No identification is free of problems. The arguments are elaborate, and I will not summarize them in detail. For much of the nineteenth century there was a consensus that the pagan of the *Carmen* is the elder Flavian. In 1870 Mommsen had no doubts, and most subsequent scholars followed him.[90]

Other solutions have been proposed. In 1960 G. Manganaro suggested that the pagan of the *Carmen* was Gabinius Barbarus Pompeianus, who was briefly prefect of Rome in 408/409, when the city was first besieged by Alaric. In the general uncertainty of the time, he reverted to pagan sacrifices to ensure the safety of the city.[91] The proposal has few advantages and raises many problems. Matthews decisively rejected Manganaro's arguments, and no one today would accept them.[92]

In 1992 Grünewald made the suggestion that the anonymous pagan of the *Carmen* is an amalgam of Flavian the elder and his son, and that the poem was written at the same time as, and was perhaps even prompted by, the rehabilitation of the elder Flavian.[93] He points out that not only was the younger Flavian urban prefect in 394, he was also the immediate predecessor of Pompeianus in that position during the siege of Alaric, at the end of 408, and as such may have been associated (justly or not) with the paganism of his successor. So, on Grünewald's interpretation, both Mommsen and Manganaro may be right: the anonymous pagan of the *Carmen* may be simultaneously the elder Flavian and Pompeianus (through his association with the younger Flavian). The possibility that the author of the *Carmen* is confusing father, son, and Pompeianus, either willfully or through ignorance, seems unlikely, but it cannot be dismissed out of hand—especially if it were written at a distance of thirty years. The poem is a polemic, in some respects a very clumsy and ill-informed one, and it has proven difficult to hold it to a standard of historical accuracy or even internal consistency. The poem might conceivably describe the actions of one person in a single situation or of one person over his entire life. Perhaps it uses a single person to stand for an entire class, and so attributes some of the general attitudes and specific actions of a variety of pagans to him. The notion that this text can date as late as the 430's, or even very much into the fifth century, however, seems impossible. The tensions it describes and its hostile tone are unexampled in texts of the period; it is far more likely to be a product of the late fourth century. Furthermore, if Shanzer is right that the *Cento Probae* copies the *Carmen*, then it cannot be dated later than the end of the fourth century.[94]

Consideration of these various proposals is now probably academic. As L. Cracco-Ruggini has shown, the pagan of the *Carmen* is almost surely Vettius Agorius Praetextatus.[95] The unnamed pagan of the poem is said to have been urban prefect (lines 25–29), consul (lines 112–114), and praetorian prefect (lines 85–86). Praetextatus held all three of these offices. It has always been recognized that Praetextatus' attested cult interests dovetail with those mentioned in the *Carmen* (lines 23–24, 38–40, 106, 108), and as Cracco-Ruggini has shown, there are many other points that make it overwhelmingly likely that the *Carmen* was directed against Praetextatus. For example, the *Carmen* alludes to the grief of the pagan's wife after his death, to her attempts to "move Acheron" (lines 115–122). According to Jerome, after his death Praetextatus did not go to reside "in a milky white palace of heaven, as his unhappy wife claims, but is held in filthy shadows" (*non in lacteo caeli palatio, ut uxor conmentitur infelix, sed in sordentibus tenebris continetur*) (*Ep.* 23.2.1; cf. 3.2). On the epitaph she set up to her husband, Paulina remarks too that she is desolate, for she had hoped her husband would survive her; "nevertheless I am fortunate because I am yours, and have been, and after death soon shall be" (*sed tamen felix, tua / quia sum fuique postque mortem mox ero*) (*CIL* 6.1779 = *ILS* 1259). Furthermore, it is possible that the title of the poem has survived: in a medieval library catalogue there is a reference to "verses of Bishop Damasus about Praetextatus the urban prefect" (*Damasi episcopi versus de Praetextato praefecto urbis*).[96]

Scholarship loves vacuums, and the desire to name the anonymous pagan has been overwhelming. Matthews subscribes to this attitude: "A decision, one way or the other, is imperative. To reserve judgement is the least defensible of attitudes."[97] There would be some gains (chiefly biographical) from a certain identification of the pagan of the poem. It is important, however, not to lose sight of the general significance of the poem for the religious history of the period, which does not depend on identifying the unnamed pagan. On any interpretation, the *Carmen* provides an account of religious tension in the Roman senatorial class near the end of the fourth century A.D.

The term that the poem uses to describe a pagan sympathizer is *sacratus*. In the fourth century, pagans themselves used this word to describe their allegiance to the old gods. It might also be translated in certain contexts as "initiated." The word is used in the *Carmen* with irony. It indicates that the pagan is given over to the gods, but there is the implication of both a positive and a negative sense: devoted and accursed.[98] The theme of pagan devotion—or accursedness—runs through the entire text. The introduction of the poem (lines 1–24) questions the general worth of this pagan devotion (lines 6, 13, 24–25). Later the poem's anonymous villain is repeatedly described as "devoted": "no one on earth was more devoted to the pagan gods than he" (*fuit in terris nullus sacratior illo,* line 34); "what good is this devoted man to the city?" (*sacratus vester urbi quid praestitit,* line 46); "none of the devoted can preserve their sense of decency" (*sacrato liceat nulli servare pudorem,* line 76); and "what good could the old gods be for this devoted man?" (*quid . . . potuit praestare sacrato,* lines 87–88).

The author of the poem seems very familiar—perhaps even a bit too familiar, for a Christian—with pagan cult and ritual. The poem begins with a virtual catalogue of pagan observances (lines 1–24). Many of the gods of traditional Roman religion are named as favorites and allies of the poem's unnamed pagan: Venus (line 87), Saturn (line 88), Neptune (line 89), Hecate (line 90), Mercury (line 92), the Lares and Janus (line 93), Terra (line 94), Ceres and Proserpina (line 96), Vulcan (line 97). The poem emphasizes his connection with Jupiter: he had hoped for the health of the Jupiter of Latium (line 122); at his death he departs for the "throne of Jupiter" (line 26).[99] He attempted to restore various rites of the old religion, in particular sacrifice (lines 36–43), and was especially addicted to haruspicy, that is, prophecy from the entrails of the sacrifice. According to the poem "he learned from Numa Pompilius himself—the first among many *haruspices*" (lines 35–36). He was a particular "friend of the Etruscans" (line 50), who were also adepts in haruspicy (*Etruscus ludit semper quos vanus aruspex*, line 8).

According to the poem, this pagan was also an adherent of certain exotic cults and rituals which were regarded by Christians as notoriously depraved. He was a participant and leader in the celebrations of Bacchus (lines 49, 69–75), and during his consulship only the goddess Flora, with her debauched festival and attendant prostitutes, rejoiced (lines 112–114). He studied the arcane and accursed arts of magic and poison (lines 51–53). His participation in the so-called "oriental" religions is especially noteworthy. He "sought the sun beneath the earth" by sacrificing to Mithras (line 47); he worshiped Bellona (or Ma, line 68) and Sarapis (lines 50, 91). Like other senators of the day, he took part in the gory sacrifices of the *taurobolium* (lines 57–62). With his friends, he escorted the silver chariot of the great mother, Cybele, and her castrated consort, Attis (lines 63–66, 77, 103–109). He went with shaved head as a suppliant to the altars of Isis (lines 95, 98–102). His family also worshiped the old gods. His heir dedicated a temple to Venus or Flora (lines 112–114), and after his death his wife used all the resources of pagan religion—prayers, offerings, even magic incantations—hoping to "move Acheron" (lines 115–122).

In addition to his devotion to the pagan gods, the villain of the poem was actively hostile to Christianity: "mad, he would have destroyed many Christians" (*christicolas multos voluit sic perdere demens*, line 78). He was even "prepared to make war in vain on the true god" (*contra deum verum frustra bellare paratus*, line 54).

PAGAN QUIETISM

The anonymous pagan described in the *Carmen* holds high public office, and his religious activities are public and provocative. As the poem emphasizes several times, the Roman senate itself follows his lead. Thus the religious attitudes attributed to him in this poem cannot be regarded as eccentric and isolated—no more than those of Flavian in 394. It is a mistake to "quarantine" individuals, especially prominent individuals who occupy positions of leadership, as if they are utterly unique. Those who attempt to argue that individuals like Flavian and Praetextatus are "merely" eccentrics have a larger purpose: by insisting on the idiosyncracy of known militant pagans, it is possible to explain away religious conflict. Nevertheless, this position raises important problems. To what extent were the religious views of Praetextatus or Flavian typical of the Roman elite? Were many Roman senators in the later fourth century belligerent in the cause of paganism? Were other pagans quiescent? If such "factions" existed, what were their social and cultural characteristics?

It is clear that Flavian was not the only belligerent pagan senator in Rome at the end of the fourth century. It is equally clear that many pagans in this period kept their mouths shut and their heads down. In 394, for example, Flavian's good friend Symmachus evidently did not support Eugenius. After the victory of Theodosius he was consequently in a good position to help the younger Flavian mend his fortunes at the imperial court. It is impossible to quantify the extent of either attitude. Furthermore, a word like "faction" or "party" would be far too strong to describe the sum of individuals with such political and religious tendencies. As Alan Cameron and others have rightly pointed out, there is absolutely no reason to think that there was a formal, organized cabal of "pagans committed to the overthrow of Christianity" in this period.[100] A word like "circle," with its connotation of a loose assemblage of like-minded individuals, might do, if the word had not been preempted long ago by scholars who, basing themselves on the evidence of Macrobius' *Saturnalia,* imagined a semiformal resistance, founded on a full-blown pagan philosophy and centering on Symmachus and his friends.

The nature and articulation of religious sympathy within the senatorial class in the late fourth and early fifth centuries and its relation to political activity have been subjected to intense and skeptical scrutiny in recent years. Traditionally scholars have been inclined to allow that there are broadly two kinds of paganism among Roman senators of the late fourth century. The first, or "traditional" variety, is manifested by allegiance to the old state cults of Rome: a senator might, for example, serve as an augur or as a member of the board of *pontifices*. The second, or "orientalizing" type, can typically be seen in activities centering on some of the famous and exotic eastern cults that flourished in Rome at this time, such as that of Attis and Cybele, Isis, Bellona, or Mithras.[101] The best-known evidence for this oriental religious activity on the part of the Roman senatorial class comes from a sanctuary of the Magna Mater, located near the Vatican known as the Phrygianum (Cybele, the Magna Mater according to tradition came from Phrygia).[102] There a series of inscriptions records that many senators, including Praetextatus and his wife, underwent the ritual of the *taurobolium,* in which initiates descended into a pit and a bull was slaughtered above them. A shower of blood rained down on the initiate, who was thus "reborn for eternity" (*in aeternum renatus*) (*CIL* 6.510 = *ILS* 4152).

Much has been made of the significance of this distinction between "traditional" and "oriental" religious affiliations for the political activities of the late fourth-century Roman senatorial class. In the past it has been generally accepted that the "oriental" strain was more personally, existentially significant than the "traditional" religion. By the fourth century, it was argued, allegiance to the Roman state religion had withered away to an empty, formalistic ritualism that was valued chiefly for its associations with tradition and that engendered only the most austere and intellectual loyalty. So modern scholars associated the characteristics attributed to these two pagan types with a political posture: the zealous adherents of the "oriental" religions were considered to have been much more politically active than those who were only perfunctorily, intellectually attached to the state religion. This interpretation finds some support in the attitudes of the early Christian fathers, who seem to have been far more hostile to the orgiastic "oriental" religions than to the bloodless and harmless "traditional" Roman gods.

This reconstruction of two pagan parties has now been largely discredited. When one looks at the attested religious activities of known Roman senators in the late fourth century, it is not easy to verify the existence of parties or even of informal social cliques founded on this discrimination between "oriental" and "traditional" religions.[103] It was normal for the pagan Roman elite of the period to have both "traditional" and "oriental" religious allegiances. Vettius Agorius Praetextatus is the best known of these pagan aristocrats. Many modern scholars have reckoned him as the "leader" of the "oriental party" until his death in 384. Virius Nicomachus Flavianus has commonly been seen as another prominent member of the "oriental" group; he is often supposed to have taken over the leadership of the pagan opposition after the death of Praetextatus. It is far more difficult to isolate members of the "traditional" party than of the "oriental" party: almost no Roman senators of this period devoted themselves exclusively to the old state cults. The crucial case (in fact, virtually the only case) is the orator Symmachus. There is a great deal of documentation for the life of Symmachus, including his own voluminous correspondence; and yet there is no indication that he took part in any of the activities of the various oriental cults of late antique Rome. Furthermore, his political gestures against Christianity, particularly his letter on the restoration of the altar of Victory, seem moderate.

Most contemporary scholars continue to accept the broad distinction between "oriental" and "traditional" cults but do not believe that exclusive allegiance to one or the other was common, or that such a focus would translate into a corresponding political activism or quietism.[104] Rather, the contrast is imagined as one of private ("oriental") versus public ("traditional") religious activity. Much of the antipagan legislation of the emperors, from Constantius II to Theodosius the Great, is directed against the "traditional" cults of Rome. The famous religious struggle over the altar of Victory was certainly concerned with the "traditional" state religion. The revolt of Flavian and Arbogast, to the extent that it was about religion at all, appears to have been concerned with Jupiter and state sacrifice, not with Cybele and the *taurobolium*.

Imagining "oriental" and "traditional" paganism in this period in terms of a dichotomy between private versus public religion also has methodological implications for modern historians of the period. If the sources are silent about Symmachus' connections with the "oriental" religions, this does not necessarily mean that such connections did not exist; the silence may rather be attributed to the private nature of "oriental" cult and the public nature of our sources for the life of Symmachus. For example, in the pair of matching statue bases, dedicated to Symmachus and Flavian in the house of the Symmachi on the Caelian hill (*CIL* 6.1699 = *ILS* 2946; *CIL* 6.1782 = *ILS* 2947), the careers of both Symmachus and Flavian are outlined. Both are described as *pontifex maior*, as "traditional" a religious activity as existed in ancient Rome. There is no mention of any "oriental" religious activities for either man. Again, the absence of references certainly does not mean that such activities never existed. An analogous inscription of that doyen of the "oriental" religions, Praetextatus, erected in the house of a relative, describes his public career but mentions no religious activities, "oriental" or "traditional" (*CIL* 6.1777 = *ILS* 1258). Just so, in the rehabilitation of 431 there is no reference to any of Flavian's religious activities whatsoever. The absence of evidence for a commitment to the "oriental" cults in the extensive correspondence of Symmachus is more troubling, although one might argue that the letters are public in character,[105] or perhaps that embarrassing references to Symmachus' "oriental" pagan sympathies have been edited out.[106]

The distinction between "traditional" and "oriental" religions, then, is not helpful for evaluating the political activity of the Roman senatorial class.

Pagan senators routinely had interests in both types of cult. If political activity at this time was associated with religion, it was associated with the traditional state religion, not with the oriental cults. Individual senators might be more or less active on behalf of paganism. Antagonism toward Christianity seems to have been haphazard. It is impossible to construct the typical profile of a religious "activist" or a "quietist"—and without the ability to identify some profile, it is pointless to discuss "factions" and "groups" and "cliques."

The evidence for the religious affiliations of Flavian can serve as a case in point. He, if anyone in this period, was politically active on behalf of paganism. Flavian's religious activities are usually thought to have paralleled those of Praetextatus: he is thus believed to have had affiliations both with "traditional" and with "oriental" religions. But while Flavian participated in the "traditional" state religion of Rome, there is very little evidence that he had anything to do with the rites of any "oriental" cults. In one letter to Flavian, Symmachus alludes to his interest in the cult of the Magna Mater (*adornare te reditum quod sacra Deum Matris adpeterent, arbitrabar*) (*Ep.* 2.34). As in the case of Symmachus, the absence of evidence for this kind of religious activity does not mean it did not exist. The diptych of the Symmachi and Nicomachi, which was probably created within a decade of the elder Flavian's death (see below), shows that his immediate descendants were involved in some of the contemporary "oriental" mystery cults—and so, without any doubt, was he.

Flavian's actions during the usurpation of Eugenius resonate far more with his activities within the "traditional" state religion than with any "oriental" mystery cults. The appeal to Jupiter at the battle of the Frigidus, for example, strikes a chord with Flavian's known activity as a member of the board of *pontifices*. This is the only priesthood that he is known certainly to have held. Perhaps significantly, Flavian's position as *pontifex* is not mentioned in the *cursus* heading Flavian's rehabilitation, though it is mentioned in the honorific inscription from the Caelian (Chapter 2 above). The *pontifices* were the chief priests of the old Roman state religion. Despite the conservative appearance and reputation of the college, however, it would be a mistake to imagine that in this period its members had no interests in the "oriental" cults. Virtually all of the *pontifices* attested from the late fourth century (again with the notable exception of Symmachus) are also known to have been adherents of various "oriental" cults. Vettius Agorius Praetextatus, for instance, was a member of the board of *pontifices*.[107]

Documentation for the activities of the college of *pontifices* at the end of the fourth century is scarce. It is a commonplace in the letters of Symmachus that the old religion (particularly as reflected in the duties of the college of *pontifices*) is being neglected at this time, and that this neglect may lead to the decline of the state itself (see *Ep.* 1.51; cf. 1.46.2 and 1.47.1). Nevertheless, there are scattered references to the board and its activities in various inscriptions honoring prominent senators of the day. In one case, the *pontifices* repair a building at their own expense (*CIL* 6.2158 = *ILS* 4944). The most important descriptions of the activities and duties of the college in these years are provided by Symmachus himself in his correspondence.[108] There appears to be substantial continuity in the duties of the college from the great days of the Roman republic and empire down to late antiquity. The college continued to be charged with general oversight of the conduct of the religious affairs of the state. For example, it was responsible for the supervision of the religious calendar; if some dire prodigy occurred or a sacrifice went wrong, it was expected to advise what expiations should be undertaken to set matters right. It also was in charge of the cemeteries of the city.

The survival of the board's traditional supervision of the cult of Vesta is particularly well attested. Praetextatus, for instance, is described on one of his inscriptions as *pontifex* of Vesta (*CIL* 6.1779 = *ILS* 1259), rather than more generally as *pontifex maior*. In fact, he was such an advocate for the Vestals that at his death they decided to honor him, an unusual gesture (the Vestals did not traditionally so honor men) that Symmachus in his capacity as *pontifex* tried to stop (*Ep.* 2.36). As we see here, Symmachus too was concerned with the administration of the cult of Vesta. Best known is his nostalgic and rather grotesque proposal that a certain Vestal who had broken her vow of chastity be punished in the ancient Roman way—by being buried alive (*Epp.* 9.147, 148).[109] So Gratian's confiscation of the endowment of the Vestals would necessarily be of great concern to the *pontifices,* to men such as Praetextatus, Symmachus, and Flavian. Symmachus in his famous letter to the emperor (the third *Relatio*) is just as concerned to see the endowment of the Vestals returned as he is to see the restoration of the altar of Victory.

Above all, the *pontifices* maintained the state cult of the Capitoline triad: Juno, Minerva, and Jupiter Best and Greatest (*Optimus Maximus*). This Jupiter, with his temple on the Capitoline hill overlooking the city center, or Forum, was the traditional protector and champion of the Roman state. As the chief priests of the Roman state religion, the *pontifices* were strongly associated with this chief god of the Roman state religion. The connection was traditional, and endured in the minds of pagans and Christians alike during the late fourth century. So in a famous passage Jerome describes a jovial Roman *pontifex* bouncing his Christian granddaughter on his knee, as she gurgles "Alleluia" at him. Jerome comments: "I think that even Jupiter would have been a Christian, had he had relatives like these" (*Ep.* 107.1). The mention of Jupiter should be understood as a reference to the religious office of the pagan grandfather.[110]

The *pontifices* were also concerned with prodigies, supernatural events through which the gods made their will known.[111] Prodigies might take a variety of forms. One common manifestation, for instance, is the appearance of birds in particular quarters of the sky. The gods, however, might make their attitudes apparent through countless other devices: odd meteorological phenomena, for instance, or monstrous apparitions. Some idea of the importance of these prodigies for Roman tradition can be derived from one of the writers who was still read by senators in late antiquity: the Augustan historian Livy. The narrative of Livy's history of early Rome proceeds by years. For many of these years he provides a list of *prodigia* that presumably derives from the records of the college of *pontifices*.[112]

The interpretation of prodigies—that is, divination—required special skill and knowledge: a college of augurs grew up in Rome, which developed a canon of rules of interpretation, the *ius augurale*. As the etymology of the name of these priests implies, originally they were particularly concerned with reading the appearance of birds in the sky. The *pontifices*, as chief administrators of the state religion, were responsible for accepting or rejecting the notice and interpretation of a prodigy. If they accepted the occurrence as significant, then they had to fix appropriate procedures, such as sacrifices, which were required to expiate it. Symmachus again provides clear evidence of the continuation of these interests of the *pontifices*.[113] In one letter to Praetextatus, for instance, he is concerned because a prodigy has occurred and no expiations seem to work (*Ep.* 1.49). In another he describes a prodigy that occurred on the birthday of the city of Rome—one of several, he says, but he hesitates to describe the others for fear that even the act of verbalizing them will itself prove unlucky (*Ep.* 6.40.1).

Not only were the *pontifices* concerned with the expiation of prodigies, but they had traditionally kept a list of them. The records of the college, the *Annales Maximi* and the *commentarii,* had contained an annual account of all such events, along with regulations for the calendar and lists of magistrates. The chronicles of the *pontifices* were among the few sources for the history of early Rome, and they were influential on the formation of later Latin history writing.[114] In certain respects these records might be imagined as the first annalistic "histories" of Rome; doubtless they were used as sources and models of organization by many of Rome's later historians. Livy provided lists of prodigies in his history, probably derived from the records of the *pontifices*, and even writers of contemporary history, such as Tacitus, could not avoid including prodigies in their history, much as they might have liked to do so.[115]

The connection between the college of *pontifices* and the *Annales Maximi* is interesting, for here we see paganism and historiography, veneration of the old gods of the state and allegiance to Roman tradition, coming together. Flavian was not simply a religious reactionary; he was also a historian (see Chapter 5 below). The *Annales* were certainly no longer kept by the college in the fourth century A.D., but any educated Roman of the day—and certainly Flavian—would have been well aware of the traditional connection between the college and these records. Flavian has left no record of his attitude toward the *Annales*. Nevertheless, for him these hoary records, with their annual account of *prodigia*, must have been an important symbol of both Roman history and religion. This connection was made by Macrobius: "The *pontifices* were assigned the privilege of keeping the record of events on tablets, and we call these annals the *Annales Maximi*, as they are the work of the *pontifices maximi*" (*Sat.* 3.2.17).

The correction of the text of Livy, mentioned by Symmachus and attested by Flavian's son and grandson (see Chapter 6 below), should also be considered in the context of this connection between history and religion. As will be seen, the corrections made to manuscripts by the elite in this period are most certainly not evidence for a coordinated and intentional project of cultural preservation. They are, however, evidence for contemporary interests and reading habits, and the process of correction is itself not culturally insignificant. Livy's history is filled with lists of prodigies that ultimately derive from the records of the *pontifices*. These prodigies are more than vestigial appendages to the history. For Livy, as for Symmachus (and, by extension, Flavian), the health of the state was intimately linked with the will of the gods. Livy claimed that prodigies were less frequently reported or expiated in his day, the time of Augustus, than they had been in the great old days of the republic. This situation, for him, was disastrous: a cause of the decadence and the decline of the state.[116] A similar attitude can be found in Symmachus (*Ep.* 1.46). During this period other pagans as well were interested in the prodigies, especially the prodigies reported in Livy. Julius Obsequens even wrote a *Liber Prodigiorum*.[117] Interest in Livy was not confined to pagans. Christian apologists and polemicists, such as Augustine and Orosius, made extensive use of the historian, though certainly for their own purposes.[118]

The reading of Livy by Symmachus and the family of Flavian fits very well with the religious activities of the elder Flavian, particularly with his position as a *pontifex*. His appeal to Jupiter at the battle of the Frigidus, his reputation for knowledge of the future, his interest in sacrifice—all of these are the usual concerns of the Roman state religion and are the special province of the *pontifices*.

To sum up my interpretation of the events of 394: religion surely played some part in the usurpation of Eugenius, even if it was not the central or precipitating cause. Flavian was not the only pagan senator who supported Eugenius in part for religious reasons, as the settlement imposed by Theodosius (described by Augustine and in more detail by Prudentius) shows. On the other hand, it would be a mistake to imagine that the senate generally was pagan, or even that all pagans supported Eugenius. Pagans in the 390's were less powerful and numerous than the old interpretation would allow; nevertheless, they were also more influential and resentful than some recent critics imagine.[119] Arbogast and Eugenius probably initiated their revolt for political reasons; it is likely that they recruited Flavian as their praetorian prefect in order to gain the support of the Roman senatorial class generally, with no particular thought of the concerns of pagans. Perhaps they were surprised that he introduced a religious agenda into their campaign against Theodosius; perhaps they were not. Nevertheless they tolerated and even supported him. Flavian's main religious concerns were more limited than Bloch argued. Like Roman senators since the time of Constantius, he wanted to see the altar of Victory restored to the senate house and to have the endowments of the priestly colleges that had been confiscated under Gratian returned. As Ambrose complains (*Ep.* 57), Eugenius granted these requests.

THE AFTERMATH OF THE PAGAN REVOLT

Even if Flavian, Eugenius, and Arbogast did not see themselves as leading a pagan revolt against Christianity in 394, the usurpation was constructed as a religious rebellion in the years following their demise. The point is made by the settlement imposed by Theodosius: in the immediate aftermath of his victory, the emperor regarded the paganism of the elite as somehow complicit in the usurpation of Eugenius. Theodosius claimed to be saddened by the death of Flavian, who had served him well in the past: he said before the Roman senate that he would have pardoned him, had Flavian allowed him the opportunity (cf. lines 16–17 of the rehabilitation and Rufinus, *HE* 11.33).[120] Nevertheless, after his victory Theodosius "desired" the remaining pagan elite to convert to Christianity, and they obliged (Aug. *Civ. Dei* 5.26; Prudentius, *Contra Symmachum* 1.506–607). The younger Flavian was only one of the many who converted to Christianity at this time.

In the years following 394 the usurpation of Eugenius was speedily enshrined as a pagan revolt, and Flavian as one of its chief architects. Whatever the biases of Ambrose, his writings against Eugenius (*Epp.* 57, 61; *Expl. Psalmi* 36) were influential. Other texts contemporary with the revolt also imply that it had a religious aspect. In the first book of his poem *Against Symmachus,* Prudentius describes the mass conversion of the elite after 394. Claudian, in his panegyric *On the Third Consulship of Honorius* (396) describes the battle of Frigidus (87–105). He says nothing about the religious sympathies of the forces of Eugenius, though he does describe the various Christian miracles that helped Theodosius.

Flavian is not mentioned in connection with the revolt of Eugenius until the 410's. Rufinus, writing his church history at about this time, mentions Flavian's predilection for sacrifice and the arts of prediction (*HE* 11.33). Ambrose's biographer Paulinus, writing in 412/413 (or perhaps 422),[121] names Flavian and Arbogast as the chief instigators for the return of the altar of Victory and the priestly endowments. He also tells the famous story of their threat to convert Ambrose's church to a stable (*V. Ambr.* 26–31). Augustine, writing about 415, is aware of the part Flavian played in the revolt, and describes the statues of Jupiter set up by the forces of Eugenius at the Frigidus (*Civ. Dei* 5.26). Orosius' account in his *History against the Pagans* (dating to 417) relies on that of Augustine; he emphasizes the paganism of Arbogast (*Hist. adv. paganos* 7.35).

The various Greek sources for the usurpation of Eugenius are all later than Flavian's rehabilitation. They are less detailed, though most confirm that the usurpation had some religious connotation. The account provided by Sozomen in his *Church History,* written about 440, relies on Rufinus; he repeats that Flavian knew how to predict the future, and, though allowing that Eugenius was a Christian, he casts doubts on the depth of his religious conviction (*HE* 7.22–24). Philostorgius, writing a little earlier than 440, says that Eugenius was a Hellene, that is, a pagan (*HE* 11.2). In the *Church History* of Socrates, which dates to this same period, an account of the usurpation of Eugenius is provided that says nothing about paganism (*HE* 5.25). In the later 440's Theodoret describes the battle of the Frigidus and provides the only evidence for the famous pagan army standards, with their images of Hercules (*HE* 5.24). The last account of the revolt of Eugenius is provided by Zosimus, ca. 600. He says nothing about any religious motivation for the usurpation (*Hist. Nova* 4.54–55).

After 394 Flavian's name was irrevocably associated in the west with paganism and the usurpation of Eugenius—at least for Christian historians and intellectuals. In addition, the battle of the Frigidus had a very important place in the ideology of the later members of the Theodosian dynasty.[122] With two exceptions—the rehabilitation and Macrobius' *Saturnalia*—Flavian is not mentioned in the fifth century except as a pagan leader in revolt against Theodosius and the true god. At the time of the rehabilitation, then, there was a substantial group in Rome who could not have heard the name of the elder Flavian without thinking "pagan reactionary." Whether or not the omission of reference to religion was routine in public inscriptions by this date, its absence from the inscription rehabilitating Flavian would surely have been felt. Furthermore, the inscription is repeatedly and unequivocally labeled a rehabilitation, but nowhere does it specifically say why Flavian was originally disgraced (see Chapter 4 below); this vagueness, too, will have directed attention to the story of the revolt of Eugenius.

In 431 many remembered Flavian and were aware of the circumstances of his disgrace and his posthumous reputation—and not only historians. The fact of the rehabilitation itself provides ample evidence of this point. Not least important were those who were ultimately responsible for the rehabilitation: the Roman senate and Flavian's family. As the inscription notes, the rehabilitation merely gives voice to what the senate has had "in heart and mind and far from any interruption of intervening forgetfulness" (lines 25–26). The senate has "protected Flavian's memory no less than the imperial person" (lines 26–27). Even forty years after the event the name of the family is impugned by his fate, no matter what their achievements: the very honor of the younger Flavian "is only half complete even when crowned by the praetorian prefecture" (line 31). Flavian has always been remembered; his disgrace has been both an incentive and impediment to forgetting him. Those addressed in the rehabilitation cannot fail to have been sensitive to the retrospective attitude toward Eugenius and Flavian. For these, too, religion surely was a prominent subtext of the rehabilitation.

Beyond the rehabilitation, there is no direct evidence for the attitude of Flavian's descendants toward him after 394. There may, however, be some evidence for their attitudes toward paganism. An ivory diptych has survived, one panel labeled "of the Symmachi" (*Symmachorum*), the other "of the Nicomachi" (*Nicomachorum*).[123] Diptychs of this kind were manufactured from the end of the fourth century through the beginning of the sixth in Rome, Milan, and Constantinople. The diptych of the Symmachi and Nicomachi, however, belongs to a more restricted group of diptychs, distinguished by their classicizing themes and style. These diptychs were produced in Rome (and, to a lesser extent, Milan) at the end of the fourth century and the beginning of the fifth. Most of the diptychs are concerned with the consulship: they seem to have been produced to celebrate the selection of a prominent individual to hold this most prestigious office. The diptych of the Symmachi and Nicomachi is unusual (but not unparalleled) in that it seems to have been produced to celebrate a marriage alliance between the two families.

The diptych consists of two facing panels, the left now in Paris, the right in London.[124] At the top of each panel within a frame (a so-called *tabula ansata*) is carved a name. On the left panel is inscribed *Nicomachorum;* another name is carved in the corresponding place on the right panel, *Symmachorum*. These two families had been friendly with each other over several generations.[125] The orator Symmachus and the elder Flavian were the best of friends. Much of Symmachus' correspondence is addressed to Flavian and then later, after his death, to Flavian the younger. Flavian the younger himself married a daughter of Symmachus; later his daughter (the elder Flavian's granddaughter) married a son of the orator (Chapter 2 above).

The coupling of these names on the diptych calls for an explanation beyond the general connection between the two families; the diptych surely must have been commissioned to celebrate some special occasion. Two possibilities come to mind: the wedding of Flavian the younger to the daughter of Symmachus, probably sometime between 392 and 394, and the wedding of the daughter of Flavian the younger to the son of Symmachus in 401. Either occasion would be appropriate, given the dating of the diptych on stylistic grounds to the end of the fourth century. The dating here has very interesting implications for the interpretation of the significance of the imagery of the diptych. In the years between 392 and 394 Flavian and his son were embroiled in the revolt of Eugenius; in 401 the emperor was firmly in control, and the younger Flavian had converted to Christianity. Like most scholars, I would favor the later date of 401 for the diptych. The decisive point in favor of this date is the erection of the matching statue bases on the Caelian hill, which can be attributed to that year or a little later (Chapter 2 above): like the diptych these bases are erected to celebrate a connection between the Symmachi and Nicomachi, specifically a marriage connection. Against this dating some might urge that the family had surely converted to Christianity by 401, and that the pagan iconography of the diptych is inappropriate to this context. Yet the statue bases, which surely do postdate the conversion of the younger Flavian, also allude to the pagan traditions of these two families. If the diptych was produced as late as 401, its overt use of the imagery of pagan cult calls for some comment.

The iconography of the diptych alludes to the mystery cults of the "oriental" religions and, most probably, to the erotic mysteries of marriage as well.[126] On the panel of the Nicomachi is carved a woman, facing the viewer, turned slightly to her right. She stands before a round altar on which a flame burns. Her right breast is bared, and in each hand she holds a flaming torch, lowered so that the flaming heads of the torches converge at her knees, as though she has taken the flame from the altar and is passing it from one torch to the other. In the background stands a pine tree, hung with cymbals.

The pine tree and cymbals are attributes of Cybele and Attis. The scene is thus set in a precinct of this pair. The woman must be a goddess.[127] The two torches held down with heads converging suggest Kore (Persephone). One element, though, is jarring. The bared breast of the figure is not appropriate for a representation of Kore. This feature would, however, be suitable if the figure were Aphrodite.[128]

The allusion (via the bared breast) to Aphrodite suggests the erotic. The passing of the flame from altar to torch to torch has both erotic and religious connotations. Torches were used in the Roman wedding celebration, and the word for torch, *taeda,* was commonly employed metonymically to mean "wedding" in Roman literature. At the same time, the torches here must also have a religious significance, alluding to sacred mysteries, particularly the mysteries of Demeter. This union of the erotic and the religious is appropriate, since the mystery religions themselves were commonly associated with marriage. In Greco-Roman times initiation into the mysteries of marriage might be combined with initiation into other kinds of mysteries.[129]

The mixing of the iconography of the cults of Cybele and Attis, Demeter, and Aphrodite is not surprising in the context of later antique paganism. One of the chief concerns of Neoplatonic philosophy was to find the unity of the divine behind its various manifestations. A classic example of this tendency toward religious syncretism can be found in the speech given by Vettius Agorius Praetextatus in Macrobius' *Saturnalia.* There Praetextatus describes all of the divine as manifestations of one spirit, which he characterizes in Mithraic terms as the "manifold power of the sun" (*solis multiplex potestas*) (Macrob. *Sat.* 1.22.1). The same sentiment is attributed to Praetextatus in an inscription, in which his wife Fabia Anconia Paulina describes him as a "learned worshiper of the manifold divine spirit" (*divumque numen multiplex doctus colis*) (*CIL* 6.1779 = *ILS* 1259, line 15). The same point can be made by considering the various cults to which Paulina was devoted. According to an inscription (*CIL* 6.1780 = *ILS* 1260) she was initiated into many cults, including that of the Magna Mater (*tauroboliatae*) and the mysteries of Demeter and Kore at Eleusis (*sacrata apud Eleusinam deo Iaccho, Cereri et Corae*).

The association of the erotic and the religious on the panel of the Nicomachi is paralleled in the astonishing epitaph of Praetextatus and his wife (*CIL* 6.1779 = *ILS* 1259).[130] On the front of the inscription is a dedication to Praetextatus and Paulina, "who lived together for forty years." On each of the two sides are poems from Praetextatus to Paulina. On the back is a long (40 lines) poem from Paulina to her husband. Like the diptych of the Symmachi and Nicomachi these poems are concerned with the paganism of the late Roman elite, with marriage and mystery religions. The parallel between marriage and initiation here carries strong connotations of gender and eroticism: husband is initiator, wife initiated.

Praetextatus says in his poem on the left side of the monument that he "has entrusted the deeply hidden secrets of [his] mind to [his] wife" (*arcana mentis cui reclusa credidi,* line 4); the pair is united "by the custom of years together, by the bond of initiation, by the faithfulness of the marriage yoke and by perfect harmony" (*iungimur . . . / aetatis usu, consecrandi foedere, / iugi fideli, simplici concordia,* lines 9–11). Paulina, too, in her poem on the back of the monument, emphasizes the link between her religious experiences and her relationship with her husband. "You," she addresses her husband, "a devoted initiate, conceal in the secret places of your mind what you discovered in the holy rites" (*tu pius mystes sacris / teletis reperta mentis arcano premis,* lines 13–14). These are the secrets (*arcana mentis*) that Praetextatus says he has entrusted to his wife. Paulina continues, noting that Praetextatus has "kindly bound [his] wife as an ally in these rites" (or "through these rites": *sociam benigne coniugem nectens sacris,* line 16). "You, my husband, through the benefit of your teaching, deliver me pure and chaste from the lot of death, you lead me into the temples and devote me as a handmaiden to the gods; with you as my witness, I am initiated into all the mysteries" (*Tu me, marite, disciplinarum bono / puram ac pudicam sorte mortis eximens, / in templa ducis ac famulam divis dicas; / te teste cuntis imbuor mysteriis,* lines 22–25). She then lists some cults in which her husband has initiated her: the *taurobolia* of Cybele and Attis (lines 26–27); the threefold secrets of Hecate (line 28); the cult of Ceres (line 29).

> Because of you, everyone proclaims me holy, everyone proclaims me blessed, because you yourself have spread my goodness throughout the world: though unknown I am known to all. For with you as my husband, how could I fail to please? The mothers of Romulus' city take their example from me and think their offspring beautiful, if it looks like yours.

Now men, now women desire and acclaim the honors that you, my teacher, have conferred.

te propter omnis me beatam, me piam / celebrant, quod ipse me bonam disseminas / totum per orbem: ignota noscor omnibus. / Nam te marito cur placere non queam? / Exemplum de me Romulae matres petunt / subolemque pulchram, si tuae similis, putant. / optant probantque nunc viri, nunc feminae, / quae tu magister indidisti insignia. (lines 30–37)

The prominence of Demeter on this panel may have some special significance for the Nicomachi. We know from Symmachus and the subscriptions to Livy that the Nicomachi owned land in Sicily (Symm. *Ep.* 4.71), more specifically in the vicinity of Enna (subscription to Livy, bk. 7). In the classical period and after, Enna was renowned for its cult of Demeter and Kore.[131] A coin of the archaic period from Enna shows a scene similar to that on the panel of the Nicomachi.[132] On its obverse, within a border of dots, a chariot is driven to the right by Demeter, who holds the reins and a torch. On the reverse is a woman standing one-quarter left before a (circular?) altar. She holds a flaming torch in her right hand. Around the edge is inscribed HENNAION.

The representation on the panel of the Symmachi also alludes to the cults of several gods. Here a female figure, crowned with ivy, stands at an altar. Viewed from behind, her upper torso is twisted so that her face and breasts appear in profile. She is taking a bit of incense from a jar in order to deposit it in a small fire atop a square altar, which is adorned with garlands of leaves. Behind the altar stands a childlike attendant, holding a vase and a bowl of fruit. Above and behind the altar stands an oak tree.

The oak tree refers to Jupiter. The ivy garlanding the head of the figure should allude to Liber. The juxtaposition of these two gods may seem odd at first glance, since traditionally the priest of Jupiter could not touch ivy or even mention it.[133] In the Neoplatonic theology popular in late antiquity, however, even Jupiter and Liber might be united as aspects of the unitary divine. As Macrobius has Praetextatus point out in his speech in praise of Sol Invictus, Jupiter and Liber are the same (*Sat.* 1.18.15–18).

If the female figure on the panel of the Nicomachi is a goddess, so should be the figure that balances it on the panel of the Symmachi. Perhaps the ivy may refer to Liber's feminine counterpart, Libera, who shared a temple with him under the auspices of Ceres in the Forum Boarium?[134] Libera was sometimes identified as Cora (Kore), the daughter of Ceres (Demeter), and as such she figures in the mystery religions of the period. Again Paulina's religious experience is illuminating. She was "initiated at Lerna into the cult of the god Liber and Ceres and Cora" (*sacrata apud Laernam deo Libero et Cereri et Corae*) (*CIL* 6.1780 = *ILS* 1260). This panel, then, like the panel of the Nicomachi, represents an aspect of the goddess Kore at sacrifice and alludes to initiation in a mystery religion.

As Kore is associated with Aphrodite on the panel of the Nicomachi, so may she be associated with another goddess on this panel. Here, though, there are no signs so explicit as the baring of the breast. Simon suggests a possible connection with the goddess Iuventas. Iuventas has associations both with the youthful, evergreen strength of ivy, and with the cult of the Capitoline Jupiter. She is also in legend a bride: her wedding to Hercules was depicted on the gable of the Capitoline temple of Jupiter.[135]

The two panels of this diptych are closely paralleled and contrasted. Two goddesses, both at sacrifice, face each other. One is seen from the front, the other from behind. In both, trees stand in the background, indicating the environment of the sacrifice, mirroring each other. On one panel is Cora-Iuventas, the virginal bride; on the other is Cora-Venus, the young wife. On the panel of the Nicomachi we find the oriental cult of Cybele coupled with Cora; on the panel of the Symmachi the tree of the Roman Jupiter shades the sacrificing goddess.

The line between Christianity and paganism was not clear in late antiquity as it was later. The use of pagan iconography in this period does not necessarily guarantee that a particular object was not commissioned or possessed by a Christian, as the inventory of the Esquiline treasure shows.[136] Still, the cupids of the Esquiline treasure seem rather innocuous when contrasted with the sacrifices represented on the diptych of the Symmachi and Nicomachi. The iconography of the diptych cannot be explained with reference to Christian uses of the Roman cultural legacy; it must be seen in the context of the religious practices of the Roman senatorial class of the 380's and 390's, of individuals like Vettius Agorius Praetextatus. The diptych shows that the pagan religious interests of the families of the Nicomachi and Symmachi continued even after 394.

This discussion should not be taken to mean that the younger Flavian was necessarily an "insincere Christian." His "sincerity" is an unresolvable question. The diptych does show at least that after 394 his family was not exclusively Christian. It is not surprising that someone who converted to Christianity under substantial pressure should retain an attachment to the religion of his father. Even willing converts, like Jerome and Augustine, were ambivalent about the traditions they abandoned. There is no reason to imagine that the younger Flavian saw any inherent contradiction in his religious beliefs; by the standards of paganism, why should he not worship both Christ and Jupiter? The diptych also suggests (as Matthews had surmised) that the family of Symmachus (and by extension Symmachus himself) were involved in the "oriental" cults.[137] The diptych was produced in the early fourth century, and there is no way of saying what the younger Flavian's interests were some forty years later, at the time of the rehabilitation. I suspect, however, that even at this late date he would not have completely abandoned the religion of his childhood.

THE PAGAN PATINA: MACROBIUS' *SATURNALIA*

The best parallel for the rehabilitation is the *Saturnalia* of Macrobius, at once the most provocative and the most problematic source for the study of the elite of late antique Rome. Like the rehabilitation of Flavian, the *Saturnalia* was written in the 430's but looks back to the end of the fourth century. In contrast with the rehabilitation, which does not mention religion, the *Saturnalia* is preoccupied with paganism and the Roman elite's absorption with it.

It was long thought that the composition of the *Saturnalia* was contemporary with the individuals who play leading roles in it. It was considered to be a firsthand description of the "circle of Symmachus" and the "age of Praetextatus," dating roughly to the end of the fourth or the beginning of the fifth century A.D.[138] However, as Cameron persuasively argued and Panciera has now confirmed, the dialogue must be dated to the early 430's. The author of the dialogue must surely be identified with the praetorian prefect in 430, the year preceding the younger Flavian's term in that office.[139] Macrobius is a contemporary of Flavian the younger, not of the elder Flavian. So the *Saturnalia* does not date to the time of the usurpation of Eugenius, but to that of the rehabilitation of the elder Flavian. The implications of this revised dating are large and complicated. No longer imagined as a manifesto for the partisan religious struggles at the end of the fourth century, the *Saturnalia* is now generally conceded to be a "tendentious and idealized portrayal . . . composed almost half a century after the death of its leading representative."[140] Even the religious sympathies of the author, Macrobius, no longer seem certain. At one time it was taken for granted that he had to be a "committed pagan." Given his prominent position at the Christian court of Galla Placidia in 430, however, it seems certain that he must have been a Christian.

The redating of the *Saturnalia* does not completely discredit it as a historical source for the pagan commitments of the Roman elite in the late fourth century, though it must be used with caution. The work is concerned with historical individuals, such as Praetextatus, Symmachus, and Flavian, and it is written only forty years after Flavian's death. Some participants in the usurpation of Eugenius still survived. Macrobius probably knew personally the younger Flavian, who was his successor as praetorian prefect. Furthermore, some of the information provided in the *Saturnalia* can be verified against documents of the fourth century. Praetextatus' famous speech about Sol Invictus (*Sat.* 1.18) is only one of the most notable examples. Inscriptions contemporary with Praetextatus attest that he was an adherent of this cult, and even from the perspective of the 430's it would be difficult to explain this interest away as harmless antiquarianism.

But the value of the *Saturnalia* as a historical source for the late fourth century is far from the most interesting or most difficult question that its redating raises. The text must also now be considered as evidence for attitudes toward paganism and the pagan past in the mid-fifth century. It is generally acknowledged that by this time Christianity had decisively triumphed and paganism had virtually vanished. How is the apparent paganism of the *Saturnalia* to be interpreted in a Christian context? Does the text exemplify the attitudes of some particular, identifiable social group, perhaps the descendants of the old pagans, the new Roman Christian elite? The text is concerned with paganism as a historical event, an element of the past. What are the differences between the attitudes toward paganism in the mid-fifth century and at the end of the fourth, and what do these differences mean?

Since 1966 Alan Cameron has sporadically attempted to draw out the implications of his redating of Macrobius: his two most important statements have appeared in short essays.[141] Traditionally Macrobius had been used as evidence for a literary and cultural aspect of paganism in the 380's and 390's.[142] Now instead he must be used as evidence for the 430's and the attitudes of the Christianized Roman elite of that period toward its recent pagan past. At the same time, Cameron argues, removing the *Saturnalia* from the 390's must cause us to revise in radical ways our understanding of that period, for modern reconstructions of a pagan "party" in this period, whose understanding of culture and politics was largely informed by its religious sympathies, and which was itself united by its belligerent attitude toward Christianity, were founded on Macrobius' representation of "the circle of Symmachus."

Removed from the context of the 390's, Cameron argues, the *Saturnalia* ceases to look like a reactionary manifesto for paganism and becomes more like a piece of "nostalgia," which has little to do with anything except literary convention: "Quite apart from his obvious nostalgic idealization of Symmachus and his friends, Macrobius does not even purport to give a true picture of their culture. His use of their names is merely a literary device."[143] So much for the historical significance of Macrobius as a source for the 380's and 390's. Nor does Cameron have anything to say about the cultural significance of the *Saturnalia* in the 430's, beyond emphasizing that it is a manifestation of "sentimental antiquarianism and nostalgic idealization of the past."[144] Its paganism is "essentially nostalgic and literary."[145] Above all, he characterizes this paganism as associated with the past, with circumstances that are lacking but much desired. "The pagan past is idealized on every page: but because it is past, not because it is pagan."[146] "Macrobius saw the *'saeculum Praetextati'* through the rose-coloured spectacles of one who had heard of it only from old men (among them no doubt the younger Flavian) who sadly contrasted the iron days of the present with the golden days of their youth."[147] This is an intellectualized paganism, a religion manifested more in literature than in ritual, prompted more by antiquarianism than by vital religious allegiance; this is not the classical paganism of the past, but a classicizing paganism. As Matthews puts it, paganism in this period has moved from the sanctuary of the Magna Mater, the Phrygianum, into the library; it has been transformed and refined into a literary activity that is not inconsistent with Christianity.[148]

To reinforce this characterization of the *Saturnalia* as a "tendentious and idealized portrayal," Cameron contrasts it with Ammianus' critical account of the Roman senatorial class, an account he takes to be historically accurate (Amm. 14.6 and 28.4). Where Macrobius represents Flavian's generation as the epitome of culture and refinement, Ammianus shows them as philistines. "It is hard to resist the conclusion that Macrobius is deliberately rebutting Ammian's accusations. . . . What more natural than that he should have sought to answer Ammian's slashing denunciations of the very men he considered the last of the Romans?"[149] Cameron certainly shows that it is informative to read Ammianus and Macrobius against each other. It is debatable, however, whether Ammianus' account should be taken as a standard of truth against which Macrobius' tendency to idealize the Roman senatorial class can be measured. The two authors disagree, but they also share some common ground. Each shows in his own way the importance of the connection between status and erudition during this period. Furthermore, Cameron (and others) understand Ammianus' criticisms of the Roman elite in a far too literal-minded way. The Roman senatorial class, after all, must have been one of the chief audiences for his history. What does it mean that Ammianus would have called his prospective readers decadent, to their faces? Would they have disagreed? Or would they have nodded their heads, saying, "Yes, yes, we live in an age of decadence and there are so few of us left to carry the torch"? As for Macrobius, the issue is more complicated than Cameron seems to allow. To be sure, considered as a historical source for the 390's, the *Saturnalia* must be subjected to searching criticism. Histories are products of their time, and this is a feature that the *Saturnalia* has in common with any history, including that of Ammianus. The *Saturnalia* may well be, in certain respects, a "tendentious and idealized portrayal" of the Roman senatorial class in decline—though it is far from clear that Ammianus would have found much in it to disagree with, or that its author would have disapproved of Ammianus' portrayal of the senatorial class in general (see Chapter 6 below).

When Cameron characterized the *Saturnalia* as a piece of "nostalgia," he did not pause to consider the implications of such "nostalgia" for elite Roman culture of the mid-fifth century. Nostalgia can connote harmlessness and triviality, and I take Cameron's point to be that in the *Saturnalia* paganism has been reduced to a kind of aristocratic daydream, which would offer "nothing at all to offend the most narrow-minded Christian."[150] So elements of the classical tradition are made innocuous and are accommodated to Christian culture. Now, even for Christians, knowledge of pagan culture can denote erudition and nothing more.

Cameron may have picked the right word to describe the *Saturnalia,* but "nostalgia" is not a trivial or harmless phenomenon—as I am sure he would be the first to agree. The implications of a "circle of the nostalgic" within the elite demands examination and exploration. At its most basic, the idea of nostalgia implies a dissatisfaction with the present and an idealization of the past, an attitude that already suggests a certain disaffection from prevailing norms. As this definition implies, nostalgia by its very nature is routinely associated with a discontinuity, whether of society or self: the age is not as good as it once was, or we ourselves are not such as we once were. Nostalgia is also a social phenomenon: it works to promote the sense of collective identity of some particular group, frequently a generational group, and the opposition of that group to the present majority.[151] If "nostalgia" is the right word for the *Saturnalia,* then that work is far from a *simple* accommodation to the Christian order of the day.

The *Saturnalia* presents a miscellany of information in the form of a dialogue, in which one of the chief interlocutors is the elder Flavian. The author claims in the preface addressed to his son that it is a compilation of things that are useful to know, ordered so as to be coherent and easily accessible (1.pref.1–13). The discussion is planned on the evening of the Saturnalia, and it takes place on each of the three successive days of the festival. The dramatic date of the dialogue is probably December 384, just before the death of the dialogue's host and leading speaker, Vettius Agorius Praetextatus.[152] The participants include all of the leading pagan senators of the day, "men who command respect for their learning no less than for their noble birth," as the grammarian Servius says early in the book (1.4.4). This ideal of status coupled with learning is a central issue in the *Saturnalia,* as it is traditionally in Roman culture.[153]

The narrative begins on the eve of the Saturnalia, at the house of Praetextatus (1.1–5). After some discussion of various Roman antiquities, the group agrees to meet during the festival, when they have the leisure to talk at length. Flavian is not present at this first meeting. His good friend Symmachus is, however, and he suggests that the company invite the participation of Flavian, "who has proved that he has surpassed that admirable man Venustus, his father, by the distinction of his character and the dignity of his life no less than by the abundance and depth of his learning" (1.5.13).

The following day the group convenes at house of Praetextatus (1.6–2.8). Flavian makes his first appearance in the work here, when he arrives at Praetextatus' house accompanied by his "good friend" Eustathius (1.6.4). The conversation soon turns to Vergil (1.24), who will dominate the discussion for the rest of the *Saturnalia.* One of the participants makes a disparaging speech about Vergil, which provokes the rest of the company. Each puts forward a particular virtue of the poet and promises to argue in detail for it: this section amounts to the *Saturnalia's* "table of contents" (1.24). Praetextatus undertakes to demonstrate Vergil's knowledge of pontifical law (1.24.16), while Flavian points out that he finds in the poet "such knowledge of augural law, that, even if he were unskilled in all other branches of learning, the exhibition of this knowledge alone would win him high esteem" (1.24.17). This comment foreshadows a discussion of augural law that Flavian should contribute on the following day (1.24.21 and 24–25).

The discussion of the second day at the home of Flavian is recounted in the third book of the *Saturnalia.* This book is unfortunately fragmentary: the beginning, including Flavian's discussion of augural law (cf. 1.24.17 and 21), and much of the middle has been lost. As preserved, the book begins with Praetextatus discussing pontifical law (3.1–12).[154]

The final four books of the *Saturnalia* are taken up with the discussions of the third day, which take place at the home of the orator Symmachus (bks. 4–7). The beginning of book 4 and the end of book 7, which contained the opening of the discussion and its conclusion—as well as the conclusion of the entire work—have been lost. Appropriately, the conversations of this third day deal for the most part with the qualifications of Vergil as an orator. Symmachus makes substantial contributions to the discussion, but most of his speeches fall at the beginning of the meeting, in the fragmentary fourth book.

Flavian is one of the most prominent persons in the dialogue. As a wealthy member of the senatorial class, his status is far higher than that of many of the other characters of the dialogue. Furthermore, Macrobius singles him out, along with Symmachus and Praetextatus, by having him host the discussion for one of the days of the festival. It thus seems odd that he plays such a small role in the preserved sections of the *Saturnalia*. His contributions to the conversation can easily be summarized in a paragraph. At the evening drinking party of the first day, Flavian comments on a particular sacrifice, called "for the road" (*propter viam*, 2.2.4). Later in the same session he quotes Varro's Menippean satire "You Don't Know What the Evening May Bring" (*quae inscribitur "nescis quid vesper vehat"*) to the effect that sweet cakes should not be served with the second course (2.8.2). Throughout the rest of the extant *Saturnalia*, Flavian makes only one contribution, a speech about the relationship between wine and heat (7.6.1–15), a subject he says that "has often intrigued me and that I have much pondered" (7.6.14).

Flavian's most important contribution to the *Saturnalia* is apparently a section that has been omitted from the manuscripts, but that is clearly marked as having been there at one time: a discussion of augural law. Augural law was well defined. Its rules were nominally secret, but several writers are known to have discussed them. Cicero's book *On Divination* is notable not least because it has survived. Several other books on divination are known from later citations; the most influential seems to have been that of Nigidius Figulus.[155] In his lost discussion Flavian must have quoted extensively from these and other such works.

In considering Macrobius' portrait of Flavian, it is also necessary to consider that part of the dialogue which is set at his home. As Praetextatus is represented as the chief authority of the group, the first part of the dialogue is set at his home and is concerned with the organization and overall subject of the dialogue. The third part, which is concerned with rhetoric, is set at the home of Symmachus, a noted orator and an authority on rhetoric. The second part of the book, which is set at the home of Flavian, is concerned chiefly with religion. Presumably the setting is appropriate because Flavian was imagined to have been interested and expert in religious matters.

Of the religious topics discussed at Flavian's house, the major surviving section is Praetextatus' elucidation of pontifical law. As we have seen, the *pontifices* were the most prestigious of the priests of ancient Rome, charged with general supervision of religious practices. They traditionally had kept a chronicle of the various prodigies that occurred from year to year, the *Annales,* and listed precedents for sanctioned religious procedures, the *Commentarii.* Praetextatus' discourse on the lore of the college of *pontifices* doubtless was based on this kind of information. The preserved sections of Praetextatus' speech deal particularly with sacrifices: what kinds of victims are appropriate for which gods, which procedures of sacrifice are appropriate or inappropriate in which circumstances.

There is also a religious overtone in the discussion of Vergil. Macrobius several times calls the poet *pontifex maximus,* chief officer of the college of which Flavian himself was a member. Servius, too, in his commentary on Vergil, refers to him by the same title. Vergil, then, is imagined as the head of the official state religion, and of the board of priests of which Flavian, Symmachus, and Praetextatus were members.[156]

PAGANISM, SILENCE, AND THE REHABILITATION

The silence about Flavian's paganism in the rehabilitation appears to be significant. Religion played a part in the usurpation of Eugenius, and even those who think it did not must concede that in the aftermath influential Christian authors such as Ambrose and Augustine conceived of the usurpation as a pagan revolt. Theodosius' requirement that surviving pagans such as the younger Flavian convert to Christianity confirms that the victorious emperor also saw the conflict in religious terms. Macrobius' *Saturnalia* shows that at the time of the rehabilitation Flavian was associated with elite paganism. So it seems clear that a contemporary reader would be aware that something was not being mentioned in the letter of rehabilitation.

It is both enlightening and puzzling to contrast the letter of rehabilitation with Macrobius' *Saturnalia.* In addition to being a pagan, Flavian was a statesman and a scholar. He embodied the traditional Roman ideal of excellence in public service and learning—an ideal that continues to be espoused in the

Saturnalia of Macrobius. So his rehabilitation may rightly be seen as a manifestation of contemporary nostalgia for the more glorious days of Rome's past.[157]

At the same time, the utter silence of the rehabilitation regarding Flavian's paganism is an enigma. Macrobius' *Saturnalia* presents us with a rehabilitated person. The letter of rehabilitation alludes to Flavian's political career and his intellectual interests (i.e. his *History:* see Chapter 5 below), but it says nothing about his religious interests, which figure so prominently in the western Christian historiography of the early fifth century A.D. Why this reticence? In the earlier part of the fifth century, in the years immediately following the usurpation of Eugenius, in the period when Flavian was still under an "interdict of silence," pagan religious offices and activities may have been unspeakable, unmentionable in public documents. Such a milieu may explain why there should be no mention of Flavian's paganism. By the 430's, however, it was possible to speak of paganism. In the *Saturnalia,* senators do not dream of the revival of paganism; they dream of their immediate ancestors, of another, earlier generation who were able to dream of a revival of paganism. The old religion of Rome has achieved a patina.

If Macrobius could have Flavian discuss augury, how should the rehabilitation's failure to mention his position as *pontifex maior* be understood? Trivial oversight? A silence dictated by the public character of the monument? A sign of some sensitivity and embarrassment regarding the pagan past on the part of his family, and hence, perhaps, an index of some vestigial investment in paganism — or perhaps the contrary? In any event, the inscription deals with this aspect of the Roman past through the strategy of silence, and that silence demands to be contrasted with the garrulousness of Macrobius.

It is risky to describe the attitude of the Romans toward their pagan past simply as "nostalgia" or "romanticism" without further discussion or qualification, because such words may conceal the continuing dangerous and disturbing connotations of that past. Paganism was never a trivial matter after the fourth century, neither to the surviving elite families nor to the other Christians who read Roman history and literature. To focus exclusively on the Christian domestication of the pagan Roman past is to understand less than half of the story. The pendant documents of 431, the rehabilitation and the *Saturnalia,* illustrate some of the tension between the domestication and dangerousness of the Roman past. To be sure, the paganism of Flavian was known — and it might even have been openly discussed, as it was by Macrobius. At the same time, though, this same paganism remained a matter of some sensitivity, as the rehabilitation shows by its vagueness every time it alludes to the circumstances of Flavian's disgrace.

As I will argue in the next chapter, silence is not merely the absence of speech; it is the implication of something that might have been said, but is not. The memory of Flavian and his pagan sympathies was certainly alive in 431. In some situations it could be spoken; in others, it might not be. The silence of the rehabilitation regarding Flavian's original disgrace epitomizes this tension: something well known is withheld. To put the problem in larger terms, when dealing with the survival of pagan culture in the Christian world it is a mistake to focus exclusively on the contemporary social dynamics of assimilation or conflict, or to concentrate completely on the prescriptions for the present and future of groups or institutions or individuals. Contemporary change and prospective action are important; so too is the retrospective attitude toward the past. There is a relationship between contemporary social processes and tradition. It seems to be increasingly common in the modern world to insist that tradition is a product of present social circumstances, a thing to be manipulated easily: what we are determines what we remember. It is equally possible to take the opposite tack, as did for example Freud, and argue that it is the past which is constitutive of the present: as he said, we all suffer from memories.[158] For my purposes, it is enough merely to insist that there is a mutual determination between memory and present being.

The chief documents of the cultural memory of the Roman senatorial class in the mid-fifth century are Macrobius' *Saturnalia* and the rehabilitation of Flavian. In them it is possible to see the preservation of certain elements of the old Roman cultural legacy in a new Christian world. It is also possible to see in them the suppression of certain parts of the past. Memory is selective, that is, assimilative; it is the process by which the past is appropriated by the present for its own purposes and ends. What cannot be assimilated is forgotten—and forgetting is as much an active process as remembering. To understand what is recollected in the rehabilitation or the *Saturnalia,* or more generally in the Christian preservation of the pagan Roman past, it is necessary to have some sense of what has been cut out and forgotten. Forgetfulness is not total: it is here that the past bites back. The inconsistencies relegated to silence and forgetfulness never vanish entirely; traces and marks of their repression remain, like scars or erasures, to trouble and resist the assimilative processes of memory. Evidence, like a silence or an erasure, is an indirect, inexplicit way of alluding to some unstated thing. It is not only the sleep of historians that is disturbed by evidence; for societies and religions, too, such traces are the causes of tension, signs of what there is in the past that resists assimilation, nagging reminders of what has been forgotten.

The interpretation of something not said will always be controversial. Even the recognition of a silence raises problems: it is certainly conceivable that some might insist there is no silence in the imperial letter; that the absence of reference to paganism means nothing. Historians, some might say, must stick closely to what is said and avoid pursuing what is not said. Because it is in the nature of silence to dissimulate its own presence, it is difficult to prove these skeptics wrong. Discussion with a critic who begins from the position that there is nothing to be interpreted is profitless. Nevertheless, any interpretation, historical or literary, necessarily requires the isolation of that which is unsaid in some sense: that which is inapparent and so subject to elucidation. Silence is at the very heart of what the historian and critic do. And, as we shall see elsewhere (Chapter 7 below), there may yet be something else unsaid within the rehabilitation that confirms the importance of paganism in it.

CHAPTER 4

REMEMBERING TO FORGET

The *Damnatio Memoriae*

THE INSCRIPTION does not speak of certain of the positions held by Flavian and his son, nor does it allude to Flavian's religious attitudes. What these omissions mean, or if they mean anything, must be a matter for discussion: there are silences in any text, and the significance of what is not said is always a matter for interpretation, or rather the essential precondition of interpretation. As suggestive as these specific silences may be, they are only manifestations of a more general and far-reaching problem, one that is central to any understanding of the inscription.

Arguably, the crucial fact about the statue base from the Forum of Trajan is that it presents itself as a rehabilitation. That is to say, the inscription asserts itself not just as a representation of the life of Flavian, but as a new and improved version, a restoration, a re-representation. It refers to certain details of the life of Flavian, but also to an earlier representation of that life and the eradication of that representation. Implicit in the rehabilitation is the evocation of an earlier silence, and this situation complicates the interpretation of the inscription immeasurably. A restoration is like a representation. No matter how faithful, it cannot be regarded as the same as the thing for which it stands.[1] The fact of the rehabilitation implies that earlier representations had somehow come to be flawed: corrupt, false, or incomplete. The rehabilitation should be seen as an improvement over the earlier silence in that it presents itself as a more complete or truer disclosure, but it should also be understood as different from the earlier representations that it restores. Those earlier representations took their meaning from an affected correspondence to the life of Flavian; the rehabilitation takes part of its meaning from an affected correspondence to the earlier representations. The rehabilitation also claims to correspond to the reality of Flavian's life, but that pretension is undermined by its acknowledgment of the editing and repression of earlier accounts. One must ask whether the rehabilitation itself is at last adequate to the truth or whether it, too, has been subject to the same processes of selection, omission, and editing. So the self-proclaimed character of the text as rehabilitation simultaneously suggests the inadequacy of earlier accounts and affirms its own accuracy.

Throughout the imperial letter, the restoration of memory and honor are emphasized. By memory the emperor means the general contemporary recollection of the elder Flavian. More specifically, though, it is a recollection that the emperor and Roman senate share. Honor—the prestige an individual accumulates through public accomplishments and recognition—is manifested in the public record of magistracies and in the material objects bestowed upon him, such as statues and inscriptions. In the very first sentence, the letter weds prestige and recollection, describing the contemplated action as "defending honor and recalling memory" (*adserere honorem et memoriam . . . revocare,* line 10). The letter returns to the pair in its formal conclusion, with a slight twist. Here *honor* is replaced with *dignitas,* and the imperial benefices to Flavian are treated as accomplished: remembrance and prestige have been restored (*redditam . . . memoriam et dignitatem,* line 35).[2]

The reputations of father and son, the elder Flavian and Flavian the younger, are improved by the rehabilitation. According to the preamble, the statue "has been restored in honor of the son" (*reddita in honorem filii,* line 4). The point is made again in the imperial letter: the worth of the elder Flavian has been proven by his teaching of his son, whose honor is only "half full" (*honor semiplenus,* line 31) though he holds the praetorian prefecture. It is the father's honor that is restored, but the restoration takes place to fulfill the honor of the son. As we have just seen, the letter says at the outset that it is "defending honor" (line 10), and later it claims that it has accomplished the "restoration of the honor" of the elder Flavian (*restitutionem honoris eius,* line 28).

The intention to restore the memory of the elder Flavian is announced at the beginning of the text, where the letter claims "to recall memory to eternal light" (*revocare memoriam in lucem aeternam,* line 10). It adds that the action is undertaken "to restore the recollection" of Flavian (*in restitutionem . . . recordationis,* lines 14–15). By the end of the correspondence, the goal has been accomplished: the memory of Flavian has been effectively restored (*redditam memoriam,* line 35).

The allusions to the restoration of Flavian's memory and honor in the imperial letter presume an earlier loss, an erasure. To speak of a restoration is a way of representing a silence. Before the time of the rehabilitation, certain things could not be said. At some point, a silence had been imposed over the life of Flavian and over some periods in the career of his son. So the fact of the rehabilitation implies that Flavian had suffered an "abolition of memory," or *damnatio memoriae,* at some time in the past.

The history of political repression of social and cultural memory in ancient Rome, of the so-called *damnatio memoriae,* has yet to be written. Even the traditional narrative descriptions of the processes by which the state attacked the memory of those deemed public enemies are out of date or incomplete. Vittinghoff's classic book is more than fifty years old and is far from exhaustive.[3] A full account of the *damnatio memoriae* would be a major project for a mature and accomplished Roman historian. The strategies by which enemies are purged were developed throughout Roman history, from the fifth century B.C. through the sixth century A.D. There is extensive evidence for the practice of the purge in general and in specific cases, ranging from explicit statements in literary sources to actual erasures on inscriptions, defaced coins, modified statues, and circumlocutions in texts. These sources have by no means been thoroughly collected and evaluated, and this situation is especially unfortunate because the particularities of the various instances of the application of *damnatio memoriae* vary immensely and the subtleties of each case can be informative.

The *damnatio memoriae* raises fascinating questions about the relationship between elite political control and collective cultural tradition, the opposition of written history and unwritten memory, and the nature of remembering and forgetting. These problems have been central to practically every field in the social sciences for the past century, and any respectable account of the *damnatio memoriae* would have to take account of the technical and sophisticated literature that has been generated on these subjects.[4] Although this literature is scattered through a half-dozen disciplines, the various accounts and theories are by no means incompatible with one another. The Freudian analysis of repression and negation is one of the most influential accounts of remembering and forgetting.[5] Another notable discussion was provided by the sociologist Maurice Halbwachs in his book on the "collective memory"; his ideas have been developed further by such scholars as Pierre Nora.[6] Martin Heidegger exemplifies the long and substantial tradition of philosophical and theological writing on the significance of silence.[7] And there is John Cage's musical masterpiece, *Silence.*[8] Recent work on the discussion of the Holocaust has taken the relation between memory and history as a central theme.[9] Recent East European writing, prompted by political developments and the opening of state archives, has developed the notion of memory as a form of political resistance.[10]

There is also an immense body of comparative material which has been examined by historians, political theorists, anthropologists, and sociologists. Rome is far from unique in its attempts to suppress representations of individuals who have been condemned by the state. Historically, all societies, including modern Western liberal democracies, have necessarily been selective about what they remember and what they forget.[11] Even contemporary American businesses may treat embarrassing executives in a manner reminiscent of the *damnatio memoriae*.[12] Anthropologists since Fraser and even before have dealt with the phenomenon of "the unspeakable" in traditional societies,[13] and practically everyone has been interested in the nature of "censorship."[14]

The most notorious instances of political manipulation of memory come from Eastern Europe, where the recollection of public enemies has regularly been purged over the course of the twentieth century.[15] Such comparative examples, however, should be used with caution. The differences between a modern Soviet purge and the ancient *damnatio memoriae* should not be underestimated.[16] To begin with, some appreciation of the differences in the available communications media of the Roman world and the Soviet Union is essential. As an archaic state, Rome had far less powerful instruments of social and cultural control than those available to modern totalitarian regimes. Furthermore, in Rome the *damnatio memoriae* was directed without exception at the internal ruling elite of the state. Stalinist purges, by contrast, had much broader scope and application: they were used not only to send a message to a narrow, privileged group within society, but to affect public consciousness of the past in the broadest possible way and to disseminate a particular image of the past to the broadest possible public. Above all, it is necessary to consider the thoroughness with which the attack on representations of the public enemy is implemented. The Roman *damnatio memoriae* was much more restricted in its effects than a modern purge. The Soviet government aimed for utter annihilation of all trace of the public enemy—something the Romans never attempted to do.

In this chapter I provide a general description of how the Roman state attempted to purge the memory of those who were condemned as its enemies, and I discuss the paradoxes that these procedures created for ancient authors, especially the historian Tacitus and the author of the imperial letter rehabilitating Flavian. Despite pretensions to the contrary, Roman political attacks on memory were not intended to *destroy* recollection of an individual; indeed, the procedures used could never have had that effect. The *damnatio memoriae* did not negate historical traces, but created gestures that served to *dishonor* the record of the person and so, in an oblique way, to confirm memory. Thus it is more accurate to describe the attack as a *damnatio* than an *abolitio memoriae*. This point has large implications both for Roman imperial politics and for historiography.

DAMNATIO MEMORIAE

Throughout the period of the republic and the empire, a span of more than eight hundred years, the state devised and implemented a variety of well-defined strategies for attacking the memory of a dead public enemy. In general outline these included the eradication of visual representations of the person, in particular of statues and busts, the erasure of his name, and a ban on the observance of the funeral and mourning. By decree of the senate (or later, of the emperor) any or all of these penalties might be imposed.

The expression *damnatio memoriae* is a modern coinage. It is often used loosely (and, from a juristic perspective, incorrectly) to sum up the various penalties used in ancient Rome to attack the memory of dead enemies of the state. It is true that approximations of the phrase can be found in many Roman authors, including historians such as Tacitus, but those instances do not refer to a legal procedure. In particular, there is a technical, juridical expression, "condemnation of memory" (*memoria damnata*), which refers not to an attack on the contemporary recollection of the dead, but to the posthumous prosecution or conviction of a person on charges of treason.[17] Even so, there was no juridical concept of *damnatio memoriae* in ancient Rome, only a more or less conventional repertoire of penalties for repressing the memory of the public enemy, which might be enacted separately or together. Nevertheless, for the sake of convenience I will here refer to the Roman attack on memory as *damnatio memoriae*, or in English as "repression" or "anathematization" or "purge."

The fact that there is no technical and recognized procedure called a *damnatio memoriae* is consistent with the goal of the purge. The *damnatio memoriae* is supposed to eradicate memory. But to recognize that there was such a technical procedure would be to acknowledge the repression, and thereby allow the existence of those of whom it was illegitimate to speak. Therefore, it is integral to the process of forgetting that it pretend not to be a repression at all, that it dissimulate itself. If the purpose of repression is to purge representation and impose forgetfulness, then it must pretend to be nothing itself—otherwise, the process would become the sign of the thing repressed, and so would produce an effect contrary to its goal.

There is no lack of information about the *damnatio memoriae*. The details of these proceedings are known from a variety of scattered sources. Juristic texts, inscriptions, poetry, and historians provide details about the means of "forgetting" and about the various specific applications of these techniques to particular enemies of the state. Many of those anathematized were as renowned (or notorious) in antiquity as they are in the present day. Livy's story of the *damnatio memoriae* of M. Manlius Capitolinus in the fourth century B.C., for example, was often repeated. The recollection of the two assassins of Caesar, Cassius and Brutus, was repressed—and that fact became famous. M. Antony, the triumvir and opponent of Augustus, also notoriously suffered an "abolition of memory." Other memorable accounts of the *damnatio memoriae* concern cases dating to the early principate. Tacitus' accounts of the treason (*maiestas*) trials under Tiberius are especially well known.[18] Recently in Spain a long inscription was discovered that verifies and elaborates many of the details of Tacitus' story of the condemnation of Calpurnius Piso in A.D. 20 (Tac. *Ann*. 3.11–18).[19] Tacitus preserves many detailed descriptions of the procedures for attacking the memory of an enemy of the state, as well as elaborate criticisms of the process. The dichotomy between memory and forgetfulness is central to his idea of history and its function. The fact that certain condemnations of memory should be as famous as they are, told and retold by Roman authors, is doubtless a paradox of a kind—a paradox that Roman critics of the penalty, particularly Tacitus, do not fail to point out.

THE *DAMNATIO MEMORIAE* OF THE ELDER FLAVIAN

Already in 393 and 394 the emperor of the east, Theodosius, had given unmistakable signs of contesting the legitimacy of the regime of Arbogast and Eugenius. For the year 393, the first full year of his reign, Eugenius had proposed himself and Theodosius as consuls (it was customary for the two emperors to share the consulship with each other in the first year of a reign). Theodosius ignored this gesture and appointed himself and Abundantius as consuls.[20] The following year, 394, Eugenius chose Flavian as his consul, leaving the selection of the second consul to the other emperor. Theodosius ignored Eugenius and chose two consuls of his own: his sons, Arcadius and

Honorius. Consequently the consular dates that survive in inscriptions from Italy dating to 394 mention only Flavian, as though he were the sole consul of the year.[21]

After Theodosius defeated the forces of the usurper at the battle of the Frigidus in September 394, he evidently took a conciliatory and generous attitude toward Flavian's reputation and toward surviving members of the family. He did not, however, have time to dispose of the various legal and administrative problems that had been created by the usurpation. He died soon after, in January of 395, leaving his son Honorius to put Italy back in order. Honorius (or his ministers) decided to make a new beginning, disavowing the illegal activities of the usurper and his confederates.[22] In a decision issued on Rome's birthday, 21 April 395, and addressed to Andromachus, then prefect of Rome, Honorius validated the day-to-day transactions of minor magistrates under Eugenius but placed the principal figures of the rebellion under an "interdict of silence":

> All transactions [of the period of usurpation] that were arranged privately are to be valid, unless fraud or coercion or intimidation can be demonstrated. We order that the names of those ill-omened consuls only be eradicated, so that reverence may be shown in the recitation [of state documents] by readers to those who administered the annual magistracies in the East under our ever victorious standard. Let the period itself be considered as if it never were, since any prescription of silence omitted at the time cannot be imposed even regarding those matters where we ourselves have so asserted.

> *stent denique omnia, quae in placitum sunt deducta privatum, nisi aut circumscribtio subveniet aut vis aut terror ostenditur. funestorum tantum consulum nomina iubemus aboleri, ita ut his reverentia in lectione recitantium tribuatur qui tunc in Oriente annuos magistratus victuris perpetuo sunt fascibus aspicati; tempus vero ipsum ac si non fuerit aestimetur si quidem tunc temporis omissa aliqua praescribtio taciturnitatis etiam de illis quae confirmavimus non possit obponi.* (CTh 15.14.9)

The settlement proposed here for the illegal regime should be contrasted with the three laws put forward by Theodosius just seven years before, in 388, after he had defeated the pretender Magnus Maximus (CTh 15.14.6–8). Then, the emperor invalidated all legal actions (with a few clearly specified exceptions) undertaken in areas under Maximus' control. Furthermore he voided all magistracies held under this usurper as well as all legal decisions rendered:

> We order that all who were advanced because of the usurpation of the tyrant and who received any illegal title of office shall produce and return their certificates of status and letters. We order that such verdicts and opinions as could not have been rendered by those who could not lawfully have the title of judge shall be removed from all offices of public record, so that the authority of these acts shall be invalidated and no one shall attempt to rely on these judgments, which are negated owing to their period and author.

> *omnes qui tyranni usurpatione provecti cuiuslibet acceperunt nomen inlicitum dignitatis, codicillos adque epistulas et promere iubemus et reddere. iuris quoque dictionem adque sententias, quas promere nequiverunt qui iudicum nomen non habere non potuerunt, ex omnibus publicorum monumentorum scriniis iubemus auferri, ut abolita auctoritate gestorum nullus his iudicatis conetur initi, quae et tempore et auctore delentur.* (*CTh* 15.14.8)

In contrast, the law decreed by Arcadius and Honorius specifies that those who served as consuls under Eugenius are to have their names struck from the record, but it says nothing about other magistracies. Even during the reign of Eugenius, Theodosius had refused to recognize the consuls appointed by the usurper and had appointed his own. It is not surprising that his sons refused to acknowledge them after the fact. It is remarkable, however, that there is no reference here to the status of other magistracies. The fact that the actions of such junior magistrates are to be considered valid might be taken to imply that those of major magistrates are to be considered invalid. It also might be understood to mean that the legitimacy of the various other magistracies is recognized. So we might mistake this law to mean that the elder Flavian's term as consul is to be unmentionable, null and void, but that his son's contemporary term as urban prefect is to be recognized.[23]

The new emperors were cognizant of the ambiguity of this preliminary pronouncement, and over the next few months they issued further legislation, designed to supplement and amplify the first decision. On 18 May 395, another constitution was addressed to the prefect of the city (*CTh* 15.14.11). Here the emperors recognized that they had not dealt with the problem of the status of the other magistracies that had been held under Eugenius, and they decreed that those who had held office were to be pardoned but that they should receive no status or advancement for their illegal service. Those who had served under the tyrant "should not endure the mark of disgrace or be contaminated by any ugly word" (*ne . . . notam infamiae sustineant aut deformi vocabulo polluantur*); rather, they "should have only such rank as they had before the time of the tyrant" (*quibus eas tantum dignitates valere decernimus, quas ante tyrannicum tempus habuerunt*).

The following month a similar constitution was addressed to Eusebius, the praetorian prefect of Italy. Again it was specified that those who had held office under Eugenius should not be penalized, but neither should they receive credit for their service:

We eradicate all disgrace of the stain, in the appearance of an honor, branded on those whom the plague of the time of the tyrant infected. Consequently we grant to all without exception of rank or order their previous status, so that all may have the same rights and occupy the status of their former rank, provided that none of them flatter themselves with honors which they obtained at that time [i.e. of the usurpation].

his quos tyrannici temporis labes specie dignitatis infecerat, inustae maculae omnem abolemus infamiam. cunctis igitur statum priorem sine cuiusquam loci aut ordinis exceptione tribuimus, ut utantur omnes iure communi, teneant statum veteris dignitatis, ita ut nihil sibi ex his quos adepti fuerant honoribus blandiantur. (*CTh* 15.14.12)

Other sources attest that these directives were carried out. Flavian the younger was not allowed to take credit for his term as urban prefect in 394, though he evidently continued to "flatter himself" by taking credit for it privately and there appears to be a subtle allusion to it in his *cursus*, included in the prescript of the rehabilitation of his father (Chapter 2 above). He was also initially required to repay the salary that his father had drawn in the service of Eugenius (Symm. *Epp.* 4.19, 51; 6.12), though he was in the end excused from this obligation (Symm. *Ep.* 5.47).

In these constitutions the emperors are quite specific about their concerns and about the extent of their "interdict of silence." The penalties they describe are well defined, aimed only at particular, unauthorized events that occurred during a very restricted period. It is only Eugenius' usurpation and its administration that shall be treated "as if none of it ever happened." There is no reference here to a more general, thoroughgoing attack on the memory of the leaders of the rebellion, that is, to a *damnatio memoriae*. In fact, there is no record of the condemnation of Flavian's memory. The major source for his anathematization is precisely the imperial letter of rehabilitation.

The rehabilitation itself never states in categorical, juridical terms that "Flavian suffered a *damnatio memoriae* and the emperors hereby rehabilitate him." Such a statement would be unusual and would contradict the impression created by other sources; the *damnatio memoriae* was not a legal concept or procedure in ancient Rome. Instead, the emperor proceeds by listing the individual privileges to be returned to Flavian and his family. The references to these privileges are rather abstruse and allusive. It occasionally takes some expertise to recognize them as references to an attack on the memory of Flavian. That they are recognizable at all is owing to the fact that the repertoire of penalties is conventional.

BAN OF REPRESENTATIONS

The imperial letter of rehabilitation proposes to "recall Flavian to the monuments and inscriptions of his worth" (*in monumenta virtutum suarum titulosque revocemus,* lines 17–18). This provision of the rehabilitation implies that the name and image of Flavian had previously been banned. This statement is iterated by the very context in which it appears: an inscribed statue base, a monument crowned with a statue, restored in honor of Flavian. As the statue has been restored (*reddita,* line 4) so has been the memory of Flavian (*redditam . . . memoriam,* lines 34–35).

The ban on material representations was perhaps the most noticeable strategy used to attack memory of the condemned. It is certainly the aspect of the *damnatio memoriae* that has attracted the most attention from modern scholars. The ban applied not only to monumental dedications, such as statues, but to all images, including busts and even coins and medallions.[24] This ban is both prospective and retrospective: there are to be no representations of the condemned in the future, and those representations which already exist are to be altered or destroyed. The ban applies to representations in all places, public and private: none are to be permitted.[25]

Many ancient statues have been modified—an original head removed, replaced, or reworked to represent someone new. Such modifications are not infrequently motivated by a *damnatio memoriae,* but they need not be.[26] Let us take only one problematic example: the so-called Barberini statue, a late republican representation of an unidentified Roman senator holding busts in either hand. The head of this statue is ancient but not original, for at some time the statue has been decapitated. The missing head may or may not reflect a *damnatio memoriae;* whatever the case, it raises the same general questions about memory and forgetting, questions that are only emphasized by the connotations of the busts carried by the headless senator. Whatever its cause, the modification to the statue is the sign of a missing person and, as the sign of someone who has passed out of representation, it poses questions as inevitable as they are perhaps unanswerable: Who might the person have been? What is the meaning of his absence?[27]

The destruction of a monumental representation such as a life-sized statue that has stood in a public space must have been an extraordinarily impressive event, as memorable for contemporary Romans as the recent destructions of statues of communist leaders in Eastern Europe have been for moderns. The practice is often described in all periods of Roman history, from the republic through the late empire. In the early empire, description of the destruction of public statues and other images of a condemned traitor was virtually a set piece of historians and poets. Easily the most famous of all such descriptions is Juvenal's vivid account of the fall from favor of Tiberius' aide, Sejanus, and the destruction of an equestrian statue of him:

> the statues come down, and follow the rope; the axe chops the chariot wheels and the legs of the unoffending horses are broken. Now the fires roar, now with the furnace and bellows that head, once adored by the people, burns and huge Sejanus melts; then from that face which was second in the entire world are made pitchers and basins, frying pans and bedpans.
>
> *descendunt statuae restemque sequuntur, / ipsas deinde rotas bigarum inpacta securis / caedit et inmeritis franguntur crura caballis: / iam strident ignes, iam follibus atque caminis / ardet adoratum populo caput et crepat ingens / Seianus, deinde ex facie toto orbe secunda / fiunt urceoli pelves sartago matellae.* (Juvenal 10, 58–64)[28]

The destruction of statues was a familiar enough penalty that it might be used spontaneously by the Roman people as a way of sending a message to the senate. According to Tacitus, when Cn. Calpurnius Piso was on trial for the murder of Tiberius' popular foster son, Germanicus, the senate hesitated to convict him. The people, who had loved Germanicus, rioted and destroyed a statue of Piso (Tac. *Ann.* 3.14), thus adopting the methods of official political repression to manifest popular sentiment. The recent overthrows of communist monuments in Eastern Europe are comparable: the methods used by society against the state have been learned from the political behavior of the state itself. For example, in August 1991 the statue of "Iron Felix" Dzerzhinsky, founder of the KGB, was toppled by a mob. The monument had stood in Dzerzhinsky Square, Moscow, in front of the headquarters of the KGB, the Lubianka Building. The overthrow of the statue was itself the occasion for a public celebration. The empty statue base now remains, covered with graffiti; the statue itself lies in a garden along with the bits and pieces of other communist monuments.[29]

An instructive parallel, roughly contemporary to the disgrace of Flavian, is provided by the *damnatio memoriae* of the eunuch Eutropius, a favorite of the emperor. In 399 he fell from favor, victim of a failed military campaign and court intrigue.[30] In a strongly worded and very rhetorical letter, the emperor ordered that "all statues, all images whether of bronze or marble . . . in both public and private places are to be destroyed" (*CTh* 9.40.17). The court poet Claudian, in his polemical poem attacking Eutropius, also mentions these statues, commenting on their proliferation and the boastfulness of their inscriptions (Claudian *In Eutrop*. 2.70–83). He concludes with the ironic wish that they should not be torn down (as had been ordered) but should somehow "remain undisturbed, as indisputable proofs of our eternal shame" (*maneant immota precamur / certaque perpetui sint argumenta pudoris,* 2.77–78). This paradoxical hope sums up the problem of "remembering to forget."

It would be easy to multiply examples of the practice. Some passages spell out the rule, however, in a general prescriptive way. So, for example, the *Digest* states that "we should know that statues of those who have been banished or exiled by reason of treason should be taken down" (Modest. *Dig.* 48.19.24).

Destruction of various images of the condemned enemy of the state seems to have been far more common in the principate than during republican times.[31] Nevertheless, authors of later periods like to cite republican precedents as justifications for the practice. The accuracy of such late authors is not always beyond reproach. In some cases it appears that they are anachronistically projecting the practices of their own day back into the republican period. So, for example, Cassius Dio cites the disgrace of M. Manlius Capitolinus in the fourth century B.C. to justify the practices of the third century A.D. As part of the penalties imposed, he claims that "the name and whatever images of Capitolinus there were were erased and destroyed" (Dio frg. 26.1).[32]

The purge of the representations of the enemy applied not only to images erected in the public space, but also to images kept in the home by the family.

Statues of the public enemy Eutropius were to be removed from "both public and private places," and there are many precedents for the practice. For example, in the early principate, Claudius' promiscuous empress, Valeria Messalina, was subjected to a similar disgrace. According to Tacitus, by decree of the senate "her name and image were to be removed from all places, public and private" (Tac. *Ann.* 11.38).[33]

Privately held representations of a public enemy were banned for the future. This interdict applied most notably to the public display of the wax portraits of distinguished family members that senatorial Roman families kept in the open receiving room of their houses, the atrium.[34] So after the posthumous condemnation of Libo Drusus, it was forbidden that his family parade his bust in future funeral processions (Tac. *Ann.* 2.32.1). Tacitus provides another famous example in his account of the funeral of the wealthy Roman woman Junia Tertulla, who had been the wife of Cassius and the sister of Brutus. Because her husband and brother had conspired to kill Julius Caesar, her family was not permitted to parade their busts at her funeral (Tac. *Ann.* 3.76, summarized at length and discussed below).[35]

Often the family was forbidden to keep the bust at hand, even if locked away in a cupboard.[36] Already in republican times, Sex. Titius was condemned by the senate for keeping a statue of L. Appuleius Saturninus in his home (Cicero *Rab. perd.* 24). The ban is also attested in the early principate. Under Claudius, C. Silius was condemned among other reasons for keeping in his home a portrait of his father, who had been condemned and executed under Tiberius (Tac. *Ann.* 11.35).[37] Those who were found to keep such statues secretly and illegally were considered guilty of the same crime as those whom they surreptitiously honored.[38] So C. Cassius was exiled under Nero for honoring a portrait of the tyrannicide among his ancestral portraits: "because among the busts of his ancestors he also adored one of C. Cassius, inscribed thus: to the leader of factions" (Tac. *Ann.* 16.7; cf. Suet. *Nero* 37 and Dio 62.27).

ERASURE OF THE NAME

The name of a public enemy might also be erased from some public documents.[39] After the disgrace and death of Valeria Messalina, it was ordered that her "name and image be removed from all places, private and public" (Tac. *Ann.* 11.38). After the death of Domitian, the senate decreed that "his inscriptions were to be erased everywhere as soon as possible, and all memory of him was to be destroyed" (Suet. *Dom.* 23; cf. *Vit. Commodus* 20.5 and Macrob. *Sat.*

1.12.37). The penalty is known from all periods. The frequency with which it was applied in various situations is suggested by the erasures of names that are often encountered in Roman inscriptions. Evidence for erasures on inscriptions has not been thoroughly collected; indeed, publications of inscriptions (particularly older editions) do not even consistently note them.[40]

Dio Cassius claims that the state was already erasing the names of public enemies from inscriptions in the fourth century B.C. He says that M. Manlius Capitolinus' name was erased from all inscriptions (frag. 26.1, quoted above). Dio is probably indulging in an anachronistic projection here, though his statement does provide evidence for the practice in the third century A.D. The earliest certain examples of the penalty date to the late republic.[41] The most important early evidence comes from Cicero: in two passages he alludes to the erasure of a name, in both cases suggesting that a consul's name should be removed from the state lists of officials, the *fasti*. Once in his *Philippics*, inveighing against Antony, he suggests that "his entire consulship should be removed from all record of the monuments" (*totus consulatus est ex omni monumentorum memoria evolsus*) (Cicero *Phil.* 13.11.26). Elsewhere, speaking of two consuls, A. Gabinius and L. Calpurnius Piso Caesonius, he remarks that these are "consuls who everyone thinks should be removed not only from memory, but even from the official lists" (*consules quos nemo est qui non modo ex memoria, sed etiam ex fastis evellendos putet*) (Cicero *Sest.* 14.33). These passages suggest that it is normal, or at least imaginable, to erase the name of those who are disgraced from inscriptions. They also seem to imply that it is possible, though unusual, to erase the names of such individuals from the consular lists.

Cicero is speaking wishfully and polemically. At all times it was unusual to erase a name from these lists.[42] Even after condemnation, if a man had legally held a consulship his name might remain in the *fasti*. Tacitus remarks that after the condemnation of Calpurnius Piso, Tiberius refused to allow "the name of Piso to be removed from the consular lists, when the names of M. Antonius, who had made war on his native land, and Iullus Antonius, who had outraged the home of Augustus, remained" (Tac. *Ann.* 3.18). This passage implies that Piso's name will be allowed to remain in the consular lists but is to be excised from other monuments.[43]

It appears that the name of the elder Flavian was banned, and we know that the emperors banned the names of the consuls of 394. However, there are a few references to Flavian's consulship in contemporary inscriptions from Italy (the only area that Eugenius controlled), all in unofficial texts, specifically a series of Christian grave-inscriptions.[44] There is no trace of his consulship in any later consular lists.[45] Even after 431 Flavian was not credited with the office: there is no reference to his consulship in the rehabilitation. Furthermore, the letter of rehabilitation has been carved over an earlier, erased text—whether an earlier inscription of Flavian or not we cannot say.

Credit for his term as consul was not restored to Flavian because it was never taken away. Theodosius never recognized Eugenius' appointments. In 394 he had appointed his sons joint consuls. So Flavian's consulship was not legitimate to begin with, and its removal from the documents of the west was not part of the attack on the memory of Flavian, but a mere correction of the record. What was never legitimately received cannot be restored.

DISCONTINUING THE NAME

Another aspect of the Roman attack on memory involved a ban on the continued use of the name of the enemy by the family. The senate could pass a decree requiring the family to discontinue the use of a particular element of the name. Most commonly the family was required to desist from using the first name, or *praenomen*.[46] The practice was archaic, little attested in the early principate, and not at all after the Julio-Claudians. Aulus Gellius claims to have heard Herodes Atticus remark on the custom:

> I hear that the ancients judged that the first names (*praenomina*) of certain Roman patricians, who had deserved ill by the republic and for that reason had been condemned, should not be given to anyone of the same family, so that their name should appear disgraced and dead along with them.

> *antiquos Romanorum audio praenomina patriciorum quorundam male de republica meritorum et ob eam causam capite damnatorum censuisse ne cui eiusdem gentis patricio inderentur ut vocabula quoque eorum defamata atque demortua cum ipsis viderentur.* (Aulus Gellius 9.2.11)

There are verifiable examples of the practice going back to the early republic. The earliest case dates to the fourth century B.C. The *gens Manlia* imposed on itself a ban of the *praenomen* Marcus because of the disgrace of M. Manlius Capitolinus: "by decree of the Manlian family it was provided that no one should be called Marcus Manlius" (*gentis Manliae decreto cautum est ne quis deinde M. Manlius vocaretur*) (Livy 6.20.14).[47] In fact, there is no Marcus Manlius attested after Capitolinus, although the *praenomen* is attested in earlier generations.[48] Because of the criminal activities of two of its members, at an uncertain date the patrician Claudii excluded the *praenomen* Lucius from their *gens* (Suet. *Tib.* 1). One L. Claudius Pulcher is attested in the late republic, mentioned by Cicero as *rex sacrorum* and *pontifex minor*.[49] However, since he is the only Lucius known among the family of the Claudii, and since Suetonius testifies that the patrician Claudii shunned the name, most suppose that his *praenomen* should be emended.[50]

The best-known instances of the penalty date to the early principate. As part of the *damnatio memoriae* enacted against M. Antonius in 30 B.C., the senate denied the *gens Antonia* the right to use the *praenomen* Marcus in the future.[51] The eldest son of the triumvir had been named Marcus,[52] but he did not survive the year of his father's condemnation. Antony's other son, Iullus,[53] survived to carry on the line, producing a boy whom he named Lucius.[54] The death of Lucius in A.D. 25 without issue brought an end to the family. The latest example of the suppression of a part of the name of an enemy of the state occurred in A.D. 20 in the case of Gnaeus Calpurnius Piso.[55] Aurelius Cotta proposed that the name of Piso be erased from the consular lists, and that half his property be confiscated; the other half of the property would go to his heir, Gnaeus, provided that he change his name (*Ann.* 3.17).[56] Tiberius would not allow the name of Piso to be erased from the consular lists (see above),[57] but the requirement that the son change his *praenomen* was evidently not modified. Gnaeus disappears, only to re-emerge in A.D. 27 as consul with a new *praenomen,* Lucius. After the *damnatio memoriae* there are no more Gnaei to be found among the Calpurnii Pisones.[58]

There is one example, dating to the reign of Tiberius, of the suppression of the *cognomen* of an enemy of the state. When the senate condemned M. Scribonius Libo Drusus in A.D. 16 it was decreed that in the future no Scribonius might take the *cognomen* Drusus (Tac. *Ann.* 2.32).[59] Except for a mistaken reference in the *De Viris Illustribus* to a ban of the *cognomen* Capitolinus among the Manlii (24.6), there is no parallel for such a penalty. Some have suspected that the ban was prompted by a desire to shelter the son of Tiberius from sharing the same name (i.e. Drusus) with an enemy of the state.[60] At any rate, it should be noted that in one of the official lists of consuls, the *Fasti Amiternini,* the condemned is named simply as M. Libo.[61] Furthermore, it seems that the ban was observed: no more Drusi are attested among the Scribonii Libones.

There is no certain reference in the rehabilitation of Flavian to the restoration of a part of his name. In line 14, however, the emperor claims to act *in restitutionem pr[.]n[..]inis inlustris et . . . recordationis,* "to restore the glorious pr[——]en and the reverend recollection" of Flavian. The context of this passage deals with an imperial restoration (*restitutionem*). Presumably some word describing an honor removed from Flavian by the *damnatio memoriae* should be restored. The size, shape, and most of the letters of the word are legible. There is a very limited range of possibility for its restoration: *praenominis* is the only word I can think of that makes sense and fits the traces. As many of my readers have pointed out to me, this restoration is vulnerable to serious objections, which I will summarize below. Because of these difficulties I have not entered this restoration in the text of the inscription. It should be noted, however, that *praenominis* is at least an epigraphically possible supplement, even if its sense is in certain respects troublesome. All of the restorations so far proposed in this place (see Appendix) are more or less innocuous in their sense; but, from an epigraphical point of view, all are materially impossible.

I find no instances of the ban of the *praenomen* after the treason trial of Calpurnius Piso. In fact, there is some question as to why such a ban would be imposed in the case of Flavian or, for that matter, in the late empire at all. The use of the *praenomen* vanishes in most families in late antiquity in favor of the *cognomen* or a *signum,* and there is in fact no indication that Flavian—or his son—even had a *praenomen*. The fullest attestation of the elder Flavian's name is Virius Nicomachus Flavianus.[62] For the most part, however, he is simply called by one of his *cognomina,* Flavianus, as was the custom in late antiquity.[63] Why should the emperor restore a part of the name that is no longer used—if it even existed? Furthermore, it should be noted that there is no mention of any *praenomen* at the head of the inscription rehabilitating Flavian. If the emperor is restoring the use of Flavian's *praenomen* to the family, why is it not mentioned at the head of this very inscription, along with the rest of his name?

Thus, if this supplement to the text were to be accepted, it would be necessary to imagine that the imperial restoration of the *praenomen* here was a formality, a bow to tradition: the measure was intended to be more appropriate than effective. The rehabilitation alludes to the restoration of another privilege that was likely superannuated in the Christian world of 431: the restoration of the *religiosum munus,* the privilege of performing the rites that were owed to the dead. Indeed, the invocation of *damnatio memoriae* and its reversal by a more or less formal rehabilitation is already by this time virtually an antiquarian activity, which summons up with it all of the dying traditions of the old Roman state.

There was antiquarian interest in the traditional use of the *praenomen* in late antiquity. One unknown but surely late author wrote a treatise on the subject.[64] Romans of the fourth century A.D. were also aware of the historical precedents for the ban of the *praenomen* in the context of the anathematization of enemies of the state, if only through their readings of classical literature. The summary (*periocha*) to book 6 of Livy, for example, mentions the *damnatio memoriae* of M. Manlius Capitolinus and the ban of his *praenomen*—though it makes the mistake of attributing the ban to a decree of the senate. In Livy the action is described as gentilitial decree. The dates of the *periochae* are unknown, though many would argue that they should be attributed to late antiquity.[65] If so, the error may reflect a contemporary assumption that, as part of an "official" attack on the memory of a public enemy, the family was required by the state to discontinue the *praenomen* of a member who had suffered disgrace.

MOURNING

In the rehabilitation it is claimed that Flavian is rehabilitated because his son "may be thought to be on trial if he is not absolved of the debt of duty owed the dead by his whole house and family" (*delatus exsistimetur nisi integer tandem et absolutus religiosi muneris debito totius domus eius familiaeque sit,* lines 32–33). The phrase *religiosum munus* refers to traditional cults and practices associated with the dead. There is no Christian connotation to the phrase here.[66] In the context of the attacks on the memory of the public enemy, this statement must mean that the family may now make the traditional offerings at the grave of the elder Flavian, and may keep a portrait of him at home, among those of their other illustrious ancestors.

As we have seen, in the earlier empire when individuals were convicted on charges of treason the family was frequently forbidden to display or even to keep portraits of them within the home. There is no evidence that such bans occurred as late as the fourth century, nor even that the Roman elite continued to preserve and parade these wax images during this period. Anyone as familiar with Roman literature as are the characters in Macrobius' *Saturnalia,* however, would have known of the custom. It is also amply attested that privately held statues of public enemies continued to be forbidden in the late empire.

It was commonly forbidden to observe the traditional rites at the grave of a public enemy.[67] Public enemies could not even be buried unless their family petitioned for the right.[68] According to the later jurists:

> The bodies of those who are condemned to death are not to be denied to their relatives: even the deified Augustus writes that he observed this

rule. . . . Today, however, the bodies of these are not buried unless permission is sought and granted, and sometimes it is not granted, particularly for those convicted on grounds of treason.

corpora eorum qui capite damnantur cognatis ipsorum neganda non sunt: et id se observasse etiam divus Augustus . . . scribit. hodie autem eorum in quos animadvertitur, corpora non aliter sepeliuntur quam si fuerit petitum et permissum et nonnumquam non permittitur, maxime maiestatis causa damnatorum.
(Ulpian *Dig.* 48.24.1; cf. Paul. *Dig.* 48.24.3)[69]

Even if the enemy was buried, the tomb was not protected from desecration, because it was excluded from the protection normally accorded to the dead, the *res religiosae*. It was thus possible "to use stones taken (from such graves) for whatever purpose" (Paul. *Dig.* 47.12.4).

Those who survived the condemned were not permitted to mourn. Surviving members of the family were forbidden to show grief for the death of someone convicted of treason (Ulpian *Dig.* 3.2.11, 3; cf. Marcell. *Dig.* 11.7.35).[70] Such mourning was itself treasonable. There are traces of bans of this kind from earliest republican times. In Livy's exemplary tale of Roman tradition, when Horatius kills his sister he remarks: "thus may any Roman woman perish who mourns for an enemy" (*sic eat quaecumque Romana lugebit hostem*, 1.26.5). Under Tiberius, "it was forbidden for the relatives of those condemned to death to mourn" (Suet. *Tib.* 61.2). The mother of Fufius Geminus was killed because she wept for the death of her son (Tac. *Ann.* 6.10.1).

Other forms of commemoration were also denied to the family. So it was illegal for the family to celebrate the birthday of a public enemy. Under Domitian, Salvius Cocceianus was penalized "because he had celebrated the birthday of his uncle, the emperor Otho" (Suet. *Dom.* 10.3). The state might even declare the birthday of a public enemy a day of ill omen, a *dies vitiosus*, as was done in the case of M. Antonius.[71] The day of the public enemy's death might become a day of public celebration. Antony, Libo, and Sejanus suffered this penalty.[72]

IMPLEMENTATION OF THE *DAMNATIO MEMORIAE*

How, in practical terms, was an attack on the memory of an individual implemented? How did the state deal with existing representations of the public enemy? Inscriptions or statues, for example, might be utterly destroyed, as was Sejanus' equestrian statue; they also might be left to stand, but altered or erased. It is clear both from literary *testimonia* and from surviving monuments that either or both methods might be used. In the case of M. Antonius we hear that "they destroyed some of his monuments, others they erased" (τὰ τοῦ' Ἀντωνίου κοσμήματα τὰ μὲν καθεῖλον, τὰ δ' ἀπήλειψαν) (Dio 51.19.3).[73] The issue is not trivial; the implications of erasure are very different from those of an utter eradication.

For obvious reasons, there is less surviving evidence for the utter annihilation of representations of a public enemy than for alteration or erasure of such representations. Annihilation leaves no trace; alterations and erasures may survive. Many examples of altered statues are known.[74] When an individual suffered a *damnatio memoriae,* representations of him were frequently reused. The head of the statue might be recarved, or even removed and replaced, as in the case of the statue of the senator carrying busts (discussed above). Likewise, inscriptions were often left to stand, with only the name of the public enemy erased. Not infrequently the name shows through the erasure. A particularly notable example, both for modern scholars and for the ancient Roman public, is the arch of Septimius Severus (*CIL* 6.1033 = *ILS* 425). No attempt has been made to erase the entire inscription. Here only the name of Severus' disgraced son Geta has been erased, and traces of the name are recognizable, even from a distance, through the erasure.[75]

The inscription of rehabilitation provides some information about the history of the monument on which it is inscribed. The text is carved over an erasure. The fact of this erasure suggests that the base itself is not a new construction but an original monument of Flavian. The statue on the base is described as "returned" (*reddita,* line 4), as is Flavian's memory (*redditam . . . memoriam,* lines 34–35). This word may be contrasted with "restoration" (*restitutio*), which is used elsewhere in the text to describe Flavian's restoration. So too his *praenomen* may have been restored (*restitutio* [*praenominis?*], lines 13–14), as was his honor (*restitutionem honoris,* line 28). It is tempting, but ultimately impossible, to insist on a precise distinction between the two. Clearly the statue is a material thing, and its return is a physical action, unlike the restoration of Flavian's honor and *praenomen*. On the other hand, the word "returned," *reddita,* is also used to describe the restoration of Flavian's memory—which, like his honor and name, is an immaterial thing. In any event, it is clear from the inscription that the original statue of Flavian was affected in some way by his disgrace: it may have been destroyed, or merely removed and placed in storage.

It is impossible to be certain that what has been erased from this statue base referred to the elder Flavian. The rehabilitation might also have been carved on a base from some other, unrelated statue. Roman statue bases of all kinds were not infrequently reused. This point is irrelevant to the evaluation of the erasure in the context of the rehabilitation: no matter what the history of the base, it is significant that the rehabilitation was carved on a palimpsest. The identification of what has been erased, however, does matter for a reconstruction of Flavian's condemnation and the history of his reputation between 394 and 431.

At the beginning of his *Book of Laughter and Forgetting,* Milan Kundera tells the famous story of a hat. In 1948 a picture was taken of two Czech leaders, Gottwald and Clementis. The day was cold, and Clementis lent Gottwald his hat. The picture became famous, known to every Czech:

> Four years later Clementis was charged with treason and hanged. The propaganda section immediately airbrushed him out of history and, obviously, out of all photographs as well. Ever since, Gottwald has stood on that balcony alone. Where Clementis once stood, there is only bare palace wall. All that remains of Clementis is the cap on Gottwald's head.[76]

Repressions leave traces, even if those traces are only a gap in the picture of a crowd or a period of historical silence. Sometimes the trace may be even more noticeable. At the outbreak of the Hungarian revolution in 1956, the fifty-foot-high bronze statue of Stalin in Budapest was destroyed. The head of the statue was placed at an intersection, with the sign "No-through-road." The pedestal, with only the boots of the statue intact, was left standing.[77] Many such traces remain of the "second Russian revolution" of August 1991. Statues lie ruinous in parks or behind buildings; pedestals capped by bronze boots, covered with graffiti remain on public view.[78] These traces were (and are) signs of resistance, unlike the the cap of Clementis, which was understood as the sign of oppression. So in Budapest in 1956, when, a week or two after the overthrow of Stalin's statue, Soviet troops retook the city, the remains of the statue were eradicated: in its mutilated state it had become a monument to the revolution.

The rehabilitation provides some grounds for speculation about the status and appearance of this particular monument of Flavian during the forty years of his condemnation, between 394 and 431. We do not know whether the base itself was removed from the Forum of Trajan and stored somewhere away from view.[79] I am inclined to think it must have remained on public view; otherwise there would have been little point in erasing it. So we might imagine that this monument, denuded of its statue, with a blank, purged face where the honorific inscription belonged, remained prominently displayed in the Forum of Trajan for some forty years for all to see: a mute reminder of Flavian's disgrace.

There is some contemporary evidence for the survival of such mutilated monuments. The Vandal generalissimo Stilicho was a friend of Symmachus and the younger Flavian. He may even have helped the younger Flavian recover the favor of the emperor after 394 (see Symm. *Ep.* 4.1, 2). In 408 Stilicho himself was disgraced and executed. He was declared a public enemy, his property confiscated.[80] Subsequently a *damnatio memoriae* was carried out, and his name was erased from many monuments. Three statue bases honoring Stilicho have been recovered from the Roman Forum (*CIL* 6.1730, 1731, and 31987). One of these (31987) was found *in situ*. This block had originally been used for an equestrian monument; later it was converted to a monument honoring the armies of Arcadius, Honorius, and Theodosius, which, under the command of Stilicho, routed Alaric and his Goths in 403. On it there presumably stood a statue of Stilicho. After the condemnation of Stilicho in 408, his name was erased from the monument. What became of the statue is unknown; the inscription with its erasure, however, was left to stand in the Forum.[81]

The thoroughness with which an attack on representations of a public enemy might be carried out should also be considered. Some sources suggest that in principle the name and representation of a public enemy were to be destroyed everywhere throughout the Roman world. The Roman empire, however, was a large place; communications were not so efficient as in the modern world, nor were the news media so centralized. A modern totalitarian dictator would have been frustrated and disappointed with the powers of a Roman emperor. As a practical matter, it cannot have been a simple thing to implement or enforce a total silence throughout the Roman world. Furthermore, it was surely no easier in antiquity to enforce a ban on private commemoration of an individual than it would be today.[82]

Another, related reason that the state did not attempt to eradicate utterly the name of a public enemy may have to do with the audience for the *damnatio memoriae*. The "message" of the *damnatio memoriae* was primarily directed at a small percentage of the populace, the senatorial elite. Many in the late antique Roman world would have known little or nothing about someone like the elder Flavian, beyond the fact that he held the consulship, and would have cared less. Given the limited objects of the anathematization, total eradication of the name would have been unnecessary and enforcement would have been easier.

The practical problems of implementation and enforcement are only apparently at odds with the goals of the *damnatio memoriae*. For the attack on memory to be effective it is necessary for it to be less than totally effective. Exceptions to the ban not only occurred, but were known and tolerated. Although the ban on images of the public enemy was in principle universal, and severe penalties sometimes were imposed on those who did not observe it, enforcement was inconsistent. Whether the sporadic enforcement of the ban was intentional, or was merely owing to the limitations of the state's power, the fact that traces of the state enemy always survived is of paramount importance to an understanding of the procedure.

In many cases, even public statues of enemies of the state were permitted to remain in full view. Although the emperor Domitian suffered a *damnatio memoriae* and most of his images were removed from the city (Plin. *Paneg.* 52.4; Suet. *Dom.* 23), a statue of him nevertheless continued to stand in Rome down to the time of Procopius (*Hist. Arc.* 8). In the reign of Augustus a statue of the tyrannicide Brutus was noticed, standing in Mediolanum. The emperor did not penalize the city, or require them to destroy the statue (Plut. *Comp. Brutus and Dio* 5). According to a speech that Tacitus puts in the mouth of the disgraced historian Cremutius Cordus, Augustus permitted statues of both Brutus and Cassius to remain on display after he had defeated them and their memory had been repressed (*Ann.* 4.35). Statues of public enemies might also be kept privately by members of the family even with the knowledge of the emperor. In one case, Augustus knew that a certain L. Sestius honored Brutus among his ancestors even though he had been forbidden this privilege. Augustus not only tolerated his behavior, but even promoted him to consul (Dio 53.32.4; App. *B.C.* 4.51).

As with the ban on images, it was possible to carry out the ban of the name only in principle. Inscriptions containing the unerased name of a public enemy have frequently survived. In fact, there is scarcely any public enemy whose name has not survived on some inscription—and often on many. Such survivals might depend on a variety of considerations, including location, importance, and type of inscription.[83] In some cases the unerased name is evidence for the practical inability of the Roman state to enforce the ban everywhere. For instance, various inscriptions of Cornelius Gallus were erased. The survival of one particularly boastful inscription in Assuan, on the borders of Egypt and Ethiopia, may be ascribed to the relative isolation and obscurity of its location.[84] The survival of the name of a disgraced consul, say, on an amphora handle or drainpipe might be attributed to the inability to locate every occurrence of the name.

Attacks on memory could not be universally enforced in part because the state was incapable of ferreting out and eradicating every occurrence of the name of a public enemy. In a sense, the intent of the authorities in leaving traces of the public enemy is immaterial; the semantic effect of the survival of such traces will be the same no matter what the state's intentions. Nevertheless, it seems clear that the state did not even attempt to erase every appearance of an offending name. In some cases, the name of the person anathematized might easily have been destroyed but was not, as is evident from the numerous surviving inscriptions of emperors who were condemned after death.[85] For example, two boundary stones from Dalmatia have been recovered, both dedicated by order of the same legate of Caligula. On one the name of Caligula has been erased (*CIL* 3.8472 = *ILS* 5948); on the other it has not (*CIL* 3.9832 = *ILS* 5949). It would have been no more difficult to locate one of these boundary stones than the other; apparently, the local authorities did not care enough to erase more than the one.[86]

The only inscription of the elder Flavian that seems to have been affected by an attack on his memory is the statue base from the Forum of Trajan, on which the imperial letter of rehabilitation has been inscribed. Only one other *public* inscription of Flavian is known: the honorific text from Lepcis Magna, which was erected soon after 377 (Chapter 2 above). There is no indication that it was affected in any way by Flavian's disgrace: the inscription was inscribed on a reused stone, but was itself never subsequently erased or reused.

The other surviving inscription in honor of Flavian is a private dedication, erected in the ancestral home of the Symmachi on the Caelian hill, probably soon after 401; and this dedication was not a small wax bust, but a full-sized statue (Chapter 2 above). The rehabilitation allows Flavian his statues once more, and so implies that all representations of him had been ordered destroyed. It follows that this dedication was erected illegally. Furthermore, this inscription inappropriately claims Flavian's term as consul, which was not regarded as valid even after the rehabilitation. In addition it should be noted that the *damnatio memoriae* imposed on Flavian did not keep authors from mentioning him. The orator Symmachus devoted the entire second book of his published collection of letters to his correspondence with the elder Flavian. Among these are letters that even mention his participation in the usurpation of Eugenius.

The attitude of Flavian the younger toward his term as urban prefect provides a useful parallel to these representations of Flavian's consulship. Like his father, Flavian the younger received his office from the pretender Eugenius. He was consequently not allowed to take credit for his tenure of this office. So in public dedications he could take credit only for his two later terms as urban prefect, as he does in the honorary inscription from Naples (Chapter 2 above). Though he could not claim the office officially, he did not hesitate to do so privately. In his subscriptions to the books of Livy which he has corrected (Chapter 6 below), he often signs as "thrice prefect of the city."

Most astonishing is the younger Flavian's *cursus* in the preamble of the imperial letter of rehabilitation. The rehabilitation does not, on the face of it, affect the career of the younger Flavian, but only that of his father. It is startling to find him described here not as "urban prefect twice," or even "urban prefect thrice," but as "urban prefect rather often" (*saepius*) (line 5; see Chapter 2 above). The word draws attention to itself by its very ambiguity, and to the third, illegal term as urban prefect, a term that he should not have been able to claim explicitly, even after the supposed rehabilitation of his father.

REPRESENTATION, MEMORY, AND SILENCE

Thus, despite the implication of its name, the *damnatio memoriae* is at best only an indirect attack on memory. More immediately, the repression is directed against representation. To use the phrase from the Theodosian Code (15.14.9), it is an "interdict of silence," not one of thought. Utter eradication of all representations was a practical impossibility for the Roman state and was not even attempted. Even those monuments which were in public view were only sporadically destroyed. In some cases the survival of such monuments was clearly not an oversight. They were permitted to stand. Furthermore, the state often chose to erase rather than utterly destroy monuments of public enemies. So the object remained on display, its mutilation a continuing reminder of the disgrace of the public enemy. Likewise, bans on mourning and mention of the name of the traitor had the effect of keeping the memory of the traitor alive, not destroying it: one can avoid using a particular name only so long as one *remembers* that it is not supposed to be used. The name of the enemy survives, and wherever it is erased the erasure itself is displayed as a sign, a reminder of what lies beneath it. Despite appearances, political repression here does not work to destroy memory, but (indirectly) to foster it.

This paradox of the *damnatio memoriae* is related to the famous paradox of "remembering to forget." The exemplary anecdote is provided by Cicero:

> What is the sense of the saying that the wise man should not let past blessings fade from memory, and should not remember past misfortunes? In the first place, is what we remember in our power? Themistocles, in any event, when Simonides (or some other such person) offered to teach him the art of memory, replied: "I would prefer the art of forgetting; for I remember even what I do not want to remember, but I cannot forget what I want to forget." He [Epicurus] had great ability; but still the fact of the matter is that a philosopher who forbids us to remember is far too demanding.
>
> *Iam illud quale tandem est, bona praeterita non effluere sapienti, mala meminisse non oportere? Primum in nostrane est potestate quid meminerimus? Themistocles quidem, cum ei Simonides an quis alius artem memoriae polliceretur, "Oblivionis," inquit, "mallem; nam memini etiam quae nolo, oblivisci non possum quae volo." Magno hic ingenio; sed res se tamen sic habet ut nimis imperiosi philosophi sit vetare meminisse.* (Cicero *De Finibus* 2.104)

Simonides was regarded as the inventor of the "art of memory," and so it is appropriate that it is he who offers to teach that art to the fifth-century B.C. Athenian statesman Themistocles. Themistocles responds that the art of memory is easy: to attempt consciously to keep something in consciousness is a straightforward task. More difficult and contradictory would be the "art of forgetting."[87] To attempt to forget a thing consciously requires one to think of the thing, and to think of the thing is to do the contrary of forgetting it. The paradox of the *damnatio memoriae* involves the same contradiction: if one must constantly remember not to mention a person, then one is surely not forgetting that person. So the enforcement of a public ban on representation of a person necessarily reinforced the memory of the unmentionable person, to the extent that the ban was enforced. Like Freudian repression, the repression of social memory requires constant effort and vigilance.[88]

The *damnatio memoriae* must reinforce memory of the public enemy because the continuance of memory is essential to the success of the repression. The penalty works only so long as those who are condemned remain in memory. Only in this way can the ban on commemoration of them be significant. If *all* recollection were destroyed, then the *damnatio memoriae* would be impossible. How or why should one forbid the representation of a person of whom there is no knowledge?

The most perceptive ancient commentator on the *damnatio memoriae* is the historian Tacitus, who is emphatic about the persistence of memory in the face of attempts to control it. He uses the fact of the survival of memory as a lever to criticize the imperial *damnatio memoriae* and, as we will see in the next chapter, this critique is central to his general historiography. He comments, for example, in the context of his description of the condemnation of the historian Cremutius Cordus, that "it is pleasant to laugh at the foolishness of those who imagine they can destroy even the memory of the next generation by their present power" (*quo magis socordiam eorum inridere libet, qui praesenti potentia credunt extingui posse etiam sequentis aevi memoriam*) (*Ann.* 4.35). The emperor may ban contemporary representations, but future memory is beyond his reach. Tacitus makes a comparable point at the beginning of the *Agricola,* when he discusses the imperial repressions of his youth: "We would also have lost our very memories together with our voice, if it were as much in our power to forget as to be silent" (*memoriam quoque ipsam cum voce perdidissemus, si tam in nostra potestate esset oblivisci quam tacere*) (*Agr.* 2). Here we see the usual contrast of representation ("voice") and memory, and an allusion to the paradox of forgetting: to forget is not "in our power." Tacitus believes that memory will persist in the face of political repression; moreover, he believes that political repression paradoxically strengthens memory. This point is repeatedly highlighted in his writing and has been duly noted by modern scholars, though few have given any attention to the logic of the paradox.[89]

A similar contradiction is highlighted in the imperial letter rehabilitating the elder Flavian. Although the letter speaks several times about "restoring memory of Flavian" (lines 10, 14–15, 35), it also concedes that the ban has been ineffective in suppressing memory of him. It was possible to outlaw the monuments and name of Flavian, but in the end his memory was invulnerable. The rehabilitation is the formal restoration of the memory of a person whom no one has really forgotten. So, for instance, many of the senators to whom the letter is addressed are said to recall the speech by Theodosius, made more in sorrow than in anger, after Flavian's participation in the abortive pagan rebellion (*plerique meministis,* line 17). Forty years later, Flavian's restoration is in the hearts and minds of the senators, far from any interruption of intervening forgetfulness (*absque interpellatione ulla mediae oblivionis,* lines 25–26). The enduring recollection of Flavian may seem vaguely treasonous, contrary to the intent of the imperial anathematization of his memory. The letter recognizes the inconsistency and condones it, claiming that the senate has guarded the memory of Flavian no less than it has the imperial person (*non minus memoriae illius quam nobis . . . praestitis,* lines 26–27). Not even the emperor himself has been able to forget Flavian. He professes to be anxious not to appear to have acted because he was reminded, rather than of his own accord (*admoniti potius quam sponte,* line 29). The rehabilitation is in a sense superfluous, because the *damnatio memoriae* has affected only the representations of Flavian, his monuments and inscriptions, the use of his name, the ability of his family to express their sorrow. The ban has not been able to touch the memory of him.

The mechanism of the *damnatio memoriae* is predicated on the traditional dichotomy between representation and memory. It is commonly imagined that the goal of representation is to stand adequately for what it represents. It is reassuring when there seems to be "sincerity," when the representation and memory seem to correspond and there appears to be a correlation between what is said and what is thought. Representation and mind, however, are autonomous and need not correspond to each other. The procedures of the *damnatio memoriae* presume the possibility of such a disjunction between the two—in fact, they rely on it. The problem can be approached by examining the dichotomy between the representation and what is represented.

A representation is a thing that stands in place of something else, and thus representations are generally conceived as untrustworthy. A thing that stands in place of something else is not actually that other thing; consequently it can be used to represent either a thing that is or a thing that is not. Because of this flexibility, there is an uncomfortable similarity between a thing that stands in place of something else and a lie. To adapt Eco's famous definition of the sign, we might say that a representation is anything that has the potential to be used to tell a lie.[90] A lie may be defined as a representation that (by intention) does not correspond to an external reality; that is to say, it is a (willful) representation of something that is not.

The correspondence of any representation to what it represents must always, on skeptical evaluation, be questionable. The relation of language to "reality" is by its nature dubious: in popular cliché, "Saying it's so doesn't make it so." This idea of the independence of representation from what it represents I will call "simulation." By "simulation" I mean an appearance that is imagined to stand in place of nothing or, at best, in place of something highly questionable. It is a representation that is conceived as having no correspondence to anything "out there," as answering to no reality. So, for example, when one simulates fear, one puts on an appearance that is not answered by a psychological truth.

Broadly speaking, representations may be imagined as standing in place of ideas held in mind and in place of physical things in the external world.[91] In either case, the thing represented, be it something in mind or something in the world, is imagined as being outside of language and appearance. Such things do not stand in place of something else, as representations do: they are only what they are. Since they do not represent but only exist, they do not have the potential to lie; a thing that is only itself cannot be false. Mendacity is a quality of representation, not of being or mind. Furthermore, the thing that is represented is also commonly imagined as independent, autonomous of its representation. In short, what is represented is imagined as the equivalent of what is real and true. Misrepresentation, or the absence of representation, is not commonly thought to be sufficient to falsify a memory, a feeling, a historical fact, or a physical object. If I refuse to give voice to a feeling, or to name an existing person or thing, that does not mean the feeling or person or thing therefore ceases to exist. What *is* will persist even in the face of silence or lies. To elaborate on the cliché, "Saying it's not so (or even not saying it at all) will not make it not so."

It may help to make the argument clearer if I diagram (in good Aristotelian fashion) the distinction I am drawing between these two relations of appearance and reality (see Illus. 2).[92]

The *damnatio memoriae* should be understood as dissimulatory, a masquerade.[93] It works to produce *significant* silences and erasures. The key is to recognize that silences and erasures are themselves signs. To be sure, they are signs that pretend to be the opposite, the negation of representation—just as the *damnatio memoriae* purports to be the destruction of memory, and not its dishonoring. To notice silences and erasures, however, is to treat them as representations: what is recognized is always a sign, and a sign is never merely itself, but always something that stands for something else. The object of perception is never a "simple reality," but always, by virtue of the operation of perception itself, a thing that refers and connotes.

The discrimination between simulation and dissimulation, as I have defined it here, corresponds to the conventional dichotomy between "realist" and "idealist" conceptions of language. Not only silence, but any representation, is dissimulatory if it is imagined as subordinate to its referent. The notion of the priority of the referent to its representation is the hallmark of a realist conception of language: language exists to reflect some reality, be it social or material, and is the product of that reality. Idealists, by contrast, argue that language creates its own reality. So, to use the hackneyed example, why should Eskimos have many words for snow, and Californians only a few?

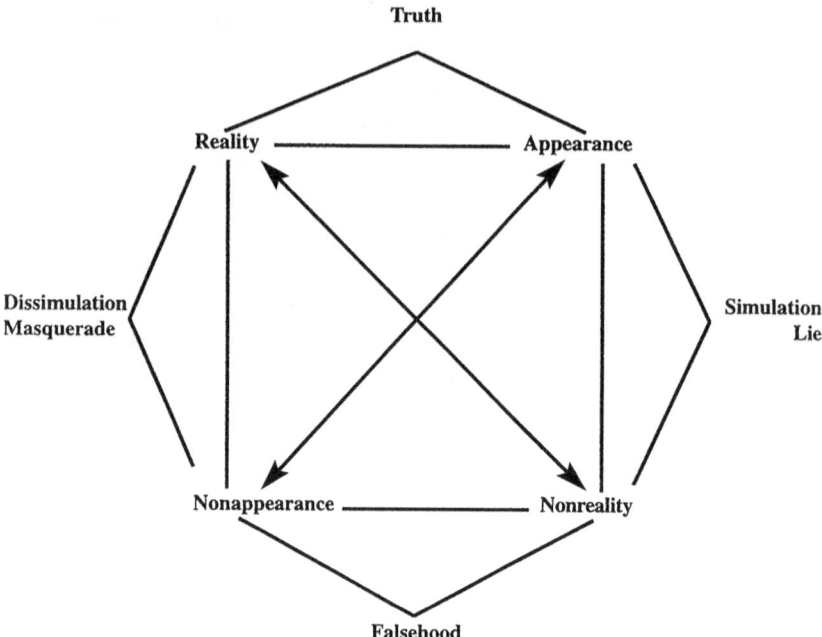

ILLUS. 2. Simulation and dissimulation

Surely the material nature of snow itself is not different in these places?[94] The realist theory of language is the more popular, conventional conception: people use words, words do not use people. Some would even argue for an association of these theories of language and broad historical periods: idealist conceptions of language do not become generally thinkable until modern times, under the influence of the technologies of industrial reproduction and the mass media.[95] Euphemism is sometimes used as an argument for the realist position. Euphemisms are used to describe uncomfortable social and cultural phenomena; they must frequently be changed as the representation is contaminated by the disconcerting things it represents. Here, then, representation appears to be dependent on what is represented, and that reality cannot be changed by merely changing its representation.[96]

This model of simulation and dissimulation, realism versus idealism, likely derives from the common human experience of the dichotomy between speech and mind. In individual experience it is possible to say what one does not think. Speech notoriously has the potential for lie. But is it possible to lie in one's own mind, to think what one does not really think? Can consciousness be false to itself? Freud thought that it could, but that remains one of his most radical positions. He also argued that, contrary to popular belief, it was in the power of the human mind to forget what it wanted or needed to forget; that forgetting was not a slip, but a highly motivated process.[97] In traditional philosophy and popular belief, mind and thought are usually imagined as present to themselves and, consequently, true. This presence of mind to itself is why it appears to be paradoxical that the mind should be able consciously to forget something. It also seems experientially obvious that it is possible to keep silent about what one has in mind, to not say what one thinks. To keep silent does not mean that there is nothing in mind. Likewise, to have a silence imposed does not mean the destruction of what is in mind.

The contingency and untrustworthiness of representation contrasts unfavorably with the autonomy and truth of the thing represented. This imbalance between the two was used by Tacitus to criticize the political repressions of the early emperors. Tacitus would say that the *damnatio memoriae* is directed against representation; it cannot touch the enduring truth of memory. Consequently the repression is ultimately a vain and delusional exercise. No matter what the tyrant does, memory will survive to vindicate the silence imposed by the tyrants of the day. In the end, a ban on representation merely confirms the truth that underlies the silence. Even Tiberius, who is for Tacitus the master of repression and dissimulation, knows this. As Tacitus has him say in a speech to the senate, Tiberius himself desires that his own memory should be kept in the hearts of men, not in unreliable monuments and statues: "These are my temples in your hearts, these are my most splendid and durable images; for those that are built of stone, if the verdict of future generations changes, are despised as sepulchers" (*Ann.* 4.38).

Tacitus' Tiberius is playing on the conventional idea of the monument, turning it upside down. One of the most basic and traditional ideas about the monument is that it should preserve memory and ward off forgetfulness. However, there is always a danger that this benign function can not only fail, but work to an opposite end. Like any representation, the monument stands in place of what it represents: memory. Used incorrectly, the monument ceases to be a reminder and becomes an unresponsive, didactic tool of political power: it tells people what they ought to think instead of submitting itself to the will of the community. Such a monument works to displace and destroy memory rather than to nurture it. This critique of the idea of the monument is very ancient. It can already be found in Thucydides (2.43), and Plato makes use of it in his general critique of writing (the *Phaedrus*).[98] In recent years, architects commemorating the Holocaust have shown great sensitivity to the idea that monuments can as easily be used to seal off cultural memories as to keep them alive: they can be fascistic or communal.[99]

Paradoxically, the great confirmation of memory and truth is the silence imposed by the *damnatio memoriae*. It may be possible and even common to imagine an utterly neutral silence, the state of nature, a silence with nothing behind it. Such a neutral silence can exist only to the extent that it is not recognized. Once recognized it must be treated as a sign, and a sign is never merely itself, but always something that stands for something else. The object of perception is never a "simple reality," but always, by virtue of the operation of perception itself, a thing that refers and connotes.

Unlike most other signs, silence pretends not to be a sign. This might be the definition of silence: a sign that affects to be the negation of representation, to be the absence of a sign; it is a sign that suggests and evokes without actually representing. So, to the extent that it is the object of perception, silence carries connotations of dissimulation. It implies an absence of some kind—something that might be said, a sound that might be made, but is not.

The experience of "keeping silent" may be the foundation of this perception of the dissimulatory quality of silence. A person may go for long periods of the day without speaking. These periods are experienced as silence, however, only when it is noticed that there is no talking. Silence exists only in light of the possibility of speech. To put it another way, one "keeps silent" when dissimulating—when one has something to say, but does not say it. The imposed silence and erasures of the *damnatio memoriae* are dissimulatory in the sense that they suggest that something is not being said.

Silence, because it is imagined as outside of representation, is frequently associated with truth. Silence can be misinterpreted, may even be intended to mislead, but can silence be a lie? Can what is not said be false? Because silence is not imagined to represent at all, it is normally not thought to be able to represent what is not. From a common perspective, silence can be regarded as the only appropriate response to truth. This idea is familiar in late antiquity in the literature of Neoplatonism and various mystic religions, particularly in the literature of apophatic (or negative) theology, as represented by such authors as Dionysius the Areopagite.[100] The only appropriate representation of a transcendental truth, such as god, is to not represent it at all. God is what is above and beyond representation, what guarantees representation; attempts to bring god into the world of representation are perversions and diminishments of the divine, as, on a realist theory of language, representation is merely a dependent reflection of the real, a secondary and inadequate substitute for the truth of being. The divine remains outside of representation, and any attempt to represent it can only diminish it. God is the unnameable.

Silence is made significant only by postulating the priority of what is outside of representation. The sense of a silence is produced by an awareness, vague or specific, of something that is or has been there, but is not being represented. What exists in memory or in fact can persist in the absence of its representation, and that is the precondition for creating the sense of the thing not said, the recognition of silence. Silence, then, is commonly imagined as the ultimate manifestation and confirmation of the truth of being. In light of such attitudes, it is a paradox that any state would imagine it could accomplish anything by attacking the truth of memory and history through the destruction of contemporary representations—but this paradox not only lies at the heart of the practice of the *damnatio memoriae*, it also provides the grounds for the many critiques of such procedures, ancient and modern.

Despite the differences between the two, ancient critiques of the *damnatio memoriae* and contemporary criticism of the Soviet purge are framed in the same terms. Both rely on the dichotomy between memory and representation, specifically on the dissimulatory or realist model of this relation. Memory, like reality, is imagined as independent of and prior to representation. The suppression of representation cannot touch it. Consequently it can work outside of representation to preserve truth even when it is forbidden—in silence. Furthermore, because memory seems impervious to political control, it is frequently regarded as the locus of popular resistance, both in the Roman empire and also in the modern totalitarian state.[101] While such reactions are stirring, this traditional association of memory, truth, and reality should be regarded critically.

The historian Tacitus believed that the political power of the emperor could be resisted through memory. The same logic underlies contemporary critiques of Soviet purges. "I always knew that truth would triumph," says Bukharin's widow.[102] Conquest says at the end of his book on the Great Terror that the Soviet government "not only annihilated people physically, but hoped to destroy the memory of them. They succeeded in the first, but not in the second."[103]

Milan Kundera suggests that resistance is possible through memory: "The struggle of man against power is the struggle of memory against forgetting," he says.[104] Memory resists even the desires of the rememberer; it is not in our power to forget. In Kundera's novel *The Book of Laughter and Forgetting*, his hero, Mirek, struggles to forget an old lover. In this, Kundera says, he is "just as much rewriting history as the Communist party." Mirek thinks that she is too unattractive for a man of his current status. Nevertheless, certain memories persist, details of their lovemaking, for example, and spring to mind unbidden, despite his self-disgust.

Many of the same essential points have been made by Václav Havel in his 1979 essay "The Power of the Powerless."[105] Havel argues that it is possible for people to acquiesce in an immoral political system (live the lie) but still preserve themselves by "living in truth." In a situation where communication is highly formalized and performative, the withholding of an expected word or gesture becomes significant. Political regimes, such as the Roman principate or Havel's Eastern Bloc "post-totalitarian systems," promote ideologies that serve to justify the system and to integrate its subjects within it. The regime itself is as much a captive of this ideology as anyone: as Tacitus knows well, even the emperor is the prisoner of the *arcana imperii*. It is not that everyone (or anyone) must accept this political ideology at face value: "Individuals need not believe all these mystifications, but they must behave as though they did, or they must at least tolerate them in silence, or get along well with those who work with them. For this reason, they must live within a lie."[106] For Havel, however, even the powerless can resist this oppressive political ideology, by "living in truth." Living in truth may be manifested in merely doing one's job well, or even in not doing certain things.[107] It is an effective form of resistance because it shows up the prevailing political ideology for the charade that it is, and so subverts it. For the ideology is necessary for the very existence of the political order. The point is also central in Tacitus: he shows in numerous anecdotes that good men are hated by the emperor, because their mere existence gives the lie to the imperial order. As Tacitus says at the end of the *Agricola*, he writes so that people will know that good men can exist even under bad emperors.

The problem of silence is more complicated than these relatively straightforward paradoxes of memory and representation. One of the chief functions of silence is to represent the very absence of representation. It would of course be paradoxical to represent what is not represented directly, explicitly. Silence proceeds indirectly, by suggestion. It may be useful to think of silence as a way of representing a limit, a boundary: "Beyond this I shall say no more." The idea of the limit suggests that there is something outside, or beyond: something that is not being represented, but that is there.[108] Silence represents silence by "circling" a thing, establishing its shape through the limits of speech. These limits can be determined by beginning and ending speech, by disappointing contextual expectations, out of the imperatives of genre or conversation, or they can be manufactured in other ways: allusion, ambiguity, and irony, for instance, are ways of suggesting limits of representation, the contours of things not said. The representations of silence can be conceived as *adumbration,* that is, drawing with shadow: shape is delineated in a negative way, through shading, without using light.

Condemned public enemies could not be mentioned directly. For example, historians were not allowed to use certain names, as we learn from Tacitus in the cases of Cremutius Cordus (*Ann.* 4.35), Arulenus Rusticus, and Herennius Senecio (*Agr.* 2). When dealing with enemies of the state, circumlocutions were safer. The emperor Augustus himself provides lessons in how not to refer (or do I mean how to not refer?) to those who have suffered a *damnatio memoriae.* In his account of his accomplishments, the *Res Gestae,* Augustus refers to several of his enemies without using their names.[109] The ostentatious refusal to name makes it clear that these people are unmentionable. So, at the beginning he claims to have raised an army to free the republic from the "tyranny of a faction" (1.1). Cassius and Brutus are not mentioned by name, but are nonetheless clearly included in the reference to "those who assassinated my relative" (2). Augustus avoids Antony's name, but leaves no doubt as to his identity, claiming to have restored to the temples of Asia those statues which "he with whom I waged war" (24.1) had stolen. Later, Augustus alludes to Lepidus when he claims to have agreed to become *pontifex maximus* only "after the death of that man, who had taken advantage of civil disturbance to seize it for himself" (10.2).[110]

There is a comparable coyness about naming usurpers in late antiquity. From the time of Constantine unsuccessful pretenders to the throne are routinely designated "tyrants" (*tyrannus*) in all sorts of public documents.[111] As a rule, their names are not mentioned, though anyone who encountered such a text would know who was meant. For example, in imperial rescripts following the revolt of 394, Eugenius' name and those of Arbogast and Flavian are ostentatiously avoided. When reference is made to Eugenius, it is as "the tyrant" (see *CTh* 15.14.9, 11, and 12).

The same kinds of circumlocutions can be found in the imperial letter rehabilitating Flavian. Even as Flavian is rehabilitated, "certain others" suffer a *damnatio memoriae.* If Flavian did wrongfully suffer the *damnatio memoriae,* who is to blame? Certainly not the emperor. Flavian was accused wrongfully, owing to certain "underhanded insinuations" (*caeca insimulatione,* line 18). Because of his virtue, he was vulnerable. His accomplishments "roused the jealousy of scoundrels" (*excitavit livorem inproborum,* line 21). The force of the references escapes us. Possibly they refer to no one; that is, they are a pretended dissimulation and serve only as an excuse for the rehabilitation. They function, however, just as do other references to condemned enemies of the Roman state, drawing attention by their very imprecision.

Curiously, the imperial letter of rehabilitation proceeds formally by the same strategy as a *damnatio memoriae*. It makes its points indirectly, through implication and innuendo, never by announcing its objects outright. References to the earlier *damnatio* and present rehabilitation are oblique and often abstruse. Although the imperial letter speaks of "memory" or "honor" as "returned," it never explicitly says why Flavian suffered a *damnatio memoriae*, or even that he did suffer a *damnatio memoriae*. Instead, it proceeds by compiling a list of honors and privileges (perhaps including an anachronistic restoration of the *praenomen?*) that Flavian and his descendants may once again enjoy. From these restored privileges it is possible for us to have some sense of the penalties that had been imposed on him. Even so, it takes a certain amount of expertise simply to recognize these allusions and their relevance to the *damnatio memoriae*.

In the visual media, one equivalent of silence is the erasure. As we have seen, the Romans did not uniformly annihilate the inscriptions of an individual who had suffered a *damnatio memoriae:* often they let them stand, complete, but with the pertinent names erased. At first glance, intuitively, erasures may seem to be merely the negation of writing: meaningless in themselves, they are merely an impediment to the decipherment of the original content of the stone. Like scars or silences, though, erasures may also be regarded as positive signs. Understood as signs, they suggest, like silence, a dissimulation: that there is something beneath, something that is or was there, but that does not come to appearance. As the erasure marks a silence, it also functions as a reminder of what is not said: it tells the reader to remember to forget, and thus to remember what is forgotten.

If we realize that silence is a sign, then its potential for lying must also be recognized. If silence is a way of representing dissimulation—a limit of representation—then, like any representation, it may do so falsely. It is, in other words, possible to suggest by a significant silence that something is not being said, when actually *nothing* is not being said: one can simulate dissimulation. Tacitus provides good examples of the ambiguity of silence. For instance, he reports that on one occasion, late in Tiberius' reign, the emperor left his retreat in Capri as though to return to Rome. But then he stopped and waited at the borders of Campania. The meaning of this hesitation was unclear to Tacitus: either Tiberius "was in doubt as to whether he should enter Rome— or, because he had decided against it, he was affecting the appearance of intending to arrive" (*ambiguus an urbem intraret, seu quia contra destinaverat, speciem venturi simulans*) (*Ann.* 6.1). The hesitation might have been sincere; that is to say, Tiberius may really not have been certain about whether to enter the city or not. Or again, the hesitation may have been a ploy. For Tiberius, the master dissimulator, to give the "appearance of intending to arrive" would be to feign the contrary, to hesitate, to dissimulate his intention. Here Tacitus suggests the hesitation itself is a simulation: Tiberius affected it because he had decided not to go. So Tiberius' dissimulations need not be true: they can be simulations. But Tacitus' famous summary verdict on the character of the short-lived emperor Galba, "a man distinguished more for the absence of vices than the possession of virtues," illustrates the treacherousness of reading too much into passivity. In the case of Galba, passivity was truth; people, however, tended to understand the vacuousness of his character as something more cunning, that is, as dissimulation. "The terror of the times masked the truth, so that what really was just laziness was called wisdom" (*Hist.* 1.49). The ambivalence of the meaning of silence is made obvious when it is "de-naturalized" and "ceases to be regarded as merely the physical absence of voice, or action, or representation.[112]

In addition to the referential aspect of silence, the gestural aspect must be considered. To utter a word is an act, and an evaluation of the utterance must involve some consideration of it from that perspective.[113] To keep silent is not only to refrain from speaking; to keep silent is to do something as well. There is a common tendency to equate silence with passivity—again, largely because silence is commonly imagined as the negation of speech, not as a positive act itself. So the contemporary rallying cry "Silence = Death" refers to the imposition of silence on people, to the oppressiveness of authority and the passivity of victims. It is common to think of political repression in analogous terms: silence imposed from above. The silence of political victims is imagined as passivity, nothing but the absence of speech. As we have seen, Tacitus alludes to this idea of silence in various places.

When conceived as a positive action, however, it becomes obvious that "keeping silent" may mean many different things. So in the modern world it has been common to speak of the macho "strong, silent type," or the "inscrutable oriental," or the "mousy housewife"—each with its own special connotation.[114] In the next chapter I will consider the broad historiographical implications of the theme of silence in history, especially in the historian Tacitus. This discussion can only be the beginning of such a discussion. A full treatment of the subject would have to attempt an analysis of the semantics of silence within the specific history. Tacitus, for example, was very sensitive to the variety of connotations silence may have. In his histories it is the sign of the oppressed, but it is also the weapon of the tyrant. It is an instrument of disgrace, but it is also the source of vindication. The dichotomy between the aggressive silence of the emperor and the slavish silence of the senate is central to Tacitus' understanding of the significance of silence.

A single example will show the range of connotation of silence in Tacitus. In the eighth year of Tiberius' reign (A.D. 22), one of the last survivors of the civil wars died: "Junia Tertulla, niece of Cato, wife of Cassius, the sister of Brutus.... Her will caused much discussion, because although she was very rich and included complimentary references to virtually every leading Roman, she omitted the emperor" (Tac. *Ann.* 3.75). The omission carries an implied insult to Tiberius; it is significant and noted. Tiberius, however, pretended to take no note of the implied insult. How could he, since it was not really there? He bore her no malice and graciously allowed her a traditional Roman funeral. At this ceremony, as was customary, the busts of her ancestors were paraded. The portraits of her husband, Cassius, and her brother, Brutus, however, could not be displayed, because both had suffered *damnatio memoriae* as public traitors. Tacitus claims that the absence of the busts served to make both more conspicuous; they became all the more noticeable to the extent that they were not seen: *praefulgebant Cassius atque Brutus, eo ipso quod effigies non visebantur* (*Ann.* 3.76). The absence of reference to Tiberius in the will was construed as an insult, and Tiberius' silence in response indicated his malevolence, whereas the absence of reference to the "tyrannicides" at the funeral was seen as a glorious vindication.[115]

REHABILITATION

The statue base from the Forum of Trajan is unusual because it is a rehabilitation. There are relatively few examples of individuals whose honor is restored after a *damnatio memoriae,* and there are no accounts of any rehabilitations even remotely as elaborate as Flavian's. Still, there are many instances of individuals who are known to have been rehabilitated after a *damnatio memoriae.* There are also occasional references to the process of rehabilitation in relatively regular, formal-sounding language. So Tacitus mentions a proposal brought by the urban prefect (and later emperor) Domitian "concerning the restoration of the honors of Galba" (*Hist.* 4.40). Elsewhere we hear of rehabilitation as a "restoration to wholeness" (*restitutio ad integrum*) (Suet. *Claudius* 9). The word *restitutio* is also used in the imperial letter rehabilitating Flavian. Since the attacks on memory by the *damnatio memoriae* do not themselves comprise a settled, institutionalized legal procedure, it seems unlikely that there would have been a technical juridical concept of a *restitutio ad integrum,* meaning a general rehabilitation. The phrase, however, does occur as a technical procedure, meaning a "reinstatement into a former legal position," which is doubtless the source of its use to describe rehabilitations.[116]

In an early instance of a rehabilitation, Claudius replaced statues of Caligula's murdered brothers Nero and Drusus (Suet. *Claudius* 9). Some years later, Otho managed to have the statues of Poppaea Sabina restored by senatorial decree. There was at the time a rumor that he intended to revive the memory of Nero as well (Tac. *Hist.* 1.78).

The most famous rehabilitations, however, are associated with the reign of Galba. When Galba took the throne, he demanded that those who had profited from the reign of Nero return their gains. He restored those who had been exiled by Nero on charges of treason, and he transferred to the mausoleum of Augustus the bones of members of the imperial family who had been murdered. He also replaced the statues that had been destroyed (Dio 64.3.4c).[117]

Galba himself was condemned under his successor. After the death of Otho, the Roman people spontaneously paraded busts of him to the city's shrines (Tac. *Hist.* 2.55; cf. Suet. *Galba* 23). Later yet, one of Vespasian's generals, Antonius, ordered that the "statues of Galba, which had been thrown down in all the disorders of the times, should again be honored" (Tac. *Hist.* 3.7). After the accession of Vespasian, an urban praetor (the later emperor Domitian, of all people) moved that the honors of Galba be restored. At the same time, Curtius Montanus moved that the memory of Calpurnius Piso also be restored. The senate passed both motions but, according to Tacitus, the latter restoration was never carried out (Tac. *Hist.* 4.40).

Some useful points of comparison for the elder Flavian's rehabilitation are provided by Symmachus' letters on behalf of Flavian the younger in the wake of Eugenius' usurpation of 394. Flavian the younger did not himself suffer a *damnatio memoriae.* The emperor was lenient toward him. By 399 he had been restored to imperial favor and was serving as urban prefect. Symmachus' letters on his behalf during this period speak of his return to favor in much the same kind of language as the letter of Valentinian uses to describe the rehabilitation of Flavian senior (see particularly Symm. *Epp.* 4.4; 5.6; 7.93, 96, 104; 8.29). For instance, the imperial letter claims "to recall the memory of the deceased to eternal light" (*memoriam defuncti in lucem aeternam revocare,* lines 10–11). In a letter to Theodorus, Symmachus remarks that "your consulship (398) recalls my son Flavian (the younger) to the light" (*filium meum Flavianum consulatus tuus revocat in lucem*) (Symm. *Ep.* 5.6). The imperial letter claims that it is the job of the emperor to defend senators against "the pitfalls of mankind's lot" (*casus condicionis humanae,* lines 9–10). According to Symmachus, in the wake of the restoration of Flavian the younger "human misfortunes have been put to rout" (*Humani casus in fugam versi sunt*) (Symm. *Ep.* 4.4).

One rehabilitation is contemporary with Flavian's *damnatio memoriae*. Flavius Eutolmius Tatianus was one of the most eminent men of late antiquity. His life is thoroughly documented, particularly from the law codes and the writings of Libanius.[118] A native of Lycia, he rose to the office of praetorian prefect, which he held from 388 to 392. In 391 he held the consulship, with the orator Symmachus as his colleague. In 392, owing to the intrigues of Flavius Rufinus, Tatianus was deposed from the praetorian prefecture; Rufinus took his place. Penalties followed in 393. Tatianus' son Proculus (*PLRE* Proculus 6), who had recently served as urban prefect of Constantinople, was lured back from hiding and executed before his father's eyes. Tatianus survived his son and this ordeal. Although condemned to death, his sentence was commuted, and he was banished to Lycia. He also survived a bit of himself, so to speak. He lost his property to confiscation, and his native land suffered as well. A *damnatio memoriae* was carried out against him. According to the late testimony of Photios (*Bibl.* 258), after his disgrace Tatianus wandered Lycia until his death, a blinded beggar. If so, he could not see that his name had been erased and was now missing from many of the inscriptions honoring him, even as his compatriots will have been forced to take notice of the erasure, and will have been reminded of the name beneath the erasure daily by the living, breathing presence of this blind man.[119] Tatianus died still in disgrace; his rehabilitation followed the fall of Rufinus, in 396.[120] The reinstatement is recorded in the Theodosian Code: the disgrace of Tatianus should no longer have any force; the blot on the honor of the Lycians has lasted long enough; it has been washed away by the cleansing powers of time itself (*nec unius viri inlustris Tatiani tantum valuerit temporalis offensio, teterrimi iudicis inimici, ut adhuc macula in Lycios perseveret, quae in ipso iam temporis absolutione consumpta est*) (*CTh* 9.38.9, dated to 31 August 396). At about this time, Tatianus' grandson (also named Tatianus) restored one of his grandfather's statues in Aphrodisias. The marble pedestal, with a verse inscription of nine hexameters, Homeric in its diction, was published by Robert in 1948:[121]

> Who am I and from where do I hail? From Lycia, preeminent occupant of the chair of governors, Tatianos, who preserved cities (of the province)

safe by his just laws. But all-mastering time would have destroyed me if my child, third in line from me, my namesake and similar in accomplishments, had not raised me up from the ground and set me on a monument (*stelai*),[122] conspicuous to be seen by all, locals and foreigners alike. He drove the deadly misfortune [i.e. plague and famine] from the land of the Karians; he gave justice to live among mortals; an envoy of the emperor, he was a succour for the people who still rejoice.

Τίς; πόθεν; ἐκ Λυκίης μέ[ν], | ἀριστεύσας δ' ἐνὶ θώκοις |
Τατιανὸς θεσμοῖς τε δίκης | πτολίεθρα σαώσας. |
Ἀλλά με πανδαμάτωρ χρόν[ος] | ὤλλυεν, εἰ μὴ ἐμὸς παῖς
ἐξ ἐμέθεν τρίτατος καὶ | ὁμώνυμος ἔργα θ' ὅμοιο[ς] |
ἐκ δαπέδων ἀνελὼν | στήλης ἐπίθηκεν ὁρᾶσ[θαι] |
πᾶσιν ἀρίζηλον ναέταις | ξίνοισει θ' ὁμοίως, |
Καρῶν ἐκ γέης ὃς ἀπήλασε | λοίγιον ἄτην, |
τὴν δὲ δίκην μερόπεσιν | ὁμέστιον ὤπασ' ἐπεῖναι |
πεμφθεὶς ἐκ βασιλῆος | ἔθ' ἀδομένοισιν ἀρωγός.

The inscription emphasizes the endurance of Tatianus' reputation (through the restoration of his monuments) and the survival of his name (through the eminence of his "homonymous" grandson). There is no mention of his earlier disgrace. As Robert says, the phrase "all-mastering time which would have destroyed me" is a "veil discreetly thrown over these earlier events."[123] The form the veil takes, however, is highly significant. The re-erection of this statue of Tatianus is described in terms of a set of themes that are common to monumental commemoration and to the writing of history in general: the destructive effects of time, "the master of all,"[124] and the necessity of combatting time by means of things that last, such as monuments or writing. This larger historiographical issue is inevitably raised by the procedures of the *damnatio memoriae*.

Symmachus claims in connection with the younger Flavian that it is a greater thing to *restore* honor than to *give* it (*maius quiddam est honorem restituere quam dedisse*) (Symm. *Ep.* 4.4.2). Greater or not, a restoration is certainly always a different thing than the original grant. A rehabilitation can never be a complete reversal of a *damnatio memoriae*, a return to some earlier integrity, even though it may advertise itself as such. A rehabilitation is not merely the straightforward expression of something—the dignity, or honor, of a person.

It is the restoration of the representation of that thing. Like Valentinian's letter rehabilitating the elder Flavian, it is a writing over the sign of an erasure. It is not just an utterance; rather, it is the expression of something that *is,* but that has heretofore been unsaid or even unsayable. A rehabilitation is the vindication of a silence. In this peculiar character, it is much like history.

CHAPTER 5

SILENCE, TRUTH, AND DEATH

The Commemorative Function of History

THE FIRST LINE of the imperial letter rehabilitating Flavian is remarkable in a variety of ways. It appears to invoke the authority of the Roman tradition of historiography and biography. It also alludes to the commemorative function of writing, which the rehabilitation has in common with the writing of history. The avowed purpose of the rehabilitation is to speak, to give voice to something that is kept in the silence of memory and thus bring it to appearance. Likewise, one of the chief and traditional functions of history is to give voice to that which has been but which has passed from being, thus vindicate it from oblivion.

The theme of silence is pervasive in most historical writing. It has been central to any kind of realistic discourse—that is, the enunciation of things that are regarded as real—at least since Herodotus. In his proem, Herodotus claims to write

> so that the occurrences owing to men may not become evanescent (ἐξίτηλα) in time and so that the great and marvelous monuments, some called to witness by Greeks, some by Barbarians, should not lose their renown [lit.: become ἀκλεᾶ, without-renown].

Here Herodotus provides an explicit and paradigmatic statement (and it is perhaps *the* paradigmatic statement) of "the commemorative function of history."[1] As in all traditional narrative history—that is, history which "merely tells a story"—the motivation for writing is conceived as being deictic: demonstrative and revelatory. The historian shows what has occurred because if things are not shown they may become "evanescent," fade from memory by "losing their renown." Historians lend their voices to the past so that it will not perish entirely, so that some part of it, in the telling, will survive. The past is spoken or written precisely in order to bring what was, but is no longer, to appearance, to ward off the decay of the sublunary world and so to preserve it against the annihilation of forgetfulness. Writing, by virtue of its permanence, can secure ephemeral events against the passing of time. The silence against which this kind of writing measures itself is imagined as a kind of neutral, natural thing. It is a silence produced by time, by the passing of things and of narrators out of existence. It is the silence of physical decay and death.

This commemorative function of history is one of the most traditional and common themes of historical writing. It is found in practically every narrative historian, in more or less developed forms. The author to whom I will give special attention in this chapter, Tacitus, has foregrounded the theme more than most and has made it more central to his historiography than any historian I know, with the possible exception of Michelet.[2]

Other motivations for the writing of history have been put forward. Most commonly it is imagined that history can be useful: it has been seen as an instructor, or as a guide to the future.[3] Nevertheless, even for historians who subscribe to an extremely utilitarian criterion for the practice of history, silence remains an issue. Thucydides, for instance, hopes that his history "will be judged useful for those who desire to have a precise knowledge of what has happened and what will happen" (1.22).[4] Yet, when he comes to consider the causes of the Peloponnesian War, he suggests that "the truest cause was the one least mentioned" (1.23).

It has long been common to criticize narrative history as "mere" antiquarianism or aestheticism, and to insist on some larger and more useful goal for the practice of history than a simple evocation of the past. More recently, scholars have tended to point out that the basic presupposition of "positivist" or "naive realist" history—that is, the adequacy of narrative to reality—is false.[5] Even so, traditional descriptive history continues to have its advocates. Arguably, practitioners of this kind of history have at least kept faith with a powerful and ancient idea: that bygone things are worth saying, merely—or perhaps especially—because they were, and that the homage of voice, however inadequate, is the only possible vindication of a past that otherwise would be dead and silent.

In modernist historiography—by which I mean here historical writing since Marx and Freud and Nietzsche—silence remains a dominant theme.

The connotations of silence, however, have changed. The traditional revelatory ethic of commemoration, of writing merely "to say what happened," has been replaced with an ethic of suspicion. Instead of speaking to show, historians speak to decipher. Silence now is imagined as a mystifying veil, which conceals the truth *for a reason*. This change in the conception of silence has coincided with a shift from classical narrative style to a more analytical figuring of history. Before, history was written *to reveal,* and the chief methodological problem was to come up with a rhetorical narrative style that was adequate and appropriate to reality, to find the appropriate name for a given action or thing. In the modern period, history was written to reveal a truth that had been misunderstood or concealed. This motive can be traced far earlier than the nineteenth century. Already Thucydides, for example, thinks of his history not merely as a statement of what has happened, but as a vindication of truth against ignorance and perhaps even hypocrisy. Certainly he imagines that history will bring to light a truth that few know and that is seldom stated. For Tacitus, as well, silence is not merely a product of the decay of time, but is manufactured by present political power for its own intentionally inscrutable purposes. As he remarks in the *Annals,* tyrants of the day may imagine that "they can destroy even the memory of the next generation by their present power." But historians such as himself through their writing will in the future tell the tale and rehabilitate public memory. So the hopes of tyrants are vain (*Ann.* 4.35).

Comparable reasoning can be found in many contemporary schools of historiography. Again, the catalogue of histories that are motivated by this sense of silence could be extended almost infinitely; the theme is particularly well developed in the work of historians of the "left"—if such a place can be conceded to exist anymore. Marxist or socialist historians may write the history of the working class, a story traditionally "untold," because of the elite biases of most historians. Practitioners of women's history aim to vindicate their subjects from the silence of the past, a silence to which they have been relegated by historians whose overwhelming preoccupation has been the traditionally male world of public civic life. Ethnic histories focus on groups that have been omitted from the record by the dominant culture. "Postcolonial" history, such as the Indian school of subaltern studies, aims to rehabilitate the voices of non-European nations and ethnicities from the silence of hegemonic historiography imposed by classical (i.e. nineteenth- and early twentieth-century) European imperialism. The point is succinctly made in the introduction to a collection of interviews with prominent historians (edited by MARHO, the radical historians' organization):

Past efforts to contest prevailing social and political arrangements disappear from dominant versions of our history—when they are not simply labeled foreign or dismissed as utopian. Yet there is a tradition of radical history writing that has worked to overcome this kind of historical amnesia. It has sought to rescue from oblivion the experiences and visions of past movements against social and political domination, and to analyze historically the structures and dynamics of domination today.[6]

The interpretation of the relation of silence to history-writing that I offer in this chapter is, I suppose, in some respects my own. I try to find inspiration in theoretical essays, not a machinery that can be adopted wholesale for brutal application to any text. I make what I find my own, with a view to my own thoughts and the demands of my texts. The influence, more or less immediate, of various authors on my thinking, however, should be recognized. It is difficult to imagine how anyone could write on silence without being influenced, consciously or unconsciously, by the Freudian arguments about repression and its effects. Baudrillard's general distinction between simulation and dissimulation has been very useful in formulating my argument. Derrida's recent essay on Dionysius the Areopagite and apophatic theology[7] contained many relevant ideas. M. de Certeau's conception of the past as "radical alterity," laid out in his *Heterologies* and in *The Writing of History,* has stimulated my thinking in many ways. Above all, I have adopted many of Ricoeur's suggestions about hermeneutics, as he has developed them from his early work *The Symbolism of Evil,* through his book on Freud, and most recently in the three-volume set *Time and Narrative.* The general distinction that I have just outlined between the traditional commemorative narrative and modernist analytical historiography, for example, derives directly from Ricoeur's "hermeneutic of revelation" and "hermeneutic of suspicion."

In contemporary historiography the theme of silence has been most prominently at issue in the recent debates about the representation of the Holocaust. The issue became decisively central to this field in the course of the notorious *Historikerstreit,* the debate among German historians during the late 1970's and 1980's about how, or even whether, it was possible to write about the Holocaust. Doubtless the centerpiece of the discussion was Wolfgang Iser's essay in which he argued that the truth of an event of this magnitude lay beyond, or outside of, representation.[8] He defined the problem of historical representation more narrowly than have I: he was chiefly concerned with the tension between specificity and generalization in narrative. This theme has continued to figure prominently in the writing of historians of the Holocaust, especially in work written and sponsored by Saul Friedländer, including the journal *History and Memory* and papers from the recent conference at UCLA entitled "Probing the Limits of Representation." The same themes surface in recent discussions of neo-Nazi revisionists, who claim that the Holocaust (i.e. the mass killing of Jews, Gypsies, Slavs, and others by Nazis) is a historical falsification, that it never really happened. In his extended essay on these writers, entitled *The Assassins of Memory,* the French ancient historian Pierre Vidal-Naquet affirms the role of the historian as guardian of memory, vindicator of silence. This attitude is perhaps best seen in his citation of Chateaubriand as an example of his ideal of the function of the historian:

> When, in the silence of abjection all one can hear is the slave's chains and the traitor's voice; when all tremble before the tyrant and it is as dangerous to incur his favor as to fall from his grace, the historian appears, charged with the vengeance of peoples.[9]

These same themes are now central even to popular presentations of the Holocaust. So, at Holocaust museums in Washington D.C. or in Los Angeles it is possible to access an enormous database of recorded interviews with concentration camp survivors—one of several projects to record as many of these experiences as possible. It is said that these interviews were compiled because that generation of survivors is now dying out, and it is important that the power of this multitude of specific concrete recollection should somehow be preserved and not go into silence with them. Here we are asked to witness the transition of an event from living memory to dead written history.

The use of the theme of silence in the historiography of the Holocaust is at heart very traditional. Silence is figured as the negation of historical speech: it provides the room in which historical speech can occur. And because silence is imagined as outside of speech it seems to provide also a guarantee of the truth of what resides within it. Silence, then, is used to confirm the truth of history, and to refute theorists who see history as founded on the simulatory fantasy of representation rather than on the dissimulatory reality of silence. Hayden White, because of his work on the simulatory aspects of historical writing—"history as representation"—has been taken as the paradigm of the opposition in this discussion. His famous essay on the contemporary political uses of the history of the Holocaust has been the particular occasion for disputing his general argument.[10] Here I am concerned to elucidate this traditional view of silence and its connection with reality. I should be clear from the outset, though, that I am not trying to support the truth claims of this position—to the contrary. Silence is not the negation or absence of representation; it is a product of representation. Silence is a sign that pretends not to be a sign, a sign that effaces or dissimulates itself: this is precisely the source of its strength and prestige for producing the illusion of reality. Nevertheless, insofar as it is recognized, silence *is* a sign. As such, like words, it represents and can give no guarantee of the truth and reality of what it represents. Like words, silence can lie, or not. As Tacitus already well knows, silence too is a simulation.

As I have said, silence is an issue not only for historians, but for anyone who aims to say something true and real. A scientist, for example, in an original piece of research, is not concerned to write what is not, but rather to write what is, but has not been said: that is, to write what exists in silence. In this sense, scientists must conceive of themselves as discoverers, not creators. Literary critics, no matter how playful and creative, aim to explain a text; that is to say, they attempt to bring into appearance something that is there, to be found in the text, but that is not explicit. If it were explicit, there would be no point in saying it. Again, their interpretation is conceived as speech over a silence. This conception of speech is produced by representing it as a restoration, as the recovery of an integrity that existed at one time but that has lapsed in some way. Again, this is speech figured as spoken over silence—or, perhaps better, and more materially, it is writing imagined as written over an erasure.

BEGINNING TO SPEAK

The beginning, the first words uttered or written, is the most concrete limit of speech. Whether literary or historical, the beginning is a difficult yet crucial thing, as anyone who has had to write one knows.[11] On the one hand, we might think of the beginning in a tautological, intransitive way; that is, in terms of what it does. The beginning is in one respect an act, a thing that does not refer to something else, but merely is: the inauguration of speech, the fact of the utterance of the first word. As such, it marks a limit between the word and what is unwritten, or unspoken: it is a boundary, like a birth or a death. On the other hand, we might think of the beginning in a more transitive way, in terms of its relationship to what precedes and follows. From this perspective, a beginning is a place of inauguration, of establishment, and as such it has a strongly prescriptive force. It looks both backward and forward, outward and inward: it situates the work against and among its various predecessors, but it also institutes what poses as a self-contained, intentional structure. To do all this, it invokes authority: the persona of the author, the omniscience of a god, the prestige of a discipline, the familiarity of a genre.[12]

Any utterance can be regarded as an attempt to say something or as an attempt to do something or, to use the jargon of speech-act theory, as "constative" (which would correspond to the "transitive" beginning) or "performative" (the "intransitive" beginning).[13] A constative utterance is descriptive and is susceptible to analysis in terms of truth and falsehood. The sentence "Thucydides wrote the history" is either so or not so. A performative utterance, on the other hand, is neither true nor false. It is not an attempt to say that something is so; it is an attempt to make something so. A statement such as "I now pronounce you husband and wife" is not a description. Rather, it must be evaluated in terms of what it accomplishes, that is, in terms of whether it is effective or ineffective (or, to use speech-act terms again, "felicitous" or "infelicitous").

The line between performative and constative speech is in principle and practice porous. A performative utterance need not be constative, but all constative statements have a performative aspect. Even the most apparently descriptive statement can also be regarded as the event of its enunciation. So, to say that "Thucydides wrote the history" is to perform an act of speaking. Construed as such, we might understand "(I assert that) Thucydides wrote the history" or "(I vouch that) Thucydides wrote the history." Speech-act theorists call such elementary performatives *locutionary acts*.

In a tautologous way these basic speech-acts perform themselves: to say anything is already to perform an act of speaking. But what are the implications of the mere act of speaking? What does such a locutionary act do? In large part, to perform the act of speaking is to assert a presence: "There is an 'I' (i.e. the speaker) here." The extent of speech marks and defines the limits of this presence. Furthermore, the presence of speech serves to imply its negation: silence. So, to put it in a positive way, to perform the act of speaking is to inaugurate voice. To put it in the more suggestive, negative way, to speak is to end silence.

The performative aspect of speech is strongly marked at its beginnings, precisely because the beginning is a boundary, the line at which silence and speech are juxtaposed and distinguished. The delimited specificity of speech here is placed into a contrast and opposition with the boundlessness of silence. At heart the distinction is one of presence and absence, being against the void, consciousness and the world "out there." In addition to this structural opposition of present and absent, though, a beginning also involves a sequential distinction of present and past. The beginning of speech is not only a structural boundary between talking and not talking, it is also the temporal moment of a transformation. Consequently speech and silence are commonly assimilated to present and past. The world of the living, the here and now, the present, is the world of speech. The past, on the other hand, is what has passed out of being, what is not here and now, what has been reduced to silence. Amorphous, mysterious, open-ended, like silence the past is delimited and defined only on that edge where it approaches the living, present world of speech.

A beginning is not only an intransitive, performative utterance. From a transitive, constative perspective (i.e. in terms of its content), the beginning is an announcement, a statement of intent for what follows. Here, the authority—that is, the persona and credibility of the speaker—is established, the rules of what subsequently will be sayable and unsayable are determined. The beginning is chosen with a view to its adequacy as a point of departure. It is conceived as a seed, or germ. In the beginning there is a unity, from which spring the consequent phenomena in some order. From the beginning "all of what follows must proceed."

It would be an error to imagine that, simply because of its sequential priority, the beginning is in every sense prior to what follows. Historians who have wrestled with problems of periodization know how arbitrary the selection of a beginning is, how closely implicated with the unity of the arguments or events that follow it. There can be no beginning without there already being something to begin. The choice of the beginning is complicit in the plan of what it is to introduce. In literature and history, then, beginnings are knowable only in retrospect. The beginning is produced from the perspective of the totality, with the end in view.[14]

As the beginning affects what follows, it also looks to what precedes. So, while a beginning is prescriptive for the work it introduces, it also positions the work among and against similar writings. Speaking and writing always occur in a context, which carries with it certain rules and norms. The structures of a history, for example, are ordered according to various received rules, which must be followed if a work is to be regarded as a history. A writing or utterance, then, will have certain continuities and consistencies with a repertoire of other, earlier texts. At the same time, a beginning must mark a discontinuity, a rupture, from what has come before it. If it did not, it would not be a beginning. The tension between these two pressures on the beginning is crucial for the integrity of the work. Continuity provides the authority of tradition for the work. At the same time, it calls into question the autonomy of the work and the authority of the author. Discontinuity, on the other hand, is an assertion of the particularity of the work. Once again, the beginning serves to locate the authority of the work and to establish the position of the author.[15]

In the contemporary world, the importance of the origin has eroded. Of course, it is still always necessary for every work to begin, but the beginnings themselves are not so strongly marked as they were in traditional literature. It is no longer fashionable to invoke the muse at the beginning of an essay. It has become increasingly common to disguise the beginning of a work—to begin by pretending that one is not beginning. Detective novels, for instance, will often begin *in medias res,* say with the description of a crime; movies more and more avoid the traditional formal beginning of title and credits and open immediately with the action. By contrast, in Greco-Roman literature (as often in traditional texts and utterances), the integrity of the beginning is as a rule carefully observed: beginnings are formal and formulaic things. The Greeks tended to invoke the gods at the beginning of a work; Latin literature more often appeals to tradition. Both strategies appeal to an authority external to the work for the initiation of speech, thus demonstrating allegiance to tradition and genre. The importance of the beginning was reinforced in a variety of ways. Greek and Roman rhetorical handbooks, for example, discuss the composition of the proem in abstract, theoretical terms. In ancient (and medieval) times, works were often even identified by their first words.[16]

The stakes at the beginning of the imperial letter rehabilitating Flavian are unique: the letter itself is quite centrally and patently about the transition from silence to speech. Flavian has been subject to an "interdict of silence"; it has been forbidden to speak of him. So, quite aside from the content of the letter, the act of representation that the letter performs is *itself* already a reversal of that silence and a rehabilitation of Flavian. From this perspective, we might say that the letter is "phatic": its purpose is not just to give an account of something, but to break silence. This is speech as self-announcement.[17] The transition of status, from purge to rehabilitation, from state of silence to state of speech, occurs most concretely and obviously at the beginning of the letter. Beginnings are largely about this transformation. The first words of the imperial letter rehabilitating the elder Flavian consequently demand special attention: they bring into play all of the issues regarding beginnings. The first line is simultaneously an announcement of intent, an invocation of the past, and a formal inauguration of voice out of silence.

The first sentence is long and weighty, grammatically and rhetorically complex, elevated in diction:

> To defend against the pitfalls of mankind's lot the dignity of men renowned and eminent in the state when corrupted to some extent by interpolations and to recall the recollection of the departed to eternal fame may be regarded as a correction, so to speak, of his fate, which is considered as a preliminary judgment and the greatest supplement of a man's worth. Senators, on this noble and auspicious occasion you join us by recognizing at last . . . (lines 9–12).

This passage does what it says: defends and recalls. The function and content of the imperial letter are the same: it is a speech about the act of imperial speaking. To speak is the function of a rehabilitation; it is also the function of the act of speech. Above all, it is the function of a beginning: to inaugurate the presence of speech and mark off a boundary from what is absent, dead, silent.

The opening sentence of the letter is framed as a general statement ("to recall the memory of a dead man to eternal light is an emendation"), and so carries some of the force of potential and purpose. The text that follows elaborates on this theme: it rehearses the fact of Flavian's disgrace and the reasons for his restoration. In its closing words the letter recurs to the introductory statement of intent: "Accordingly, rejoice with us, senators, in an excellent work of our reign, as you join with us in our revision; approve the restoration of the remembrance of the prestige of that senator both to you and to the country: in his company your senatorial dignity was increased and through his descendants you continue to thrive in our esteem" (lines 33–36). The language here echoes the proposals made in the beginning of the letter. Now, however, the rehabilitation is represented as accomplished, rather than prospective: the senate is invited to approve the memory and prestige that have been restored by the letter.

Announcement of intent and statement of accomplishment: the prospective proposal of the introduction and the answering, retrospective claim of the conclusion combine to form and emphasize the effective character of the imperial letter. The letter is represented at the beginning as intended to do something, and at the end as having done this same thing. This performative force is further emphasized. The letter states at its beginning that the deed is inaugurated with good and auspicious omen (*bono faustoque omine*, line 13). In its final lines, the letter, or rather the rehabilitation accomplished by it, is explicitly described as an act, "the most excellent work of the emperor's reign" (*optimo imperii nostri opere*, line 34).

The object of the imperial letter is to make it possible to speak of Flavian. Memory of him had been purged. Representations of him, visual and verbal, had been forbidden. In the mere act of speaking Flavian's name, then, the emperor is reversing "the interdict of silence" and making it permissible by his example for others to do the same. At various places the letter speaks about itself, describes what it is doing, and so provides some further detail about the force of this elementary act of speaking. Above all, the act of speaking here is intended to recall memory to mind. So in its first sentence the letter speaks of "defending honor and recalling memory to eternal light" (lines 10–11). Later it says that the author is "restoring everyone's sacred recollection of Flavian" (lines 13–15). At the end of the letter, the senate is invited to "approve the memory that has been restored" (lines 34–35). The statement "We know that what we do today has been in your hearts and minds and far from any interruption of intervening forgetfulness" (lines 25–26) only serves to confirm that the mention of Flavian is intended to shore up the memory of him. The relationship between representation and memory here is not trivial or casual. This connection is bound up with the historiographical ideas that inform the *damnatio memoriae*. It is also central to the traditional Roman practice of history.

There is a formality and weightiness to the beginning of the imperial letter, which suggests an allusion to earlier, canonical works of Roman literature—and, in particular, to Roman historiography. The use of an allusion or quotation at the beginning of a work is common in formal beginnings of most periods and literatures. Like an invocation of the divine, a reference to another work helps to set the work in the context of a tradition. Certainly it is a common feature of the Roman literary tradition to begin a writing with an allusion to some exemplary work. This practice continues down into the world of late antiquity.[18]

The connotations of an allusion or quotation are very much like those of a rehabilitation. To recognize a citation is to conceive of a piece of writing as a rewriting, or reinscription: the evocation of another, preexisting (even if inapparent) text. In a more general way, the citation also works to defer the authority for its utterance elsewhere. It is not an original statement, but the rehearsal of a statement made on the authority of someone else. The invocation of authority is, as we have seen, one of the basic functions of any beginning, and is one of the objects that motivate beginning a work with a citation or an allusion.[19] The issue of authority is a problematic and even sensitive topic in the rehabilitation of Flavian (see Chapter 7 below).

The opening reference to "famous and distinguished men" (*clarorum adque inlustrium in republica virorum,* line 9) immediately suggests a context of biographical writing. In particular, the beginning of the imperial letter of rehabilitation is comparable to one of the most famous and quotable beginnings in all of Roman historiography: the first line of the earliest and most venerable of all Latin histories, Cato's *Origines.* Cicero says that he has always considered it "magnificent and remarkable" (*Pro Planc.* 66). In this beginning Cato remarks that "it is appropriate that there survive an account no less of the leisure than of the affairs of famous and great men" (*clarorum virorum atque magnorum non minus otii quam negotii rationem exstare oportere*) (frag. 2 Peter).[20] Cato's reference to "famous and great men" here is programmatic: the function and purpose of his writing is precisely to provide that account. In the *Origines* he traced early Roman history, emphasizing in particular the biographies of outstanding senators.

Whether or not the *Origines* was still well known in late antiquity (and it most likely was not much read), the line quoted above was familiar, even proverbial. Two contemporaries of the elder Flavian allude to it in their writing. His good friend Symmachus makes use of it, appropriately enough, in the first letter of his correspondence, addressed to his father. "It is pleasant," he says, "to provide an account no less of leisure than of business" (*libet enim non minus otii quam negotii praestare rationem*) (Symm. *Ep.* 1.1.2). Flavian's great adversary, Ambrose, also knew the line: he alludes to it in the introduction to his work on duty (*De officiis ministrorum*) where he contrasts speech and silence, and discusses the eloquence of silence:[21]

> Should we then be mute? Not at all. "There is a time to be silent and a time to speak." Furthermore, if we "give an account of our leisured word," we should be careful that we do not equally give an account of a leisured silence. Because there is also a busy silence, as in the case of Susanna, who did more by keeping silent than if she had spoken. In fact, by keeping silent among men, she spoke to God, and she found no greater proof of her chastity than silence.
>
> *Mutos nos esse oportet? Minime. "Est enim tempus tacendi et est tempus loquendi." Deinde si pro verbo otioso reddimus rationem, videamus ne reddamus et pro otioso silentio. Est enim negotiosum silentium ut erat Susannae quae plus egit tacendo quam si esset locuta. Tacendo enim apud homines locuta est Deo; nec ullum maius indicium suae castitatis invenit quam silentium.* (Ambrose, *De off. min.* 1.3.9)

The biographical impulse is as old as the Greco-Roman tradition of historiography. The notion that there is a particular value in passing on an account of the deeds of famous men is a topos in ancient historiography, with a tradition going back as far as the *Iliad*. In the ninth book of the *Iliad*, after the insults of Agamemnon, Achilles sulks in his tent, weeping and consoling himself by singing the "renowned deeds of men," the κλέα ἀνδρῶν (*Il.* 9.189). Roman biography and history are influenced by the ancient custom of delivering a laudatory commemorative oration (the *laudatio funebris*) at the funerals of distinguished men (*clari viri*).[22] In the *Origines*, Cato describes the evolution of the earliest Roman histories. He suggests in a celebrated passage that history-writing developed out of lays, or traditional oral tales, in which the exemplary exploits of famous men were recounted. At the same time, he points out that the beginning of his own work alludes to this tradition. So he says that history is in origin and essence an account of "the praises and virtues of famous men" (*clarorum virorum laudes atque virtutes*) (Cato *Origines*, frag. 118 Peter).[23]

The beginning of the imperial letter also may be compared with that of another Roman historical work, more recent and quite suggestive. Tacitus' *Agricola* begins with a similar general statement of purpose: "to transmit the deeds and habits of famous men to later generations was the custom of ancient times" (*clarorum virorum facta moresque posteris tradere, antiquitus usitatum*) (*Agr.* 1).[24] In this short and early work, Tacitus recounts the career of his father-in-law, a distinguished Roman general whose career was curtailed by the jealousy of the tyrant Domitian. Tacitus addressed his biography to future generations as a kind of rehabilitation: a posthumous justification of Agricola's life. The general structure of the *Agricola* is traditional; many of its notable features are typical of the genre of the Roman funeral oration.[25] An allusion to this work would be eminently appropriate at the beginning of a real rehabilitation, this one an imperial letter that posthumously praises the life and deeds of a Roman senator.

It cannot be proven that the first line of the imperial letter of rehabilitation certainly alludes to Cato's *Origines* or Tacitus' *Agricola*—any more than it can be conclusively demonstrated that the opening line of Tacitus' *Agricola* really alludes to Cato (as is generally thought). Unlike explicit references such as bibliographical citations, allusions and metaphors and irony and the like leave much to the imagination: they insinuate and evoke rather than assert. The work of making the connection is left to the audience. It is this sense of a thing which is there but unsaid—that is, a silence—which creates the freedom and even the possibility of interpretation.

There is nothing implausible in the idea that there might be an allusion to Tacitus in this letter. In fact, it would be surprising if the author of the text did not know Tacitus. Tacitus' writing seems to have had little currency among his contemporaries and immediately succeeding generations, but he seems to have enjoyed a resurgence of popularity in the fourth and fifth centuries, among Christians as well as pagans.[26]

An early and significant reference to Tacitus comes from the Christian apologist Tertullian in the third century. Tertullian, while criticizing Tacitus' account of Jewish religion in book 5 of the *Histories*, refers to the historian with an evident punning allusion to the meaning of the name Tacitus, or "silent one," as *ille mendaciorum loquacissimus*, "that chatterbox among liars" (*Apologeticus* 12).[27] Later, there are many more allusions to and citations of Tacitus' works. In the fourth century, the *Historia Augusta* (*Vit. Aurelian* 2; *Vit. Probus* 2) groups him with the greatest of Roman historians. In an important passage, Jerome refers to thirty books of Tacitus, which cover from "after Augustus down to the death of Domitian" (*Comm. on Zacchariah* 14.1, 2 [3, p. 914]). Servius, in his commentary on the *Aeneid* (*ad* 3.399) cites Tacitus for an obscure bit of geography. In the fifth century Sidonius Apollinaris mentions the historian several times (*Epp.* 4.14.1, 4.22.2; *Carm.* 2.190–192, 23.153). Orosius cites and quotes Tacitus extensively (*Adv. Paganos* 1.5.1, 1.10.1, 7.3.7, 7.9.7, 7.10.3, 7.19.4, 7.27.1, 7.34.5).[28] Surely the most important of the authors influenced by Tacitus in the late fourth and early fifth century, however, must be the historian Ammianus Marcellinus. Although Ammianus does not refer to Tacitus by name, verbal echoes have been detected. Furthermore, Ammianus begins his history in A.D. 96 with the death of Domitian, where Tacitus leaves off. Ammianus thus implicitly announces himself as the successor of Tacitus.[29]

Various causes have been proposed for this revival of interest in Tacitus. The author (or authors) of the *Historia Augusta* attributes some of the responsibility to the emperor Tacitus (A.D. 275), who supposedly regarded himself as a descendant of the historian, and who consequently arranged for Tacitus' portrait and books to be distributed to public libraries (*HA Tacitus* 10.3).[30] Another reason for the interest in Tacitus is tied to the rise of Christianity: many of the citations from Tacitus in the fourth and fifth centuries come from the fifth book of his *Histories*, which was of special interest to Christian intellectuals since it is concerned with Jewish antiquities.[31]

Tacitus is not the only classical Roman historian who was being read during this period. Much better attested is the interest taken in Livy by pagans and Christians alike during the late fourth and early fifth centuries. As we will see (Chapter 6 below), both the family of Flavian and the family of his close friend Symmachus seem to have had a particular interest in this historian. A manuscript of the works of the historian circulated among them, to be copied and corrected. Tacitus may have been read during this period for some of the same reasons that Livy was read.

FLAVIAN THE HISTORIAN

The allusion to historiography in the first line of the imperial letter of rehabilitation has other resonances. The person being rehabilitated here, the elder Flavian, was himself a noted historian. On the statue base from the Caelian hill (*CIL* 6.1782 = *ILS* 2947, line 7; reproduced in Chapter 2 above), his grandson-in-law Memmius Symmachus refers to him as a *historicus disertissimus*, a "most learned historian." Flavian's activities as a historian are recognized in the letter of rehabilitation itself. The writing of these histories is not represented in the letter of rehabilitation as merely an indulgence of private antiquarianism: they had evidently helped to mitigate Flavian's disgrace after his defection and death, and they are said to be one reason for the enduring affection of the emperor toward him, and a significant factor in his rehabilitation. So, as the letter says, the emperor Theodosius had been most impressed by these histories: the senators will recall "the kindness the emperor tendered to him [i.e. Flavian] and even to the *Annales*, which he desired his quaestor and prefect to dedicate to him" (lines 19–20).

Although practically nothing is known about Flavian's *Annales*, much has been written.[32] No fragment of these histories is known to have survived. In fact, aside from the references to the histories in his inscriptions, we know only that one of his descendants may have been inspired by them to write a history in his turn. According to Cassiodorus, around 520, Q. Aurelius Memmius Symmachus "released a history in seven books, in the manner of his relatives" (*parentesque suos imitatus historiam quoque Romanam septem libris edidit*).[33] Nevertheless, despite (or perhaps because of) the lack of information, a great deal has been made of this history. Most notoriously it has been proposed that Flavian's *Annales* were a major source for the *Historia Augusta;* the younger Flavian has even been suggested (surely wrongly) as the author of this compendium.[34] More recently there have been attempts to identify Flavian's *Annales* as a major source for the account of the years 270–378 in Eunapius and Zonaras (via Petrus Petricius)[35] and for Jerome's *Chronicle*.[36]

It would be rash to make too much of such conjectures, since practically nothing can be known with certainty about the character and theme of these histories, or even about their subject matter. If the imperial letter uses the title *Annales* precisely, Flavian's book should be an account that is organized chronologically, not by some thematic or geographic principle. It cannot be determined from the title whether it was a history of larger or smaller scope. According to the letter of rehabilitation, the emperor Theodosius was impressed by the work; elsewhere we hear that Theodosius particularly enjoyed reading about the history of the republic (*Epit. de Caes.* 48, 11–12; cf. Aug. *Civ. Dei* 5.26).[37] Perhaps, then, we should imagine Flavian's *Annales* as a history of the republic, in the manner of Livy (though it should be noted that in such a case these *Annales* would certainly not be a suitable source for the *Historia Augusta* or Petrus Patricius or Eunapius).[38] Flavian's heirs, Flavian the younger and Dexter, corrected the text of Livy (see Chapter 6 below). Macrobius says that Flavian was interested in prognostication and the interpretation of prodigies such as are frequently listed in Livy's history. In the *Saturnalia* (1.5.13) he comments on augury in Vergil. As *pontifex maior* he was a member of the Roman priestly college that traditionally had shared the responsibility for keeping track of these prodigies and recording them. The old *Annales* of the college of *pontifices* had been an important source for the traditional kind of annalistic history that Livy wrote, and they (or the tradition of their connection with the pontifical college) may have been an inspiration for Flavian's history as well.

Although these *Annales* seem to have been Flavian's chief literary accomplishment, they were not his only writing. By 431 he was remembered for broadly based learning: Macrobius says that his discourse was informed by a supply of deep erudition (*Sat.* 1.5.13). He is known to have attempted at least one translation of a Greek text. Sidonius Apollinaris mentions his translation of Philostratus' life of the notorious Hellenistic shaman Apollonius of Tyana (*Ep.* 8.3.1).[39] There are also indications that he had some interests in philosophy, even if we know of no philosophical works from his pen. Macrobius makes a point of emphasizing his friendship with the philosopher Eustathius (*Sat.* 1.6.4). In one of his letters to him the orator Symmachus jokes about Flavian's unseemly familiarity with the costume and haircut preferred at the time by pretentious philosophers (*Ep.* 2.61).[40]

Recently there has been an interesting attempt to recover and analyze some writings of Flavian. Noting that the imperial quaestor was responsible for drafting imperial legal decisions, and that Flavian served in this office in 389–390, Honoré has collected the legal decisions from the Theodosian Code dating to these years. He then analyzes the style of these texts.[41] He concludes that the quaestor "can turn a phrase on almost any topic. But he is an extremist, who likes categorical statements and dislikes nuances." In particular, Honoré imagines that these texts demonstrate the "intransigence" of their author.

Honoré also suggests that a particular speech in the *Historia Augusta* should be in substance attributed to Flavian (*HA Tacitus* 6.7),[42] believing that it, like the letters of the Theodosian Code, is marked by a particularly intransigent tone. According to the *Historia Augusta,* this speech was delivered by a senator, an ex-consul by the name of Maecius Faltonius Nicomachus, on the occasion of the appointment of the emperor Tacitus and his restoration of the senate. This person is not otherwise known. The speaker praises the emperor although he is elderly, and rails against the appointment of children as emperors, using the famous line: "May the gods forfend the selection of children as emperors!" (*di avertant principes pueros*). Honoré argues that "the supposed third-century context [of this speech] is inappropriate."[43] There is no indication, apart from this speech, that the emperor Tacitus had children or that any child was his rival for the throne. A much more appropriate context, Honoré suggests, would be the revolt of 394, just a few years before the composition of the *Historia Augusta*. It will be recalled that the child emperor Valentian II had died or had been assassinated, and that the generalissimo Arbogast had taken this opportunity as the occasion to make emperor his own creature, the elderly and learned Eugenius. These two, along with Flavian, then led a rebellion. The emperor Theodosius had countered the usurpation by making his eight-year-old son Honorius emperor of the west. Honoré suggests that now Flavian, who was energetically promoting the cause of Eugenius, delivered the substance of the speech reported in the *Historia Augusta* before the Roman senate.

HISTORY AND SILENCE

"History is a resurrection," says the inscription on Michelet's tomb.[44] The inscription from the Forum of Trajan, on the other hand, is the rehabilitation of a historian. It has a strongly marked commemorative function, and it begins with a line that has the potential to evoke the traditional historiography of Rome. Here history is a rehabilitation. The association of history and rehabilitation suggested by the first line of the letter is quite appropriate: the emperor's power to rehabilitate is very like the historian's self-conception; the rationale for the rehabilitation finds close parallels in common motives and justifications for the writing of history. In the sense that the rehabilitation aims to speak a name that heretofore has been unspeakable, it is like traditional narrative histories, which aim to represent what has gone without representation.

The motivation for simple narrative is commemorative. The logic supporting this commemorative function of history is dissimulatory, in the sense in which I outlined this idea in Chapter 4. Traditional history is founded on a realist conception of language. Events and their representations are imagined as autonomous of one another; and ultimately the event takes primacy over its representation. The fact that a thing should fail of its representation, "lose its renown," does not falsify the thing, or damage its reality. So, for example, in Herodotus' proem, there is no question that the truth (i.e. the facticity) of past events will be annihilated by time, only that they may "become unrenowned" and fail of their representation. Even if the events of the past are forgotten, they are not for that reason conceived as any the less real, nor even as utterly excised from mind: it is always possible to be reminded of what one has forgotten. Rather, they fail of their representation to mind. The failure of representation does not destroy what is not represented; it merely dissimulates the thing. Failure of representation; loss of renown—such by-products of the passing of time produce the sense of silence.

A sense of dissimulatory silence, of something that is unsaid but sayable, is essential for any representation. One speaks, for example, out of the experience of something that needs to be said—and that, by necessity, has not been said. This experience of the "need to speak" may be seen as generated out of some external imperative: someone asks a question, for example, that demands an answer. In a more basic, experiential way, however, the link between representation and silence is manifested as the link between speech and thought. Thought is imagined as silent, while speech is the overt representation of that thought. Speech proceeds out of and is prompted by thought: so it may be considered a dependent reflection of mind, a form of "thinking out loud." In this scenario, representation is literally produced out of a dissimulatory silence.

A sense of silence remains a necessary condition of possibility for any form of analysis or criticism—literary, philosophical, or scientific. Authors of fiction give representation to themselves, their feelings and thoughts, and, as we have just seen, such self-representation is imagined as the dissimulatory dichotomy between representation and mind. In scientific or historical or critical literature, however, the silence that is explored is usually conceived as external to the writer, whether its reference is to the natural world, the past, or a text. So the dichotomy between representation and thought is reconfigured as one of representation and reality. The silence of thought is projected out onto the external world. In this way the historian or scientist aims to uncover something, to bring it to representation. No realist discourse aims to say what is not, nor as a rule does it aim to say what is obvious. Analysis typically aims to elucidate that which is, but which is not explicitly expressed. The analyst will begin by charting the boundaries of what is said (and, at the same time, a part of the contours of what is not said). It is the recognition that something is there albeit unspoken that produces both the freedom and the compulsion to talk. Without the construction of such silence there would be nothing for the analyst to say. For a scientist, for example, there is the silence of the universe: the sense that there are rules of behavior in the physical world, and that, though these rules are not apparent, they are nevertheless "there" to be "discovered"—that is to say, uncovered, or brought to appearance. For the literary critic there are the silences suggested by context, metaphor, and symbol—all of which beg explanation. For the historian there is the silence of the past, the sense of things that were but are no longer; because they are no longer, they are not immediately apparent and must somehow be brought to appearance.

When a thing is understood as a representation, it is conceived as standing in place of something. What it stands for need not be present; in fact, by serving as substitutes, representations work to displace what they stand for. If the representation is conceived as true, however, then the thing represented must be imagined as being, or as having been. If representation were only or merely adequate to what it represents, then texts would be transparent, meaning would be entirely exposed, and there would be nothing to interpret: the only comment possible would be quotation. For analysis to be possible, it is necessary to imagine that representations implicitly say more or less than the truth of what they refer to. For example, it might be imagined that the text has a figurative dimension—manifested through metaphor, citation, allusion, and so on—that exceeds its overt referentiality. So it would be possible for a text to "mean more (or less) than it says" and, consequently, to be the object of interpretation.[45]

The recognition of silence—gaps or lacunae—in a text also suggests a hermeneutic problem. What is the motivation for this silence? Why do texts not say everything? Why is there always something to explain? If something is meant, why is it not said outright? Following Ricoeur, let us take two extreme alternatives.[46] We might propose, for example, that the unspoken is not hidden, but merely unnoticed. To decipher the immanent presence of god in the world, or in the book of nature, one need only understand the language, recognize a symbol. The process of labeling, the deictic indication of the indisputable existence of some existing sign, might be described as a "hermeneutic of revelation." Most traditional "commemorative history" tends to fall on this side of the "hermeneutic spectrum." At the other end of the scale, we might imagine that what is unspoken is concealed for some sinister, ulterior reason. Consequently, to get at the truth of the human libido, or of labor, or the will to power requires the ability to see through cynical and self-serving lies—the "hermeneutic of suspicion." Modern interpretation, beginning especially with Freud and Marx and Nietzsche, has gone a long way down this road. The imperial letter of rehabilitation is the vindication of the victim of a repression. Nevertheless, it does not present itself as a decipherment of lies or as the disclosure of something long repressed. Rather, it represents its relationship to the earlier silence in a more innocuous and benign way: Flavian's name has always been obvious, apparent to all even in those years in which it was unmentionable (see lines 25–26). It need only be recalled. By speaking out, the emperor is only making explicit what has always been obvious. This is the attitude of the political authority that is responsible for the rehabilitation, but that had also been responsible for the original purge. One might accordingly see this representation of the silence that had so long covered Flavian as just another cynical and manipulative attempt at concealment: from the perspective of those who have been subject to such power, it will seem disingenuous, to say the least. In his historical writing, on the other hand, Tacitus expresses an attitude toward silence that might be characterized as a "hermeneutic of suspicion." The truth of the past is explicitly represented as having been hidden, concealed behind lies and ambiguous silences. The truth is suppressed for cynical, political purposes, and it is the job of the historian to find the truth behind such intentionally misleading and oppressive representations and silences.

If the "hermeneutic of revelation" is predicated on a recognition of the symbolic, the "hermeneutic of suspicion" is predicated on a decipherment of the sign of the erasure. Both symbol and erasure indicate something that is or has been there, but that is not or is no longer overtly represented. Unlike the symbol, though, the erasure connotes a temporal aspect to the removal of the referent, and at the same time suggests that the referent has been concealed—that it has been intentionally removed or hidden, for reasons that may be more or less apparent.

So far, I have been discussing silence in synchronic structural terms: the dichotomous relationship of speech and mind or of representation to what is represented. For historians, however, silence is a temporal production. There is a correspondence between the structural construction of silence through analysis and the temporal construction of silence through historical narrative. It would be a mistake, though, to reduce the implications and connotations of the experience of time to a structural model. History is about the past, about what was at one time but no longer is: the evanescent, as Herodotus says. In concrete, human terms, history is about those who once were living but now are dead; who once could speak for themselves but now are silent. So the dead past provides the referential object for history as its silence produces the condition of possibility for historical discourse.

Historians value the silence of the past because it seems to provide a guarantee for the truth of the representations of the present. It is a largely unspoken scandal for history (as for other "realist" discourses) that it is a representation at all.[47] History regards itself as dealing with truth, and there is a gap between the truth of the thing that history represents and the representation that history itself self-evidently and necessarily is. Any history can be only a simulation of the past; it cannot be the past itself. The contrary of simulation may be imagined as dissimulation: a silence that stands in front of something true. Because silence is thought to be the negation of representation, it seems true: what is not a representation cannot lie. The silence of history is a temporal production. Historians do not imagine themselves to be merely representing a thing but, rather, to be *restoring* it to appearance. The writing of history, like the writing of a rehabilitation, is portrayed not as an inscription, but as a reinscription, a writing over an erasure. So the representative character of historical writing is mitigated: history is figured not merely as the production of an appearance, but as the restoration of what has been effaced from appearance. Heidegger's explanation of the etymology of truth (*aletheia*) as a thing that is "un-covered" and "un-forgotten" confronts these same issues.[48]

Another reason for the importance of silence in historiography is that it provides historians with a space in which to speak. Unlike the analyst, who elucidates, the historian restores. As with any analysis, history must be true, and must stand in some relationship to certain sources. History cannot be a sheerly imaginative product. It must be composed with reference to "what really happened." On the other hand, it must also say something that has not been said. "Say something once, why say it again?" So historians must say what is true and what has not been said—that is, they must say what is preserved in silence. The dead, defined broadly as the past, or as what has passed out of being, provide an excellent object for this kind of discourse. What is dead is simultaneously real and not real; it remains true, though it exists no longer. Furthermore, the dead have passed out of the world of the living:

they are no longer explicitly there, self-evident to those who blindly encounter them indirectly through the traces they have left from time to time. The dead endure only in memory and silence, to the extent that they endure at all. Their only remedy is representation, which "stands for" them, in their place.

The temporal idea of silence is manifested in the historical conception of the source. History has no access to the past except through documents, "traces," survivals out of a time that has vanished.[49] For example, a ruin is a survival, a material object with a pronounced temporal dimension. The ruin exists in the here and now and it brings certain things to explicit appearance.[50] By and large these things are tautological, descriptive aspects of the ruin itself: a ground plan, a masonry style, and so forth. At the same time, however, the ruin suggests an absence: something that is not there, but that has been. The ruin evokes, without bringing to appearance that thing which is not there; it indicates that something existed at some time in the past, and that this thing exists no longer. So the ruin effaces the past at the same time that it makes it visible (on this subject see further Chapter 7 below). If the ruin is viewed by an analyst, say an archaeologist, this suggestion of temporality may be felt as an imperative to interpret. The romantic poet might feel this urge more accurately than the archaeologist: that is, as a vague and inexpressible sentiment of "melancholy,"[51] or, perhaps better and more commonly, as a feeling of "nostalgia." The scientific archaeologist proceeds with apparent bloodlessness to an explanation of the ruin's production.[52] In a very general way, though, ruins and other historical documents, like symbols and erasures, may be viewed as traces or survivals, as indications of the evanescence of an indeterminate something. In this way, the historical document indicates a dissimulatory silence that is produced by the passing of time.

This ambiguity, while most strongly marked in historical discourse, must in the end be admitted to be the quality of any sign. In popular thought the sign is often confused with what it represents. Nevertheless, on reflection it should be clear that it is the essence of the sign to "stand for" what it represents: it evokes the presence of its signified, because the sign is meant to be comparable to the signified. At the same time, it should also be clear that every sign also suggests the absence of its signified, because it is only comparable and not identical to it. To "stand for" a thing is both to represent it and to replace it. So all representations are perceived *in rasura;* they carry with them the intimation of absence and silence because such qualities are in the nature of the movement of the trace.

The implications of this logic for the practice, justification, and motivation of history are far-reaching. Historians are frequently imagined as the "avengers of silence." They are seen as providing a voice for those generations of the dead who have had no voice, and who, being dead, can have no voice unless a champion speaks for them. As we saw in the introduction to the present chapter, one of the high moral justifications for writing the past has typically been the rehabilitation of those whose story has not been told: the poor, women, minorities, and other groups that exist on the margins of the dominant civic polity.[53] There is also an answering contemporary ideology of activism, most obviously associated with the slogans "Silence = Death" and "Breaking Silence."[54] Rather than approach the problem of history and silence through such large generalizations, however, let us look at a particular text. The thematic of silence can be illustrated in practically every traditional history, and in many literary texts from late antiquity (see only Ambrose's *De officiis ministrorum,* discussed above). In the present context, though, it will perhaps be most appropriate to discuss the historian whose very name means the "silent one": the author of the *Agricola,* Tacitus.[55]

THE HISTORIAN OF SILENCE

The beginning of the *Agricola,* like the opening of the letter of rehabilitation, is a formal inauguration of speech out of silence; and it raises the same issues as the letter of rehabilitation. It is a commemorative work, a history whose function is, from its outset, precisely to say what has been. By lending his voice to the past, Tacitus assures that some part of it, at least, will survive in the telling.[56]

In terms of its larger structure and motivation, the *Agricola* is cast as a kind of rehabilitation. Gnaeus Julius Agricola had been Tacitus' father-in-law. Agricola had served the emperor Domitian faithfully and with distinction. After the successes of his military career, moreover, Agricola was popular with the Roman people; when danger threatened, they asked for his leadership, contrasting his excellence with the failings of other generals. Such praise beat on Domitian's ears like a whip. So it was precisely because of Agricola's excellent qualities that Domitian began to hate him: this was an emperor who was "unfriendly to virtue" (*Agr.* 41). In the end, Agricola did not suffer a *damnatio memoriae*—but he was forced by the hostility of the emperor to cut short his career and to withdraw from public life.

For Tacitus, the story of Agricola begins with his demise. "Now, as I was about to tell the story of the life of a man who was dead, I have needed indulgence—an indulgence that I would not have sought had my intention been to condemn him—so cruel and hostile to virtues are the times" (*Agr.* 1). To speak of virtue, to admire good character, was permitted neither by the times nor by the jealous nature of the emperor. As Tacitus says in his conclusion to the work, "Let those whose habit it is to admire what is not permitted know that good men can live under bad emperors" (*Agr.* 42.4). Agricola had not made a gross display of his virtues but had practiced them quietly, with dignity. "Most people, who are accustomed to judge great men by their ostentatious displays, though they watched and observed Agricola, questioned his reputation, and few deciphered it" (*Agr.* 40). Tacitus saw it as his duty to bring his father-in-law's unmentionable merits to light, for the benefit of those who had been unable to discern them. Even in death Agricola had been unremarkable, unpretentious, nothing like those vain and self-indulgent senators who sought fame through an ostentatious suicide (*Agr.* 42).[57] Because of the modesty of his life and death, because of the temper of the times, which, like the character of the emperor, was "hostile to virtue," Agricola was quickly forgotten. "No one, when the death of Agricola became known, was glad or—at least immediately—forgetful" (*Agr.* 43). In this environment, where everything is motivated by jealousy and ambition, and thus conspires against the representation and recollection of virtue, it is the duty of the historian to look beneath dissimulatory appearances, and to write, in order to recover and preserve the memory of merit.

Even from this brief account it is apparent that the narrative of Agricola's life is centered on a thematic of memory and silence. This point is even more clearly illustrated by the programmatic and general remarks Tacitus makes in the introduction (*Agr.* 1–3) and conclusion (*Agr.* 44–46) of the work.

In the first chapters of the Agricola, Tacitus provides a remarkable autobiographical note about his own life and his development as a historian. In his youth he had lived through a period of autocratic rule, during which the brave had perished and the wise had kept their mouths shut. At this time, the writings of historians were burnt and even casual conversation was curtailed:

> We certainly have provided a wonderful example of our submissiveness. Just as the last generation saw the extreme of freedom, so we saw the extreme of slavery, when informers deprived us even of the give-and-take of speaking and hearing. We would have lost our memory along with our tongues, if it were as much in our power to forget as to keep silent.
>
> *dedimus profecto grande patientiae documentum; et sicut vetus aetas vidit quid ultimum in libertate esset, ita nos quid in servitute, adempto per inquisitiones*

etiam loquendi audiendique commercio. memoriam quoque ipsam cum voce perdidissemus, si tam in nostra potestate esset oblivisci quam tacere. (*Agr.* 2)

Times have improved, and under the new regime of Nerva and Trajan it has become possible to write history once more. By telling the story of Agricola, Tacitus is not only vindicating the life of a man who perished in obscurity during this period. He is also vindicating himself from the silence that had been imposed on him for those many years: "It will not be unpleasant to have written a memorial of our former slavery and a witness to our present blessings, even with unpracticed and rusty voice" (*non tamen pigebit vel incondita ac rudi voce memoriam prioris servitutis ac testimonium praesentium bonorum composuisse*) (*Agr.* 3).

The final paragraphs of the *Agricola* read like an exposure of the vanity of the *damnatio memoriae*. Tacitus insists that representations of the dead are vain; rather, the ineffable and unrepresentable qualities of the person should be kept alive in memory, which is beyond the power of anyone to harm.[58] So he advises Agricola's surviving relatives:

> I would give the following advice to his daughter also and his wife: that they cultivate the memory of father and husband in such a way that they contemplate each word and deed in their hearts, and that they cling to the form and feature of his spirit rather than of his body. It is not that I think that the representations which are fashioned of marble or bronze should be forbidden, but images of the face are vain and evanescent; the shape of the mind is eternal, and you cannot hold it or show it through alien media or craft, but only by your way of life. Whatever we have loved in Agricola, whatever we have admired, remains and will remain in the hearts of people through the endless procession of ages because of the reputation of his accomplishments.

id filiae quoque uxorique praeceperim, sic patris, sic mariti memoriam venerari, ut omnia facta dictaque eius secum revolvant, formamque ac figuram animi magis quam corporis complectantur; non quia intercedendum putem imaginibus quae marmore aut aere finguntur, sed, ut simulacra vultus imbecilia ac mortalia sunt, forma mentis aeterna, quam tenere et exprimere non per alienam materiam et artem, sed tuis ipse moribus possis. quidquid ex Agricola amavimus, quidquid mirati sumus, manet mansurumque est in animis hominum, in aeternitate temporum in fama rerum. (*Agr.* 46)

The problems that Tacitus addresses at the beginning and end of the *Agricola* should be familiar from the discussion of the *damnatio memoriae:* memory versus representation, truth versus appearance, silence versus speech. He is concerned in each instance to give precedence to memory, truth, and silence. This priority is the grounds for Tacitus' critique of the *damnatio memoriae* (see Chapter 4 above). It is also at the heart of his general historiography.

The theme of silence runs not only through the *Agricola* but also through the surviving fragments of Tacitus' two major historical works, the *Annals* and *Histories*.[59] The issue is pervasive: there is scarcely a page in these works where the theme of dissimulation is not addressed. Seldom has the issue of the rehabilitating function of the historian been so prominently figured. Even casual research into the role of silence and the *damnatio memoriae* in Tacitean historiography quickly provides enough material for a rather long book—and I intend to treat the matter here in only a short digression.[60] I will spend the remainder of the present chapter discussing anecdotally the strategic ways in which Tacitus uses silence in his historiography, showing how these examples illustrate and support my general arguments about the relation between silence and historiography. I concentrate upon examples taken from the *Agricola,* though I will provide parallels from his other works as well.

TACITUS ON HISTORY, REPRESENTATION, AND SILENCE

As I have been at pains to point out in these past two chapters, one of Tacitus' central concerns in his historical writing is the relationship between representation and reality. As he claims, those who possess power in the present imagine that by suppressing or creating representations, they can alter the truth as well (*Ann.* 4.35). Tacitus' writing itself is a refutation of this idea. Representation is at best only a distorted, distant reflection of reality. What is true, Tacitus believes, is autonomous of its representation and will endure even when it is unexpressed. So silence is not a means to destroy the truth; to the contrary, it is the essential and characteristic index of truth. These ideas figure prominently in Tacitus' description of his various historical actors, in his critique of sources, in his general remarks about history, even in his style.

The issue of dissimulation is most obvious and ubiquitous in Tacitus' portrayal of the political relationship between emperor and senate. The insincerity of the Tacitean emperor has always drawn the attention of commentators. Dissimulation seems to be a prerequisite of the imperial office, for in one way or another, all of Tacitus' emperors are dissimulators.[61] What they dissimulate is very frequently hatred and anger. For Tacitus there is a link between hatred or anger and silence. For example, Tacitus says that the emperor under whom Agricola served, Domitian, had "by nature a violent temper and, to the extent that he was secretive, he was the more unrelenting" (*natura praeceps in iram, et quo obscurior, eo inrevocabilior*) (*Agr.* 42). Nero "dissimulated his hatred for the present, but it soon returned" (*dissimulatum ad praesens et mox redditum odium*) (*Ann.* 16.5.3). Even the bumbling and innocuous Claudius was capable of dissimulation—although in his case Tacitus insinuates that the line between dissimulation and vacuousness was uncertain: "In the days following" the execution of his treacherous and lecherous wife, Messalina, "he gave no sign of hatred, satisfaction, distress, or any other human feeling—even when he saw the accusers exulting and his children mourning. His forgetfulness was helped by the senate, which decreed that her name and images should be removed from places public and private" (*ne secutis quidem diebus odii gaudii, irae tristitiae, ullius denique humani adfectus signa dedit, non cum laetantis accusatores aspiceret, non cum filios maerentis. Iuvitque oblivionem eius senatus censendo nomen et effigies privatis ac publicis locis demovendas*) (*Ann.* 11.38).

The prince of all Tacitean dissimulators, however, is Tiberius. Like Domitian, Tiberius was accustomed to "lay up his hatred for a long time, in order to store it away and bring it out increased" (*odia in longum iaciens, quae reconderet auctaque promeret*) (*Ann.* 1.69.5). His pretence and insincerity are everywhere chronicled in the first six books of the *Annals*. One or two examples can stand for a multitude. According to Tacitus, Tiberius was by nature secretive. After he became emperor, his natural tendency was encouraged. "Even in matters where Tiberius was not intentionally deceitful, his words, either by nature or custom, were always hesitant and unclear. Now indeed that he was trying to hide completely his real feelings, his language became even more twisted, uncertain and ambiguous" (*Tiberioque, etiam in rebus quas non occuleret, seu natura sive adsuetudine, suspensa semper et obscura verba; tunc vero nitenti ut sensus suos penitus abderet, in incertum et ambiguum magis implicabantur*) (*Ann.* 1.11). In A.D. 20 he presided at the trial of Cn. Calpurnius Piso, who had been brought before the senate on charges of treason. Popular feeling ran high against Piso. The senators cried out in anger when he appeared. Piso, however, "was frightened by nothing more than he was by Tiberius," who sat inscrutably "without pity, without anger, stony-faced—locked and closed against any outburst of human emotion" (*nullo magis exterritus est quam quod Tiberium sine miseratione, sine ira, obstinatum clausumque vidit, ne quo adfectu perrumperetur*) (*Ann.* 3.15). Knowing from Tiberius' very inscrutability that he was doomed, Piso returned home and committed suicide. On another occasion, Tiberius wrote to the senate expressing vague fears of sedition and plots against his person. He did not, however, name any names. One brave senator proposed that Tiberius should speak more explicitly: tell the senate whom he feared, so that the traitors could be destroyed. Tiberius was furious: "Of all his—as he considered them—virtues, there was none that he loved more greatly than his dissimulation." So he greatly disliked disclosing what he had suppressed (*nullum aeque Tiberius, ut rebatur, ex virtutibus suis quam dissimulationem diligebat*) (*Ann.* 4.71).

The silence of the emperors was ominous, even threatening. The Roman senate, on the other hand, adopted a defensive silence. So Tacitus remarks that Agricola wisely kept quiet and spent much of his time in leisure, even when he held public office. He did so not because he was lazy, but because he was "aware of the temper of the times under Nero, in which passivity was taken for wisdom. His term as praetor was marked by the same silence" (*gnarus sub Neronem temporum, quibus inertia pro sapientia fuit. idem praeturae tenor et silentium*) (*Agr.* 6). As informers tattled shamelessly and emperors became more sensitive to the slightest sign of an offense, senators became ever more silent. "People behaved secretively even among their intimates; encounters and conversation, the ears of both friends and strangers were avoided. Even voiceless, inanimate objects, ceilings and walls, were examined anxiously" (. . . *sui tegens adversum proximos; congressus, conloquia, notae ignotaeque aures vitari; etiam muta atque inanima, tectum et parietes circumspectabantur*) (*Ann.* 4.69).

According to Tacitus the prominent figures of his history typically spoke and acted in an ambiguous and deceptive manner. This would not pose a problem for later historians if, as some of his modern critics suggest, this deceptiveness were his own creation, mere innuendo.[62] Tacitus, however, claims to find these qualities in the sources themselves. Thus he comments about his sources for the actions of Tiberius:

> Regarding the election of consulships, from the time Tiberius first became emperor and later, I scarcely dare to make any definitive assertions. The evidence in the historical authors, and even in his own speeches, is conflicting. Sometimes he suppressed the names of candidates, but described their birth, career, and service records, so that it might be understood who they were. On other occasions he removed even these clues, but merely warned the candidates not to disturb the elections by bribery—promising his own assistance to the same end. . . . In terms of his words, his policy was specious. In terms of his deeds, it was meaningless, or deceitful, and

to the extent that it was concealed under the appearance of a greater liberty, it would issue into an even more loathsome slavery.

de comitiis consularibus, quae tum primum illo principe ac deinceps fuere, vix quicquam firmare ausim: adeo diversa non modo apud auctores, sed in ipsius orationibus reperiuntur. modo, subtractis candidatorum nominibus, originem cuiusque et vitam et stipendia descripsit, ut qui forent intellegeretur; aliquando, ea quoque significatione subtracta, candidatos hortatus ne ambitu comitia turbarent, suam ad id curam pollicitus est. . . . speciosa verbis, re inania aut subdola, quantoque maiore libertatis imagine tegebantur, tanto eruptura ad infensius servitium. (*Ann.* 1.81)

The interpretation of silence is thus also an issue of source criticism for Tacitus. The problem is created and manifested not only in the dissimulation of actors and sources, but in the rationale that Tacitus uses to choose what he will say. Tacitus is concerned to tell what others have ignored. For example, he comments that other historians have not described the unending series of trials under the early *principes:*

I am not unaware that most writers omit the dangers and punishment of many men. They tire of the quantity of material, or fear that what they found lengthy and depressing may affect their readers with a comparable boredom. But I have found much worth knowing, even if unrecorded by others.

Neque sum ignarus a plerisque scriptoribus omissa multorum pericula et poenas, dum copia fatiscunt aut, quae ipsis nimia et maesta fuerant, ne pari taedio lecturos adficerent verentur: nobis pleraque digna cognitu obvenere, quamquam ab aliis incelebrata. (*Ann.* 6.7)

Examples of the uses of silence in Tacitus could be expanded almost endlessly. Practically every character in his historical writings is frequently silent—or silenced. For Tacitus, the period of which he writes, and in which he lives, is marked by a profound dysfunction of communication: signs have become misleading, twisted, and warped; representations have lost their correlation to what they represent. Always beneath the cloudy surface of representation lurks an oppressive political reality. This situation has profound political implications for Tacitus: the threatening silence of the oppressor and the acquiescent silence of the oppressed are the very instruments of the political stability of the Roman principate. For Tacitus, to speak explicitly and accurately of a thing is to bring it out of the world of silence and into the light of representation, to consciousness, where there must be acknowledgment—surrender or resistance. For example, Nero was shocked by a conspirator who dared speak the truth to him, for Nero "was as ready to commit crimes as he was unaccustomed to hear them mentioned" (*qui ut faciendis sceleribus promptus, ita audiendi quae faceret insolens erat*) (*Ann.* 15.67).

As for the principate, the unspoken truth was known or suspected by all: what was in name a republic had become the rule of the first man, or *princeps*. To speak this truth, however, would be dangerous—not just for the speaker, but for the stability of the political regime itself. Consequently Tacitus has his emperors advised to guard very carefully the *arcana imperii*, "secrets of rule." As Augustus' widow Livia was told, "it is a principle of empire that the books balance only if there is a single accountant" (*eam condicionem esse imperandi ut non aliter ratio constet quam si uni reddatur*) (*Ann.* 1.11). Not only must there be secrecy, but in order for this secrecy to be a secure basis for political power, the secrecy itself must be dissimulated, effaced. Just so, the *damnatio memoriae* must be dissimulated in order to be effective, and for forgetfulness to work it must somehow escape notice. Late in Tiberius' reign a senator proposed to increase the explicit powers of the emperor. Tiberius refused the proposal, not because it was an increase of his power, but because it made his power explicit:

> There was no doubt that this proposal went deeper (than its appearance) and attacked the secrecy at the heart of the principate. But Tiberius replied as if the provision actually envisaged an enlargement of his powers. . . . [B]y means of this speech, which had a popular appearance, he kept possession of the power of his sovereignty.
>
> *Haud dubium erat eam sententiam altius penetrare et arcana imperii temptari. Tiberius tamen, quasi augeretur potestas eius, disseruit. . . . favorabili in speciem oratione vim imperii tenuit.* (*Ann.* 2.36)

Any explicit increase in an emperor's power—because it is *explicit*—is actually a diminution. Accordingly Tiberius cleverly pretended that the proposal was an increase of his powers and declined it. By doing so, he actually reinforced the illusion that the emperor was not an autocrat: it is this sleight of hand that was precisely the secret of his power.[63]

While Tacitus takes dissimulation to be one of the leading political realities of his time, he does not approve of it. To the contrary, his honorable actors uniformly behave in a forthright manner. Perhaps the best example of this is provided by his encomium of his father-in-law, Agricola. Agricola's character is the antithesis of that of a Tiberius or Domitian. Some, we are told, thought that Agricola was an excessively harsh critic: a friend to the deserving but equally unpleasant to the wicked. Be that as it may, "out of his anger nothing remained hidden, so that you would not fear his silence: he thought that it was more honorable to give offense than to hate" (*ceterum ex iracundia nihil supererat secretum, ut silentium eius non timeres: honestius putabat offendere quam odisse*) (*Agr.* 22). Note that what Agricola does not dissimulate is exactly what the emperors do dissimulate: hatred and anger.

Silence is significant even at the level of style: no author has ever made more extensive and effective use of innuendo, irony, and sarcasm than Tacitus. His writing is replete with elaborate and pregnant silences, vague hints, and wicked allusions.[64] In one of many examples, he implies that Agricola did not die naturally but was murdered, without actually saying that this was the case: "the persistent rumor that his life was cut off by poison enhanced the sympathy [for his family]: I have discovered no evidence that would allow me to confirm this" (*Augebat miserationem constans rumor veneno interceptum: nobis nihil comperti, adfirmare ut ausim*) (*Agr.* 43).[65] Tacitus attempts to program his readers to be suspicious, to be on the lookout for omissions and hidden, ulterior meanings in his writing. Thus, after a particularly awful imperial atrocity, he notes that the senate responded with its usual nauseating obsequiousness. He goes on to say that this slavishness was too common for him to mention every example. Rather, he proposes to restrict himself to signally disgusting occasions:

> What is the point of recounting that offerings were decreed for the temples in response [to such murders]? Anyone who comes to know the events of this period from my writings or from the writings of other authors should take it for granted that as often as the emperor ordered exiles or murders, prayers of thanksgiving were made to the gods, and what once had been a sign of prosperity now indicated public misfortune. Even so, I will not keep silent in cases where a decree of the senate illustrates some novelty of flattery or extreme of groveling.

> *dona ob haec templis decreta quem ad finem memorabimus? quicumque casus temporum illorum nobis vel aliis auctoribus noscent, praesumptum habeant, quotiens fugas et caedes iussit princeps, totiens gratis deis actas, quaeque rerum*

secundarum olim, tum publicae cladis insignia fuisse. neque tamen silebimus si quod senatus consultum adulatione novum aut patientia postremum fuit. (*Ann.* 14.64)

So the issue of silence is emphasized in Tacitus' relationship to his sources, in his decision to talk about what others have left unrecorded, and even in his own style of writing. The theme is finally elevated to a virtual principle of his historical method. The connection between silence and anger, or oppression, provides the motivation for his practice of history and is illustrated in his accounts of earlier historians who spoke unmentionable truths and suffered the consequences. Because both are, like Tacitus, historians, and because their stories are embedded in his history, there is a reflexiveness in his account of them.

The first anecdote concerns a historian who perished unjustly during the reign of Tiberius. "The year (A.D. 25) began with the prosecution of Aulus Cremutius Cordus on a new and previously unheard of charge: praise of Brutus in his *History,* and the description of Cassius as 'the last of the Romans'" (*Ann.* 4.34). Brutus and Cassius had suffered the *damnatio memoriae,* and under Tiberius they were regarded as unmentionable. Tacitus claims that Tiberius' face was grim at the trial of the historian: a fatal sign. Nevertheless, Cordus defended himself admirably:

> Among us there has always been complete uncensored liberty to speak about those whom death has placed beyond hatred and partiality. . . . Cassius and Brutus are known by their statues—even the conqueror did not remove them. And they have their place in the historian's pages. Posterity gives everyone his due honor. If I am condemned, there will be no lack of those who will remember not only Cassius and Brutus but me as well.

> *sed maxime solutum et sine obtrectatore fuit prodere de iis, quos mors odio aut gratiae eximisset. . . . quo modo imaginibus suis noscuntur, quas ne victor quidem abolevit, sic partem memoriae apud scriptores retinent. Suum cuique decus posteritas rependit; nec deerunt, si damnatio ingruit, qui non modo Cassii et Bruti, set etiam mei meminerint.* (*Ann.* 4.35)

As this passage itself attests, Tacitus is among those who would later remember Cassius and Brutus, and Cordus as well. Cordus' claim that those who have died are beyond hatred or partiality is remarkable. For Tacitus, hatred is the preeminent quality that emperors tend to bury in silence. It is the emotion that forthright men such as Agricola do not conceal. It is also the very quality that Tacitus himself claims to eschew in his own historical writing (see below).

Cordus did not wait for a verdict but left the senate and starved himself to death. The senate ordered his books to be burned—but a few copies survived, hidden away to be republished years later. The futility of the book-burning prompts Tacitus to comment:

> For this reason one is inclined to laugh at the foolishness of those who imagine that by present despotism the remembrances of the next generation can be extinguished. To the contrary, the influence of genius, when it is repressed, only grows. Nor have alien kings and those who imitate their cruelty achieved anything but to produce shame for themselves and glory for their victims.

> *quo magis socordiam eorum inridere libet, qui praesenti potentia credunt extingui posse etiam sequentis aevi memoriam. Nam contra punitis ingeniis gliscit auctoritas, neque aliud externi reges aut qui eadem saevitia usi sunt, nisi dedecus sibi atque illis gloriam peperere.* (*Ann.* 4.35)

In the *Agricola* Tacitus tells a similar story about two historians who were his own contemporaries: Arulenus Rusticus and Herennius Senecio.

> We read that when Thrasea Paetus was praised by Arulenus Rusticus and when Helvidius Priscus was praised by Herennius Senecio, it was a capital crime, and that punishment was directed not only at the authors themselves, but against their books as well; the job was given to the public executioners of burning in the *comitium* and Forum the legacy of our noblest spirits. They doubtless thought that the voice of the Roman people, the freedom of the senate, and the conscience of mankind were destroyed in that fire; particularly because the votaries of wisdom were in addition expelled and all liberal culture exiled, in order that nowhere might anything of good report present itself to men's eyes.

> *Legimus, cum Aruleno Rustico Paetus Thrasea, Senecioni Herennio Priscus Helvidius laudati essent, capitale fuisse, neque in ipsos modo auctores, sed in libros quoque eorum saevitum, delegato triumviris ministerio ut monumenta clarissimorum ingeniorum in comitio ac foro urerentur. scilicet illo igne vocem populi Romani et libertatem senatus et conscientiam generis humani aboleri*

arbitrabantur, expulsis insuper sapientiae professoribus atque omni bona arte in exilium acta, ne quid usquam honestum occurreret. (*Agr.* 2)

It is interesting that Tacitus claims to have *read* about these two historians: from the outset, we see that condemnation of them has already failed. As in the case of Cordus, "someone will remember them, also." In each case the crime of the historian was to praise virtue. Tacitus, too, as he claims in the introduction to the *Agricola*, has taken it as his task to commemorate virtue, though emperor and times may be hostile toward it.

HISTORY: A SURVIVOR'S STORY

In commemorative historical writing everything happens as though the historian is bound by some obligation: the nature of the obligation, how and why it has been incurred, generally remains unspoken. This sense of speech as something owed is a quality that historians share with witnesses (or survivors). Tacitus is clearer than most historians about the commemorative function of his history and his relation to it. This motive is expressed in the first line of the *Agricola*, and he makes the point even more forcefully elsewhere: "I think that this is the chief duty of the history: that virtues should not be kept in silence, and that for vicious words and deeds there should be fear of posterity and infamy" (*praecipuum munus annalium reor ne virtutes sileantur utque pravis dictis factisque ex posteritate et infamia metus sit*) (*Ann.* 3.65).[66] Tacitus also explores to a remarkable degree the reasons why he feels honor-bound to speak of the past. Speech and silence are not only issues in the composition of the *Agricola*, he says, but have also had a deeper, existential significance for his own life and his choice to write history. At the end of the introduction to the *Agricola* Tacitus talks about his contemporaries and his own youth:

> For a period of fifteen years, a large portion of a person's life, many of us perished through chance incidents, the bravest by the cruelty of the emperor; a few of us, so to speak, survived not only our contemporaries but ourselves. For so many years have been removed from the middle of our lives, in which the young men among us reached old age, and old men came almost to the very edge of life—all in silence.
>
> *si per quindecim annos, grande mortalis aevi spatium, multi fortuitis casibus, promptissimus quisque saevitia principis interciderunt, pauci ut ita dixerim,*

non modo aliorum sed etiam nostri superstites sumus, exemptis e media vita tot annis, quibus iuvenes ad senectutem, senes prope ad ipsos exactae aetatis terminos per silentium venimus. (Agr. 3)

Tacitus returns to the issues of the introduction in the conclusion of the *Agricola*. The last line of the work sums up his theme:

> Whatever we have loved in Agricola, whatever we have admired, remains and will remain in the hearts of people through the endless procession of ages because of the reputation of his accomplishments. Forgetfulness has buried many of the ancients, as though they had neither reputation nor quality. Agricola will outlive death as his story is told and handed down to posterity.

quidquid ex Agricola amavimus, quidquid mirati sumus, manet mansurumque est in animis hominum, in aeternitate temporum, in fama rerum; nam multos veterum velut inglorios et ignobilis oblivio obruit: Agricola posteritati narratus et traditus superstes erit. (Agr. 46)

This concluding line alludes to the first line of the introduction to the work: "to hand down the deeds and habits of renowned men to posterity..." (*clarorum virorum facta moresque posteris tradere*) (*Agr.* 1). The reference to *survival*, however, calls to mind the concluding section of the introduction: under Domitian, many perished—including Agricola. Only a few, who were both lucky and discreet, managed to survive their friends. Tacitus was one of these.

Survival, however, came at a price. For Tacitus to live on, it was necessary for him to submerge himself in silence. The experience of those years left him with ambivalent feelings regarding his relationship to those who perished.[67] On the one hand, he recognizes himself as a collaborator in the worst excesses of the regime. The best spoke out and perished; Tacitus' survival, which he owed to his silence, is evidence of his guilt and complicity in their deaths. Through his very passivity he was a participant in Domitian's murders. As Tacitus says toward the end of the *Agricola*, Agricola was fortunate in the time of his death, for he was not required to observe or take part in the worst atrocities:

> Soon our hands dragged Helvidius to prison; the look that Mauricus and Rusticus gave shamed us; Senecio stained us with his innocent blood.

> *mox nostrae duxere Helvidium in carcerem manus; nos Maurici Rusticique visus adflixit, nos innocenti sanguine Senecio perfudit. (Agr. 45)*

At the same time, though, Tacitus is ready to excuse his own complicity. In one place, he criticizes those who did not cooperate with Domitian, choosing instead an ostentatious death. Such deaths were wasteful and self-indulgent, and accomplished nothing except to gratify a suicidal lust for glory:[68]

> Let those who are inclined to admire what is not permitted know that great men can live even under evil emperors, and that submission and moderation, if industry and energy are present, can scale the same heights of glory as those who have more frequently achieved fame by a precipitous path which brings no benefit to the state, that is, through a pretentious death.

> *sciant, quibus moris est inlicita mirari, posse etiam sub malis principibus magnos viros esse, obsequiumque ac modestiam, si industria ac vigor adsint, eo laudis escendere, quo plerique per abrupta, sed in nullum rei publicae usum, ambitiosa morte inclaruerunt. (Agr. 42)*

Such ambivalent sentiments are familiar in the modern world, particularly among the survivors of wars, concentration camps, and other catastrophic situations in which certain individuals survive their loved ones. Psychologists even have a name for the specific phenomenon: "survivor guilt."[69]

Tacitus emerged from these years of tyranny alive, but not intact: not only did he survive his contemporaries, he also survived a piece of himself. By writing history, Tacitus rehabilitates, resurrects the memory of those who died, thus satisfying the debt he owes both to them and himself. In Tacitus' narrative some part of Agricola, too, may now survive. The narrative, however, cannot make good what has perished. It is no more possible for Tacitus to become whole again than it is for Agricola to live again. In each case it is possible only to *evoke* what has been lost, not to *recover* it as though it had never been missing at all. The account of Agricola—and of that portion of the historian himself which has been lost—is like the rehabilitation of the elder Flavian: it is an account written over the sign of an erasure. It is like a history or monument: it stands in place of, but is not identical with, the life of Agricola and the lost youth of Tacitus. The writing of the *Agricola* may (for survivors) evoke the memory of what has perished. But at the same time, it confirms that those things have perished. Because history and monuments and documents of other kinds are substitutes for the past, and are not the past resurrected, they are a confirmation, or reinscription, of death, absence, and loss, not a remedy for them. There is a sense here, however, that the writing, while it cannot replace what is gone, can somehow vindicate it. What is dead is gone, to be sure; this much is implicit in the fact of its writing. Yet it is important that what is dead not perish utterly. In memory, what is dead can still live in part. It is the job of the historian, through representation, to evoke that memory.

We might say that for Tacitus, himself a survivor, it is the job of the historian to create survivals. A survival is a thing that has endured beyond, outlasted, something past. We might characterize the survival as a witness, or evidence, of death, as a kind of trace. A trace, as defined above, is a thing with a marked temporal dimension, which suggests in its enduring existence that something has perished. It is a survival.

In the introduction to the *Agricola,* Tacitus speaks of survivors, not survivals. Moreover, he claims that he is himself a survivor. Unlike the survival, the survivor is a living, conscious agency. The survival can merely suggest in a more or less vague way. The survivor can speak. Where the survival can only indicate the past, the survivor can recall it. For a survivor the traces of the past continue to exist, but in silent memory. In a sense, of course, we are all survivors: we are continually in a process of outliving our present, and the traces of our memories make us creatures who both live and have lived, who exist both now and through the past. Tacitus makes this point in asserting that he, the historian, is a survivor as well—and not merely the survivor of the reign of a cruel and oppressive emperor, or of some other external catastrophe, but of a part of himself, a part that until now had been kept only in memory and silence. He rehabilitates that "part of himself," just as he rehabilitates "a part of Agricola," by giving an account, through his history.

Tacitus sees his writing as somehow owed. So far, however, we have only been circling around the central problem of the constitution of this obligation. Tacitus does have more to say about his reasons for speaking out. His most famous remarks about his motivation are negative. He claims that "those who profess honesty must write without partiality or hatred" (*sed incorruptam fidem professis neque amore quisquam et sine odio dicendus est*) (*Hist.* 1.1) and that he intends to write "without anger or partisanship; I am far removed from the motives to do so" (*sine ira et studio, quorum causas procul habeo*) (*Ann.* 1.1). These qualities are the same qualities that fester and grow when emperors keep them in silence, and that Agricola purged from himself by giving them expression. Had Tacitus been angry and resentful, he presumably should not have written at all. There is a correlation between his distance from these qualities and his willingness and ability to speak. Tacitus here is not announcing a standard of objectivity and his own freedom from bias, as is frequently imagined; the notion that Tacitus is an utterly objective and unbiased witness is obviously laughable. Rather, he is describing the enabling motivation for writing history, or for speaking at all.[70] As he says at the beginning of the *Agricola*, in days of old "the greatest talents were led to publish an account of virtue without partisanship or ambition, but as the price of a good conscience" (*celeberrimus quisque ingenio ad prodendam virtutis memoriam sine gratia aut ambitione bonae tantum conscientiae pretio ducebatur*) (*Agr.* 1). Tyrants might burn the accounts of these splendid talents, but in vain (*Agr.* 2).

For Tacitus, history-writing should not be motivated by a contemporary political commitment but by a sense of duty to the past. Tacitus does not explain precisely how this feeling of duty is generated, though for him it is clearly internally imposed: a matter of conscience (*bona conscientia*). It is the writing of history that satisfies conscience. So the compulsion to speak comes out of the survivor's memory, out of the present experience of silence as a quality of one's own memory. Good conscience is secured by speaking out.

How can speaking out produce good conscience? Tacitus claims that representation is of itself inadequate to the larger objectives of history and to the duty that the living owe the dead. In the last chapter of the *Agricola*, he addresses himself to the wife and daughter of the great man. The history he is now concluding, Tacitus suggests, is (like other forms of representation) vain. External representations are alien from mind and memory. The essence of Agricola can be kept only through a way of life, or, to use a loaded modern term, through re-enactment; by bringing the past not just to representation, but to true consciousness:[71] "images of the face are feeble and evanescent; the shape of the mind is eternal, and you cannot hold it or show it through alien media or craft, but only by your way of life" (*simulacra vultus imbecilla ac mortalia sunt, forma mentis aeterna, quam tenere et exprimere non per alienam materiam et artem, sed tuis ipse moribus possis*) (*Agr.* 46).

Tacitus' statements about his own practices and motives for writing history suggest a profound historiographical problem: What is the motivation for telling stories about the dead? Why do people feel the need to speak of, or even remember, the past? In the *Agricola*, Tacitus provides clues as to his own more or less developed ideas, clues that might take us in a variety of different directions. We have already spoken of one standard answer: that historians speak to instruct.[72] It would also be possible to focus on the social functions of the act of storytelling, as anthropologists and others have done for years with mythology.[73] Tacitus, however, suggests a personal or, in modern terms, a psychological motivation for writing.[74] Tacitus' decision to write is motivated by a death: by the guilty sense that he was a participant in the murder and so has survived not only his friend and father-in-law, but a bit of himself as well. These same feelings lie at the heart of Primo Levi's writing. As Levi remarks in his brilliant essay on witnessing and survival, *The Drowned and the Saved*,

> We, the survivors, are not the true witnesses. This is an uncomfortable notion of which I have become conscious little by little, reading the memoirs of others and reading mine at a distance of years. We survivors are not only an exiguous but also an anomalous minority: we are those who by their prevarications or abilities or good luck did not touch bottom. Those who . . . have not returned to tell about it or have returned mute, . . . they are . . . the submerged, the complete witnesses, the ones whose depositions would have a general significance.[75]

I would not presume to equate the middle-class history of a contemporary Californian with the experiences of a survivor of Auschwitz like Levi; nevertheless, it seems to me that his remarks have a generalizable significance. Loss is the common everyday experience of time, and memory is simultaneously the evidence and solace of that loss. After his *damnatio memoriae*, Tatianus was blinded and left to live (see Chapter 4 above). He ended his life wandering blind among his erased monuments in his homeland. This experience is typical. Everyone stumbles among the detritus of their lives, remembering some things, remembering that they have forgotten others. The human world is evanescent. What is now will someday be no more; but it will leave traces of its passing in memory and in the material world. These traces subsist, as does memory, to suggest the thing that is no longer there, to call it to mind, but also to remind us of the fact that this same thing has indeed been irretrievably lost.

It is the experience of time through memory that makes us all simultaneously creatures of the past and inhabitants of the present: in this sense, we are (to use Tacitus' phrase) survivors of ourselves, and so can bear witness to what is no longer. It is through memory that the silent dead infest the living, and it is through memory that the authority of the past is internalized.[76] Certainly for Tacitus, the obligation to write history has much in common with the feelings that give rise to "mourning and melancholy" and to nostalgia.[77]

The same "sense of loss" that supports history and mourning also supports the *damnatio memoriae,* which is both an enforced and a denied nostalgia. There must be a sense that something has fallen out of representation, that it was at one time but is no longer—a sense that something has been lost. If not, then memory truly fails and with it the force of the *damnatio memoriae.* The force of the rehabilitation has much more to do with the re-enactment of the death and condemnation of Flavian than with an account of the events of 394. The survivors have always remembered Flavian, but it is only after the rehabilitation that they can "satisfy the debt of duty owed the dead" (*religiosi muneris debito,* line 33)—that is, acknowledge the irremediable fact of his loss, through the act of mourning. The writing of history, too, is motivated more by guilt and a desire to mourn than by a desire merely to evoke. The survivor is the one who remains to see that the proper rites are performed for the dead and for that part of the self which has perished, and in the end compulsively to rehearse that loss once again by writing the history.

CHAPTER 6

REHABILITATING THE TEXT

Proofreading and the Past

A METAPHOR running through the imperial letter suggests an equivalence between the rehabilitation of Flavian and the correction (*emendatio*) of texts. Most immediately the metaphor alludes to the comparability of a political rehabilitation and the practice of history, but there is more to the allusion. The elder Flavian himself wrote a history—the imperial letter mentions his *Annales*—and his two descendants who are involved in the rehabilitation, Flavian the younger and Dexter, are known to have corrected manuscripts of portions of Livy's history. This correction of manuscripts is an activity they shared with other members of the elite, and for that matter with most other readers.

For modern readers, who have been reared to expect the standardized and relatively "clean" texts of the print media, it can be difficult to appreciate just how regularly scribal culture produces texts with serious flaws, from misspellings to omissions to complete gibberish. In this environment the process of correction is a fundamental part of the act of reading. Correction—*emendatio*—was routine for anyone who read anything. There can be no question of imagining, as did Herbert Bloch, that it is a specialized activity like modern textual criticism, employed exclusively by a small intellectual elite for propagandistic purposes. At the same time, it would be a mistake to follow the trend of recent scholarship (epitomized in the writing of Alan Cameron) and to imagine that because correction is routine it must therefore be strictly functional, without any larger cultural significance.

One might begin to approach the problem of the various connotations of the practice of correction by asking why readers of the period bothered to correct at all, why they circulated their corrected manuscripts and signed their names to them.[1] These subscriptions, along with the corrections, were reproduced in subsequent copies made from the manuscripts. Certain corrections were considered more valuable and valid than others, whether because of the fame of the correctors or because of the quality and intelligence of the corrections. Some corrected copies were regarded as superior to others. In a subscription to Cicero's *De lege agraria,* for example, a certain Statilius Maximus says that he corrected his text of that work against a copy which had been in the possession of Cicero's secretary, Tiro. Gellius says that he had seen a text of Ennius, one with corrections in the hand of Lampadio (*Lampadionis manu emendatum,* 18.5.1). Donatus, following Suetonius, says that the *Aeneid* was corrected in a rough way (*Aeneid summatim emendata*) after the death of Vergil by Varius and Tucca (Donatus *Vit. Verg.* 39; Suet. *Praef.* 2.12). Jerome mentions that Cicero corrected the text of Lucretius (*Chron. Euseb. ad ann.* 94). These examples show that corrected manuscripts circulated, that the corrections and subscriptions to them were noticed, and that credit for the corrections was attributed to particular people.

The correction and annotation of errors in manuscript is bound up with the desire to recover the integrity of something that has been damaged, a desire that also supports the practice of history (see Chapter 5 above). That integrity may be associated only with the text itself or with the intentions of the author. In making such corrections the Romans evidently had the notion that the text, like a historical document, is a kind of trace, which embodies certain intentions that should be reconstructed, understood, and respected. In a scribal culture, these intentions are self-evidently fragile things, susceptible to corruption and even destruction. Authors occasionally corrected copies of their own work, and such corrections were regarded as authoritative. In a famous case, Martial addressed a friend who wanted him to furnish a text of the epigrams corrected in his own hand: "Pudens, you require me to correct my little books with my own pen and hand. Oh, how excessively you appreciate and love me, you who want to have an original of my trifles" (*Cogis me calamo manuque nostra / emendare meos, Pudens, libellos. / o quam nimium probas amasque, / qui vis archetypas habere nugas!*) (*Ep.* 7.11). Boethius corrected a copy of his own work on arithmetic (subscription to the *De arithmetica*).[2] When Augustine sent a copy of his *City of God* to a friend, he says that he too had corrected the books (*Ep.* 1A.4). So, in a very general way, the practice of *emendatio* is an entirely appropriate metaphor for the practice of history, which is also frequently conceived as being about the recovery of an originating intelligibility or integrity from the corruptions and wasting power of time.

In this chapter I will be concerned to determine the nature of the practice of *emendatio* in late antiquity and some of the more specific reasons for the use of the metaphor in the letter of rehabilitation. I will also attempt to isolate some of its larger cultural connections, particularly its association with the reconstruction of the past and with the transformation of popular attitudes toward pagan religious experience. I certainly would not argue that these are the only connotations which the practice of *emendatio* might have, any more than I would agree that there was an unlimited range of associations. Different social and cultural groups understood the practice in different ways.

THE METAPHOR

The first line of the imperial letter provides a definition of the goal of the rehabilitation and suggests a comparison of this process with the practice of history. The letter goes on to equate the rehabilitation with the correction of a text: "to defend the dignity of men renowned and eminent in the state when it has been corrupted to some extent" (*clarorum adque inlustrium in republica virorum . . . interpolatum aliquatenus adserere honorem,* lines 9–10) and "to recall the recollection of the departed to eternal fame" (*et memoriam defuncti in lucem aeternam revocare,* lines 10–11) are characterized as "seeming to be a kind of correction" (*emendatio quaedam . . . videtur,* lines 11–12).

The word *emendatio* may have a range of meanings. For example, it is regularly used to indicate a general sort of repair. On any interpretation, however, an *emendatio* is not literally the same thing as a rehabilitation. Here the word is used metaphorically, implying a comparison between the rehabilitation and some process of *emendatio*. The fact that the word is used here in an extended, figurative sense is clearly signaled in the text itself. To begin with, *emendatio* is singled out and emphasized by the structure of the sentence: this word is the predicate to everything else in the sentence. Furthermore, *emendatio* is modified and marked by the qualifying adjective *quaedam*, which is often used to soften a harsh metaphor.[3] Also, the rehabilitation is not said "to be" the equivalent of a correction, but "to seem like" (*videtur*) a correction: the two are comparable but not equivalent.

Metaphors are like silences, symbols, quotations, and other forms of allusion: they insinuate something without saying it overtly; they suggest without bringing the thing to explicit appearance. Consequently they demand comment, or at least some minimal interpretation. More specifically, a metaphor invites comparison of two things: here, a rehabilitation and a correction. So it is necessary to examine the specific force of the word *emendatio* in this context and to discern the reasons why the letter singles it out as a fitting description of the rehabilitation.

One of the more specialized, technical meanings of *emendatio* is "emendation," as in the correction of a text.[4] This interpretation of the use of the word is supported here by the description of the dignity of those whom the emperor is to protect as having been "corrupted to some degree" (*honorem interpolatum aliquatenus,* line 10). On a strictly etymological interpretation, the verb *interpolare* means to "modify by insertion," or "interrupt." In practice the word has a wider range of meaning than its derivation might suggest, being used to describe a broad range and variety of textual corruptions, and not only scribal insertions. Nevertheless, the range of its usage is much more restricted than that of *emendare,* since it almost always describes some kind of damage suffered by texts from a scribal error.[5] As in the case of *emendatio,* the letter itself draws attention to a metaphorical use of the term here, qualifying the word with a softening adverb, *aliquatenus,* "to some extent." The juxtaposition of "emendation" and "interpolation" in the same sentence is decisive: the word *emendatio* here suggests specifically the correction of manuscripts. So the imperial rehabilitation and, by extension, the practice of history, is regarded as somehow like the correction of texts.

As the letter of rehabilitation begins with an allusion to correction of texts, so it returns to this theme at its end. In the conclusion, the emperor invites the senate to "join with us in our revision [of Flavian]; approve the restoration of the remembrance of the prestige of that senator both to yourselves and to the country" (*nobiscum recognoscitis et redditam vobis et patriae senatoris eius memoriam et dignitatem probate,* lines 34–35). The word translated here as "revise" is *recognoscere.* Like *emendare,* this word has a variety of uses. It may, for example, mean in a general way "to recall." It also has the more specialized meaning of "to reread [manuscripts]." Thus, Pliny the younger couples this verb with *emendare,* speaking of "rereading and correcting books" (*Libellos recognoscere et emendare*) (*Ep.* 4.26.1). The verb *recognoscere* is used in this sense in imperial correspondence of all periods.[6] It is also so used in a contemporary subscription. In the subscription at the end of book 9 of Apuleius' *Metamorphoses,* a certain Sallustius claims that he "read and corrected" (*legi et emendavi*) the text in 395; he goes on to say that later, in 397, he revised (*recognovi*) the text. (On this and other subscriptions, see below.)

The textual metaphor may be further elaborated in the imperial letter. The allusion to "emendation" is followed by an ambiguous relative clause: "[This rehabilitation] may be regarded as a kind of correction of his fate, which is considered a preliminary judgment and the greatest [——]ment of worth" (*emendatio quaedam eius sortis videtur, quae praeiudic[ium sum]mumque [——]mentum virtutum exsistimatur,* lines 11–12). Grammatically, the antecedent of the relative "which" (*quae*) here could be either "correction" (*emendatio*) or "fate" (*sortis*). De Rossi chose the latter alternative; he has been followed by all subsequent editors. Consequently he was obliged to interpret the reference to a "preliminary judgment" (*praeiudicium*) in a negative light, and to restore a word with it that would continue this negative tone. He chose to supply a bland, generic word, as much for the sake of example and to provide the general sense he thought was required as from any certainty about the correctness of his supplement: *[detri]mentum* (see Appendix). So the clause should be understood to mean that Flavian's end is considered "a prejudicial (in the modern sense of the word) preliminary judgment and the chief diminishment of his virtues." It is the function of the imperial rehabilitation to render the final judgment and to fill out the account of Flavian's honor. On this interpretation, the force of the present tense of *exsistimatur* must be temporal: people of the present day, some thirty-five years after the event, think of Flavian's death as a disgrace, a blot on an otherwise exemplary life.

On the other hand, the word *emendatio* might be understood as the antecedent of the relative clause. On this interpretation, the present tense of *exsistimatur* should be understood as generalizing rather than temporal: the relative clause provides an approximate definition of *emendatio:* a *praeiudicium* and something else (the word has not survived entire), a *[——]mentum.*

The word *praeiudicium,* like *interpolatum,* is a technical term. It is attested with virtually no other meaning than a narrow, legal one. When a suit was lodged, a preliminary hearing might be held to determine some issue in advance of the trial: for example, it might be necessary to determine the status of one of the litigants. The preliminary judgment that issued from this action was called a *praeiudicium.* It is not necessary to follow De Rossi in imagining that the word has a negative sense. Since the preliminary decision might have an effect on the outcome of some principal suit that had been lodged, and since this decision might even make it unnecessary or impossible to try the suit, the word comes occasionally to be used with the modern, negative connotation of "prejudice" or damage.[7] Nevertheless, in Roman law the idea of the "preliminary verdict" is neutral, with no necessary positive or negative connotation.

No matter what the antecedent of the relative clause, the word is used here in some extended, metaphorical sense: neither the emperor's "correction" nor Flavian's fate is literally a "preliminary verdict." The verb of the relative clause, *exsistimatur,* confirms this figurative use: it (Flavian's fate or the emperor's emendation) *is considered to be* a preliminary judgment. In part, the "preliminary judgment" may well allude to Flavian's term as "circuit judge" (*vicarius*) in Africa. The imperial letter refers favorably to Flavian's judicial eminence at various places: so he is honored for his legal acumen and virtue (see lines 4 and 22–24; cf. Chapter 2 above). At the same time, the procedure of a "preliminary judgment" (taken in an extended, neutral sense) describes the imperial "correction" quite adequately, and puts a nice twist on it: as Flavian adjudged and settled the problems of provincials, so the emperor adjudges and settles the life of Flavian. As the historian judges and settles the past, so the corrector corrects the text. On this interpretation of the relative clause, the letter couples Flavian's reputation as a judge with the imperial rehabilitation, with the theme of historiography, and with the practice of textual correction.

If the imperial "correction" is taken as the subject of the relative clause, then De Rossi's restoration, *[detri]mentum,* must be discarded. To the contrary, a noun describing some *improvement* to Flavian's condition should be restored. Given the proximity of *emendatio* and *praeiudicium,* the restoration might have textual or legal overtones. Restoration here is difficult: the range of possibility is too great to allow for a really persuasive resolution of the word. A host of words will fit the space and traces of *[———]mentum.* A bland and generic restoration, which might be proposed merely for the sake of example, would be something like "improvement" (say, *[aug]mentum* or *[purga]mentum*). More interesting would be the restoration I have suggested: *[supple]mentum.* The verb *supplere* was used in antiquity to mean "to complete or supplement an unfinished literary work."[8] So the rehabilitation would be the "completion" or literary "fulfillment" of Flavian's virtues, which, like those of his son, were only half full, owing to his disgrace. It would be a mistake to put too much weight on this or any restoration: readers should keep in mind that the rehabilitating "supplement" of the emperor here is only my modern editorial supplement.

The invocation of *emendatio* parallels the process of the rehabilitation itself. Is not the correction of a text much like the rehabilitation of a person? At the same time, it is a provocative metaphor for the writing of history. The elder Flavian was a historian, and his eminence is mentioned in the imperial letter (lines 19–20) as one of the motives for his rehabilitation. The rehabilitation itself can be compared to the writing of history (see Chapter 5 above).

The idea of correcting manuscripts is well suited for use as a metaphor for dealing with the past. Alan Cameron has kindly drawn my attention to an analogous use of this metaphor of textual "correction" in the third *Relatio* of Symmachus. Symmachus here argues against following a precedent set by the emperor Constantius. The policy was flawed, and Constantius himself would never have followed it had it been possible for him to learn from the example of some earlier emperor:

The slip of a predecessor corrects one who follows, and from the criticism of an earlier instance arises the correction.

corrigit enim sequentem lapsus prioris et de reprehensione antecedentis exempli nascitur emendatio. (Relatio 3.6)

As in the letter rehabilitating the elder Flavian, the sentence is summed up by the word *emendatio*. Other vocabulary in the sentence also suggests the processes of a specifically textual correction: *corrigit* and *lapsus*. Symmachus begins with a felicitous reversal of the commonplace idea about correction: it is not only that errors are to be corrected; they also serve to correct those who encounter them. It is only with the apprehension and criticism of a mistake that the possibility of correction comes into being, and this apprehension is not only an improvement of the error, but an improvement of the person making the correction. The idea supporting the metaphor here is even more traditional than in the letter of rehabilitation: it is not that the past is to be "fixed"; rather, it is exemplary. Whether the example is good or bad, those in the present can learn from it.

There is still another aspect to the metaphor of emendation in Flavian's rehabilitation. Flavian the younger and Dexter, the two descendants of Flavian who participated in the erection of the inscription recording his rehabilitation, are not known to have been historians themselves.[9] Both, however, *are* known to have participated in that general activity of most ancient readers: they were correctors of the text of one of the greatest of all Roman historians, Livy.

THE CORRECTION OF LIVY

An author of the Augustan period, Livy wrote a history of Rome, from its beginnings down to his own day. The preserved title of the work is *Ab urbe condita (From the Foundation of the City)*.[10] A sprawling work, filling 142 books, Livy's history was far too voluminous to be contained in a single scroll, or, for that matter, by the fourth or fifth century, in a single codex. Because of its unwieldiness, the history was divided into smaller sections. This division was only a matter of convenience for those who copied the history, though it might be argued that Livy's tendency to organize his history in shorter groups of books made the compartmentalization of his history by later scribes easier.[11] These groups of ten and five books, so-called decades and pentads, constitute the basic units in which the later tradition of Livy's history is preserved. The first, third, and fourth decades have survived, along with the first half of the fifth decade. Each of these units has come down to modern times through a separate manuscript tradition.[12]

In one of his letters Symmachus mentions that he has a copy of the entire text of Livy's history. He had evidently promised a copy of the text to one of his friends, a certain Valerianus. So he writes in a letter dating perhaps to 401 that "the gift of the complete works of Livy which I have promised is even now delayed owing to the diligence of correction" (*munus totius Liviani operis quod spopondi etiam nunc diligentia emendationis moratur*) (*Ep.* 9.13).[13] Symmachus writes another, comparable letter to Ausonius, accompanying a copy of Pliny's *Natural History* which he sends as a present: "in these books the scribe, who is careless of accuracy, will not please your lavish learning. But the negligence of the correction will not be to my discredit. I have preferred to find approval with you because of the promptness of my gift, rather than because of [the accuracy of the correction, which is owing to] someone else's labor" (*in quis [libellis] opulentae eruditioni tuae neglegens veritatis librarius displicebit. sed mihi fraudi non erit incuria emendationis. malui enim tibi probari mei muneris celeritate, quam alieni operis examine*) (*Ep.* 1.24).

As these two citations show, correction was regarded by Symmachus as a procedure that should ideally be applied to every manuscript after it had been copied, and one that he might have been expected to carry out (though he did not scruple to ignore the procedure on occasion in the interests of time). Symmachus did not necessarily correct his own books, any more than he would have copied them with his own hand. It is significant, then, that in a famous series of subscriptions appended at the ends of the books of the first decade of Livy, several friends of the orator sign their names as correctors of the text.[14] One of these occurs at the end of each of the first nine books. In it, a certain Tascius Victorianus says that he has made the corrections on the behalf of the Symmachi: "I, the noble Victorianus, corrected (this text) for the lordly family of the Symmachi"; *Victorianus, v(ir) c(larissimus), emendabam dominis Symmachis.*

In his subscription, Victorianus claims to be a gentleman of senatorial rank, a *vir clarissimus*. Nothing is known of any of his public activities or of his family.[15] Consequently some have thought, doubtless rightly, that he was a grammarian who enjoyed his promotion to the clarissimate as an acknowledgment of his learning and of his special services to prominent families such as the Symmachi.[16] He is known to have rendered comparable services to the family of Flavian. A friend of Sidonius Apollinaris had presumably asked for a copy of a translation of Philostratos' *Life of Apollonios of Tyana*. Sidonius responded that "as you had requested, I have sent the biography of Apollonios the Pythagorean; not as Flavian the elder wrote it out from the text of Philostratos, but as Tascius Victorianus wrote it from the raw draft of Nicomachus; in my hurry to oblige, the confused, precipitate, and rustic business of transcribing it resulted in a hasty copy" (*Apollonii Pythagoricii vitam, non ut Nicomachus Senior e Philostrati, sed ut Tascius Victorianus e Nicomachi schedio exscripsit quia iusseras, misi; quam, dum parere festino, celeriter eiecit in tumultuarium exemplar turbida et praeceps et Opica translatio*) (Sidonius Apollinaris, *Ep.* 8.3.1).

What precisely Sidonius means to say about the relationship between the texts of Philostratos, Flavian, and Victorianus is not clear. Some, arguing that *exscripsit* here means merely "to copy," believe that this passage shows that Flavian copied out the Greek text of the *Life of Apollonios*, and that this text was in turn copied by Victorianus.[17] Most have found it difficult to believe, however, that Flavian would have copied out eight books of Greek.[18] Of course, it would also be difficult to believe that many of the wealthiest and most important men in the late empire took the time to correct manuscripts of literary authors, and took pride in this labor, or that they spent their free time practicing calligraphy, were there not substantial evidence proving that they did so. Such activities may have been more or less routine for the elite in the later empire, but from a more general historical perspective they seem remarkable and odd: they will be discussed further below. Even so, there is no indication that men of such high status spent their days in the common activity of scribes, copying out texts. Furthermore, the use of the word *schedium* to describe Flavian's work tells against it being only a copy of Philostratos. Consequently most scholars follow Mommsen, who proposed that Flavian had written a rough translation of *The Life of Apollonios* and that Victorianus polished this translation.[19]

The word *schedium* may be used to refer to a piece of writing in a modest or deprecating way: as "notes" or "jottings." More important, though, the word is used by Sidonius to refer to the odd bits of writing from which he compiled the ninth book of his letters: "When I came home, working as a copyist I immediately and hurriedly wrote out all of my jottings which lay about in disorder on crumbling and worn-out papers" (*cum domum veni, si quod schedium temere iacens chartulis putribus ac veternosis continebatur, raptim coactimque translator festinus exscripsi*) (Sid. *Ep.* 9.16.2). The word he uses here to describe the transfer of his writings from notes to finished manuscript is *exscribere*. This word is frequently used to describe the activity of copying; here, though, it refers not to the mechanical copying of a scribe, but to the copying and redrafting that an author does in producing the finished version of a work. This meaning would well suit Victorianus' dealings with the "notes" of Flavian. Certainly this word would not suit a scribal transcription. As for Flavian's relationship with the text of Philostratos, *exscribere* can also have the meaning "to translate"; or even "to render," that is, to translate in a freer and more literary manner. Thus Sidonius, in praising a translation of Origen, says that it makes even the greatest renditions of Greek authors look poor, so that by contrast one would have said that even Cicero did not "translate according to the standards of idiomatic and proper Latin" (*in usum regulamque Romani sermonis exscripserint*) (*Ep.* 2.9.5). *Exscribo,* then, is used in two senses in Sidonius' letter concerning the *Life of Apollonios*. That is the point of the contrast of the two clauses: "not *in the manner* that Flavian wrote it out . . . but *in the manner* that Victorianus did" (*non ut . . . sed ut*).[20]

On balance, it seems likely that Sidonius here refers to a Latin translation of Philostratos' *Life of Apollonios of Tyana* which in turn had been polished and organized by Victorianus. The fact that Sidonius mentions this detail in his correspondence is itself tantalizing. Sidonius lived in the latter half of the fifth century, mostly in the south of France, though he also spent a great deal of time in the city of Rome. There is no indication in his letter as to how he came by his information about Flavian and Victorianus, nor is it clear what or how he expects his correspondent to know about these two. Clearly Sidonius has in his possession a copy of Philostratos, probably a Latin version translated by Flavian. Some have supposed that Sidonius had somehow gotten possession of the book collection of the Nicomachi,[21] and that Sidonius knows two translations of the text: a rough version by Flavian and a more polished rendering by Victorianus. More likely, however, his statement derives from a note appended to Sidonius' copy of the translation, more or less like a subscription, in which Victorianus described his editing (and, if Mommsen is right, editing here is not too strong a word) of Flavian's text.[22]

The grammarian Victorianus, then, seems to have been a kind of secretary or literary assistant to both Symmachus and Flavian. Or should we imagine that Victorianus worked mainly for Symmachus, and that he was detailed to "polish" Flavian's "jottings" after his death? In any event, the overlap here is suggestive. Victorianus may have been only a librarian or perhaps a glorified secretary; his employment by both Symmachus and Flavian shows that there was some communication between them about their literary activities.

Flavian, in his capacities as historian and *pontifex maior,* may well have been a reader of Livy (see Chapter 5 above): if he was still alive when Symmachus first acquired the text of Livy and had it corrected, Flavian might have borrowed or have had copied parts of the book. But perhaps Symmachus did not acquire his text of Livy until after his friend's death: there is no indication that the elder Flavian knew of Symmachus' text of Livy or had any hand in the correction of it. There is evidence, however, that his heirs did. Flavian the younger and Dexter, precisely the two descendants of Flavian who are mentioned on the rehabilitation, are known to have corrected books of Livy, books that ultimately derived from Symmachus' manuscript, already corrected by Victorianus. They describe their corrections in a series of subscriptions which, like those of Victorianus, are appended to the books of the first decade of the history.

The subscriptions of Flavian the younger are found after the text of three different books of the first decade: 6, 7, and 8. Each of the subscriptions is slightly different from the others. The subscription to book 6 is the simplest of the three: "I, the noble Nicomachus Flavianus, thrice prefect of the city, corrected (the text of this book)"; *Nicomachus Flavianus, v(ir) c(larissimus), ter praef(ectus) urb(i) emendavi.* The other two subscriptions specify the place where the younger Flavian undertook his corrections. The subscription to book 7 mentions Enna, in Sicily: "I, the noble Nicomachus Flavianus, thrice prefect of the city, corrected (the text of this book) at Enna"; *emendavi Nicomachus Flavianus, v(ir) c(larissimus), ter praef(ectus) urb(i) apud Hennam.* The subscription to book 8 mentions "Thermae," evidently some spa or hot springs, located perhaps, like Enna, somewhere in Sicily: "I, the noble Nicomachus Flavianus, thrice prefect of the city, corrected (the text of this book) at Thermae"; *emendavi Nicomachus Flavianus, v(ir) c(larissimus), ter praef(ectus) urb(i) apud T(h)erm(as).*[23]

The period of the younger Flavian's activity correcting his copy of Livy can be approximately dated by his description of himself as "thrice prefect of the city." This claim is disingenuous, for he held the position legally no more than two times: his first term in the office coincided with the usurpation of

394, and was later disallowed by Theodosius the Great. His last tenure of the office (his second legal term and third overall) probably dates to 408, or at least to sometime after 402 (see Chapter 2 above). Furthermore, Flavian the younger does not mention his term as praetorian prefect in 431: a supreme honor for a Roman senator, one that he can scarcely be imagined to have omitted had he already held it. So, conservatively, he read and corrected the first decade of Livy sometime between 402 and 431. His activities, then, are later than Symmachus' letter mentioning "the correction of the entire works of Livy." The reference to Enna might be taken to confirm that the subscriptions date soon after 408: these were troubled times for the western empire. Rome itself was sacked, and Italy was repeatedly ravaged by the invading army of the Visigoths. It is known that the family of the younger Flavian had an estate somewhere in Sicily (see Symm. *Ep.* 4.71 and Chapter 2 above). Perhaps this was at Enna. Flavian the younger would not have been the only Roman senator who withdrew from the political life of the city for the relative safety and tranquillity of some country property in Sicily at this time.[24]

Flavian the younger's son Dexter, the same who supervised the erection of the statue base bearing the imperial letter of rehabilitation, also took part in the correction of the text of Livy. Subscriptions in his name are found at the ends of three books from the first decade: 3, 4, and 5. The subscriptions to books 3 and 4 are identical and simple: "I, the noble Nicomachus Dexter, corrected (the text of this book)"; *Nicomachus Dexter, v(ir) c(larissimus), emendavi*. The subscription to book 5 is more elaborate and interesting, providing some specification of what the process of *emendatio* involved: "I, the noble Nicomachus Dexter, corrected (the text of this book) against the copy of my relative Clementianus"; *Nicomachus Dexter, v(ir) c(larissimus), emendavi ad exemplum parentis mei Clementiani*.[25] The date of Dexter's correction of his books of Livy is even less certain than that of his father's. Since he does not mention his term as urban prefect in his subscriptions, he must have made the corrections before his term in that office. His time as urban prefect can itself be dated only to sometime before the erection of the inscription rehabilitating his grandfather in 431.

The fact that the subscriptions of Flavian the younger and Dexter have been transmitted together with those of Victorianus may be taken as proof that the manuscript which the Nicomachi corrected was itself copied from the text of Symmachus, which had already been once corrected by Victorianus. So, when Dexter says that he "made his corrections against the copy of his relative, Clementianus," he is not claiming to have made his corrections by comparing his manuscript with its exemplar; rather, he has taken the trouble to compare the readings of his text to those of an independent authority—certainly not an unparalleled procedure in antiquity.[26] The subscriptions of Flavian the younger and Dexter show only that they were reading a text already corrected at the behest of Symmachus, not that they were themselves cooperating as helpers in the lengthy project he had assigned Victorianus.

The word *emendatio* in the first line of the letter of rehabilitation alludes to the process of correcting texts. It might be taken to refer more specifically to the corrections to the text of Livy made by the Nicomachi. If so, it would be necessary to imagine that their interest in the text of Livy either dates to or continues into the years immediately before the rehabilitation. It is also possible (and indeed likely) that the younger Flavian and Dexter made corrections to other manuscripts as well, perhaps including other books of Livy, of which no trace has survived. In either case the reference to "emendation" in the rehabilitation should be construed not only as a nod to the family's attested activities and interests, but also in a more general way: the correction of manuscripts was an interest of the senatorial elite in late antiquity, a manifestation of cultural and social prestige.

The correction of manuscripts continues as long as manuscripts are read. Elite interest in the correction of texts, such as is displayed by Symmachus and the Nicomachi, is in evidence down into the sixth century. The habit can be shown to continue even within these same noble families. In one famous case, which dates to the later fifth century, the great-grandson of the orator Symmachus (who was also related to the Nicomachi by the marriage of his grandfather to the daughter of the younger Flavian)[27] corrected the text of Macrobius' commentary on Cicero's *Somnium Scipionis*. Macrobius was also the author of the *Saturnalia,* in which the orator Symmachus and Flavian the elder were leading characters. In his subscription he says that "I, the noble Aurelius Memmius Symmachus, corrected and punctuated my copy at Ravenna with the noble Macrobius Plotinus Eudoxius" (*Aurelius Memmius Symmachus v.c. emendabam vel distinguebam meum Ravennae cum Macrobio Plotino Eudoxio v.c.*). His collaborator here, Macrobius Plotinus Eudoxius, was doubtless some relation of the author.[28]

THE MEANING OF *EMENDATIO*

"A rehabilitation is like a correction, so to speak." The meaning of the metaphor may seem at first glance simple and obvious to a modern scholar. The connotations of *emendatio,* though, even when used in this relatively restricted textual sense, require some examination. Modern textual criticism, despite the common vocabulary it shares with ancient textual criticism, is a development of the past two hundred years.[29] The basic, determinative goal of modern textual criticism—the establishment of a homogeneous edition (i.e. identical multiple copies) of a text that will be circulated and serve as a standard for all readers—is impractical and unimaginable without the modern reproductive technology of the printing press. Contemporary methods for realizing such a text—viz., the composition of a systematic recension, the collation and categorization of extant manuscripts, and the use of considered and argued conjectural emendation to correct passages where the mechanical collation of manuscripts does not produce an acceptable reading—is irrelevant, or at best is relevant only with extensive qualifications, to the activities of Flavian the younger and Dexter. To understand the metaphor in the imperial letter of rehabilitation, we need to look at the meaning of ancient *emendatio* more closely. As it happens, specific information about the interactions of these Nicomachi with the text of Livy has been isolated.[30]

A modern systematic recension shows that the manuscript tradition of the first decade of Livy may be divided into two broad classes. The first class is represented by only one manuscript, a very ancient codex commonly cited as V (Verona XL [38] = *CLA* 4.499). It contains a palimpsest of parts of books 3–6 of Livy's history, written in uncial script, dating to the early part of the fifth century A.D. Gregory's *Moralia* was written over the text of Livy in the early part of the eighth century. This manuscript is often taken to represent the state of Livy's text in the late antique world—up to the time of Symmachus and Flavian. The second class is represented by all of the numerous manuscripts of Livy's first decade that have been transmitted through medieval cathedrals and monasteries, all of which probably go back to a common archetype: the corrected text of Victorianus, Flavian the younger, and Dexter.[31] This hypothetical exemplar is commonly designated N, for the "Nicomachean recension." To describe what the Nicomachi did as a "recension" is an anachronism or an overstatement or both. In only one case do the correctors specify that they have consulted a manuscript other than the original from which their text was copied: in the subscription to book 5, Dexter notes that he checked his corrections against the manuscript of his relative Clementianus. It should be said, rather, that this class of manuscripts of the first decade of Livy derives ultimately from the corrected manuscript of the Nicomachi.

As the manuscripts preserved in the medieval tradition derive from the text of the Nicomachi, some traces of the corrections made by the younger

Flavian and Dexter to Livy's text may be expected to have survived in them. By using these, it may be possible to elaborate the specific kinds of procedures meant by the term *emendatio*. J. E. G. Zetzel has made an attempt to define the practices of the subscribers of Livy in precisely this way.[32] I will review his arguments and conclusions briefly.

One important point is provided by the format of the subscriptions themselves. The subscriptions are written at the ends of the various books of Livy. The lettering that marks the end of the book (the colophon) normally contains in addition to these subscriptions the author's name (*Titi Livi*), the title of the work (*Ab urbe condita*), and a notice that one book has ended and another begins (e.g. *explicit liber, incipit liber*). As Zetzel notes, the subscriptions of the correctors must have originally been sandwiched between the lines of the text that was being corrected, rather than written continuously, as an independent paragraph.[33] So the subscription at the end of book 7 would have been laid out in the following way:

emendavi Nicomachus Flavianus
TITI LIVI
vc ter praef. urbis apud Hennam
AB URBE CONDITA
Victorianus vc emendabam domnis Symmachis
EXPLICIT LIBER VII INCIPIT LIBER VIII

The fact that the subscriptions were originally divided in this way, rather than written in one continuous unit, implies that they have been inserted into a preexisting manuscript. So Victorianus, Flavian the younger, and Dexter apparently did not copy out a new text of Livy as part of their corrections; rather, they inserted their corrections over erasures, between the lines, and in the margins of an existing manuscript. It should not be imagined that the correctors here are attempting to create a new, "clean" manuscript as a modern textual critic would.

One manuscript, the famous tenth-century Medicean Livy commonly designated M (Laur. 63.19), probably provides the best witness for the fully corrected text of the Nicomachean Livy.[34] The text of Livy contains, as do many other ancient texts, a certain number of "doublets," that is, variant readings imbedded side by side in the text, of which only one can be correct.[35] Such doublets are produced by scribal correction and conjecture at all periods of transmission, ancient and medieval. The text of M, however, in several places preserves an unusual form of doublet, which in all likelihood was produced not in the medieval period but in late antiquity.[36] This doublet is signaled by the abbreviation *i.a.* (*in alio*); that is to say, "in another (manuscript)." So, for example, at Livy 4.13.6 the author must have written "Agrippa Menenius was assigned to him as a colleague" (*collega additur ei Agrippa Menenius*). The text of M at this place reads "Agrippa in another manuscript Manilius [M]enenius was given to him as a colleague" (*collega additur ei Agrippa i.a. Manilius ⟨M⟩enenius*). No doubt scribes often corrected their texts through their own commonsense conjectures. Here, however, the alternative readings are not the product of conjecture but of collation, of comparison with the passage in a different manuscript—that is, a manuscript other than the immediate exemplar. There is no indication that this collation was in any way systematic, as would be that of a modern stemmatic recension. There is not even a way of determining how many manuscripts were examined. As we have already seen, Dexter claimed in the subscription to book 5 to have corrected his copy of Livy with reference to an independent copy, that of his relative Clementianus. While these doublets are almost certainly ancient, they need not have been produced by Flavian the younger or by Dexter. Nevertheless, they do provide some sense of how alternative readings deriving from another manuscript might have been entered in the text, and they also demonstrate that books other than 5 were at some point proofed against an independent copy.

The way in which the doublets appear in the Medicean Livy also provides a clue as to the nature of the manuscript that emerged from the "Nicomachean recension." In these cases the reading of the manuscript was unchanged. The variant was introduced in addition to the base reading, perhaps as a marginal note, and there was evidently no attempt to select and present one of the readings as the correct one.

Another feature of the Nicomachean recension may have been the insertion of annotations. The Medicean Livy includes quite a number of these. Most cannot be dated with any confidence. One, however, almost surely goes back to late antiquity: at 8.15 Livy discusses how the Vestal Minucia is buried alive. The annotator discusses this practice, and concludes that he is amazed "that when he (Livy) says she was buried, he does not mention that this was mandated by the Sybilline books, as I recall that I myself have read in the poetry of precisely that period, cited in Phlegon" (*miror autem, cum defossam indicat, omississe illum ex libris Sibillinis hoc esse praeceptum, ut legisse me in ipsis apud Flegontem temporis istius versibus recolo*).[37] Phlegon of Tralles, who wrote in Greek, was a historian of the time of Hadrian. Phlegon's work was certainly known in late antiquity: in fact, the only references to him in

Latin literature are to be found in the *Historia Augusta* and Jerome, both of which are roughly contemporary with the rehabilitation.[38] The interests and knowledge that are betrayed by this note are entirely consistent with what we know of Flavian and his family—and, for that matter, with the themes of the rehabilitation. The author, for example, can read Greek, and he is interested in historical writing. Furthermore, the interest in the Vestal Virgins is appropriate for a member of the pontifical college: it will be recalled that Flavian's friend Symmachus was interested in the ancient precedents for burying Vestals alive, and even went so far as to propose reviving the custom in his own day (Symm. *Epp.* 9.147 and 148). Praetextatus' solicitousness prompted the Vestals to grant him the unexampled honor of a statue (see Chapter 3 above). Pagan interest in the cult of the Sibyl was also high in the late fourth and early fifth centuries, as was Christian hostility to it. In 407 Stilicho had the Sibylline books burned.[39]

The correction of Livy by the younger Flavian and Dexter is far from the only such activity known in late antiquity. There is a substantial corpus of subscriptions to other works as well, including legal texts and Christian and secular authors. The subscriptions to secular authors have been rather thoroughly collected and discussed;[40] the subscriptions to Christian authors and legal texts, though numerous and important, remain to be assembled and edited.[41] The bulk of these subscriptions date from the end of the fourth century on. This surge in the number of subscriptions, however, is probably an accident of preservation, owing to radical changes in the method of book production at this time: namely, the introduction of the codex and of uncial letter forms.[42] They are not the product of some imagined innovation in the practice of correcting manuscripts. The practice of correcting and subscribing texts has a history that goes back before this time, and many subscriptions to legal texts are known before this period.[43] There is also one earlier subscription to a literary text. The remarkable note to Cicero's speech *De lege agraria* dates to some time in the second century A.D. Here a certain Statilius Maximus claims to have corrected a copy of Cicero's speech against no fewer than six other manuscripts, including one that he claimed was actually (or had been copied from) the personal copy of Cicero's secretary, Tiro: "I, Statilius Maximus, again corrected [this manuscript] against a copy of Tiro's, one of Laecanianus, one of Domitius, and three other old exemplars. An extraordinary speech" (*Statilius Maximus rursum emendavi ad Tironem et Laecanianum et Domitium et alios veteres III. oratio eximia*).[44]

The preserved subscriptions must represent only a small fraction of the corrections made by readers on their manuscripts in late antiquity or, for that matter, at all times. In many cases readers will have made their corrections without adding a subscription. Even when subscriptions were made, their survival would depend on the later circulation of the manuscript. Most subscriptions, like those of the first decade of Livy, are known only from later copies of the manuscript. When the corrected version of the text was copied, so were the subscriptions to it. If the corrected manuscript was not copied, then the record of the subscriptions will have been lost. Even if the corrected manuscript was copied, the subscriptions originally attached to it need not have been.

As in the case of the Nicomachean subscriptions to Livy, subscriptions were as a rule written in the colophon following the text emended, sandwiched between the notices of the end of one work (the *explicit*) and the beginning of the next (the *incipit*). The language used in the subscriptions to describe the activities of the correctors is consistent, practically formulaic. The consistency of the language and presentation may be taken to suggest some common ground among the various subscribers.[45] The same vocabulary that is found in Flavian's rehabilitation also occurs frequently in the subscriptions. Most often subscribers claim to have "emended" the text (*emendavi*). They may also say that they have "reread and corrected" the text (*recognovi*). A variety of other words are used as well, some quite specific and informative, others frustratingly vague. Thus, subscribers "annotate" (*adnotavi*), "punctuate" (*distinxi*), "correct" (*correxi*), or "review" (*recensui*—this word does not mean to systematically compare available manuscripts, as does its English cognate "recension" for a modern critic). On the other hand, subscribers may simply say that they have "read" or "reread" (*legi* or *relegi*), or "written" (*scripsi, descripsi*).[46]

Correction of a text might (but need not) involve comparison of it with another, independent copy, as Dexter corrected his copy of Livy against that of his relative Clementianus. For instance, a certain orator named Felix corrected his copy of Martianus Capella "from the most corrupt copies" (*ex emendosissimis exemplaribus emendabam*);[47] a certain Dracontius corrected his copy of the *Declamations* attributed to Quintilian against the manuscript of his brother, Hierius (*descripsi et emendavi . . . de codice fratris Hieri*).[48] The most extensive use of collation is attested by Statilius Maximus' subscription to Cicero, quoted above: he claims to have used no fewer than six manuscripts in correcting his text. In a few cases, subscribers mention that they have not used a copy in making their corrections. So a soldier named Sabinus who corrected a copy of Persius at Barcelona says that he has tried to make his correction without its exemplar (*temptavi emendare sine antigrapho meum*).[49]

Such qualifications, however, serve only to confirm that correction was frequently done with appeal to another copy of the text.

In attempting to reconstruct what these ancient correctors were attempting to do, it would be enlightening to examine the autograph copy of a corrected and subscribed manuscript. Such things are unfortunately rare. The famous fifth (?) century Medicean text of Vergil (Laur. 39.1 + Vat. lat. 3225 fol. 76 = CLA 1, p. 5; 3.96) contains the lengthy (and, in part, metrical) subscription of Asterius, consul in 494. Although this subscription has been separately added to the completed manuscript, it is not certain whether or not it is an actual autograph or a scribal copy of the autograph.[50]

One manuscript has survived that certainly contains an autograph subscription: the subscriptions of Caecilius in the text of Fronto's letters originally from Bobbio (Ambros. E.147 suppl. + Vat. lat. 5750 = CLA 3, p. 19 + CLA 1.27). These subscriptions appear frequently throughout the collection, and in different forms.[51] The accompanying texts provide many examples of the subscriber's activity. In general these modifications have the same characteristics as those of the Nicomachean text of Livy: marginal annotations, variant readings, and corrections are included. The relationship between corrections and variant readings is especially interesting. In some cases, Caecilius has merely added a marginal or interlinear note to the effect that a different reading shows up in another manuscript; in other cases, he has actually erased a word and replaced it with another. In many cases it is clear that both derive from collation, rather than conjecture. The reason for the difference in presentation is not immediately obvious. Zetzel's tentative explanation is surely best: corrections derive from the immediate collation of the manuscript with its exemplar, while variant readings derive from other manuscripts.[52]

The picture that emerges from a consideration of this corpus of subscriptions generally confirms the reconstruction of the practices of the younger Flavian and Dexter which has been sketched above. In some cases (as, for example, Felix's corrections to Martianus Capella), correction may have been a more rigorous and "scholarly" process.[53] As a rule, however, the process was more perfunctory, more like modern proofreading. Corrections may occasionally have been made by conjecture, particularly of passages in which corruption and remedy is simple and obvious. Corrections to texts were also frequently produced with some reference to another manuscript: either by comparing the manuscript with the text from which it was made (its exemplar) or by comparing it with an independent copy. The unusual subscriptions to Persius' *Satires* give some indications of what the optimal conditions for correction would have been, through the various qualifications that the subscriber provides concerning his work with the text. In one of his subscriptions he says that he "tried to correct his manuscript without the exemplar," showing that it was at least desirable to compare the text with the manuscript from which it was copied.[54] Similarly, in a subscription to Vegetius it is also claimed that the corrections were undertaken without even the exemplar of the text in hand. Corrupt passages may have been erased and corrections written over them, or corrections may have been added in supplementary notes and commentary, written in whatever space was available on the manuscript.

As is clearest in Caecilius' text of Fronto, the goals and practices of the late antique corrector seem to have been different from those of the modern textual critic. The purpose of correction was not to produce a unified text, purged of all errors to the extent possible, and approximating the original words of the author, as it is in modern textual criticism. Instead, variants, notes, and conjecture jostled side by side, without discrimination. As Zetzel concludes, "We have no reason to believe that Caecilius or any other corrector felt that only one reading in any passage was true: more than one was transmitted, and all were worthy of thought."[55]

THE SOCIOLOGY OF THE SUBSCRIPTIONS

The notes that Flavian the younger and Dexter attached to their copies of Livy are probably the most famous of all late antique subscriptions, in part because we are relatively well informed about their activities, but mostly because of the high status and prominence of the Nicomachi and Symmachi in the historiography of the period. In attempting to understand the significance of the practice of correction in late antiquity, it is necessary to have some regard for the social context in which it took place.

The correction of manuscripts was part of any reading in a scribal culture, something that anyone who read a manuscript would have done the first time (or even every time) that they read a given manuscript. The activity was general and routine among the literate population, and it was by no means restricted to the political elite. The fact that the correction of manuscripts was a routine part of reading, however, does not mean that the process had no other significance; nor does the fact that the process was common to the whole literate population mean that the cultural associations of this correction must have been the same from one social group to the next. For a student, correction will have been something done as part of school exercises;

for a scribe or a grammarian, such as Tascius Victorianus, as part of his livelihood; for a senator, such as Flavian the younger, it was a cultural activity. Consequently it is necessary to have some sensitivity to the various statuses of the subscribers.

In three cases, subscriptions seem to have been made by students.[56] A certain Crispus Sallustius says that he corrected the text of Apuleius as part of a rhetorical exercise: "I read and corrected this text at Rome, fortunate, in the consulships of the noble Olibrius and Probinus, arguing [or "doing rhetorical exercises"] in the Forum of Mars with the orator Endechelius; again in Constantinople I collated the text, in the consulships of Caesarius and Atticus"; *ego Sallustius legi et emendavi Romae felix Olibrio et Probino, v(iris) c(larissimis) cons(ulibus) [395], in foro Martis controversiam declamans oratori Endechelio; rursus Constantinopoli recognovi Caesario et Attico cons(ulibus) [397]*.[57] The precise significance of the phrase *controversiam declamans* is difficult to determine. Perhaps Sallustius means that he read the manuscript back to another who made corrections; more likely it is a metonymy for "in the course of education." In another, more straightforward case, a student by the name of Niceus corrected a text of Juvenal in the school of Servius: "I Niceus read and emended the copy at Rome, with the teacher [grammarian] Servius" (*Legi ego Niceus Romae apud Servium magistrum et emendavi*).[58] The corrector whose name has survived attached to the text of Martial, Torquatus Gennadius, is very likely another student.[59]

Professionals—grammarians, instructors, and orators—are also known to have made corrections to texts. A certain Felix appears as corrector in a subscription to the text of Martianus Capella. He says that he made his corrections "with the assistance of Deuterius, a rhetorician and my student, in Rome near the Capena gate" (*emendabam contra legente Deuterio scholastico discipulo meo Romae ad portam Capenam*).[60] This same Felix assisted Vettius Agorius Basilius Mavortius with his correction of Horace (see below).

In some cases it is stated that corrections were made with the assistance of a grammarian. The form of this assistance may have been some advice from the professional: perhaps he simply "read the text back" with the owner (*contra legente*). Or again, the professional may have furnished the exemplar from which the copy was made and against which it was corrected.[61] A certain Dracontius claims in his subscription to the *Declamations* attributed to Quintilian that he "read and emended (this text) with my friend (H)ierius, the incomparable orator (?) of Rome in the school of Trajan, with good fortune" (*legi et emendavi ego Dracontius cum fratre Ierio incomparabile arico* [sic] *urbis Romae in schola Trajani feliciter*).[62] The subscriptions to Persius' *Satires* were written by a certain Flavius Iulius Tryphonianus Sabinus, in 402.[63] Sabinus is unusual in that he is not a student or a professional intellectual or a member of the political elite, but a bureaucrat and soldier (*protector domesticus*) stationed in Spain far from the intellectual centers of the empire.[64] In one of his subscriptions he remarks that he "corrected and annotated as best I could without the help of a teacher" (*prout potui sine magistro emendans adnotavi*). Yet he presumes (as do the authors of the other subscriptions) that it is good to make corrections from the original of the text, and to do so in the company of a professional.

Unlike these men, Flavian the younger and Nicomachus Dexter are senators, members of great houses. As the subscriptions attest, Flavian the younger is already well advanced in a very distinguished public career—three times prefect of Rome—when making his corrections to Livy. The names of many other eminent figures are to be found in the subscriptions to various authors. Although Symmachus did not actually correct his text of Livy himself, he did have Tascius Victorianus do so, and mentioned the fact in a letter. Aurelius Memmius Symmachus was consul in 485, a descendant of the famous orator, and father-in-law of Boethius. He, along with the grandson of Macrobius, corrected the text of Macrobius' *Commentary on the Dream of Scipio*. Turcius Rufius Apronianus Asterius was consul in 494; at the same time (what duties did a consul of this period have?) he corrected a text of Vergil and did for the text of Sedulius' *Carmen paschale* what Tascius Victorianus did for the elder Flavian's translation of the *Life of Apollonios of Tyana*.[65] The name of the consul of 527, the distinguished Vettius Agorius Basilius Mavortius, is found in the subscriptions to the *Epodes* of Horace and in those to the manuscripts of Prudentius.[66] In the first half of the fifth century, even the emperor, Theodosius II himself, spent time correcting texts. A number of his subscriptions to Solinus have survived: these manuscripts were corrected "by the zeal and industry of the most unconquered and most Christian emperor, Lord Theodosius" (*studio et diligentia domni Theodosii invictissimi et christianissimi imperatoris*).[67] Theodosius was also interested in another aspect of book production; he even had a nickname, inspired by this activity: Calligraphos (cf. Georgios Monachos 604.8; Soz. *Praef.* 4.7–8, 10–12, 18; Soc. 7.22.6).[68]

PAGANISM, CHRISTIANITY, AND *EMENDATIO*

The general social and cultural significance of the subscriptions has been given its most influential treatment by Bloch, in his 1964 essay "The Pagan

Revival in the West," a summary of his paper of 1945. Here he very briefly asserted that the surge in the number of surviving subscriptions that began at the end of the fourth century A.D. and continued through the fifth century was the symptom of a revival of aggressive, even belligerent, pagan religious sentiment. Bloch supposed that many of the subscribers to secular Latin texts were pagans, and that they were interested in these texts as part of a general program of cultural preservation. This notion of a cultural heritage was itself integrated with the old ideal of a civic religion, on which depended the prosperity of the Roman state and the correct ordering of society. Bloch himself sums up his position best, in the famous concluding paragraph of the essay:[69]

> And yet, while their fight for the ancient religion ended in failure, they gained on another front a victory which has made their names immortal: they rescued the works of the great Latin authors out of the darkness into which they had fallen during the anarchy of the third century, copied and emended them in a fashion inherited from the great scholars of Alexandria and so prepared editions which were improved texts, and which were to form the starting point for the mediaeval tradition of these authors. Without the assiduous activity of these men, much of Latin literature that has come down to us would have been irretrievably lost. The same Church which had frustrated all attempts to restore their religion, under the leadership of the order of St. Benedict, took over this legacy to hand down to us the Latin literature which had been saved from destruction by the last pagans. This is the historical achievement of the pagan revival at the end of the fourth century.

Bloch appears to be saying here that the subscriptions are to be understood not merely as a manifestation of pagan concern for the old culture of Rome, but as evidence for a conscious and coordinated project, whose goal was nothing less than the salvage of the neglected remains of Roman literary culture for posterity. The correction of the texts of the classic Roman authors in late antiquity was thus a conscious, systematic attempt by the pagan elite to collect and improve the neglected texts of those authors, and to disseminate the improved texts in a propagandistic way among those with the taste, erudition, and sympathy to appreciate them—that is to say, among other members of the pagan elite. Using their leisure and wealth, senators such as Symmachus, Praetextatus, and Flavian would have accumulated substantial libraries, filled with rare volumes, meticulously "edited"—private libraries which served as centers for discussion and debate between senators and even favored grammarians, as meeting places for "circles" such as we find described in Macrobius' *Saturnalia*. Over time these libraries would have been passed through the generations to the heirs of these individuals, who by the mid-fifth century A.D. were predominantly Christians. Eventually, then, the books would have been donated to churches and monasteries. Thus the corrected texts and personal libraries of the pagan senators of late antiquity came to be the foundation of the great monastic collections and ultimately of the medieval manuscript tradition of the various secular Latin authors.

For Bloch and others, the key figure connecting these libraries with the the medieval Christian tradition was Cassiodorus. A distant relation of the family of the Symmachi, Cassiodorus was a Roman of eminent family. He had a prestigious public career, holding the highest offices of state. At the same time, though, he was a devout Christian who used his wealth to found the Christian religious community at the Vivarium, or "Fish Pond," at Squillace in southern Italy.[70] Those who joined this retreat were expected to pass much of their time reading and copying manuscripts. Consequently, Cassiodorus furnished the Vivarium with a library of its own, and that library has been seen as a crucial point in the history of the transmission of secular Latin literature. Traditionally, scholars have thought it consisted of Cassiodorus' family collection, including books of the sort that had been corrected by pagans such as Flavian and Praetextatus. From the Vivarium it was imagined that these texts made their way to the Irish monastic foundation at Bobbio, and thence into the medieval tradition of transmission.[71]

This old interpretation of the historical and cultural significance of the subscriptions remains very influential. Yet, its gross oversimplification of an extremely complicated and ill-documented problem has generated some vigorous criticism in recent years. In two influential articles, Alan Cameron has attempted to minimize in practically every respect the social, cultural, and intellectual significance of the subscriptions.[72] These criticisms must be seen in connection with Cameron's larger revisionist project: since the publication of his famous article redating Macrobius' *Saturnalia* from the end of the fourth century to the middle of the fifth century and debunking the "circle of Symmachus," he has argued against the notion of a pagan revival at the end of the fourth century, and against the position that a conflict of pagan and Christian religious ideology plays a role in the political, social, and cultural behavior of the period.

Cameron undeniably registers some devastating points against Bloch's position. To begin with, the importance of the subscriptions for the larger preservation of Latin literature is not so clear as earlier scholars had imagined.[73]

While it is certain that the manuscript traditions of certain authors go back to some of the copies subscribed by late antique pagans, as the text of Livy goes back to the "Nicomachean recension," in general the practicalities of the transmission of Latin classics during this period must be more complex and irregular than has frequently been imagined. So in the case of Cassiodorus' Vivarium, close examination of the evidence for the library shows that it included very few texts of secular Latin authors—and these were predominantly rhetorical handbooks. Most of the books were Christian texts.[74] Even granting that Cassiodorus was attempting to combine to some extent the Christian and secular traditions of the texts through an institutionalized ethic of manuscript production, it is clear that this was an isolated experiment which was not replicated elsewhere.[75] It may well be that the family library of his contemporary and relative Memmius Symmachus included many more and more various pagan texts than the Vivarium, but it is not known how or even whether libraries such as this were absorbed by the Christian institutions that would survive and preserve Latin literature through the medieval period.

The subscriptions that have survived were somehow assimilated into the medieval Christian manuscript tradition. But this accident of preservation does not mean that the subscribers had intended their work to be part of some project of cultural preservation. As Cameron insisted so strongly, the subscriptions are only one manifestation of a correction that was routinely made to manuscripts when they were first read: it is in this respect more like modern proofreading than like modern textual criticism. Cameron says that the subscriptions show only that the owner of the manuscript "corrected his own copy. . . . It was at once a standard academic exercise and the normal way of checking the work of a not always very literate copyist or calligrapher."[76] This point has been elaborated at great length by Zetzel in his various essays on the criticism of Latin texts in antiquity. Zetzel is chiefly concerned to distinguish the activities of ancient correctors from those of modern scientific textual critics. He argued persuasively that the correction of texts in late antiquity was never intended for the public: "What . . . the Nicomachi did was not addressed to posterity or even to contemporary readers. It is the result of private study, and for private use; it is the collection of material for thought, not the public presentation of any considered judgment."[77] In addition, as Cameron remarks, few of the texts containing subscriptions were in danger of being lost in late antiquity. Many of them, like Asterius' Vergil and the younger Flavian's Livy, were school texts, as popular with Christians as with pagans. So the subscriptions are clearly not a manifestation of some scheme consciously concocted by certain pagans to preserve their cultural heritage.

Most notably Cameron argues against Bloch's central thesis that there was a strong religious, pagan motivation prompting the subscriptions: "Is it helpful to study either the late Roman aristocracy or late Latin literature in terms of Christian versus pagan? Is it true that pagan aristocrats used Classical literature as a weapon in their battle against the new religion?"[78] To both questions, Cameron's answer is an unqualified no. Bloch made the connection between pagan religion and the correction of manuscripts in part because the subscriptions first appear in large numbers at the end of the fourth century, at the same time as "the last pagan resistance to Christianity." The perceived pagan character of the subscriptions was reinforced by the bibliography on the subscriptions: Jahn, in his pioneering study of the subject, had deliberately restricted himself to the subscriptions in the texts of secular Latin authors, excluding from consideration the numerous subscriptions to Christian authors.[79] The absence of a complete corpus of late antique subscriptions surely handicaps and to some extent dictates Bloch's interpretation of their cultural significance, and this gap remains an impediment to any discussion of the subject.[80] Nevertheless, as Cameron so well points out, the correction of manuscripts is not an especially pagan activity. In fact, pagans do not even have a monopoly on the correction of secular manuscripts. From the end of the fourth century, Christians are involved in correcting the texts of pagan as well as Christian authors. For example, the subscription to book 9 of Apuleius' *Metamorphoses* was written by a certain Sallustius in 395, "in the Forum of Mars, doing rhetorical exercises for the orator Endelechius." This Endelechius is surely to be identified with the Christian orator of the same name. So here we have a Christian involved in correcting not only a secular text, but a text that is concerned with the "oriental" cults which were so important to the pagan elite at the end of the fourth century.[81]

Furthermore, it remains to be demonstrated that any of the subscribers were pagan. "Remarkably not one [of the subscribers] has been identified as a pagan. Most were quite certainly Christians."[82] Almost without exception, the subscriptions date after the revolt of Eugenius—and in the wake of the battle of the Frigidus most of the pagan senatorial class of Rome converted to Christianity. Flavian the younger converted at this time. By the middle of the fifth century, when many of the subscriptions were written, the Christianization of the western Roman empire was largely complete: it should be presumed, unless the contrary can be proven, that figures such as Symmachus' descendant Memmius Symmachus, the mid-fifth-century corrector of

Macrobius, and for that matter the author of the *Saturnalia* himself, had embraced Christianity (see Chapter 3 above).

THE CULTURAL SIGNIFICANCE OF CORRECTION

For Cameron, the practice of correcting manuscripts is ultimately to be regarded as culturally insignificant. "The only reason such unimportant details [as subscriptions] have come down to us at all is that these chanced to be copies that found their way to a monastery where some not very bright fellow copied out the owner's imposing looking signature as though it were a permanent part of the book."[83] Certainly in the 1950's and 1960's it was fashionable in some circles to argue that elite intellectual activities, including the basic technologies of reading and writing, were culturally unimportant. This position was in part a projection of scholars' attitudes about their own activities: for objective history and philology to be possible, reading and other tools of knowledge must be functional and not ideologically motivated. It is an effect of knowledge to know everything but itself, as Nietzsche remarked in *Wir Philologen*. If the basic practices of scholarship are more than only routine and unmotivated, then scholarly activity too must be seen in historicist terms—as culturally, ideologically, and socially based. Since at least the 1960's it has been a basic principle among those who study "the history of the book" that such behavior is always profoundly ideological, that it is not only founded in larger cultural attitudes but also supports those attitudes. The explanatory power of this approach has been demonstrated time and again by scholars like Chartier, Darnton, Genette, Martin, McKenzie, and Petrucci.[84] While it is easy to see the merit of many of Cameron's specific arguments, from a generalist's perspective his conclusion will seem profoundly unlikely.

To emphasize this point it will be useful to consider briefly the problem of the cultural significance of textual correction from a broader historical perspective. One of the time-honored uses of history is to "defamiliarize" practices like proofreading, which through daily contact have come to seem natural and meaningless. Both Cameron and Zetzel insist that late antique *emendatio* is in no way comparable to modern scientific, systematic textual criticism. This discrimination is useful in certain respects: modern textual criticism, unlike late antique *emendatio,* is the privileged field of a small group of specialists; its practice is governed by a set of clearly articulated principles; it is practiced within a highly formal and exclusive institutional context. At the same time, the goals of textual criticism and *emendatio* are similar: the establishment of a "clean" and readable text. In this sense, it is reasonable to compare the two. Modern textual criticism certainly does have pretensions to be a purely functional, scientific procedure, and that claim is one of its most powerful ideological features.[85] Yet it, too, clearly has an ideological aspect. For instance, as Timpanaro argues, Lachmann's theory of textual recension is closely related to an idea of patriarchal genealogy of a variety peculiar to the nineteenth century and Europe.[86] So even modern academic textual criticism is implicated in broader cultural norms.

Admittedly, late antique correction of manuscripts is really comparable to modern textual criticism only in that both are concerned with the correction of manuscripts: otherwise they are profoundly different in almost every respect. It may be better to restrict our discussion to less "elevated" forms of correction, like proofreading. When one looks for parallels for the late antique subscriptions, it is striking how unusual they are. It is not that there are no parallels for the correction of manuscripts, or even for the subscriptions themselves. Errors occur in written texts in all times and places, and these errors are frequently fixed by checking the text against its exemplar. Wherever there is writing there is evidence for its correction, though this correction is usually haphazard and inconsistent.[87] In the Roman world the practice of correcting and subscribing manuscripts goes back at least to the second century A.D., as Statilius Maximus' subscription shows.[88] Some authors claim to have seen much older corrected manuscripts: for example, Gellius claimed that he had seen a text of Ennius corrected by Lampadio (18.5.1). Christian subscriptions are to be found in Greek manuscripts after about A.D. 300, some of them formally quite like the late antique Roman examples.[89] So there is nothing new in the correction of manuscripts. What is unusual in late antiquity is that now men of high status are to be found among the correctors; that they provide elaborate information about their careers in their subscriptions; that they refer to the correction of manuscripts in their letters, and even (in the case of Praetextatus) in an inscription. The emperor himself was known among his courtiers for his interest in this kind of activity. Certainly one should ask why the wealthiest and most eminent men of the empire, including the emperor himself, should spend their time on such things, when a wealth of other leisure activities was available to them—Ammianus lists many—and why they should bother to attach their names to these corrections.

Emphasis on the production of flawless texts does not become pronounced in Europe until the advent of the printing press—and even then, printers and authors tend to be very lax and even indifferent about the correction of errors until the nineteenth century. In a scribal culture a correction can be applied to only a single copy of a text; in a print culture, corrections can be widely disseminated. "Erasmus or Bellarmine could issue errata; Jerome or Alcuin could not."[90] The correction of an error in a single manuscript affects only that manuscript, not the tradition—unless the manuscript continues to circulate. This point should not lead one to the conclusion that the correction of manuscripts in late antiquity is merely routine. Rather, it should lead to another question: Before the arrival of printing, what is the incentive to correct at all? Why should readers of manuscripts care to spend their time annotating or making mechanical corrections to the manuscripts that they happen to read?

There is a time before the advent of the printing press when the correction of manuscripts is regarded as an important matter: the period of Renaissance humanism in Italy. Italian scholars are often seen as the progenitors of modern philology; from this perspective, their work with texts has been regarded as essentially disinterested and objective.[91] It should also be noticed, however, that their activities were overtly political.[92] The correction of texts was the occasion for remarkably personal invective (as it has continued to be for many modern textual critics). Corrections were used to justify territorial claims, dismiss rivals, and cement alliances. Valla's famous essay on the "Donation of Constantine" is only the most notorious example of the link between textual scholarship and politics during this period. As Stephanie Jed has recently shown in her brilliant analysis of Coluccio Salutati's discourse on the rape of Lucretia, there is also a strongly gendered, even erotic, component in the humanistic corrections.[93] Salutati and others speak of their corrections as "castigations," that is (literally) as "making the text chaste." In his essay on the rape of Lucretia, Salutati brings together this attitude toward the text with an account of a literal rape, which is followed by the politically charged account of the foundation of a republic by Brutus, the "castigator of tears."

Proofreading, on the other hand, as the name suggests, is a practice that comes into existence with the printing press. It is scarcely more closely comparable to late antique *emendatio* than is textual criticism. Then again, it should be kept in mind that proofreading is not in all places and all times the same thing. Attitudes toward it, even within the narrow confines of Europe, have varied as much as the procedures by which it is practiced.[94] Montaigne, for example, claimed repeatedly that he never proofread. As a point of fact, this claim was inaccurate: he did read galleys, though for him this process was much more like writing another draft than it was the simple correction of errors. Nevertheless, he deprecated proofreaders as craftsmen, mere laborers. His own creative writing, by contrast, he characterized as "play." Here we are enmeshed in the modern distinction of art and craft. This dichotomy is related to the development of the legal notion of intellectual property, which was emerging at this time, and the necessity of distinguishing the contribution and rights of author and of press.[95] Newton professed a similar disdain for proofreading, but for a different reason, which would not seem unreasonable to those who lived before the advent of printing. In one letter he told his editor not to bother trying to correct all of the typographical errors in the second edition of his *Principia;* intelligent readers, he said, would be able to make the corrections themselves.[96] In the seventeenth and eighteenth centuries there is a notorious (and far from insignificant) tendency to think of the natural world as a book, and of god as the author and proofreader.[97]

In the contemporary world (i.e. since the nineteenth century), the idea has developed that a book should be perfect. This is an idea that medieval Christian scribes would have shared, at least regarding sacred books. The cultural underpinnings of the idea in these two cases are quite different. In the case of the Bible, a scribal error might mean the difference between salvation and damnation for a reader. For the modern press, the goal of perfection has links to the ideals of industrial capitalism:

> The object of the proofreader's inspection is the master, in other words, a tool, not a finished product. It follows therefore, that if we regard the matter in engineering terms, the standards to be applied are those of the toolroom, not those of the production line. . . . [P]erfection is seldom attained; nevertheless, no lower target will suffice for the man or the firm wishing to get to the top.[98]

Of course, not everyone approves of proofreaders. Some think the perfect book is not necessarily to be desired. It might be argued for example that no book should be better than it deserves to be. As a practical matter, one must weigh the costs of editing against projected sales of a book. "How much is gained by enhancing the text, how much in sales, in prestige, in general good?" So the relation between the cost of editing and the final quality of book is conceived as a commercial transaction, and no more time and energy should be invested in a book than the profit it is expected to return.[99] Jacques Barzun thinks that proofreaders are the enemy; the process has gone too far, and nowadays editors are allowed to reduce legitimate peculiarities of style to homogeneous pablum.[100] Some editors despise authors equally: "Authors are saved from their foibles and shortcomings [by the proofreader]. Their reputation is enhanced, and perhaps each [author] learns something during the editing process. The next book will be better."[101]

Although it remains to determine the specific cultural associations of textual correction in late antiquity, it should be obvious that these cannot be the same as all of the associations that correction has taken on at these various times and places. The reason for these differences is that texts, including the circumstances of their production, correction, and circulation, are implicated in their specific cultural, social, and historical situations. Cameron makes many valid criticisms of Bloch's position. At the level of the most general question of whether or not the late antique correction of texts has a larger cultural significance, however, Bloch's affirmation is preferable in every way to Cameron's denial.

For example, Bloch argues that the subscriptions are part of some grand coordinated scheme, a propagandistic effort on the part of the pagan elite to preserve their cultural heritage for posterity. Cameron reasonably criticizes this idea but then says that the correction of texts in late antiquity is a private enterprise and that we know of it only because of chance and the mindlessness of the textual transmission. That Bloch is wrong and Cameron contradicts him does not make Cameron right. As prominent as the "history of manners" is today, from the *Annalistes* to Foucault to Gay, it is only prudent to regard characterizations of certain behaviors as "merely private" with considerable suspicion. What would it mean to behave in a way that is not supported or sanctioned by some historical and communal ethic? Would such behavior be comprehensible to a historian, or for that matter to the contemporary society, or would it be regarded as irrational and nonsensical? What might be some examples of such "private" or "personal" behavior? Sexuality? Diet? Gardening? The writing of diaries? The fact that the language of the subscriptions is uniform already demonstrates that they are not just the idiosyncratic productions of individuals, but are supported by some larger cultural institutions: namely, the rather informal "system" of contemporary rhetorical education and the practice of reading. Like all forms of human behavior, the correction of texts in late antiquity is intensely socialized. Furthermore, as we will see in more detail, corrected manuscripts certainly were circulated in late antiquity, and the quality of the corrections was an issue in this circulation. At the most elementary level, texts were sometimes borrowed in order to verify further corrections in another manuscript. Again, wealthy individuals might make gifts of books to their friends: significantly, in the notes that accompany these gifts the donors occasionally comment on the state of the text, deprecating the quality of the corrections that have been made to it. Finally, reference is made to the correction of texts in at least two inscriptions, including the rehabilitation we are considering here.

Again, Bloch suggests that the subscriptions are evidence for a pagan program to preserve secular literature in particular. Cameron responds that pagans and Christians alike are demonstrably concerned with secular literature, and that the texts of the Latin classics should consequently be regarded as common ground, with no religious connotations. But Bloch and Cameron are both focusing on the character of the texts that are corrected; this is evidence only for reading habits, a point that is relevant but also peripheral to the evaluation of the ideological significance of the practice of correction. Reading habits are evidence for an ideology, and in late antiquity the reading habits of pagans and Christians are different: pagans as a rule read only secular texts, while Christians (especially Christian intellectuals) read both secular and Christian works. This is a point that has long been recognized and discussed. I do not propose to rehearse my arguments from Chapter 3 here again; briefly, the idea that reading habits and attitudes toward authors are not affected by religious and cultural background is one that only a modern professional academic could entertain. In the modern world, specialists in late antique history (including myself) are paid to read all sorts of texts which have no bearing on their own lives and tastes, that is to say, which have no pertinence or interest for contemporary culture and society, which are boring or even distasteful. This is a central ideological feature of modern scholarship. Most readers throughout history, however, have read what interests them—and "what interests them" should not be lightly dismissed as an idiosyncratic personal matter.

There is no reason to imagine that because pagans and Christians both read secular literature it must necessarily be common ground for them. One might as easily argue that because classicists and Afrocentric historians both are interested in Cleopatra, she is common ground for them, or that the relative silence of classicists about Afrocentrism signifies their acquiescence. A common ground can as easily be a site of conflict as of concord. The presumption that underpins Cameron's argument here is analogous to the presumption that underlies the philological reading of texts: words or texts or other phenomena are conceived as having a single, uniquely correct meaning which will be the same for anyone who encounters them. This meaning is usually identified either explicitly or implicitly as what the author intended.[102] In reading a text it is rather necessary to have some sensitivity to the variety of interpretations to which it opens itself up or, perhaps better, to which it is susceptible. These meanings need not be mutually consistent; in fact, as Derrida has shown, utter consistency in language, even in rigorous philosophical texts, is not to be expected, and for good reason (see Chapter 7). The meaning of any single text can never be more uniform than the social and cultural backgrounds of its readers. A common object of interest does not necessarily imply agreement in interpretation of the significance of that object. To put it more concretely, it is extraordinarily unlikely that a Symmachus or a Flavian would have had the same understanding of Livy as an Augustine or an Orosius—or even as a Tascius Victorianus or a Servius. Nor would a Praetextatus have felt the same ambivalence reading Cicero as did a Jerome.

Regarding the subscriptions, the first issue for consideration should not be the nature of the authors who are corrected but the ideology of the process of correction itself. The fact that the wealthiest and most influential men in the empire, including the emperor Theodosius II himself, occupied themselves with the correction of manuscripts is already a strong indication that the practice has some social significance. Men like these were able, after all, to delegate such tasks to their dependents, as Symmachus delegated the correction of Livy to Tascius Victorianus. It should also be noted that there are approving references to *emendatio* elsewhere than in the subscriptions: in the letters of Symmachus and Sidonius; here, in the letter rehabilitating Flavian; and in the tombstone of Praetextatus (see below for all of these). There may even be an allusion to Theodosius II's scribal pursuits in an inscription from Lambaesis in North Africa. This text is a fragmentary hexameter epigram. Enough survives to verify that there is a contrast in it between Theodosius' preoccupation with texts and the more serious and belligerent policies of the rulers of the west, Valentinian III and Galla Placidia: "Valentinian, great ward of Placidia, mounting the gleaming stars of his earthly domain, consecrating the rule of arms, puts aside his thunderbolts; Theodosius, reveling in peace, practices his learned craft" (*[Fulgida conscendens] terra[e]ni sidera regni / [imperiu]m de[dic]ans armorum fulmina [co]ndit / [Placidiae] gra[ndis t]utela Valentinianu[s]: / [pace fruens doctam exerc]et Theodosius artem*) (CIL 8.8481 = ILS 802).

The subscriptions are yet another manifestation of the well-known link between status and learning in late antiquity: as Kaster has explained, one of the chief marks of elite status in the later empire was literary learning, the ability to participate fully in the culture of letters of the day.[103] So the association of grammarians with the elite in the subscriptions is not surprising. As is seen most clearly in Macrobius' *Saturnalia,* grammarians had a crucial role in the education of these elites, and a continuing function in their cultural activities (Chapter 3 above). The grammarian Servius was the most modest participant in Macrobius' dramatization of the dinner debates of Praetextatus, Flavian, and Symmachus. His betters are condescending toward him; he is represented as hesitating even to speak in such company. As he says in the often quoted preamble to his own comments, "It is more fitting for me to learn than to teach in this gathering, to which reverence is due no less for its learning than for its nobility. I shall nonetheless obey the will and bidding of Symmachus and speak" (*in hoc coetu non minus doctrina quam nobilitate reverendo magis mihi discendum quam docendum, famulabor tamen arbitrio iubentis et insinuabo*) (*Sat.* 1.4.4).[104] The refinement required to read and correct an author like Livy was one of the marks that distinguished a member of the elite from the rest of the population. Possession of this culture served to set them apart from those who did not matter. Evidence of this culture—refinement of speech, antiquarian knowledge, texts of favorite authors corrected with erudition, avoiding display of ignorance through the survival of errors—necessarily circulated as a kind of currency, displayed like a membership card to those who belonged, or perhaps like a supercilious sneer to those who did not. The activity of correcting is important for the opportunity it affords the elite to distinguish themselves.

For the correction of manuscripts to have a social significance, knowledge of them must somehow be circulating among some social group. The subscriptions cannot serve as a mark of cultural and social prestige if no one but the subscriber ever sees them. The social and cultural significance of the subscriptions must be considered in the context of the circulation of books in late antiquity.[105]

As at any time before the introduction of cheap writing material (e.g. paper) and a means of mechanical reproduction (e.g. the printing press) the production of a book is an expensive process: expensive in material and expensive in labor.[106] In such circumstances, books are rare things. Their value as symbolic objects and status symbols rises in direct correlation to their uniqueness and scarcity.[107] In late antiquity the possession of books seems to have become a kind of status symbol.[108] Ammianus' caustic comment about the Roman senatorial class of his day makes this point (among others): the wealthy of Rome, he says, possessed many books that they never read; and they kept their family libraries locked up as tight as a mausoleum (14.6.19). This statement, like Ammianus' digressions on the senate (14.6 and 28.4), is usually interpreted as a straightforward statement of fact, demonstrating the author's general hostility toward the members of the Roman senatorial class. On this interpretation, Ammianus would not have numbered any patrons or readers among the senators of Rome.[109] The significance of the passage is surely more complicated, however: Ammianus does not say that senators no longer read; he says that they no longer read *the books that are in their possession*. There is an apparent contradiction in the passage. Why should he say that the wealthy maintain libraries if they truly no longer read the books within them? Moreover, what is the point of these criticisms if the elite truly does read no more? His comments imply that libraries are necessary features of wealthy households, and that literary culture continued to be regarded as an important quality among the senatorial class; otherwise, there would be no reason to mention such things, even as criticism. Moreover, it is clear from other sources, not least the letters of Symmachus and the *Saturnalia* of Macrobius, that literary culture remained a badge of prestige in the fourth and fifth centuries. At least some senators continued to compete in erudition. So a man like Symmachus might easily have nodded his head to these passages, thinking of the decline of his class and of the virtue that he and his friends alone continued to display.

The culture of book-giving and the importance of textual correction in it is demonstrated by two letters of Symmachus and one of Sidonius (all quoted in a different context above). These letters either accompanied or discussed the gift of a book. In 401 Symmachus wrote to a certain Valerianus, excusing the delay in delivery of the complete history of Livy, which was owing to the "diligence of correction" (*Ep.* 9.13). Elsewhere he writes to the poet Ausonius, making a present to him of Pliny's *Natural History:* "in these books the scribe, who is careless of accuracy, will not please your lavish learning.... I have preferred to find approval with you because of the promptness of my gift, rather than because of the diligence [of the correction that is owing to] someone else's labor" (*Ep.* 1.24). When Sidonius Apollinaris gave a copy of Philostratos' *Life of Apollonios of Tyana* to one of his friends, he wrote that his hurry to oblige resulted in a hasty copy (*Ep.* 8.3.1). In each of these cases, the letter writer apologizes for the condition of the book and the quality of the correction; this presumes that the writer himself would normally have made the corrections before sending the manuscript. At the same time, each compliments the learning of his recipient, assuring him fastidiously and disingenuously that his own humble gift will not be worthy of the massive erudition that will be brought to bear upon it. The apologies for the lack of correction in these passages demonstrates that it was unusual in elite circles to circulate uncorrected manuscripts. The donors, fearing that the state of the manuscript will offend the "lavish learning" of their friends, anticipate some opprobrium for themselves for the shoddy state of the manuscripts they send.

In many cases, subscribers corrected their own copies of books with no apparent intent of circulating them. But many of the subscriptions include salutations, evidently addressed to the person who is to be the recipient of the copy of the book.[110] For instance, the subscriptions of Torquatus Gennadius to Martial include such salutations as "Quirinus, may you prosper. Read it in good health" (*Quirine floreas. Lege feliciter*).[111] A subscription to *ad Herrenium* addresses a certain Romanianus: "Long live Romanianus" (*Romaniane vivat* [sic]).[112] The most famous example of these salutations is to be found on the Calendar of 354, which was a product of the calligrapher Furius Dionysius Filocalus: "Valentinus, may you prosper in god; Valentinus, may you read it in good health; Valentinus, may you live and prosper; Valentinus, may you live and be happy; Furius Dionysius Filocalus did the lettering (*Valentine floreas in deo; Valentine lege feliciter; Valentine vivas floreas; Valentine vivas gaudeas; Furius Dionysius Filocalus titulavit*).[113] Filocalus was the calligrapher, he did not correct the manuscript. The emperor Theodosius II also liked to do calligraphy (see above); he probably also circulated examples of his work among his friends and retainers (how else would we have come to know about it?), probably with the kinds of disclaimers that we find in Symmachus.

It was also expected that the books might circulate in unanticipated ways among unknown readers (e.g. through inheritance). So subscribers occasionally address future readers in generic terms. The consul Asterius, in his subscription to the *Eclogues,* speaks to "you, whoever you are, who read, may you reread with fortune, and kindly pardon [any slips]" (*quisque legis relegasque felix parcasque benigne,* line 14).

The metaphor at the beginning of the letter of rehabilitation shows that textual correction might be associated with the preservation of tradition. There is another inscription which shows that correction might have a religious, and more particularly a pagan, connotation. This text is the famous funerary inscription of Vettius Agorius Praetextatus, which was erected for him by his wife, Paulina, in the year that he died (384) or soon after (*ILS* 1259, back; see Chapter 3 above). Praetextatus was a pagan, and in this text his activities as a corrector are linked to his religious beliefs, to his political achievements, to his prestige among the senators of Rome, and even to the erotics of his relationship with his wife. As Paulina sums it up at the beginning of the poem:

> Agorius, you who are sprung from a proud seed, you bring glory to your country, to the senate, and to your wife through your integrity of mind, your character, and your learning all at once.

*Agori, superbo qui creatus germine, patriam, / senatum coniugemque inlumi-
nas / probitate mentis, moribus, studiis simul.* (lines 4–6)

By "learning" she means more particularly his ability to "improve the texts of the wise," that is, his activities as a corrector of manuscripts.[114] In fact, the very first achievement of his that she mentions is precisely his work with such books:

> For whatever has appeared in either language owing to the meticulousness of the wise, for whom the door of heaven lies open, whatever poetry the skilled have composed, whatever has been produced with loosened measure (i.e. in prose), you restore these to a better state than when you had taken them for reading.

Tu namque quidquid lingua utraq(ue) est proditum / cura soforum, porta quis caeli patet, / vel quae periti condidere carmina, // vel quae solutis vocibus[115] *sunt edita, / meliora reddis quam legendo sumpseras.* (lines 8–12)

Paulina then says that these activities are "trivial" (*sed ista parva*, line 13)—a statement that certainly should not be taken literally. The fact that they are mentioned at all shows that they are far from trivial. She proceeds to contrast them with his other achievements. She describes his occult knowledge (lines 13–17): learned, he worships the manifold divine spirit (*divumque numen multiplex doctus colis*, line 15) and is initiated into the sacred mysteries. Compared to such matters, he regarded his many offices and honors as unimportant (lines 18–21). By the goodness of his teaching, he delivers Paulina herself pure and chaste from the lot of death (*Tu me, marite, disciplinarum bono, puram ac pudicam sorte mortis eximens*, lines 22–23), presiding over her religious transformation through various initiations (lines 22–29). Then there is a section about Paulina's own fame (lines 30–37): Praetextatus has "disseminated" her virtue (*me bonam disseminas*, line 31) throughout the world; Roman matrons take their cue from her (*exemplum de me Romulae matres petunt*, line 34); everyone approves the outstanding qualities that he, her teacher, has given her (*quae tu magister indidisti insignia*, line 37). Finally, she says that though she mourns for his death, she is happy in that she is his, and has been, and that soon, after death, will be (*tua quia sum, fuique postque mortem mox ero*, lines 40–41).

A lot might be done with this extraordinary text.[116] To begin with, it shows that status might accrue and be confirmed from the correction of manuscripts: Praetextatus is honored for improving what he reads. This honor presumes some wider knowledge of the activity. At another level, the inscription compares the transformation of texts through correction with the transformation of individuals through initiation into mystery cults. Praetextatus is learned. By his reading, he improves the texts of the wise. Presumably afterward he "disseminates" these texts either by giving them as gifts to his friends (as did Symmachus), or by lending them out so that others might check their own texts against them (as did Dexter's relative Clementianus). Those who used his books will then have made the appropriate noises about his awesome and unapproachable refinement and skill, and will have marveled at the improvements he wrought: his corrections to texts must have been known somehow, or there would be no point mentioning the activity here on the inscription. "But this is a small matter," says Paulina. Praetextatus is also learned (*doctus*) in the mysteries. He transforms his wife as well, using his teaching or knowledge (*disciplina*) to make her pure and chaste[117] and to save her from death. He then disseminates (*disseminas*) her throughout the world, and everyone marvels at the improvements that he, the *magister*, has wrought. Roman women will copy her, she is their *exemplum*. Much of the vocabulary used to describe Praetextatus' mastery of religion, his transformation of his wife and his subsequent "dissemination" of her, might equally (and occasionally even better)[118] have been used to describe his relationship to a text he is correcting. The equation of literary learning with initiation in a sacred mystery is not unique to this text,[119] though I find no other case where the correction of texts is specifically associated with initiation.

We do not know which authors Praetextatus read and corrected. The inscription does not say, and none of his subscriptions has survived: either his subscriptions were not copied along with their manuscripts, or his copies did not enter into the medieval tradition. It is clear, however, from the broad context of the poem that the authors he corrected were significant to him in some more or less religious sense. Paulina speaks generally, saying that her husband gave his attentions to "wise authors, for whom the gate of heaven lies open" (*soforum, porta quis caeli patet*) (*ILS* 1259, back, line 9). The heaven she mentions here is most assuredly not the heaven of the Christians. According to Jerome, after the death of Praetextatus, his widow imagined that he had gone to live "in a milky white palace in the sky" (*in lacteo caeli palatio*) (*Ep.* 23.2.1 and cf. 3.2). Jerome would allow that Christians may live on happily after death, but he pours scorn on the notion that a pagan should be resurrected in such a place in comfort and happiness.

I find no other evidence for the association of paganism and textual correction, and yet I think that it is very unlikely that the attitude is unique to this text. As Paulina says, these activities bring glory to Rome and the senate; and if Roman matrons take their cue from her, so too do Roman senators generally emulate Praetextatus. Above all, this equation of correction and religion is made on a funeral stone, a public monument, which would have been accessible to others.

Yet Christians also corrected the texts of secular as well as Christian authors. Certainly no one will imagine that Jerome associated the process with the same cultural activities that Paulina did. A detailed account of Christian attitudes toward correction is beyond the scope of this book. Pecere has usefully covered the essentials, with bibliography.[120] Briefly, Christian attitudes toward the book and correction are influenced not only by the practices of the Roman elite, but also by an eastern and Judaic tradition. By the time of Jerome, one can already see the beginnings of ideas that will be so important in medieval scriptoria: the sense of the intrinsic sacredness of the book; the notion of a connection between the integrity of the text and the salvation of the reader. None of these attitudes necessarily implies that the material procedures by which a Christian corrected texts (e.g. comparison of manuscript against exemplar) were different from those used by Flavian the younger or Praetextatus.[121] The humblest and most common and most traditional work of the scribe—the mere copying of texts—is invested with a spiritual significance, with the result that important people, like Jerome, might spend their days copying out entire books. The association of these ideas continues as late as Johannes Trithemius' *Praise of Scribes (De laude scriptorum)*—a work which that author had printed.[122] My essential point is that religion does play a role in Christian attitudes toward books, and more specifically their correction, even as early as the fourth century.

THE POLITICS OF "PROOFREADING"

The allusion to the correction of manuscripts in the imperial letter rehabilitating the elder Flavian has wide-ranging social and cultural connotations. There is no hint of a religious subtext in this metaphor, as there is in the account of Praetextatus' correction of the texts "of the wise, to whom the door of heaven lies open." In fact, we have so far been unable to find any allusion to paganism at all in the rehabilitation. This silence is significant: in the 430's Flavian was surely associated with paganism and "the last pagan revolt against Christianity." The Roman empire, however, was a very different place in the 430's than in the 380's (see Chapter 3 above). By this time, practically all of the Roman senatorial class had converted to Christianity; Roman society as a whole might fairly be characterized as Christian. The picture that has been sketched of this period by scholars such as Matthews and Cameron is in its large outlines correct: the paganism of this period is associated not with practice but with memory.

In his writing since the famous article on Macrobius, Cameron has wanted to distinguish between the 390's and 430's, between paganism and Christianity, in a very sharp way. So when he speaks of Macrobius' representation of the paganism of Praetextatus, he describes it as "nostalgia" or "antiquarianism." He minimizes the ambivalence of the Roman senatorial class of this period regarding its pagan past. For example, some modern scholars have wondered whether the younger Flavian's conversion to Christianity was sincere: perhaps he only went underground with his pagan sympathies.[123] On the face of it, this does not seem like an unreasonable position. Certainly by the time of the rehabilitation of his father, Flavian the younger had been a Christian for some thirty years. However, he had spent his youth and early adulthood as a pagan, and had converted to Christianity only under severe pressure, after the failure of the revolt of Eugenius (see Chapters 2 and 3 above). Cameron says that he prefers "to suspend judgment."[124]

It is too simple to draw a sharp line between the 390's and 430's, to see Flavian the younger and his fellows ca. 431 as either straightforward Christians or crypto-pagans, either utterly assimilated or intransigent reactionaries. This is a period of transition, and the problem to be explained, I think, is ambivalence, the cohabitation of contradictions. Should we completely discount the ties of kinship that bound Flavian the younger to his father? Even in 431, did he regard the old Roman gods as a literary curiosity, as mere objects of erudition, as sacred figures to be venerated—or perhaps as something else? How did he and his friends think of their reading and correction of the text of Livy? As an antiquarian pastime? Or as a deeply felt "debt of duty owed the dead?" Should Flavian the younger have been any less ambivalent about his past than Jerome and Augustine were about theirs? In the 430's the *Saturnalia* could not have been circulated (certainly not under the real name of the author) had it been generally regarded as a manifesto against Christianity; likewise Flavian would not have been rehabilitated if he were still in any sense a threat. At the same time, neither the *Saturnalia* nor the rehabilitation would have been written had there been no piety and regard for earlier times and for paganism. The rehabilitation of Flavian, like the *Saturnalia,* is evidence of both the demise of the past and its survival.

Paulina places Praetextatus' correction of manuscripts in a context that unmistakably associates it with the mystic transformation of religious initiation. It might be possible to argue for certain similarities between this idea and the association of *emendatio,* rehabilitation, and history in the imperial letter. For example, she uses the word *reddere,* "to restore," to describe the corrections (*ILS* 1259, back, line 12). This verb is also used in the imperial letter of 431 to describe the rehabilitation of Flavian (see Chapter 4 above). She also speaks of her religious transformation as saving her from death (line 23), a notion that has some common ground with the idea of rehabilitation as a form of history, which is presented in the imperial letter—and in Tacitus (Chapters 4–5 above). More significant, though, are the differences between the two texts. Paulina speaks of correction in a context dealing with religious transformation; the rehabilitation speaks more broadly of correction as a form of historical transformation.

The imperial letter begins as though it were itself a history, and proceeds to liken the labor of rehabilitation to the work of the corrector. In the rehabilitation, to correct is "to defend the dignity of men renowned and eminent in the state when corrupted to some extent by interpolations," it is "to recall the recollection of the departed to eternal fame." The correction of texts is here equated with the dynamic of memory, which governs the historical relationship of present and past. As we have seen (Chapter 5), history is a central concern in the letter, as it was for Flavian and his family. The elder Flavian was himself a noted historian. His son, Flavian the younger, and grandson, Dexter, corrected the text of Livy. What the corrector does for the text of the author, the historian does for an individual's career. What Flavian the younger and Dexter do with the words of Livy, the imperial letter does for the life of another historian—the elder Flavian. And I suppose that what the imperial letter does for Flavian, I am doing for the letter and for Flavian.

One of the qualities of history (and of narrative generally) is that it allows for the cohabitation of contradictions, as systematic analysis traditionally does not. Logically one should not say that a particular entity is both x and not-x: "Flavian the younger was pagan and he was Christian." In narrative, such statements are to be expected: "Flavian the younger was pagan and (then) he was Christian." The reason historians can say such things is that narrative proceeds sequentially. Its founding principle is transformation: if nothing changes, then there can be no sequence (or for that matter no time, as Aristotle would say). The fact that a thing is transformed does not, for a historian, mean that it leaves its past behind, even if that past contradicts what it has become. What things are, for historians, is a function of what they have been.

The United States is no longer a slaveholding society, but the contradictory fact of the past remains part of the identity of the present. I am no longer a child, but my personal history is a large part of who I am. Just so, the society of the Roman elite in 431 was *no longer* pagan.

Historical consciousness involves a negotiation between the synthesizing understanding of the present and the inconsistencies inherent in the narrative of the past.[125] The contradictions inherent in historical process are experienced both as a contemporary value and as change. History reconciles the tradition with the present. So the transformations addressed in Flavian's rehabilitation—religious conversion, rehabilitation, and textual correction—come to be treated as positive contemporary values.

In the 430's the relationship of the Roman senatorial class to its past was deeply problematic: the present was a Christian present, a world of Bibles and saints, while the past was regarded as pagan, a world of "final revolts against Christianity," of prodigies and "oriental religions." The imperial letter's self-presentation as history and rehabilitation and *emendatio* is an attempt *to explain and reconcile present and past.* By providing a model for the transformation of the past into present, the letter suggests how the two can and do coexist. Inevitably, the attempt is not fully successful. The introduction of a concept such as rehabilitation or emendation could never provide a completely satisfying resolution of the problem that the past, recent and ancient, posed for a Roman senator of the 430's. In English, the words "rehabilitation" and "correction" may convey a kind of benign objectivity; they can also suggest a violence inflicted on the past or on the text, a change willfully initiated to modify something unacceptable; this is also the vocabulary of the American prison system. In Latin, the language is on the surface also benign: *restitutio* or *emendatio* suggest restoration rather than revisionism (in its modern sense). The emendation and rehabilitation of Flavian purports to be the return of the pristine and uncorrupted truth. The errors of the past are conceived as interpolations—matter that is not integral or original to the truth, mere corruptions. Nevertheless, there is a profound uneasiness in the imperial letter about the changes it is introducing into the history of the life of Flavian (Chapter 7 below). Every history does violence to the past, in that each must begin from some ordering principle of interpretation that requires decisions of selection and exclusion.[126] And "every correction of a textual error is necessarily a historical contamination, for the very reason that it is a contemporary intervention on a transmitted text."[127] By posing as restorations rather than alterations, histories and rehabilitations traditionally efface themselves. But, as Freud says, "The distortion of a text is not unlike a murder. The difficulty lies not in the execution of the deed, but in the doing away with the traces." [128] Even the most careful emendation leaves vestiges of what it "fixes"—marks of erasure and insertion that remain to disconcert the corrector and the reader. In the manuscripts of the Flaviani and their contemporaries, there was no concern to eliminate the traces of the emendation: corrections were introduced directly into the corrected manuscript, written over erasure, inserted between lines and in margins. Here the sign of the correction is the disturbance it causes in the text. Just so, the sign of the rehabilitation is the erasure, which literally lies perceptible beneath the surface of the history of the new and improved Flavian.

CHAPTER 7

SILENCE AND AUTHORITY

Politics and Rehabilitation

MANY OF THE PROBLEMS addressed in this book are traditional, if controversial. The activities of the Roman senatorial class have long been regarded as having played an important part in the transition from the later Roman world to the medieval period, the shift from paganism to Christianity. The production of literature, the writing of history (Chapter 5), and even the routine correction of texts, or *emendatio* (Chapter 6), in this period all contributed to the preservation of what was, from a Christian perspective, the pagan Roman tradition and the reconciliation of a Christian consciousness with that heritage (Chapters 3–5). Flavian is an exemplary figure. His rehabilitation provides important, if ultimately ambiguous, evidence for the politics of culture during this period. Although the text raises large questions, it does not provide many explicit answers. For example, is the inscription maintaining a silence about Flavian's paganism or not? And if it is, what does that silence mean? To understand the historical significance of the inscription, the reader is required to interpret what the inscription does not say overtly, to take an imaginative position regarding its silences and their motivation. This ambiguity is in large part attributable to the fact that the text is a rehabilitation.

Interpretation of the rehabilitation of Flavian requires some consideration of a more general, historiographical problem: the relationship between realistic narrative and silence (Chapters 4–5). This large and abstract issue is central to any understanding of the *damnatio memoriae* and rehabilitation. A rehabilitation is about speaking over a silence, writing over an erasure. The inscription is a palimpsest: it has been erased and reinscribed (Chapter 1 and

Appendix). Furthermore, the imperial letter emphasizes Flavian's status as a historian and subtly alludes to its own character as a kind of history (Chapter 5). It even compares this process to the correction of manuscripts (Chapter 6).

What the inscription says is shadowed by *how* the inscription says it. The rehabilitation does not make its meanings known forthrightly. Instead of indicating in obvious and literal ways, it proceeds by intimation: it implies, suggests, dissimulates. The most important issues it does not mention at all. The ambiguous allusions to illegal offices, the use of metaphors and allusions to literary texts, the suggestive circumstances of the erection of the inscription, the abstruse description of the procedures of the reversal of the *damnatio memoriae*—all of these convey meanings, but in roundabout and indirect ways.

HISTORY, EVIDENCE, AND SILENCE

History is by definition a story that relies on evidence,[1] and most historians tend to think of evidence as what is there and available or explicit, not what is not; in other words, some historians might argue, a historical interpretation of an inscription or of any text must necessarily rely on what it says, not on imaginative reconstructions of what it does not say.

A piece of evidence should be understood as a trace: folded into it are the connotations of survival and evanescence.[2] Evidence is something present and existing, which is used to construct something else, which is not present or existing. So when a thing is conceived as evidence, it is by definition a thing that the historian must go beyond. To refuse to do so is to treat the thing as something other than evidence and to refuse to do history. Certainly among historians it is a habitual and necessary preliminary step to "describe the evidence," but description is inadequate. A thing becomes "evidence" only when it is used to recover something other than itself. To move from the text of Tacitus to the events of first-century A.D. Rome is to make a leap from a concrete text to imaginary things, things that have no existence except in the mind of the historian. And no text, not even a contemporary inscription or an autograph manuscript or an archaeological relic, has a relationship to a past world that is any more secure than this. To practice history is always to make as much of the evidence as possible, to go beyond the evidence and interpret and fill in the ambiguous silence that the evidence by definition evokes.[3]

There is nothing new in the idea that the historian is not and should not be limited to what the evidence says explicitly. The discussion of "historical evidence" in Collingwood's *The Idea of History* (1946) makes the point as well as anyone has. Collingwood discriminates broadly between two types of historian: the "scissors-and-paste" historian and the "scientific" historian. "Scissors-and-paste" history is characterized by the historian's complete abandonment of judgment in favor of the authority of the sources; it is "constructed by excerpting and combining the authorities of various historians." This, Collingwood says, is not really history at all. His ideal of history he describes as "scientific": "the scissors-and-paste historian reads [the sources] on the understanding that what they did not tell him in so many words he would never find out from them at all; the scientific historian puts them to the torture, twisting a passage ostensibly about something quite different into the answer to a question he has decided to ask." For Collingwood, where the scissors-and-paste historian asks, "What does the source say?" the scientific historian asks, "What does the source mean?"[4]

Even though historical interpretation is an imaginative activity, it is nevertheless bound by certain conventional restrictions. Not everything is admissible in a "legitimate" historical interpretation.[5] Postmodern theories of interpretation notoriously treat texts as unstable structures, a fluid mix of signifiers within which readers and critics must constantly reorient themselves.[6] To put this position in the language of historical research, the meanings of sources are not fixed. Instead, the sources are multivalent and ambiguous, their meaning produced by the desire of the historian. Many historians would object that such an attitude toward the sources fails to distinguish the perspective of the historian from those of the sources. By the traditional standards of history, this failure would be characterized as an anachronism: and while anachronism may be acceptable in a literary interpretation of a text, it is anathema to a historical interpretation of a source.

Despite the attempts of historians to remove anachronism from their work it must be acknowledged that every history is by its very nature anachronistic, in the sense that all history is always written after the event. The temporal distance implicit in the anachronistic position of the historian makes possible the ideal of objectivity and "suprapartisanship" even as it creates the old historicist problem of anachronistic relativism. As Koselleck says, "the emergence of historical relativism is identical with the discovery of the historical world."[7] That sense of separation which links the historian in the present to the absent events of the past both reinforces and undermines the position of the historian: because the past is dead and over, removed from the living world of politics and flux, it can be imagined as passively offering itself up to be understood objectively. As Tacitus puts it in a celebrated line, he is able to write "without malice or partisanship, because the incentive for these is far removed" (*sine ira et studio, quorum causas procul habeo*) (*Ann.* 1.1).

The problematic relationship of the historian to past events can also be discussed in terms of silence. As I have argued above (Chapters 4–5), historical discourse, like other realistic forms of narrative, prefigures itself as speech over silence, reinscription over erasure. This figuration of the space of historical writing as a silence or erasure makes it possible to dissimulate the authorial function of the historian. The historian does not write history, in the sense of being a creator; rather, the historian is imagined as rewriting a text that existed at one time but has fallen out of representation. Consequently the historian cannot be held responsible as author of the history, any more than a scribe can be held responsible for the content of the text that is being copied. Objectivity is possible: what is represented is a re-representation of a text that existed before, a copy or reproduction. At the same time, the historian can also disavow any part in the production of silence: silence is a sign that pretends not to be a sign, and a thing that is not a sign can only be natural and not the product of any author—except perhaps god.[8]

One effect of the use of this figure of silence is to create a text with connotations of objectivity and authorlessness. At the same time, however, the notion of silence creates problems for this ideal. Silence suggests only that some vague and undefined thing may have existed; it does not say precisely what. The historian can never know exactly what silence means, because silence does not indicate explicitly. In replacing a silence with something specific, the historian must exercise the imagination; he must create something and so become an author. Thus, locating the authority for a history in silence both strengthens and undercuts the authority of the historian.

AUTHORS, AUTHORITY, AND SILENCE

The idea of the author is closely linked to that of authority, in all of its more extended uses.[9] In the case of the rehabilitation of Flavian, literary authorship and political authority are coupled. The authority of political and historical speech, the warrant to speak, is lodged in an entity, the author, which the text constructs for us. This author is not only imagined as making the act of speaking possible, but also as guaranteeing the meaning of what is said. The rehabilitation, like history, presumes the logic of the *damnatio memoriae*: its representations are dissimulatory. Consequently the position of authority, like the position of the historian, is equivocal. Certainly the rehabilitation is—must be—"authorized." At the same time, however, there is an attempt to defer that authority into the silence from which all that is real emerges. In the rehabilitation, as in history, the authorial function is dissimulated.

This dissimulation of the author does not work to eliminate authority. Rather, it defers it to a place where it is incontestable. One commonly imagined characteristic of the real is that it preexists representation. Another is that it is authorless. What *is* needs no authority, other than itself, for what it is. The same is true of silence: it is frequently conceived as the negation of representation, and as such it can have no author. The political function of the dissimulation of authority, the effect of the invocation of the real, is the naturalization of an order. In the case of the *damnatio memoriae* and rehabilitation of Flavian, we are dealing with a political order (the Roman empire) that arrogates to itself the authority to pronounce the past existence or, through silence, to pronounce the nonexistence of certain of its subjects. This privilege is also commonly understood as the preserve of the historian. The project is predicated on a realist philosophy of language: what is not said does not therefore cease to exist (as an idealist would have it) but is "kept in silence." What realism reveals in spite of itself is that this silence is the product of an authority.

The authorization for speech that pretends to be "real" or "true" is typically deferred away from the speaker. In the past, such speech has most frequently been warranted by appeal to some external authority. So, for example, Homer and Hesiod claim to be inspired by the Muses.[10] Historians, like Thucydides and Tacitus, may either cite the authority of particular documents or witnesses, or appeal to their own suffering and experience.[11] Medieval thinkers may appeal to Aristotle, theologians to god.[12] In these cases, appeal to an outside authority removes the authorial function from the act of speaking or writing and places it elsewhere.

It is a truism that with the Enlightenment a development began that saw the "death of the author" (to use Barthes' phrase) in European literature and science.[13] Instead of vesting authority in the prestige of authors and books of the past, writers began to look to the justification of experiment and reason. Authority is derived not from the prestige of an authority, but from testable facts. Empiricism, with its slogan that one should "use one's own eyes and trust nature, not books," becomes the model of replicable research.[14] The same distinction comes to dominate history as well, as can be seen for example in Collingwood's discrimination between the "scissors-and-paste" historian and the "scientific" historian (see above): the former relies on the authority of a source, the latter on the ever replicable "experiment" of inference.[15] Whereas previously the warrant for the text existed in a linguistic entity—viz. the authorial intention embodied in a text—it is now deferred to a field that exists outside of language: to the "real."

This distinction is useful and, in broad outlines, correct. Nevertheless, the notion that the Enlightenment constitutes a hard-and-fast historical boundary between these two attitudes is certainly vulnerable to criticism. Thucydides, for example, is far from uncritical in his dealings with the authority of any source.[16] In particular, when realistic discourse relies on authority (rather than on empirical reason) the prestige of that authority is imagined as itself ultimately resting on experience. So in both cases the authority that warrants realistic discourse is in the end the access to something that does not depend on representation, something that exists outside of representation: it is a thing that exists in silence. The function of the appeal to this authority (whether it is imagined as indirect, through the witness of another text, or as direct, through experiment and reason) is again to dislocate the authorial function from the text. This dislocation is a hallmark of realistic discourse: a thing can never be true merely because the author says it, but only for some other reason.

One of the chief issues at stake in this discussion of authorship and authority is the control of historical meaning. Any text will contain ambiguities, and so be vulnerable to a variety of interpretations. If there is no control of meaning, then, a historian might say, the source cannot be protected from the manipulations and misinterpretations of the malicious or pretentious or excessively clever or stupid: to such readers, a historical document might mean anything. Traditional history tends to locate the meaning of the source in the intention of the author. Modern history, by contrast, usually locates that meaning in the contemporary social context of the document.[17]

The idea that the meaning of the document is defined by its contemporary cultural context should be familiar to most contemporary historians. This argument allows for a variety (though not an unlimited variety) of legitimate meanings. Furthermore, as the context is redefined or changes, so will the allowable meanings. By insisting on an arbitrary limitation of context to a particular time and place, the historian is able to restrict the range of admissible meanings of the source.[18]

The other, and more traditional, location of meaning for the historical source is in the intention of its author. Authorial intent and motivation are used as controls to protect the text from such abuse and to guarantee the correctness of historical interpretation. Who wrote the document? What was the intent of the author? To what extent does the proposed interpretation agree with these perceived purposes? I do not think that the interpretations of contemporary historians should necessarily be constrained by "authorial intent."[19] The relationship of a text to the conscious intent of its author can never be any more secure than the relationship of a document to the past. There is never any direct access to the intentions of the author; when we look for them, all we ever encounter are more texts, whether these take the form of writings or oral utterances.

It is possible to explore these issues of historical authority in relation to the rehabilitation of the elder Flavian and my interpretation of it. The inscription comments in an emphatic way on the motivation for its writing and on its author. In fact, it is no exaggeration to say, this text is obsessed with problems of motivation and authorship. As will be seen, however, the authorship of the rehabilitation is far from a straightforward problem.

MOTIVATION AND REHABILITATION

The letter of rehabilitation is sensitive about the issue of authorial responsibility and motivation. The problem begins with its account of the *damnatio memoriae* that was imposed on Flavian by Theodosius the Great. The avowed intention of the letter is to rehabilitate Flavian, and to rehabilitate him is to reverse the earlier *damnatio memoriae*. By rehabilitating Flavian, the letter confirms the merits of his life against his earlier disgrace. At the same time, the rehabilitation might be understood as an admission that an emperor, Theodosius the Great, made a mistake—and so, might consequently be construed as a censure of that emperor. Galla Placidia and Valentinian were members of the same dynasty as Theodosius, and they regarded him as one of their eminent and prestigious ancestors. In one inscription, Placidia honors him among other members of the house (*ILS* 818).[20]

Because the letter implicitly criticizes Theodosius the Great, its representation of that emperor bears close scrutiny. From the outset it is clear that the narrator of the imperial letter, Valentinian III, is concerned to give due respect to his predecessor. So he spends some time speaking of Theodosius' virtues, and then says that he hopes he has made his own filial devotion toward his predecessor sufficiently clear (*abunde causas pietatis adstruximus*, line 21).

At several points the inscription draws attention to the special friendship that Flavian enjoyed with the emperor. In the preamble, for example, Flavian is not described as "imperial quaestor" (*quaestor sacri palatii*), but in an unparalleled phrase as "quaestor at the court of the divine Theodosius" (*quaestor aulae divi Theodosi*, lines 1–2). The emperor had admired Flavian's historical writing, and had wished that his quaestor would dedicate these books to him (*annalium quos consecrari sibi a quaestore et praefecto suo voluit,* lines 19–20). He had showered kindness on him (*in eum effusa benevolentia,* line 19). Furthermore, Theodosius had been saddened by Flavian's passing; he had actually desired that Flavian "survive for us and be spared for you," and had said as much himself (*vivere nobis servarique vobis,* line 16). Flavian's condemnation and disgrace were not owing to the anger of Theodosius; what occurred was "far from that emperor's wish" (*procul ab eius principis voto,* lines 18–19).

As Theodosius' love for Flavian is emphasized, his responsibility for the *damnatio memoriae* is minimized. It is clear from the letter that Theodosius is to be exonerated from any charge of maliciousness or fallibility. He had no motive to condemn Flavian, and he had not wished to do so. If it is now necessary to reverse the *damnatio memoriae* and rehabilitate Flavian, it is not because Theodosius was himself mistaken, nor is it the fault of Flavian himself. It is the result of a great and impersonal force, the *casus condicionis humanae* (lines 9–10), the common lot that afflicts all mankind.[21] So it is possible to claim that the rehabilitation, far from implying any criticism of Theodosius the Great, should actually be understood as an homage to him (*venerationem esse,* line 15).

The original *damnatio memoriae* could not have been the emperor's fault, for it was not the idea of the emperor to censure Flavian. Theodosius had been misled by "underhanded insinuations" (*caeca insimulatione,* line 18) of those wicked men whose jealousy (*livorem improborum,* lines 19–21) had been aroused precisely by the love and kindness that Theodosius showered on Flavian. The emperor was implicated in these insinuations in only the most indirect and innocuous way. Blame is deflected from Theodosius onto certain unnamed individuals. At the beginning of his third *Relatio,* Symmachus does the same thing, even using the word *improbi* to describe certain overzealous aides who stopped him from seeing the emperor. In this case, the decision to bar the door was obviously Gratian's, but Symmachus pretends that it was the decision of these *improbi,* acting without the authority of the emperor (*Rel.* 3.1–2; cf. *Ep.* 19).

In the end, the inscription attributes blame for Flavian's disgrace, but not to Flavian or to the divine Theodosius—or, for that matter, to anyone in particular. Rather, Flavian suffered owing to underhanded insinuations (*quidquid in istum caeca insimulatione commissum est,* line 18) and the jealous machinations of certain unnamed scoundrels (*livorem inproborum,* line 21). This language is remarkably vague, to the point of drawing attention to itself. It suggests that something is not being said and describes the shape of a silence.

The text, then, has its scapegoats: responsibility and blame are redirected away from those who are to be glorified by history and toward those who will languish unmentioned.

The emphasis that the imperial letter gives to motivation and authority is mirrored by disclaimers. The text demonstrates its concern with the motivation for the rehabilitation paradoxically, by claiming that the rehabilitation is absolutely *unmotivated*. It is hoped that the emperors will not "seem to have undertaken any part of the rehabilitation prompted rather than of our own accord" (*ne quid erga restitutionem honoris eius admoniti potius quam sponte fecisse videamur*, lines 28–29; cf. line 21). The letter then proceeds to provide profuse justification. Flavian is rehabilitated for the sake of Theodosius the Great (lines 15–17); for his own sake (lines 22–25); for his son's sake (lines 4, 29–32); for the sake of the Roman senate (lines 36–37). The entire Roman community, past, present, and future, seems happily united in the desire that Flavian's good name be restored. The only people who might not wish Flavian's rehabilitation are the anonymous, jealous scoundrels (line 22), the sort of people who cast underhanded aspersions (line 18) and so caused his fall from grace. Uniting the community against a nameless enemy is a classic scapegoating strategy. It is the strategy of the *damnatio memoriae*.

The text's representation of its motivation is manifested in disclaimers. To understand the reasons for Flavian's *damnatio memoriae* and rehabilitation here, we must understand why the text dissimulates these reasons; again, we must attempt to interpret a silence. The avowed motivations of this text are no help as a control on our reading of the text. To the contrary, they would make possible virtually any interpretation the reader might wish.

AUTHORITY AND THE REHABILITATION

Rather than considering the motivations that the text alleges, it may be more useful to consider the author of the text and try to imagine what such a person might have intended to say on behalf of Flavian. First we need to distinguish clearly between the narrator of the text and its author.[22] By "narrator" I mean the persona that is constructed as speaker by the letter itself; the "author" would be the person who actually wrote the letter. The two need not be identical: any author may take on any fictional persona in a given work. In the case of the imperial letter, there is no question about the narrators: Theodosius II and Valentinian III, after all, are explicitly named as "saluting their senate." It is clear, however, that these two are not actually the authors of the letter.

In certain respects, Theodosius II would make an appropriate author for the letter of rehabilitation. In 431 he was about thirty years old.[23] He had held the title Augustus from infancy and had been sole ruler of the eastern portion of the empire since he was seven. At this time he was sponsoring the compilation of that treasure house of the Roman juridical tradition which so resembles our inscription in matters of style, the *Codex Theodosianus* (see Appendix). He seems to have had a special interest in the copying and correction of manuscripts. He was notorious for staying up late into the night with his manuscripts, his pen and knife in hand. Because he enjoyed copying out neglected codices, and because his hand was so fine, he came to be known by the nickname Calligraphos.[24] The imperial letter of rehabilitation alludes to this practice of correcting manuscripts (lines 10–11, 12?, 34; cf. Chapter 6 above).

It is, however, inconceivable that Theodosius II had a hand in the composition of the letter rehabilitating Flavian, or even that he was consulted about the matter. Rome was a part of the western empire: this letter should certainly have emanated from Valentinian's chancellery. Although it was customary for both emperors to "sign" correspondence as a gesture of imperial solidarity, in practice the eastern and western empires were separate regimes.

It is also unlikely that the other narrator, Valentinian III, was the author of the letter.[25] Certainly the narrator speaks with Valentinian's voice at various places in the letter; so, for example, at line 30 the letter describes Theodosius the Great and Honorius as "our relatives" (*parentes nostri*, line 30).[26] Theodosius I was the father of Valentinian's mother, Galla Placidia, and Honorius was her half brother. Admittedly, these two were also relatives (grandfather and uncle) of the emperor of the east, Theodosius II. Other references in the letter, though, are unambiguous. In lines 30–31 it is said that Flavian the younger has been proven true "to us and our relatives" (*nobis parentibusque nostris*) as praetorian prefect. Flavian the younger was serving as praetorian prefect in the west, at the court of Valentinian, in 431 (lines 5–6).

Valentinian, however, cannot have written the letter either. In 431 he was only twelve years old and was ruler in name only. He had become emperor some six years before, in 425, through the efforts of his mother, Galla Placidia, and the military aid of his relative, the emperor of the east, Theodosius II. In 431 Valentinian's regent, the *de facto* ruler of the western empire, was his mother, Galla Placidia.[27]

Some have suggested that Galla Placidia is the author of the imperial letter. It may well be that she was responsible for the advancement of Flavian the younger to praetorian prefect in 431. She may also have supported the rehabilitation of his father. She was at the time embroiled in an ultimately futile struggle against the ascendant influence of her most prominent general, Aëtius. By rehabilitating Flavian and advancing his son, she may have hoped to gain the favor and support of the family's friends, other Romans of the senatorial class.[28] On the other hand, it might as easily be argued (as indeed many scholars have) that Aëtius himself was behind the rehabilitation of Flavian, and for the same reasons: to gain the support of the senatorial class against Galla Placidia.[29] In later years he followed such a policy. Flavius Merobaudes, for example, supported Aëtius and delivered a panegyric in his honor. His statue in the Forum of Trajan (discussed below) may have been erected with the approval and sponsorship of Aëtius in 435.[30]

Although either Galla Placidia or Aëtius must have had a hand in the rehabilitation of Flavian, the actual writing of the letter was normally done by a secretary. The voluminous correspondence of the emperor was handled by a battery of assistants.[31] This secretary will not have operated without approval. He must have had some instruction from superiors as to what to say, and he probably submitted his copy for approval.

The most distinguished of the imperial secretaries in late antiquity was the the *ab epistulis,* or *quaestor sacri palatii*. This official was recruited from the ranks of the elite, from the grammarians, jurists, orators, and Roman senators—that is, from the society of the Flaviani.[32] The elder Flavian himself served as just such a secretary under Theodosius the Great, as the rehabilitation twice emphasizes (lines 1–2, 20). A fair quantity of dated imperial correspondence has been preserved in the legal decisions collected in the various juridical codes—the bulk of these written by the imperial quaestor.[33] Although it is possible to compare some of the imperial decisions written by the quaestor in 431 with the text of the imperial letter, the name of the secretary who served in this year is unknown.[34] Given the society from which the quaestor was drawn, this official may have been a friend or dependent of Flavian the younger. Given the high rank of Flavian the younger at the imperial court in this year, he would surely have had influence with the imperial chancellery.

The possibility should also be considered that the younger Flavian himself wrote the letter. A leading reason for the elder Flavian's rehabilitation was the importance of his son in 431, as the letter says more than once (lines 3, 29–33). The younger Flavian would have had a greater and more personal interest in the rehabilitation of his father than anyone else at the imperial court. Furthermore, the letter betrays a close familiarity with even the minor details of the elder Flavian's political activity some fifty years before, as well as a close knowledge of his activities as a historian and of his descendants' interest in the correction of manuscripts. Then again, there is the cautious and yet detailed description of Theodosius' role in the condemnation of Flavian, and an account of the emperor's regret of the necessity of censuring his old familiar in this way. There can have been few at the imperial court in 431 who were in possession of all of this knowledge besides the younger Flavian. He had served as urban prefect for the pretender and had suffered for it. He had personal knowledge of Theodosius and his settlement of the revolt. As praetorian prefect in 431, he was in a position to compose the letter, if he wished. In sum, the younger Flavian was qualified as no other to write this letter, and I would propose to identify him as the author.

Even if the younger Flavian was the author, the issue of authority remains complex. Although the two emperors, Valentinian and Theodosius, certainly did not write the letter, their authority was necessary to legitimate the rehabilitation. In this sense they are *the* authorities for the validity of the document, and their imperial intentions must be considered. If, for example, the text included their names without warrant, if they as emperors did not actually approve and sanction the rehabilitation, our understanding of it would be substantially different.

THE DEDICATION OF THE REHABILITATION

There is more to the inscription than the imperial letter alone. Other agencies and intentions must have all played their parts in making this monument, and if we are to insist on a meaning that is limited by "what the author intended" we must take these factors into account. Then there are the difficult careers at the head of the stone (Chapter 2 above), which may or may not have been written by the same person who wrote the imperial letter. Or again, there are the circumstances of the dedication, which must have been determined by someone, and which, as we will see, mirror the content of the career and imperial letter in several respects. The letter is addressed to the Roman senate: in fact, the senate is explicitly constructed as the reader of the imperial letter throughout (lines 13, 16–17, 19, 21–22, 25–26, 27–28, 33–36). On the other hand, the senate must also be regarded in another sense as "authorizing" the monument, because it presumably gave its permission to have the statue erected, in a particular place, on a particular day.[35] Furthermore, the senate's importance in the accomplishment of the rehabilitation is emphasized by the imperial letter on several occasions: they are to approve the imperial decision (see lines 22–24, 35). So the authority of the senate is sought and invoked as a way of validating the rehabilitation—and in this sense the senate may legitimately be regarded as an "author" of the inscription. Then again, Flavian's grandson, Dexter, supervised the erection of the statue (lines 37–38) and probably paid for it as well. He may then have played a role in determining the circumstances of its dedication, and also may have composed his grandfather's career. In doing this he may have been acting on his own initiative, or he may have been carrying out the instructions of Flavian the younger.

The statue base says that it was "dedicated on the Ides of September, in the consulship of the eminent Bassus and Antiochus (431)." Monuments were frequently dedicated on significant days, and this fact is routinely recorded on the inscription.[36] An awareness of the various historical anniversaries and festival days of the Roman calendar was part of the knowledge that set men of refinement apart from the vulgar, uneducated masses;[37] and a mastery of the list of holidays, of the historical significance and origins of the significance of particular days, was a part of the basic education of an upper-class Roman.[38] Even in the Christian world of the fifth and sixth centuries, the traditional Roman calendar remained in use and Roman senators continued to pride themselves on their intimate knowledge of it.[39] So on one occasion when the elder Flavian presumed to remind his friend Symmachus of some festival or other, Symmachus bridled: "You are performing the duty of a good brother, but quit reminding me. The rituals of the gods and the established religious festivals are well known to me" (*fungeris boni fratris officio, sed desine memorem commonere. Notae nobis sunt caerimoniae deorum et festa divinitatis imperata*) (Symm. *Ep.* 2.53). Macrobius' *Saturnalia*, which the author in his proem recommends to his son as a compendium of the sort of information that a well-educated young man should know, contains many discussions of Roman festival days. Praetextatus, for example, is made to give a substantial speech on the topic of the Roman calendar in general (*Sat.* 1.12–16). He is prompted by Symmachus, who urges him to "continue to expound in your pleasant manner of speaking also about the year, before you undergo the bother of someone asking, if by chance any one in this present company should be ignorant of the arrangement of the year among the ancients, or of the more exact rules by which it has subsequently been changed" (*Pergin, Praetextate, eloquio tam dulci de anno quoque edissertare, antequam experiaris molestiam consulentis, siquis forte de praesentibus ignorat quo ordine vel apud priscos fuerit, vel certioribus postea regulis innovatus sit*) (*Sat.* 1.12.1). Praetextatus proceeds to give a serial account of the months, including some of the major festivals celebrated in each, as well as historical events associated with the month. Doubtless by 431 many of the ancient pagan festivals were no longer celebrated (though some, such as the Lupercalia, may have continued to be observed: see Chapter 3 above). Nevertheless, the elite continued to cultivate the traditional knowledge of them. So there may be some significance to the selection of the day for the dedication of the inscription and statue rehabilitating that old pagan historian Virius Nicomachus Flavianus.

Interestingly, Macrobius has Praetextatus say that September, like October, is a "rehabilitated" month. Its name, like that of Flavian, had been erased and restored. As the fifth month, Quinctilis, was renamed July in honor of Julius Caesar, and the sixth month, Sextilis, was renamed in honor of Augustus, so Domitian attempted to rename the seventh and eighth months.[40] His attempt at self-commemoration, however, did not survive him:

> The month September keeps its original name. Domitian indeed had imposed on it the name of Germanicus and had given his own to October. But, when it was decided to erase the unfortunate word (i.e. Domitian's name) from every monument of bronze or stone that bore it, these months also were stripped of this encroachment of a tyrannical name. The prudence of subsequent emperors, who were careful to avoid the evil consequences of an ill omen, preserved the ancient names of the months from September to December.

> *Mensis September principalem sui retinet appelationem. Quem Germanici appellatione, Octobrem vero suo nomine Domitianus invaserat. sed, ubi infaustum vocabulum ex omni aere vel saxo placuit eradi, menses quoque usurpatione tyrannicae appellationis exuti sunt; cautio postea principum ceterorum diri ominis infausta vitantium mensibus a Septembri usque ad Decembrem prisca nomina reservavit.* (Sat. 1.12.36–37)

One salient historical event seems to have left its trace on the Ides of September: the *damnatio memoriae* of Libo Drusus. Like many condemned for treason, Libo anticipated his punishment (or pardon, as Tiberius would have had it) by committing suicide. As it happened, he killed himself on the Ides of September. Sycophantic senators immediately proposed that the day of his death be considered a public holiday—implicitly contradicting the spirit of the *damnatio memoriae* (Tac. Ann. 2.32). The case was notorious in Roman history and literature of the early empire. The establishment of the Ides of September as a day of celebration for the death of Libo is also noted in one of the many known Roman calendars, the *Fasti Amiternini*.[41]

The Ides of September traditionally had been a festival day, sacred to Jupiter. In fact, the Ides of every month were consecrated to this god. Macrobius provides various etymological explanations for the calendrical notation "Ides" before offering the opinion that the word derives from a root meaning "to divide" (*Sat.* 1.15.14–18). Most of the other interpretations he cites refer in some way to the cult of Jupiter. For example, he mentions one explanation which takes the origin of the word from the Etruscan *itis,* meaning "pledge of Jupiter" (*Sat.* 1.15.14–15). Another explanation he mentions derives the word from *idulis,* "sheep of the Ides," an Etruscan sacrifice to Jupiter (*Sat.* 1.15.16).[42] As others also note (cf. Varro *De L.L.* 5.47; Fest. 372L), this "sheep of the Ides" was regularly sacrificed to Jupiter each month on the Ides by the *flamen dialis.* The sacrifice took place on the Capitoline. So, for Macrobius as traditionally for Romans, "all the Ides are assigned to Jupiter" (*Idus omnes Iovi . . . tributas*) (*Sat.* 1.15.18).[43]

If the Ides of every month were consecrated to Jupiter, those of September were especially important.[44] According to Roman tradition it was on this day in 509 B.C. that the most ancient temple of Jupiter Optimus Maximus on the Capitoline, originally vowed by Tarquinius Priscus, had been dedicated by Marcus Horatius Pulvillus.[45] A variety of activities associated with the cult of Jupiter and the temple on the Capitoline occurred on the anniversary of the foundation. A sacred banquet, described in some calendars as the *epulum Iovi,* or "feast for Jupiter," was held in the Capitolium; the entire senate and all magistrates attended.[46] The Vestal Virgins also participated in the banquet, making an offering of sacred cakes called *mola salsa* (literally "salted meal"), a mixture of grain and salt that they had prepared from the first fruits of the previous spring's harvest.[47] The Ides of September was also the day on which the annual nail was driven into the wall of the temple of Jupiter Optimus Maximus (see Livy 7.3.5).[48]

All of these activities made the Ides of September one of the most important and remarkable days in the Roman religious calendar. Given that one of the chief ceremonies of the day was a banquet which they attended *en masse,* the senatorial class of Rome cannot have been ignorant of the association of this day with the cult of Jupiter. Macrobius provides a description of a banquet, which had once been provided for the pontifical college on the ninth day before the Kalends of September by the *pontifex maximus* Metellus (*Sat.* 3.13.10). That passage gives some sense of how elaborate such public banquets might be, and of the continuing interest in such activities by some members of the senatorial class during late antiquity.

Flavian was a member of the board of *pontifices.* Reference to this office is omitted from his *cursus* on the rehabilitation. Some scholars have argued that the omission is insignificant in this context. The inscription, however, was dedicated on a day that was sacred above all to Jupiter Optimus Maximus. The board of *pontifices* was traditionally charged with the cult of the gods and with the Roman state religion (see Chapter 3 above). Jupiter Optimus Maximus was the supreme god of the state religion: no cult was of more immediate concern to the *pontifices* than his.

It is remarkable that the statue was dedicated on such an important day of the old Roman state religion, a day that would have been particularly significant to the elder Flavian in his position as *pontifex maior*. Although Jupiter may have been well on his way to becoming innocuous by the 430's, even at this late date the god must have had rather evil connotations to Christians when linked with the elder Flavian. In the Christian historiography of the "pagan revolt" that had developed by this time, it was Flavian's adherence to the old state religion against Christianity that resulted in his original disgrace and *damnatio memoriae*. After all, at the battle of the Frigidus, Flavian and Arbogast supposedly erected statues of Jupiter overlooking the battlefield (see Chapter 3 above).

Any reader of Macrobius—and many Roman senators of the 430's— would easily and naturally have made this connection between the Ides of September and the cult of Jupiter. Consequently, the omission of any mention of Flavian's priesthood from this inscription is a very significant silence, one that we must consider in the interpretation of the text. If the inscription is dedicated on a day sacred to Jupiter, why is the priesthood not mentioned? Here the inscription leaves itself open to the imputation of a subversive intent. By the 430's, paganism was no longer practiced among the Roman elite. Its demise may have made it possible to discuss it openly, as Macrobius has his interlocutors do in the *Saturnalia*. If an allusion to paganism is recognized in this public inscription, however, it must be understood to be subtle—even furtive. And that fact is paramount for an understanding of the significance of religion in the rehabilitation, and for that matter for an understanding of the role of religion among at least some members of the Roman elite in the 430's. Open discussion might be passed off as innocuous or antiquarian, as Cameron argues is the case in the *Saturnalia*. But if there is no continuing sensitivity to the subject, what is the motivation for concealment?

It might be objected here that the significance of the date of the dedication is uncertain, and that we should suspend judgment. The dedicators of the inscription might have had some other reason in mind for selecting the Ides of September to erect the inscription, or they may have chosen this day merely by chance—in other words, the date of the dedication may mean nothing. But the intent of the dedicators is not all that is at issue here. What *is* crucial is how the inscription was understood, and certainly the inscription leaves itself open to the interpretation I am proposing.

The *Saturnalia* shows that paganism was far from forgotten among the senatorial class in the 430's. The silence about paganism in the rehabilitation of the elder Flavian shows, however, that there was some desire to forget at least certain aspects of it. The fact of the rehabilitation is already an acknowledgment of an earlier disgrace, even as it is the removal of that disgrace. The inscription says little about religion—for that matter, it says little about the reasons for Flavian's fall from honor. Such things *cannot* be discussed in a rehabilitation: they must be minimized or ignored, because it is precisely those facts which were regarded as contributing to his purge from public representation. Consequently these same facts must be repressed if his honor is to emerge unscathed. In this sense, the rehabilitation is very much like the *damnatio memoriae*. To be manipulated, memory must be silently evoked.

The statue base recording Flavian's rehabilitation was discovered in the Forum of Trajan, the latest and most impressive of the imperial fora of Rome in late antiquity (see Illus. 3). The imperial fora were extensions of the old Roman Forum, expansions and elaborations to the north of the traditional town center, built to accommodate the rapidly expanding population of the imperial city.[49] This development had begun already in the first century B.C., when Julius Caesar created his forum around the temple of Venus Genetrix (dedicated 45 B.C.).[50] His successor, Augustus, followed Caesar's example, creating a forum complete with a temple of Mars Ultor, dedicated in 2 B.C.[51] The next forum in this complex, the Forum of Nerva, contained a temple of Minerva; it was situated to the east of the Forum of Augustus and was completed in A.D. 97. Through it passes the Argiletum, the long road that ran from the old Roman Forum up to the Subura; hence this area is also known as the Forum Transitorium.[52] The Forum of Trajan was built to the west of the Forum of Augustus between ca. 104 and 113.[53] Adjoining it were built a basilica (i.e. a hall for the administration of justice), two libraries (one Greek and the other Latin), and a temple of Trajan. This group of structures was completed only under Trajan's successor, Hadrian. By late antiquity, the Forum of Trajan had become the most important complex in Rome. Thus, in his famous description of the center of Rome, Ammianus, when he arrives at the Forum of Trajan, claims to be at a loss for words: it is marvelous, "unique under heaven" (Amm. 16.10.15).

The imperial fora, like the old Roman Forum, had a variety of functions:

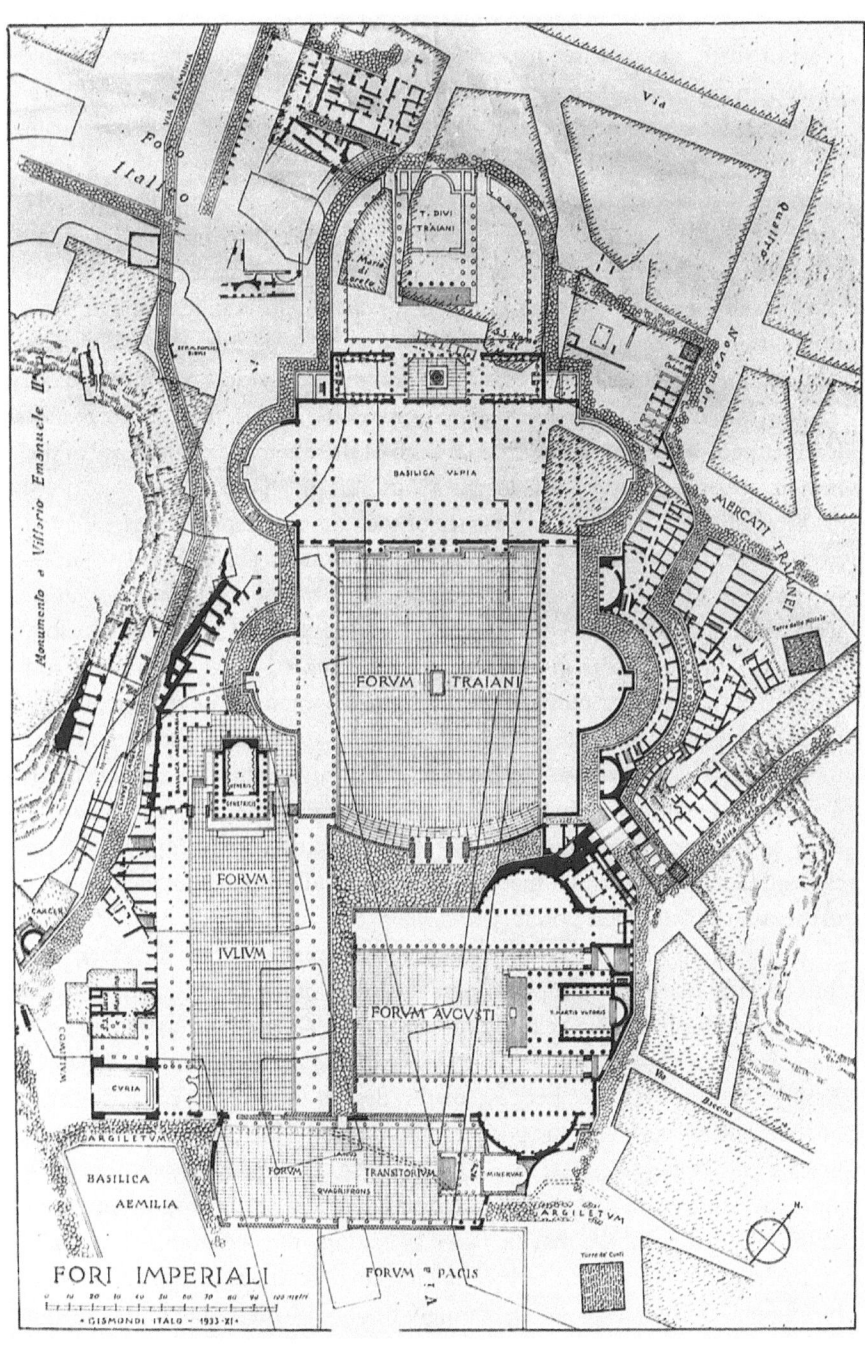

ILLUS. 3. Plan of the imperial fora. *Courtesy of DAI.*

political, legal, social, and economic.[54] As did the forum of any Roman town, great or small, the multiple fora of Rome together served as the civic center of the city. As such, they were a prominent place: it was a great honor for anyone to have a statue displayed here. The Forum of Augustus served from its foundation as a kind of national "Hall of Fame," where statues of great Romans from all periods were displayed.[55] Augustus originally ruled that only generals who had extended the boundaries of the empire should be so honored (Suet. *Aug.* 31); he seems to have considered these statues analogous to the ancestral portrait galleries that senatorial Roman families kept in their homes (see Dio 56.34). In time, though, statues were permitted to individuals distinguished for a variety of reasons. With the foundation of the Forum of Trajan, this function was usurped to some extent: now the luminaries of Rome might be honored in either or both of these two fora (take note of the honorific statues granted to Bassaeus Rufus, *CIL* 6.1599 = *ILS* 1326).[56]

From its foundation, then, statues of senators and generals were erected in the Forum of Trajan.[57] The dedications continue unabated into late antiquity; in fact, a significant portion of the inscriptions discovered by excavators, if not the majority, date to the fourth and fifth centuries A.D.[58] In this period, as earlier, eminent Romans continue to be honored for their military and political achievements. Now, however, there is something new: increasingly, statues are erected in honor of individuals who are distinguished chiefly for their literary achievements. By the time of Flavian and his son, the Forum of Trajan had become famous for its statues of literary men. Authors boast of their own statues there, and of those of their fellow writers, and emphasize the enthusiasm with which the Roman senate and people view these monuments and applaud their books.

By the middle of the fourth century, contemporary literary men were not infrequently honored with public statues. Julian himself (355–361) awarded a statue to the historian Sextus Aurelius Victor (Ammianus 21.10.6).[59] Already in 334 a statue was erected at state expense in the Forum of Trajan to Anicius Paulinus Junior "because of the deserts of his high birth, his eloquence, his fairness, and his good judgment, for which he is renowned in private and in public" (*CIL* 6.1683 = *ILS* 1221).[60] Paulinus was a man of eminent family who had held the highest offices. Nevertheless, the emphasis on his rhetorical abilities may be taken as marking the beginning of a trend.

Later in the fourth and fifth centuries, men distinguished only for their prominence in literature are increasingly honored with statues in the Forum of Trajan. The famous teacher of rhetoric Marius Victorinus was granted a statue in 354 (Jerome *Chron.*, *ad ann. Abr.* 2370 = 353; cf. Aug. *Conf.* 8.2.3).[61]

The statue base honoring the poet Claudian was also erected in the Forum of Trajan during the reign of Honorius and Arcadius, sometime between 400 and 402 (*CIL* 6.1710 = *ILS* 2949).[62] In the preface to one of his poems, Claudian mentions this very statue, emphasizing the prominence it has given him and his poetry with the Roman public. In the future, he claims, expectations of his writing will be so much the higher, now that he is on display in the middle of the Forum (Claudian, *De bello Gothico,* praef., 7–14).

One of the most famous statues of a literary figure to stand in the Forum of Trajan was that of Flavius Merobaudes.[63] Merobaudes was accomplished in the practice of both the pen and the sword, and the inscription on his statue base, which was dedicated in 435, persistently couples the two activities (*CIL* 6.1724 = *ILS* 2950). The connection between military and literary excellence was well established by this period. The dedication to Theodosius and Valentinian from Lambaesis contrasts the two (*CIL* 8.8481 = *ILS* 802), and Sidonius plays with the association in his poetry (e.g. Sid. *Carm.* 9.289–295). This statue was frequently mentioned by contemporary writers. Merobaudes himself mentioned it in one of his orations (Merobaudes *Pan.* 1 f. 3A, 2–3). Sidonius also knew of the statue and describes its location in a poem (Sid. *Carm.* 9.296–301). The chronicler Hydatius calls on Merobaudes' statues as witness to his eloquence and the elegance of his poetry (Hydatius, *Chron. min.* 2, p. 124 [= *MGHAA* v. 11]). Above all, the inscription on Merobaudes' statue base makes it clear that by the mid-fifth century the Forum of Trajan was considered a traditional and appropriate place to locate statues honoring literary figures as well as military men (*antiquitas honorabat, CIL* 6.1724 = *ILS* 2950, 10–15).

The poet Sidonius Apollinaris, too, was honored with a statue because of his literary excellence. Sidonius came from a noble family in Gaul. He was best known for his writing but did achieve distinguished office. He was appointed urban prefect of Rome in 468, though, as he says himself, that honor was a reward for a particularly notable panegyric, not recognition for his skill as an administrator. His statue was probably granted in 455 and erected in 456 in the Forum of Trajan.[64] As Sidonius remarks, the statues of many other writers already stood here, and his would stand among them for all time (see lines 21–28 of the poem embedded in Sid. *Ep.* 9.16).[65]

Flavian's statue, then, stood in a place traditionally well known for its statues of literary men.[66] Flavian was clearly notable for many reasons, not only for his skill as a writer. As can be seen immediately in the career at the head of the inscription, he was a far more prominent political figure than such authors as Victorinus or Claudian or Sidonius, or even Aurelius Victor; of the known statues of literary men, the figure who comes closest to his prestige in public life is Flavius Merobaudes. Nevertheless, the letter of rehabilitation does emphasize the fact that Flavian wrote a history that was appreciated by the emperor (lines 19–20). There are also other, less obvious allusions in the imperial letter to Flavian's activities as a writer, and the idea of rehabilitation itself here has historiographical implications (see Chapters 4–5 above). This literary aspect of Flavian's career and rehabilitation is also emphasized by the urban environment in which the statue stood. In the Forum of Trajan, near the great libraries, among the statues of other literary figures, the allusions to his activities as a historian will have taken on special meaning. Given this context of the statue base, readers must have been especially sensitive to the reference to his *Annales,* and modern scholars should also give this aspect of his life special weight.

The association of the Forum of Trajan with the intellectual life of Rome in late antiquity was explored in 1932 by H.-I. Marrou.[67] As Marrou showed, at the end of the fourth century areas of the adjoining Fora of Augustus and Trajan were being used as meeting places by grammarians and their students. As these fora became increasingly a center of scholarly and literary activity, statues of poets, orators, and historians began to appear among the figures of generals, officials, and politicians.

The activities of grammarians in the imperial fora during late antiquity are mentioned in several subscriptions. In the note appended to Martial 10.3, which dates to 401, a certain Torquatus Gennadius says that he corrected his text "in the Forum of the divine Augustus, that is, of Mars."[68] The "Forum of Mars" is an alternative name for the Forum of Augustus, deriving from the temple of Mars Ultor which stood there. The use of this alternative name was common in late antiquity and the Middle Ages. The Forum of Mars adjoined the Forum of Trajan immediately to the east.[69] Again, in the famous subscription to book 9 of Apuleius' *Golden Ass* (which was twice corrected, in 395 and 397) a certain Sallustius says that he corrected the text "doing rhetorical exercises (*declamans controversiam*) in the Forum of Mars with the orator Endelechelius."[70] Marrou understood the phrase *declamans controversiam* to imply a public aspect to the correction of texts: *emendatio,* he thought, was a scholastic performance, perhaps something like a lecture; here, he suggests, Endelechius gave lessons on the *Metamorphoses,* and his student Sallustius, as part of the study, corrected the text.[71] As we have seen, however (Chapter 6 above), the correction of texts seems to have been a routine activity, not a specialized scholastic undertaking. So perhaps it is only necessary to understand Sallustius' subscription as meaning that he corrected his copy of Apuleius at the same time that he was reading this author with Endelechius: the correction he mentions was a by-product of the study of the text, not the purpose of his lessons.

The subscription to one of the declamations attributed to Quintilian was written in the company of an orator at something called the *schola Traiani* (subscription to [Quintilian] *Declam. maior.* 10).[72] This "school" may also be known from an inscription. A funeral inscription commemorates a certain Bonifatius, a humble grammarian who was associated with something called the *atria Traiani*.[73]

These subscriptions show that some kind of rhetorical instruction was taking place in the imperial fora during late antiquity and that the correction of texts occurred in connection with this instruction. The use of these names, the *schola Traiani* and the *atria Traiani*, suggests that there was a more or less formal and regularized meeting place for this instruction in the Forum of Trajan. The subscriptions originating in the Forum of Augustus suggest that there may have been some comparable arrangement there as well. Such use of public space by grammarians during this period is not unparalleled.[74] In fact, it may well have been officially sanctioned by the emperor. In 425 Theodosius II decided to put grammatical and rhetorical instruction at Constantinople under the supervision of the state (*CTh* 14.9.3). As the ultimate supervisor of these instructors, he took it upon himself to ascertain that classes would not poach on the meeting places of the governing bodies, such as the senate house.[75] He proceeded to specify places where courses might meet. In particular he allowed that instructors might meet their students on the Capitolium of Constantinople, evidently an open area surrounded by porticoes; they might meet in *exsedrae*, rooms of a kind, often semicircular, "which seem to be attached to the southern portico" (*CTh.* 15.1.53).

The meeting places used by grammarians in these two fora have been identified by Marrou. The Forum of Trajan, like the Capitolium of Constantinople, is an open area surrounded by porticoes—such as the one in which Sidonius said his statue stood. At the northern and southern ends of the forum, semicircular additions that are quite similar in shape to a classical greek *exedra* abut onto the rear of the porticoes. The word *schola* appears to be a general word for a meeting place, often semicircular in shape.[76] *Scholae* (which served a range of functions) are known in both Pompeii (*CIL* 10.831 = *ILS* 5619) and Lambaesis (*CIL* 8.2554)[77] to have occupied semicircular structures. So the *schola* of the Forum of Trajan would seem to be located in one or both of these semicircular additions. A comparable arrangement exists in the Forum of Augustus, where the temple of Mars Ultor is flanked by porticoes and *exedrae*. If the identification of the *schola Traiani* is correct, then these *exedrae* were also likely used as meeting places by grammarians in late antiquity.

Literary activities continued in the imperial fora all the way down to the end of antiquity. As late as the sixth century, poetry readings were given in the Forum of Trajan. Venantius Fortunatus twice mentions such performances. In one place he mentions that "venerable Rome has scarcely heard in the Forum of Trajan such ostentatious poetry" (*Carm.* 3.18.7–8). In another he remarks that Vergil was read out there (*Carm.* 7.8.25–26).[78]

It is more difficult to trace the literary activity in the Forum of Trajan before the mid-fourth century. The Library of Trajan, with its Greek and Latin collections, flanking the founder's column, was one of the great libraries of Rome; in late antiquity, it seems to have been the most famous and important library in the city.[79] It had been an important landmark in the literary landscape of Rome immediately from its foundation in A.D. 112. Like a modern university, this grand establishment doubtless fostered a variety of related (though institutionally unaffiliated) activities in its immediate area. Nevertheless, as Marrou argued, there is no reason to think that the grammarians and orators of the *schola Traiani* worked in the library or used its resources, even though the proximity of the building may have been one of the attractions that drew them to the area and held them there.[80]

A more practical and immediate reason for the concentration of grammarians in the imperial fora may have been the long-established presence of copyists and booksellers. Their shops were well established there by the first century A.D., when the area was already identified as the great book market of Rome. The bookshops of the Argiletum are mentioned by Martial several times. As noted above, the Argiletum is the long street that ran from the old Roman Forum to the Subura, passing through the Forum of Nerva, or Forum Transitorium. It is here that Martial locates the bookmarket of Rome. He says on several occasions that his books can be found "in the shops of the Argiletum" (Mart. *Ep.* 1.3.1), "by the Forum of Nerva" (*Ep.* 1.2.5–8), or "opposite the Forum of Caesar" (*Ep.* 1.117.8–13).

An identification tag from a slave collar (*CIL* 15.7190 = *ILS* 8730) shows that the book trade continued in this area down into late antiquity. The tag, discovered on the Caelian hill, likely dates to the fourth or fifth century. On one side it urges the reader to "hold me [i.e. the attached slave] and return me to the Forum of Mars, to Maximianus the bookseller" (*tene me et revoca me in foro Martis ad Maximianum antiquarium*).[81] On the other, a second inscription advises the reader to "hold me because I ran away, and return me to the Caelian to the house of the eminent Helpidius"; *tene me quia fugi et revoca me in Celimontio ad domu(m) (H)elpidii, v(iri) c(larissimi)*. This Helpidius should almost certainly be identified with an attested friend of Symmachus, or at least with a member of this friend's family.[82] As we see here, he too had his residence on the Caelian, in the neighborhood of the mansions of Symmachus and Flavian (see Chapter 2 above).

It is not known how the two texts came to be inscribed on either side of the slave collar from the Caelian. There may be some connection between Helpidius and Maximianus the copyist, or there may not. Nevertheless, the conjunction of the two at least suggests an interesting problem: What is the relationship between the mansions of the great and the humble literary life of the Forum of Trajan? It is clear that the elite and the grammarians did have some personal contact.[83] In the *Saturnalia* the grammarian Servius is represented as a participant in learned discussions at the dinner parties in various luxurious mansions of the wealthy. But then, eminent individuals with literary pretensions were always present at the lessons of the *scholae* of the Forum of Trajan—if not in body, then in spirit, through their portrayal in the statues that stood nearby in the porticoes.

Finally it should be recalled that the letter rehabilitating the elder Flavian begins by alluding to the correction (*emendatio*) of manuscripts (lines 9–12; cf. Chapter 6 above). In light of the literary activities that went on around this statue, the allusion takes on even greater significance. As the representation of the author of a history, Flavian's statue and inscription would have resonated with the texts that local grammarians read (as did the statues of the other literary paragons). One wonders what the grammarians made of the base during the years in which it likely stood erased in the Forum. Did any of them compare it to an old, indecipherable book, damaged by generations of sloppy copyists? The metaphor in the first line of the imperial letter suggests this analogy. The rehabilitation of Flavian and the reinscription of the base is represented as corresponding to the critical act of reading by which grammarians and other readers improved their own texts. In this way, Flavian's rehabilitation is also a monument to the literary culture of the Forum of Trajan, in which grammarians, authors, and elite participated.

The imperial letter represents the authority that warrants it as ambiguous to the point of self-effacement. From the beginning, the text prevaricates about its author: even the preamble of the inscription is cast in an unusual passive form, making it possible to omit any reference to those responsible for the dedication (see Chapter 2 above). Nowhere is the author or informing intent clearly revealed. Various reasons might be given for the problematic status of the author of this text. Some might say that it is a function of the genre of the imperial letter and the character of a bureaucracy: anonymous secretaries routinely write such texts at the behest of various officials, but always in the name of the emperor. I think there is more to the problem. In part, the author is concealed here because of the potentially subversive character of a rehabilitation. To rehabilitate Flavian requires the reversal of a decision of the emperor Theodosius, and that reversal carries with it an implicit criticism of the emperor: Theodosius made a mistake. The ways in which the letter deals with Theodosius—the claim of extenuating circumstances, the description of his regrets, and so forth—demonstrate that this is a delicate problem. In such circumstances the writer of the letter was only wise to keep a low profile.

Another, more important reason for the discomfort with the representation of author and motivation in this text, however, has to do with the theme of silence and its relationship to the ideas of the *damnatio memoriae* and rehabilitation. One thinks of the famous anecdote about Tiberius, as told by Tacitus: Tiberius had written to the senate, expressing vague fears of sedition. He did not name any names, however. When asked for elaboration, he was furious: "Of all his self-ascribed virtues, there was none which he loved more greatly than his dissimulation. So he greatly disliked disclosing what he had suppressed" (*nullum aeque Tiberius, ut rebatur, ex virtutibus suis quam dissimulationem diligebat*) (*Ann.* 4.71; cf. Chapter 5 above). Here, merely to draw attention to dissimulation as authored was a threat to Tiberius' power. This is a paradox of the *damnatio memoriae:* to draw attention to the fact of the suppression is to threaten the status of the suppression itself (Chapter 4 above). To treat a silence as authored is to recognize it as a sign, rather than as the nothing it pretends to be. So the *damnatio memoriae* is not represented as an act, authorized by the emperor, but as the opposite of an act: a fact. And so, the letter reversing the *damnatio memoriae* is not to be imagined as an authored activity, but, like history, as a restoration.

History, we learn from the imperial letter, is a rehabilitation. Following the imperial letter, we might say, the ancient editorial practice of *emendatio* is also a rehabilitation. In modern times, too, the silences of history and textual criticism are constructed by the speech of historians and editors. Historians and textual critics conceive of themselves as speaking over a silence—as writing over an erasure. They do not think of themselves as creating but as restoring. As a point of fact, it may well be that every restoration is a new creation, but historians and editors do not imagine their activity as such. The idea of silence is necessary for their vision of historical or editorial activity: they think of themselves as bringing to light something external to themselves—something that is, but that is not apparent. Obviously in a sense historians and editors are authors, but only in a peculiar sense. The authority for what they say, they pretend, is not in their present power to dictate, but in an external, if inapparent, reality. On the contrary, historians and critics suppress their own role as authorities for what they say: they are merely discoverers, messengers, conveyors of the real. So they construct the authority for their utterances as something depersonalized and external to their discourse. And what authority can be invoked to guarantee truth and reality other than its own self-evidence? It is the job of historians and critics to point out precisely what is, after their activities, self-evident. So in the end the acknowledged authority for historical utterance is the truth of what is outside of representation: silence.

On one level, at least, the imperial letter of rehabilitation is posing as a history or, better, as a corrected copy of a text of the life of Flavian. Given the ambiguity of the imagined authorial status of the historian or corrector, it is perhaps less surprising that the text is so squeamish about its own author. For, to a historian or textual critic (and a textual critic is merely a scientific corrector), the author of the events recounted or edited is someone other than the historian or critic. Housman may have edited Manilius, but his edition is not for that reason shelved alongside copies of *A Shropshire Lad*. If we take the allusions to history and the correction of texts seriously, then how should we imagine the imperial letter? As a history? Or perhaps as the note of a corrector, as a kind of subscription? In the latter case, we might understand the letter as following the historical account of the life of Flavian. Like a subscription, the letter says that the text preceding it has been corrected, restored, improved. So the text of the corrected history here would be the text of Flavian's life—his *cursus*. And who could the narrator of the *cursus* be except the elder Flavian himself? As in a narrative history, the authority for the narration is constructed as the facts themselves. The narrator vanishes into the text. Admittedly the text of Flavian's life has been corrected, but surely Flavian must remain (at least by the dissimulatory principles of history and *emendatio*) its author.

Many will think that I am going off the deep end here. They would be right. Within the context of the metaphor of the correction of texts, we must still regard the self-effacing historian and corrector as the author and creator of the text of the life of Flavian, just as we must generally regard modern historians and textual critics as authors, despite their dissimulations of themselves. The editor or historian chooses what is to be included or excluded, what to be mentioned, what to be passed over in silence, what to be simulated, what to be dissimulated. Just so, the imperial letter has selected and corrected certain sections of the *cursus* and has, by this practice, rewritten and reconstituted the text, or history, of Flavian's life.

CONCLUSION: HISTORY AND THE LACUNA

One of the signs of time, perhaps its chief sign, is damage.[84] "All mastering time would destroy me," says the inscription of Tatianus (Chapter 4 above). Piranesi, we have seen, claimed that his book "vindicated the traces of the eternal city from the rubble and the injuries of time." The point is made clearly by the fourth-century A.D. poet Ausonius, in his collection of conventional epitaphs:

> One letter shows up clearly, set apart by double points, and that single mark in this way [L:] indicates the praenomen. Next an M has been inscribed thus [M], I think. The entire letter is not visible: the damaged apex has broken off from the remains of the stone. Whether a MARIUS or a MARCIUS or a METELLUS lies here, no one can know on the basis of secure evidence. With their shapes damaged, all the letters are destroyed, and when the characters are confused, all sense is lost. Do we wonder that men die? Monuments decay, death comes even to stones and to names.

> *una quidem, geminis fulget set dissita punctis/ littera, praenomen sic [L:] nota sola facit. /post M incisum est: puto sic [M]. non tota videtur:/dissiluit saxi fragmine laesus apex. /nec quisquam, MARIUS seu MARCIUS anne METELLUS/hic iaceat, certis noverit indiciis. / truncatis convulsa iacent elementa figuris, /omnia confusis interiere notis. /miremur periise homines? monumenta fatiscunt;/mors etiam saxis nominibusque venit.* (Ausonius 6.32)

Damage, unintelligibility, age, and death: even the casual, accidental wear that accumulates on the monument is significant and is linked to a complex of historical ideas. Editors have always remarked how difficult it is to read the inscription rehabilitating the elder Flavian: the marble itself has been worn away, and the letters have largely vanished (see Appendix). This damage should not be regarded merely as an impediment to deciphering the text; it is also the evidence of the antiquity and historicity of the document. For the inscription recording the elder Flavian's rehabilitation is a text, but it is also a monument. Its meaning is bound up not only in what it says, but in what it is. The procedures of the *damnatio memoriae* and rehabilitation, and the historiographical notions that they presume, are deeply implicated in the qualities and connotations of the Roman monument.

The leading quality of the monument (and for that matter of the historical document) is its specificity or uniqueness. This attribute is connected to the material being of the text, not to its content. It is emphasized in a variety of ways: through the differences that set it apart from other texts, through its localization in space and endurance in time. Above all, specificity can be acquired in time—through the damage and wear that a thing accumulates as it lasts and is used, its patina.

Damage can also be inflicted on an object intentionally, as when a name is erased because of a *damnatio memoriae*. Thus, the *damnatio memoriae*, by creating new damage, both attacks and, in a backhanded way, confirms the historical prestige of the monument (see Chapter 4 above). So the inscription rehabilitating Flavian is not only heavily worn, but it has also been erased once. The erasure can be regarded as wear intentionally inflicted on the inscription. Because the inscription is a monument, the connotations of this damage are different than they would be if it were a modern, reproduced text. To spray-paint an "X" over the groin of a public statue has different connotations than to use a felt-tip pen to draw a moustache on a picture of the Mona Lisa in an art history book. An inscription is an "authentic original," and to damage it is to assault the very quality it shares with an art object and a historical document, a quality that is not to be reduced to its simple content.[85] As a rough parallel, one might think of the difference between destroying a photocopy of a contract or check and destroying the document itself. In the latter case, the eradication of the document is equated with the cancellation of the act that the document embodies.

Certainly it is also possible to destroy or alter a modern reproduction, and to make a statement by doing so. It would be possible to make a political gesture, for example, by dishonoring an American flag, by burning a record album or CD, or by destroying a photograph. Nevertheless, there is a difference between destroying a reproduction and destroying an original, as there would be a difference between burning my generic flag and burning the one that Betsy Ross stitched up, or the one that flew over Fort Sumter.

Modern censorship depends for its effect on a universal implementation. When the Soviets proceeded against enemies of the state, they attempted to eradicate all trace of their existence. If a book was offensive, all copies of it had to be destroyed or altered. As we have already seen (Chapter 4), however, the Romans were evidently not concerned that their purge of a condemned public enemy be thoroughgoing: inscriptions were not destroyed utterly, but were left to stand, with legible erasures; other memorials of the public enemy were allowed to remain utterly undamaged. The reason for this difference of approach, it seems to me, is to be located in the opposition between the modern conception of the text and the ancient conception of the monument. Since the printing press, modern censorship has of necessity seen texts purely in terms of their content. Control of a text, whether through state purge or copyright, means control over what it says, not over what it is.[86] In the case of the *damnatio memoriae,* the issue is much more the physical character of the text than its content. The point of erasing an inscription is not to destroy its message, but to dishonor the medium. Where the purge of the totalitarian state aims at annihilation, the *damnatio memoriae* aims not to destroy the monument but to re-create it as ἀκλεής (to use the term from the Herodotus' proem).

The modern totalitarian purge is, in its way, a denial of the reality of history. It is an assertion that the state can control not only the present but the past as well; that the truth of the past is dependent on the representations of the present, and thus exists only at the pleasure of present power. The *damnatio memoriae* was understood by Roman critics like Tacitus as a confirmation of memory, not the destruction of it (Chapters 4 and 5 above). The erasure can be viewed from one perspective as an assault on the monumental qualities of the inscription, but from another it may be seen as yet another trace. So the erasure, along with the other casual damages the text may have suffered, contributes to the "patina" of the monument, to use another of Benjamin's words for the aura of authenticity.[87] The erasure, too, asserts the historicity of what it eradicates, even as it eradicates it. It is through activities such as erasure that authentic, historical documents are created.[88]

The authenticity of the text resides in the lacuna, to use the language of textual criticism. Like silence, the lacuna suggests the nonpresence (lack) of something that has been there but is there no longer: this is the only kind of presence the past can have. For example, there is an earlier text, visible now only through shadowy, indecipherable traces and the marks of its erasure (see Appendix) beneath the letter rehabilitating Flavian. Or again, at line 14, the letter of rehabilitation claims to restore something to Flavian—the word is not recoverable (*restitutionem pr[.]n[..]inis inlustris*). At some point in the past, the traces faded to unintelligibility. Still, the size and shape of the word, and many of its letters, can be determined. Even if the word resists satisfactory restoration, even if we cannot know what stood here, nevertheless we can feel sure that *something* was here. This vague sense is produced by the monumental, and it is the foundation of the idea of history.

The accidents that traditionally have been seen as the bane of texts, then, have also contributed to the prestige of texts. In the culture of manuscripts, a text can be "corrupted" in many ways, intentional and unintentional: through erasure, scribal negligence or error, contamination, and so on. Occurrences that damage a text, however, also contribute to its particularity and make it more "monumental." Even within a manuscript culture, such errors can be corrected, lacunae filled out. As we have seen (Chapter 6), Romans of this period corrected (*emendare*) their manuscripts as they read them. So far as this procedure can be reconstructed, though, it did not involve the eradication of problems within the text. "It is evident that the subscribers did their *emendatio* on a preexistent complete text; they made their corrections and annotations between the lines of, and in the margins of, a manuscript of Livy without intending to write or supervise the writing of any subsequent 'edition.'"[89] This form of ancient correction did not create a "clean" text, purged of all trace of corruption and error. Rather, it caused yet more damage to the text, imposing yet another layer of writing and alterations. Such corrections, like scribal errors, only contribute to the patina of the manuscript, and the patina is the sign of historical authority and authenticity.

It is an irony that modern textual criticism, which was intended from its origins to ameliorate and safeguard the manuscript,[90] in practice works to destroy its traditional monumental qualities. In the premodern world a modification to a text, whether intended as an attack (like the *damnatio memoriae,* or, to put it in more blatantly textual terms, *interpolatio*) or as a restoration (e.g. a rehabilitation or *emendatio*), only contributes to the monumental aura. These procedures are themselves products of a traditional culture, and presume particularity as a leading quality of the text. Textual criticism, by contrast, is a creation of the age of printing, and its presumptions and goals are those of reproduction. It aims to create a homogeneous and uniform text out of the various and corrupt attestations of a manuscript tradition. It accomplishes this goal by eliminating deviations and making good the damaged text. But history is in essence the discipline that concerns itself with the exceptional detail, the particular fact, the critical instance that contradicts the abstract generalization; it is the science that takes as its object damage and deviation.[91] Consequently, one of the central effects of modern textual criticism is the elimination of the material aspect of texts and with this the historical authority of the particular.[92] The particularity and monumental character of the text can be attacked only in the age of mechanical reproduction, because until that time an alternative to these qualities was impractical and imaginable only with difficulty. Before the printing press, it would have been pointless and impossible (outside of the painstaking work of the forger) to make a text homogeneous with all its exemplars. All objects are particular and unique. Thus, at least in their monumental and historical aspects, they can have no relationship of dependency on one another. With printing, the production of absolutely homogeneous copies becomes not only imaginable, but practical. Stemmatic criticism develops only after the proliferation of printed books: it becomes possible to criticize the manuscript tradition not as the production of unique and discriminable objects, but as a flawed process that provides many varied and mutilated versions of a single idealized archetype.[93] The depreciation of the particularity of objects in favor of a hypothetical and abstract archetype—or should I say prototype?—is the essence of the logic of reproduction. The methods and goals of stemmatic criticism find their parallel in the laws of copyright and patent, which themselves come into being in answer to problems raised by the technology of mass production: here, as in textual criticism, the goal is not the control of the individual text, but of the abstract content.

In a famous series of baroque paintings, the artists Guercino and Nicolas Poussin depict the encounter between pastoral life and death. In Guercino's painting, which is the earliest of the three (1621–1623), a pair of shepherds have come across a ruin; they ponder a skull, which sits on top of a wall. An inscription, *et in Arcadia ego,* runs along the top of the wall. The letters cannot be seen by the shepherds: the inscription faces away from them and toward the viewer. Several years later (1630) Poussin made a painting using this same theme. Now the shepherds are examining a tomb. Again, a skull is shown on top of it. But in this painting it is in a much less prominent position; it is ignored by the shepherds. They concentrate instead on an inscription on the side of the block. One shepherd appears to be deciphering the stone, following along with his finger as he reads. His hand blocks some of the letters of the inscription from the viewer of the painting; nevertheless, the text is easily recognizable: *et in Arcadia ego.* Poussin made a second version of this same painting (1635). Now the skull has vanished altogether. The shepherds gather around a tomb. One reads, again using his finger as an aid. Another points to something on the stone. They seem to be discussing some problem of decipherment or meaning between themselves. The inscription itself, however, is from the perspective of the viewer of the painting quite illegible.

The inscription represented in these paintings was originally understood to mean "even in Arcadia, I (i.e. death) am present" (so, for example, in the Guercino painting). Over time, however, it became canonical, and the understanding of it altered slightly: "I, too (i.e. the occupant of the tomb), once lived in Arcadia."[94] The text plays on several themes that were common in pastoral literature of the baroque period, and that had been traditional since at least the time of Vergil: nature, which eternally renews itself, versus the corruptible works of humankind; the enjoyment of life versus the inevitable fate of all; the "melancholy" that comes from the contemplation of love and death, even in the midst of pleasures.[95] Most important for my purposes, however, is the representation of writing in these paintings as something that is difficult to read, or even as something that is not read at all, and the association of this illegibility with death. Interestingly, actual inscriptions of the baroque period were often made to be more or less illegible. The effect might be created by creating a writing surface (say, a plaque) which is then left blank. Again, part of the text might be blocked off, as with Bernini's tomb of Urban VIII in St. Peter's: there the figure of death writes the pontiff's name on a cartouche of black bronze, but by his placement of the writer, Bernini has blocked the view of the inscription.[96]

In their material character, texts carry certain broad meanings, which can be understood independently from the words they bear. In an elementary way, whether it is read or not, a scroll or book or stele will be formally recognizable as a vehicle for writing. Of course, writing itself is recognizable in this same way. To understand marks as writing, it is not necessary to decipher *what* they mean; it is only necessary to recognize that they *mean*. In late antiquity, as at most times in human history, the vast majority of the populace could not read.[97] Yet, I think, it is these people who have always understood the essential character of writing best. For someone who cannot read, writing may evoke something known or unknown, familiar or mysterious—but in either case (and this is the important point), it patently refers to a thing that is not present in the writing itself. The literate, for whom letters may be transparent to the point of vanishing, have always been vulnerable to scriptural immanence and the illusion of its imminence: to the notion that writing, by virtue of its endurance, somehow contains its content; that what the writing says is identical with the writing itself. In this they are like historians who cannot discriminate between the document and the past it evokes. This illusion manifests itself in the cliché, criticized already by Plato, that writing provides a way of fixing and securing the evanescent meanings and consciousness that produced it: the idea, already present in the proem of Herodotus, that writing and monuments can somehow cheat death and preserve unchanged what has perished.

Even for the literate, though, it has traditionally proven difficult to maintain this illusion of the identity of writing and a fixed meaning. Writing, particularly when contrasted with speech, has disturbing connotations. In particular, it has always been difficult to escape the feeling that writing is an alienated form of representation. Speech emanates directly from its author; it occurs and vanishes with a specific context; its meaning seems guaranteed by the apparent unity of voice and consciousness in the person of the speaker. Writing, on the other hand, as Plato said in the *Phaedrus,* "has no father to protect it." It endures, separate from its author and from the context of its production; it has been cut off from the living, intending consciousness that gave it its meaning.[98] Writing is always irreconcilably other than what it pretends to be. If speech is commonly equated with a presence of speaker, meaning, and consciousness, writing (even while evoking these things) is at the same time commonly associated with their absence. And this association is the reason for coupling illegibility with death in the paintings of Poussin and Guercino.

An erasure, we might say, is not the negation of writing, but rather an exaggerated form of it. Here the literate are confronted with the same truth that the illiterate have always known: this mark here, on the stone before me now, indicates something that is not there, and not apparent. Historical research might usefully be imagined as a reading of the lacuna. History has traditionally been strongly identified with writing. The connotations of traditional forms of writing, like those of the monument, reinforce certain ideas about the past, and about the practice of history itself: writing is fixed, permanent; at the same time, and most important, it reiterates the sense of a separation. In its very medium, then, history replays the relationship between writing and its content, present and past.[99] In this way, writing—and by extension history and the monument—is not merely prompted by the lacuna; it is also the construction of a lacuna.

APPENDIX

Concerning the Text of *CIL* 6.1783

A HISTORY OF PUBLICATION

Despite its importance and difficulty, there have been few editions of the text, and none in this century. It will be convenient to list here (in chronological order) studies pertinent to the establishment of the text. These will be cited by author's name only in the remainder of the Appendix.

> Matranga 1849; De Rossi 1849; Cavedoni 1850; G. Henzen, supplement to Orelli 1828–1856, v. 3, no. 5593; G. Henzen and E. Bormann, eds., *CIL* 6.1783 (1882); Seeck 1883, cxii–cxiii; Paribeni 1933, 493, no. 167; Barbieri 1969, 73–74 with photographs, figs. 1–3.

The text of the inscription has often been reproduced in epigraphic collections, though usually without the complete text of the imperial letter (e.g. *ILS* 2948). I know of no translation of the complete text into English, though translations do exist in French and German.[1]

The main part of the inscription was discovered in August 1849. Workmen constructing a drain uncovered it in the Forum of Trajan, at the west porch of the Basilica Ulpia. With it was found another inscription, a statue base dedicated by the Spanish provinces in 364 to Flavius Sallustius, who was consul in 363 (*CIL* 6.1729 = *ILS* 1254).[2]

The inscription was first published in 1849 by Matranga and was re-edited later that same year by De Rossi. This edition has been the basis for all subsequent publications. So, for example, the editors of the *CIL,* Henzen and

Bormann, examined the stone to verify more difficult readings, but depended on De Rossi for most of their text.[3] Though I have examined the stone, my text also owes much to De Rossi.

On the left side of the statue base (as one faces the inscription), a fragment of a consular date survived.[4] More of this date was discovered in 1933, when a fragment was unearthed in the vicinity of the Basilica Ulpia. The editor recognized that the fragment contained a consular date, but incorrectly ascribed it to the time of Septimius Severus. In 1969 G. Barbieri managed to join the fragment to the left side of Flavian's base.

The inscription is now kept in a storeroom built under the modern street to the side of the ruins of the Greek library of the Forum of Trajan. The base and the fragment are located in different parts of the storeroom: one near "cancello" IV, the other near VI. The statue base bears the inventory number 3434.

THE TEXT

The text of the inscription can be divided into four sections: the two *cursus* of Flavian and his son (lines 1–6); the imperial letter of Valentinian III and Theodosius II (lines 7–36); a postscript stating the circumstances of the erection of the inscription (lines 37–38); and the formula providing the date when the inscription was set up (left side). The original of the imperial letter would have been written in a less durable medium. The recipients of the letter have reproduced it here for public display. The other sections were composed specifically for the inscription.

The dedication of the inscription is unusual. The first lines of the text contain a double *cursus,* and the honorific language is ambiguous. The inscription is dedicated "to the father" (in the dative) and "in honor of the son" (in the genitive following *in honorem*). The passive construction of the dedication is odd as well (see Chapter 2). The imperial letter is literary and rhetorical, both sophisticated and convoluted. Comparable examples of bureaucratic prose can be found in the imperial letters reproduced on inscriptions all over the empire, or in the juristic writings collected in the Theodosian Code and the Justinian Code, or in Cassiodorus' *Variae*.[5]

The precise nature of the imperial letter is not clear. De Rossi described it as a *diploma* (288, 315 n. 1, 348–356). Most subsequent scholars have characterized it more generally as an imperial letter *(epistula)*.[6] Strictly speaking, a *diploma* was a document composed of two leaves (whence the name), sent by the emperor to individuals as evidence of certain privileges *(beneficia)* granted them. So a traveler might receive a *diploma* attesting the right of free transport and lodging, or a soldier might receive such a text attesting the rights of citizenship.[7] The rehabilitation of Flavian and the restoration of the son's honor is an imperial benefice—and imperial *diplomata* were granted to individuals in comparable disgrace. For example, after the condemnation of the lovers of Julia, Augustus granted them *diplomata* so that they could travel safely (Seneca *De Clem.* 1.10.3). This letter, however, is addressed to the Roman senate and not to some individual descendant of Flavian. Moreover, it is specifically denied that the letter is a rescript to a petition by the senate (lines 28–30). Instead, the letter takes the form of a hortatory address to that body. The emperor was technically a member of the senate and had the right to address it. The letter alludes to such an oration by an earlier emperor, Theodosius the Great, in which the emperor regretfully condemned Flavian and the other leading figures of the usurpation of 394 (lines 16–21). In practice, however, the emperor was seldom in Rome, so his addresses to the senate often took the form of letters *(epistulae),* recited aloud to the senate by someone else.[8]

THE STATUE BASE

The height of the statue base is 1.51 m, the width .725 m. At some time before its discovery, the rear of the statue base was sheared away (see De Rossi, 288). The maximum preserved depth is .425 m. The base is crowned by a molding .22 m high. The front face of the molding is more elaborate than its sides, which are simple, outward curves. The horizontal top is partially preserved. Because of the crown moldings, the top is wider and deeper than the rest of the base: it was at a minimum .76 m wide. Two cuttings, presumably for a statue of Flavian, are preserved on it.

The field of the inscription measures 1.05 × .675 m. It is recessed, creating the appearance of a raised frame at its sides and bottom. This raised surface is narrow at the sides, measuring in each case about .025 m. The lower edge of the base has broken away, so it is impossible to tell whether there was a molding or other ornament at the foot of the inscription. The stone continues for about .24 m from the lower edge of the recessed face to the bottom of the statue base.

There are several indications that the inscription was carved over an erasure. First, the area of the inscription was originally surrounded by an inner frame, which mediated the difference between the recessed plane of the inscription and the higher face of the statue base. This inner frame survives now only at the top; at the sides and bottom, it has been carved away; now the edges of the inscribed face curve gently up to meet the raised boundaries of the inscription. In some lines the letters of the text creep up onto this curved section. Second, the field on which the text is carved undulates subtly. Such wavy unevenness is a typical product of erasure. Third, on close inspection occasional traces of earlier letters show through. These figures are shadowy, vague, and illegible; nevertheless, where they appear they seem regular in size and distribution, as one would expect if they are surviving traces of letters from an earlier text.

LETTERING

The letters of the inscription were drawn freehand in a style that epigraphers once called *scriptura actuaria*. This lettering has affinities with the recognized bookhand used for deluxe texts of this period, the so-called *canonical capitalis* (formerly called rustic capitals).[9]

As a rule, Roman inscriptions begin with large letters and use smaller letters below.[10] The lettering of the first eight lines is typically larger than that used in the body of the imperial letter, ranging consistently between .018 and .02 m in height. The interlineation in the first eight lines is slightly greater than that in the rest of the inscription, running to approximately .011 m. In the imperial letter, characters are noticeably smaller, measuring consistently about .015 m in height. Here the interlineation is approximately .01 m. Throughout, certain letters (L, F, I, and T) may be cut larger than the others, up to .025 m in height.[11] I do not indicate these here: see the photograph (Illus. 1) and De Rossi's drawing.

The density of the written line (i.e. the crowding of letters next to one another) creates the impression that the letters are elongated. In fact, the characters throughout this inscription are not remarkably high in relation to their width: the ratio of height to width is regularly about 2:1. There is no consistent shading of letters. Letter strokes are uniform, with little or no noticeable variation in depth and breadth. Vertical and horizontal strokes alike may have serifs.

ORTHOGRAPHY

Abbreviations are seldom used, except for the offices and titulature mentioned at the beginning and end of the inscription. There are practically no abbreviations in the imperial letter. The manuscripts of the contemporary

Theodosian Code observe a comparable usage. The Roman senate had urged specifically that no mystifying abbreviations (especially no legal abbreviations) be admitted into the Theodosian Code (see among the acclamations of the *Gesta Senatus de Theodosiano publicando*, 5, 11). Consequently the constitutions of the Code are relatively free of abbreviations. Headers and footers (*inscriptiones* and *subscriptiones*) to these texts, however, regularly abbreviate offices, names, and actions.[12]

The conventions of orthography are also comparable to those of the Theodosian Code.[13] The use of *adque* instead of *atque* (see line 9) is a uniform feature of both. The spelling *aput* is preferred to *apud* (lines 14, 16, 21, 24, 36). The diphthong *ae* is once preferred for *e* (*piaetas*, line 21), as we often see in the manuscripts of the Theodosian Code. The spelling *intelligo* is preferred to *intellego* (line 13; see De Rossi, 287, and the critical apparatus below). In one instance *qu* is replaced by *c* (*cottidie*, line 32). In prepositional prefixes, *s* is retained following *x* in *exsistimo* (lines 12, 32); the prefix *in-* is not modified to *im-* (or *il-* etc.) where context might seem to demand it (*inproborum*, line 21; *inlustris*, lines 9, 14; *inmerito*, line 27); likewise, the *d* of *ad-* is retained before *s* (*adstruximus*, line 22; *adservata*, line 24).

The few abbreviations commonly admitted into the imperial letter are useful for purposes of comparison with the Theodosian Code: *q.* for *q(ue)* (passim); *b.* for *b(us)* (lines 22, 23, and 25); *res p.* for *res p(ublica)* (lines 9 and 23); *p.c.* for *p(atres) c(onscripti)* (lines 13, 27, and 34). In one case, the final *-um* of a genitive plural, *provinciar(um)* (line 22), has been abbreviated at the end of a line. These same abbreviations, along with a few others, are admitted into the constitutions of the Theodosian Code.

The abbreviations for offices, because they are typically found in inscriptions and other texts of this period, are not diagnostic for a similarity with the Theodosian Code. In the careers, abbreviations are commonly (but not uniformly) marked by a supralineate bar.[14] More significant abbreviations in the imperial letter are also so indicated: for instance, *-q.* for *-q(ue)* and *-ib.* for the dative/ablative plural ending *-ib(us)* are not marked by the supralineate bar; *provinciar.*, *res p.*, and *p.c.* are so marked. I have indicated these in the text (cf. De Rossi's drawing of the text). There is only one ligature in the inscription: the N and T have been combined in *reverentiae* (line 24).[15]

Word divisions are consistently observed at line breaks. There are exceptions at lines 13, 14, 17, 19, 24, 25, and 29, but even in these cases syllabic divisions are always observed. Word division is also indicated in the text by the use of "interpuncts." These are used frequently in the careers, but seldom in the imperial letter, where they are found after the abbreviations *-ib(us)* and

-q(ue). Several marks are used for the interpunct: a simple dot or intersecting lines in the shape of an "×" or "+." A leaf is carved at the end of line 5 as a decorative filler and to divide the careers from the imperial letter. I have not indicated the punctuation in my text; see De Rossi's drawing.

TEXTUAL NOTES

The text of the inscription is difficult to read. Many of the letters have been worn away and are scarcely decipherable. The difficulty is increased by the cutting style of the stonemason: letters are faint and inconsistent, so that they are easily confused with one another. Furthermore, the inscription is a palimpsest, and in some places indecipherable traces of letters from the previous text seem to survive. Where the damage is worst, traces from the earlier and later version may easily be confounded. In general I restrict my comments here to passages in which the reading is in doubt.

The inscription poses very basic problems of decipherment. In places words are faint but (if I do not deceive myself) legible. In other places the traces of the letters are so faint that they cannot be read, though they are sufficient to exclude certain readings and to confirm the possibility of others. In such cases, the text is not exactly a restoration—though it is not really an "objective reading" either. In view of such elementary problems of transcription, it would be laughable to pretend that my own expectations have had no influence on the text I present here. Moreover, it would be dishonest to deny the influence of the readings of previous editors. On the other hand, my text is not merely a product of my own imagination. I have always measured my interpretations and readings against the traces on the stone. As De Rossi remarks (p. 288), in this text it is difficult to draw a line between objective reading and editorial restoration.

Line 4: By slip of the pen, *CIL* prints *Nicomaghi* in its diplomatic text.

Line 5: Matranga read *praef. urbis Appius,* not *praef. urbi saepius.* I have verified this reading, as did De Rossi, who admitted he could read nothing else, even though he found the reading inadmissible (p. 286). Henzen and Brunn confirmed the reading: see De Rossi, 314–315 and n. 1.

If the text is not corrected, then the prefecture is described by the genitive, *urbis,*[16] and the interpretation of the dedication becomes much more complicated. Appius Nicomachus Dexter (see line 37) would be the subject of the dedication, and *reddita (sc. statua,* line 4)[17] would have to be emended to *redditam.* The office of *praef. praet. Italiae Illyrici et Africae* (lines 5–6), would no longer apply to the younger Flavian (line 4), but to Appius. There is no evidence that Appius was ever praetorian prefect. The younger Flavian, however, did hold that position under Valentinian III and his mother, Galla Placidia (Chapter 2 above); the text of the imperial letter alludes to his current tenure of the office (lines 29–33).[18] Finally, it would be extremely odd if Appius were described only by his *nomen* and as *nunc praef. praet.* in the preamble, but by his full name and as *ex praef. urb.* in the postscript.[19]

In spite of what the stone says, it is necessary to keep Appius out of the preamble. A number of solutions have been proposed. Borghesi suggested *praef. urbi sacr. ter* or *praef. urbis aet. ter*.[20] De Rossi at first wanted to correct the text to *tertium* or *iterum*. The younger Flavian held the urban prefecture three times in all. One of these terms, though, he received from a pretender to the throne, Eugenius, so either emendation was possible. In the end, he selected neither, but decided that the first P of Appius was not so certainly inscribed that it could not also be an E. Whether or not this reading is correct (and I can perceive nothing but a P here), as a correction it is economical and elegant, producing a subtle and appropriate sense indeed: *praef. urbi saepius* (see Chapter 2 above). Henzen and Brunn verified the reading, and Borghesi gave his seal of approval (*apud* De Rossi, 359).

In the years since De Rossi's article, there has been no acknowledgment of the problem here. The word *saepius* has come to be treated as an unproblematic, objective reading. It appears in subsequent editions of the text without comment (so e.g. Henzen *apud* Orelli; *CIL*).

There is now a parallel for De Rossi's conjecture. In 1992 Silvio Panciera published an inscription in which the tetrarch Maxentius is described as having held the consulship "rather often" *(saepius)*. Panciera was also able to point to a Greek inscription of the third century (*AE* 1902, 244), in which a certain L. Egnatius Victor Lollianus is described as "proconsul of Asia rather often" (πολλάκις).[21]

Line 11: The letters following *lucem* are difficult to read. De Rossi, in his diplomatic text, estimated that there was space for eight or nine letters, and thought that the word here should begin with MV, NVM, VMA or VMM (pp. 285 and 286). Earlier Matranga had produced the same reading (p. 270). De Rossi proposed a variety of restorations: *publicam* or *urbanam* or *vitamque* would fit the traces he perceived and provide the sense required. He finally opts in his critical text for *hominum* (pp. 286–287 and 348). Other supplements have been proposed. Bormann *(apud CIL)* suggested *[antiquam?]*. Seeck proposed *a[etern]a[m]*. The first letter of this word appears to me to be certainly an A. I can make out some horizontal *hastae* following, which would suit a variety of letters; I can find no trace of the rest of the word. The sense of Seeck's restoration seems to me more appropriate than that of Bormann, and I have adopted it in my text.

Line 12: The deceptively simple restoration of *[sum]mumq(ue)* is on close examination problematic. Matranga, like De Rossi, can read MVMQ. Allowing for the three final letters of *praeiudic[ium]*, Matranga then estimates room for four letters before MVMQ. De Rossi reads an M separated off before the second M of *summumq.* by a small space. Later editors, such as Henzen (*apud* Orelli and in the *CIL*) apparently read this M as the end of *praeiudicium,* rather than as the middle of *summumq.* However one reads this letter, it wreaks havoc with the restoration of the text. To judge by De Rossi's drawing, there is not even space for one letter between the two M's, and there appears to be inadequate space to accommodate the restoration before the M. De Rossi acknowledges the problem (p. 287).

I have not been able to verify these readings. I can make out the usual shadowy traces between PRAEIVDIC and MVMQ, though I would be unwilling to insist on a connection between any of these and a particular letter of the restoration. The space available here is certainly appropriate for the restoration proposed. Since I have been unable to discern the troublesome second M, I cannot comment further on the problem raised by the readings of earlier editors here.

Of the following word, the letters ENT are certain: they were read by both De Rossi (p. 287) and Matranga. The amount of available space between these and the word preceding, *summumq.*, is variously represented: Matranga suggests seven letters; De Rossi, in his diplomatic text, suggests four or five; Henzen (*apud* Orelli) estimates six; Henzen and the other editors of the *CIL* represent five. The space available after ENT is, according to De Rossi's diplomatic text, sufficient to accommodate two or three letters. Later editors, including Henzen (*apud* Orelli) and the editors of the *CIL,* profess to be able to read MENTVM in this space. De Rossi, however, adds one final, contradictory specification (p. 286): the first letter of the word seems to him to be an A, the last an E. He then goes on to restore tentatively *summumq. detrimentum* in this space. De Rossi himself was very cautious about the restoration, even proposing a wildly different alternative: *damnumq. aeminentiae.* He comments that this restoration, while contradicting his reading of the first word, would fit the discernible traces of the second word well.

The reading of MENT is certain. The final letters are faint: I see no question about the V; only the vertical *hastae* of the M are certain, so there is a range of possibilities here. Given the irregularities in the size and disposition of letters in this text, any attempt to provide an exact count of letters missing in a lacuna should be greeted with skepticism. I do not find the estimates of any of the previous editors impossible. Presuming that no space has been left between words (and such spaces are occasionally left in this text), four letters at the minimum should be restored here. I think it would be difficult (though not impossible) to fit seven letters into the space available.

Given the uncertainty of the space and letters, I hesitantly put forward an alternative: *[supple]mentum*. That this word is one letter longer than De Rossi's estimate of the space should cause no uneasiness, given the difficulties of determining such matters in this inscription. For the argument justifying this restoration, see Chapter 6 above.

Line 13: After PC, there follows a space that can accommodate on the order of ten or twelve letters. De Rossi thought he could make out the traces of the first three letters, and suggested that they might read either PAV or FAV, and the last four are certainly MINE or MINI (p. 287, with his diplomatic text, p. 285, and the drawing). Matranga read [......] S [......]MINI in this space. Between these, De Rossi can make out only the tip of one letter. I have not been able to make out the first three letters, or any of the letters in this space. The last four I read as MINI.

There follows a jumble of letter strokes, which are difficult to decipher. From this confusion De Rossi reads *intellegitis,* and Henzen verified this reading (p. 287). In support of the reading, De Rossi cites the orthography of the word in the Theodosian Code. The final five letters of this word, GITIS, seem to me certain. The other letters appear as a series of vertical strokes, which individually could be interpreted as any number of letters.

Having established the general shape of the line, De Rossi suggests a specific reconstruction: *bono nobiscum p.c. faustoq. omine.* He sees no other possibility that does not diverge far from the perceptible traces on the stone. He suggests that if he were not constrained by the traces on the stone, he would propose to read: *bono nobiscum p.c. statim animo* (p. 287).

Line 14: After *restitutionem* there follows a large, illegible space before *inlustris.* The first editor, Matranga, read DIGNIT, followed by the traces of fourteen more letters in this space. De Rossi came to the same estimate of the number of letters available but did not read any of the letters printed by Matranga (p. 288). He did, however, note that the last four letters of the space seemed to be INIS. He says also that he has been able to isolate one additional letter in the lacuna, but he never specifies what that letter might be.

De Rossi believed that any restoration in this space should include *honoris* or *memoriae* and, at the end of the space, *nominis,* but he was ultimately unable to make these impressions agree with the space available on the stone. Finally, he left the passage for others to read, noting that any restoration must be accommodated to the visible but illegible traces on the stone. In his critical text, he printed *[honoris ac nominis]*.

The editors of the *CIL* were able to make some progress with this passage. They read considerably fewer letters than De Rossi and Matranga had, and they deciphered several additional letters. In their diplomatic text, they printed PR.M...INIS. No convincing restorations came of this reading. In their critical text, the *CIL* prints De Rossi's restoration, suggesting tentatively an alternative proposed by Bormann: *pr[imitivam nom]inis*. The following year, Seeck suggested another restoration: *pr[istini honor]is*. None of these accounts for the space and traces perceived on the stone by the editors of the *CIL*.

The reading *-inis* is not in doubt. The first two letters are more difficult. I believe that the traces of the second can be nothing but an R. The first admits a range of possibilities: I can make out an upright and at least one crossbar. This letter could be a P or an F or an E, for example. The traces that the editors of the *CIL* interpret as an M seem even less certain to me. I perceive several straight lines at facing angles: these might be traces of A, M, or N. It is difficult to gauge the number of letters that should be restored in the lacuna. I cannot imagine that more than two or three letters could conceivably have stood between the R and the angular traces at the center of the lacuna, and a like number of letters must have stood between the angular traces and the *-inis*.

With much hesitation, I would propose the restoration *pr[ae]n[om]inis* here. Given the physical space available and the visible traces on the stone here, this is the only restoration yet suggested that is physically possible. It is also appropriate in the context of the rehabilitation of Flavian from the *damnatio memoriae* he had suffered. Nevertheless, this restoration too is problematic, as I am well aware and as my benevolent readers have pointed out to me. For this reason I have not printed it in my text. For this restoration and the problems it causes, see Chapter 4 above.

Line 15: The name of Flavian in this line was seen only by Matranga in his initial transcription of the stone. Soon afterward, the inscription was vandalized, and the name was entirely obliterated (De Rossi, 288).

Line 20: With *annalium* we must understand *libros* or some other such word, which has either been omitted accidentally from the stone or is to be supplied. If the problem here is not owing to the stonemason, then we might perhaps understand some word such as *eos,* which can be inferred from the following relative pronoun. As commonly in Greek (and rarely in Latin), the antecedent may have been absorbed into the following relative pronoun.[22]

Line 30: Matranga read the final word of the line as *fili,* and represented space for five additional letters following. De Rossi has a similar estimate of the space available at the end of the line, for he restores *fili[us ei]* here. I believe that I find a trace of the left-slanting vertical of the V here. I am not certain that there is space for another word following, even one as short as *ei*. In any event, the context does not require further specification, so I have not restored this word.

Line 32: De Rossi restores *abs[q. ullo]* here without comment; later editors have found the conjecture convincing. The restoration is adequate to the sense required and to the space available on the stone. The word *absque* can be used either to mean *et ab* or as a synonym of simple *ab* or *sine*. In this context, following *integer et,* the latter sense is required. Elsewhere in this inscription, *ab* is used once (line 18) and *absque* is used once, in the sense of *et ab* (line 25). Two examples can scarcely be taken to establish a general rule. De Rossi's restoration is plausible.

There is another possible restoration: *abs[olutus]*. The word to be restored here should be an adjective to balance *integer.* This adjective should have legal connotations in order to continue the tone set by *delatus* and *integer;* it must govern the ablative. In context, when used with *debito,* the word we seek should have the meaning "exonerated of." The point of the passage is that the family owes a religious duty to the deceased which it has not been allowed to expiate: until it has redeemed this debt, its honor is not complete. The word *absolutus* meets all these requirements "absolutely." The restoration is one letter longer than De Rossi's, but this detail should not be unduly troubling: the right-hand margin of the text is ragged, and there is ample space on the stone to accommodate an additional letter.

Lines 29–33: The lines comprise a single clause. The reading here is difficult but relatively secure. Interpretation is difficult, though, because the lines are ungrammatical (cf. De Rossi, 288, 315 n. 1, and 348–349).

The passage begins with a subordinate clause *(cum . . . delatus exsistimetur)* and continues with a further subordination *(nisi integer . . . sit)*. It is difficult to locate the main verb on which all this depends. R. Kaster suggests to me that it should be taken as a circumstantial clause, loosely relying on the *ne* clause ("lest we seem") above. This is the simplest solution. Certainly these clauses are intended as continuing justifications for the rehabilitation of Flavian. The word *alioqui,* "furthermore," refers back to the justifications already alleged by the emperor with some adversative force, thus clarifying the construction.

There is a much greater difficulty at the beginning of this section: there appear to be two subjects for the clause introduced by *cum*. The words *ipse* (line 29) and *probatus* (line 30) both evidently refer to the younger Flavian. It is for this reason that De Rossi restored *fili[us]* in apposition with them at the end of line 30. On the other hand, these words might equally describe *honor semiplenus*, which is also a nominative, and which has equal claim to be the subject of the clause.

Various solutions to this problem have been proposed. De Rossi proposed to end the clause introduced by *cum* with *filius*, and to take *honor* as the subject of *exsistimetur*, which then becomes the main verb of a complete sentence. To that end, he restores *ei* before *honor*. Some verb meaning "to be" would have to be supplied (p. 348). As De Rossi emends it, the sentence might be paraphrased as follows: *cum probatus fuerit Flaviani filius, ei honor semiplenus delatus exsistemetur, nisi integer sit* ("although the son of Flavian has been proven true, his half-full honor may be considered on trial, unless he is exonerated").

Cavedoni found this interpretation forced and remarked that a suitable sense could be obtained without any restoration. He suggested that *fili* (line 30) should not be restored as *filius*, but should be taken as a genitive, and that *honor* could then stand as the subject of the entire clause (pp. 158–159). The clause might then be translated as follows: "when the honor of the son of Flavian, proved true, may be thought to be on trial, half complete as it is. . . ." Henzen (*apud* Orelli) followed this interpretation. So I have rendered it in my translation.²³

If the reading of *filiu[s]* is correct (see above ad loc.), this interpretation would have to be rejected. There would be no easy solution. So, for example, the editors of the *CIL* returned to De Rossi's restoration of *fili[us]* in their critical text. They take note of the grammatical problems in a footnote, however, and suggest the following correction: *ips⟨i⟩ etiam de institutione illius probat⟨o⟩ saepe nobis parentibusque nostris Flavian⟨o⟩ fili⟨o⟩ honor*. Here *honor* becomes the subject of the clause, and the other difficult nominatives are subordinated to it as datives.

NOTES

PREFACE

1. His explanation of the image and account of the dispute are so detailed as to make further commentary superfluous. He recollects the palimpsested inscriptions from the *Antichità* as if on the wall of a museum in tav. 8 of the *Lettere* (reproduced as the frontispiece of this book). The text of the *Lettere* is reproduced in Wilton-Ely 1972.
2. P. R. L. Brown 1961; see Chapter 3 below.
3. So he argues in publications from the late 1960's through the 1980's. A more nuanced interpretation of the *Saturnalia* is forthcoming from Cameron.
4. For essays on traditional versus modernist history, see Koselleck 1985a. Hayden White's essay "The Burden of History," reprinted in White 1978, remains worthwhile.
5. The classic essays on the subject are H. Bloch 1945 and 1964.
6. Of his many articles I would single out Cameron 1977 and 1984. For a comparable argument, see also O'Donnell 1978. For an attempt to summarize the significance of this train of thought, see the effort by Averil Cameron (1993, 156–157).
7. See e.g. Hunt 1989, 1–22.
8. This subject has been explored from a very different perspective by R. A. Markus (1990), who speaks of "the creation of the secular."
9. See H. Bloch 1964, Cameron 1977, and Cameron 1984.

1. A PALIMPSEST

1. See most notably H. Bloch 1945 and 1964. For consideration of this, see Chapter 3.
2. The words *clarus* and *inlustris* also have implications of rank: both traditionally refer to the nobility, but *clari viri* were inferior to *illustres*. See further Chapter 2.
3. For the significance of this odd statement, see Chapter 6.
4. For the metaphor, see again Chapter 6.
5. The antecedent of "which" (*quae*) here may be either "correction" (*emendatio*) or "fate" (*sortis*). For the meaning of the subordinate clause here, see the textual notes in the Appendix and Chapter 6.
6. In the Appendix see the textual notes ad loc. for this phrase.

2. *CURSUS* AND CAREER

1. Cagnat 1914 contains an excellent general discussion of the Roman *cursus*. For a more recent discussion, see Calabi-Limentani 1973, 164–167, with the bibliography by Attilio Degrassi, 446–450.
2. Callu 1974; *PLRE* I, Flavianus 15; O'Donnell 1978; Vera 1983; Matthews 1989a; Errington 1992. I find two exceptions to my generalization: Grünewald 1992 is concerned more with the rehabilitation of Flavian than with his career; Wytzes 1977 is mostly interested in the religious implications of the text. Cf. now, however, Matthews 1997, 211–213.
3. This interest dates back to Roman antiquity: see Nep. *Att.* 18.1–4. Much of the traditional research on the *cursus* was compiled and systematized in the great prosopographical dictionaries of the end of the nineteenth century. Generally on the history of epigraphical interest in the *cursus* and prosopographical research, see Galsterer 1990, 5–6.
4. Galsterer 1990, 8–9.
5. Galsterer 1990, 1–20, and the preface to Raaflaub and Toher 1990, xiv–xv.
6. Syme 1952, 7.
7. Syme 1952, preface, vii.
8. Syme 1952, preface, vii; cf. Syme's general comments about prosopography later in the preface.
9. So Cicero complains of factual errors in certain inscriptions: *ad Att.* 6.1.17.
10. On the rhetorical effect of the list, see White 1980, who is chiefly concerned with medieval Annals.
11. Galsterer 1990, 7. Cf. Syme 1952.
12. Cameron 1985b.
13. Thus O'Donnell 1978, 131 treats some of the ambiguities in the careers of Flavian and his son as "merely a bit of boasting" or "a bureaucratic nicety of detail." Cf. Errington 1992, 442 n. 15.
14. Other words used for "magistracy" in late antiquity are *dignitas* and *administratio:* see Jones 1964, 368, 377–378.
15. The problems and difficulties of the preamble have not been clearly recognized since Borghesi (in De Rossi 1849, 359).
16. The more important of these are conveniently assembled and summarized in *PLRE* I, Flavianus 15.
17. The letters addressed to Flavian are chiefly those of the second book of correspondence, *Epp.* 2.1–91.
18. He may also be the author of a number more: see Honoré 1989b.
19. "Nickname" is a loose and occasionally inaccurate translation of the notion of the *signum*. Generally on the use of the *signum* in Late Roman inscriptions, see Kajanto 1966 [i.e. 1967] and Cameron 1995.
20. Cf. Platner 1929, 191; Collini 1944, 282 and 420.
21. Cf. Bloch 1945, 210; Matthews 1973, 187.
22. So argued by De Rossi 1849, 290–293, 300–310; he has been followed by many later scholars, including the *ILS*. For the most recent assent, see Honoré 1989b, 10–11.

23. Cf. O. Seeck, *RE* ser. 2, 4, 1 (1931), Symmachus 27; *PLRE* 2, Symmachus 10; O'Donnell 1978, 129 n. 3.
24. For this *signum* of Flavian see Cameron 1995, 256.
25. For *agentis* on the stone it is necessary to understand *agenti:* see *IRT* ad loc.
26. So De Rossi (who regarded Virius as the gentilitial of the family) explained the omission of the name: De Rossi 1849, 291. There is no general account of the rules of nomenclature in late antiquity: see e.g. Gordon 1983, 22–23, which provides some bibliography. The point of departure for work on late antique nomenclature now must be Cameron 1985b; see further Eck 1993.
27. See in particular Cameron 1985b, esp. 171–177.
28. Cf. Averil Cameron 1993, index s.v. Nicomachi, and p. 79, where the name Virius is treated as a *praenomen*. The best discussion of Flavian's family background remains De Rossi 1849, 291–293.
29. See Conway 1897, index 3, s.v. Viria (*gens*) and nos. 106 and 109.
30. Generally for this family, see the *RE* s.vv. Virii, Virrii. For the consulars in the family, Barnes 1982b, index s.v. Virius. For Virii contemporary with Flavian, see e.g. Virius Lupus, a *consularis Campaniae* at about the time of Julian (*PLRE* 1, Lupus 7), and Virius Audentius Aemilianus, who was active around 378–383, serving as *consularis Campaniae* and also in Africa (*PLRE* 1, Aemilianus 4). For further Virii see the cross-references in the *PLRE* s.v.
31. On the nature of this class, Matthews 1975, 1–31. The extent to which this group had shared cultural values has come to be controversial: see Chapter 3 below.
32. Cf. *PLRE* 1, Venustus 5; De Rossi 1849, 291.
33. Seeck 1883, cii–cxiv. Cf. *PLRE* 1, Flavianus 8, Paulinus 14 and 17. Generally on the Anicii, see Matthews 1981.
34. See Cameron 1985b, 173.
35. For the senatorial *cursus* in the late empire, see Matthews 1975, 12–17.
36. If the so-called "poem against the pagans" (*Carmen contra paganos*) was in fact directed against Flavian, as some have thought, it would provide a date for Flavian's birth. According to the *Carmen,* its unnamed pagan villain died at age sixty (line 67). Flavian committed suicide after the battle at the river Frigidus, in 394, so he would have been born in 334. It is unlikely that the *Carmen* is directed against Flavian (see Chapter 3 below); still, the date must be approximately right in order to accommodate the rest of Flavian's career.
37. For these offices see Jones 1964, vol. 1, 530; Chastagnol 1960, 74–75, 405–406; Chastagnol 1958, 221–253.
38. See De Rossi 1849, 293.
39. Matthews 1975, 14.
40. Seeck 1883, cxiv; id., *RE* Flavianus 14, col. 2507; *PLRE* 1, Flavianus 15, sec. b.
41. Cf. *PLRE* 1, Venustus 5.
42. The governorship of Sicily in this period was commonly held by Roman aristocrats, not all of whom had estates on the island: see Matthews 1975, 14, and *PLRE* 1, *fasti*.
43. This *constitutio* of Gratian is addressed to *Florianum vic. Asiae;* the name here has been emended to *Flavianum vic. Africae.* See O. Seeck, *RE* 6, 2 (1909), Flavianus 14, col. 2507.

44. For the imperial *vicarii*, see Jones 1964, 481–482; Chastagnol 1960, 417–418. Roman senators were often appointed to the post: see Matthews 1975, 15, 27–30; *PLRE* 1, *fasti*, 1079–1080.
45. For this episode see Matthews 1989b, 281–282, 384–387, with bibliography cited on 536 n. 2. Of the earlier essays, see particularly Guey 1950 and Warmington 1956. For general discussion of Roman North Africa in late antiquity, see Lepelley 1979.
46. Cf. *IRT* 526, which provides reasons for the dedication of the people of Lepcis Magna to Flavian's partner in Africa, Hesperius: *iustitiae quam causae Tripolitanae del(e)gatae . . . exhibuit*.
47. On the Donatists, Frend 1985.
48. See Guey 1950, 84 n. 4. O'Donnell 1978, 130 n. 7, interprets the passage literally, explaining that Augustine has mistaken Flavian for a Donatist, as does Honoré 1989b, 10 and n. 22.
49. See G. Wesener, *RE* 24 (1963), quaestor, col. 822.
50. See further Vera 1983, 49–50, who discusses other reasons for Flavian's appointment to the court of Constantinople.
51. Generally on the *quaestor sacri palatii* see Jones 1964, vol. 1, 387, 504–505, 541; Voss 1982, 33–39; Harries 1988; Honoré 1994. For Flavian's quaestorship, contrast now particularly Honoré 1989b, 9–10, and Errington 1992, 446–448.
52. Symm. *Ep.* 3.81 and esp. 3.90: *quaestorem antehac fratrem, nunc rectorem praetorianum litteris nuntiasti*. Cf. Honoré 1989b, 13, for general discussion of the practice of moving immediately from one office to the next. O'Donnell 1978 tries to separate quaestorship from first term as praetorian prefect by six years, putting the quaestorship in 383 and first term as prefect in 389. It is also barely conceivable, as argued in Errington 1992, that Flavian first held the praetorian prefecture, then held the quaestorship, then held the prefecture for a second time. For a response to Errington, see now Matthews 1997.
53. For the praetorian prefecture see Jones 1964, index s.v.
54. This date was first supported by Seeck 1883, cxvi. Seeck has been followed by Hartke 1940, Callu 1974, and O'Donnell 1978. Cf. now Errington 1992, 456–461.
55. For the date of the younger Flavian's proconsulship, see below. The letters of Symmachus that establish the connection between the father's time at the imperial court and the younger Flavian's appointment as proconsul are *Epp.* 2.19, 22, and 24. Matthews (1989a) has recently criticized this argument. He maintains that *Ep.* 2.24 must refer to the son's proconsulship, and that it is not clear that Flavian is praetorian prefect; that *Ep.* 2.19 is certainly addressed to Flavian at the imperial court, but that there is no clear reference to the younger Flavian's proconsulship; that *Ep.* 2.22 likewise clearly places Flavian at the imperial court, but does not unequivocally refer to the son's proconsulship. Matthews is right, in my opinion, about *Ep.* 2.24. His arguments about *Epp.* 2.19 and 22 are less convincing.
56. This was the position of Seeck 1883, cxvi. The date has been accepted and argued by others, including Hartke 1938, 430–436; Callu 1974, 73–78; O'Donnell 1978, 133–136; and Vera 1983, 41–43.

57. On the history of the arrangement of the provinces in this period, see Vera 1983.
58. Callu 1974, 75–76. Cf. Matthews (1989a), who points out that this argument is not necessary: senators from the west did serve in the east in this period.
59. Levy 1971, 248–249.
60. Seeck came to support this date some years after his edition of Symmachus: Seeck 1919, 116, 261. The imperial constitutions supporting 383 would then have to be redated to 391. His argument has been seconded by Levy (1971, 245–249), who dated the quaestorship to 389/390; cf. e.g. *PLRE* I, Flavianus 15, sec. d. Matthews (1975, 231) argued that Flavian was quaestor in 388–389 and praetorian prefect for the first time in 389/390; cf. Honoré 1989a, 10, and Matthews 1989b, 479 n. 7, maintaining this position. See the extensive bibliography and critical remarks of Errington 1992, 448–456.
61. For the history of Theodosius I, his war with Magnus Maximus, and his administrative settlement of the western empire, see e.g. Matthews 1975, 223–252.
62. Honoré 1989b, 15; cf. Matthews 1989a, 24.
63. Errington 1992, 446–448, 456–457. Against Errington see now Matthews 1997. Cf. Harries 1988, 157.
64. These rescripts from the Theodosian Code (7.18.8 and 9.29.2) are addressed to the praetorian prefect, Flavian (i.e. to Flavian the elder), and are dated to 383 in the manuscripts. Editors have dealt with them in different ways. Mommsen emended them, redating them to 391: Mommsen and Meyer 1905 [repr. 1962], 1 and 2, p. 346. Seeck emdended the name of the addressee, giving them to Flavian the proconsul of Asia (i.e. Flavian the younger): Seeck 1919, 116, 261; cf. Stein 1934, 333, and *PLRE* I, Flavianus 14.
65. De Rossi 1849 argues brilliantly that all the offices held by Flavian under Eugenius were regarded as illegitimate. See further Vera 1983, 53–58. Honoré (1989b, 11–12) suggests that only that consulship was regarded as illegitimate.
66. Seeck 1883, cxvi–cxviii. Recently Callu (1974) and Vera (1983) have attempted to resurrect this argument. O'Donnell (1978) has an unusual interpretation: he places the quaestorship in 383 and the first term as prefect in 389. For the continuity of Flavian's last term, see now Errington 1992, 444–446.
67. Seeck, *RE* 6, col. 2509 (1909).
68. Seeck 1919, 453, col. 3, 23–26.
69. The dates and circumstances of Flavian's prefectures are, to say the least, controversial. For a review of earlier interpretations and an organized presentation of the evidence, see O'Donnell 1978. J. F. Matthews disapproves of O'Donnell's arguments: see Honoré 1989a, 10, and Matthews 1989b, 479 n. 7. My presentation here follows some of the arguments of Vera 1983.
70. Illyricum was a prefecture in the east at this time: see Fl. Eutropius (*PLRE* I, Eutropius 2), who was praetorian prefect of Illyricum from 380 to 381. See further the discussion of Vera 1983. Italy and Africa were under Gratian's control in 383. The province of Flavian in this year was first identified as east Illyricum by Callu (1974, 73–78). For the date, see *CTh* 7.18.8 + 9.29.2 and Vera 1983, 43–51, 53, 61–62. In the second half of his article, Vera describes the vicissitudes of the prefecture of eastern Illyricum during

the fourth century. For dissent on the date of the prefecture, see Honoré 1989a, 10, and Matthews 1989b, 479 n. 7.
71. Cf. Matthews 1989a, 47 n. 110.
72. For the prestige of the ordinary consulship in late antiquity, see Jones 1964, 532–535; more recently and in more detail, the introduction to Bagnall et al. 1987, 1–95.
73. These eight texts are cited in Bagnall et al. 1987, 322–323, comment ad ann. For an older account of the consulship of Flavian and the earlier consulship of Eugenius, see Bloch 1945, 227–229.
74. See Hartke 1938 and Callu 1974. O'Donnell (1978, 131) attempts to explain it away. There is a clear summary of the issue in Errington 1992, 442–443.
75. Honoré 1989a, 11. It is difficult to follow him: see Errington 1992, 440–441.
76. Cf. Spinazzola 1893, 520–525. The base was dedicated sometime after the younger Flavian's second legitimate term as urban prefect, ca. 408, and before he held the praetorian prefecture in 431.
77. If Honoré (1989a, 11) is right that all offices held under the usurper were regarded as legitimate with the exception of the consulship (and I do not think he is), then the younger Flavian's first term as urban prefect would have to be included in this count. In that case, this base would have to be redated to sometime between 399 and ca. 408, that is, between his second and third terms absolutely as urban prefect.
78. Cf. Paribeni 1933, 434–436 no. 7, with pl. 10 (= *AE* 1934.147).
79. Cf. *PLRE* 1, Flavianus 14.
80. Chastagnol 1962, 239.
81. Certainly the statue base from Naples was dedicated many years after his tenure as *consularis* of the region. For the office of *consularis Campaniae* see Chastagnol 1963, 362–365, and the *fasti* of the *PLRE* 1, 1092–1093. For the place of this office in the *cursus* of a Roman aristocrat in the late empire, see Matthews 1975, 14, 26.
82. For instances contemporary with the time of the elder Flavian, see *PLRE* 1, Aemilianus 4 and Lupus 7. There are others earlier, as well, who can be recovered by checking cross-references listed in *PLRE* s.v. Virius. Unfortunately, the listings of this office in the *fasti* of the *PLRE* do not include the gentilitial: *PLRE* 1, 1092–1093.
83. Cf. D'Arms 1970, 226–229.
84. See *PLRE* 1, Dexter 4, known only from a dedication in Naples: *CIL* 10.1479 (= *ILS* 4196). Cf. O. Seeck, *RE* 6, 2 (1909), Flavianus 15, col. 2511.
85. See the *TLL* s.v. *originalis,* col. 980 v. 19.
86. Seeck 1883, lii.
87. This constitution was addressed to *Flaviano proc. Asiae.* Symmachus mentions the younger Flavian's departure for Asia: *Ep.* 2.24. For the proconsulship of Asia, see Malcus 1967, 91–160, esp. 118. Cf. Matthews 1989a, 18.
88. See Vera 1983, 44–49.
89. This speech dates to 385. The law that the younger Flavian ignored dates to 381; it is to be found in the Theodosian Code (12.1.85).
90. Symm. *Ep.* 7.104: *Video Flaviani filii mei* (i.e. the younger Flavian) *honorem propterea hucusque jacuisse, ut ei testis melior eveniret. Incidarat in tyranni beneficium judicio bonorum*

temporum reservandus. Sed praestitit illi amisso praefecturae quod mutavit auctorem. Symmachus also appears to allude to the younger Flavian's illegal prefecture in *Epp.* 4.7 and 7.93. Cf. *CTh* 15.14.11. For his first, illegitimate term as urban prefect, see *PLRE* 1, Flavianus 14; Chastagnol 1962, 239–242.
91. Cf. *PLRE* 1, Flavianus 14, and O. Seeck, *RE* Flavianus 15, col. 2512.
92. See further the discussion of the younger Flavian's return to prominence in De Rossi 1849, 317–318.
93. Generally on his career, see *PLRE* 1, Flavianus 14; Chastagnol 1962, 243.
94. *RE* 6, 2 (1909), Flavianus 14, col. 2513.
95. *CIL* 6.1718 (= *ILS* 5522). Note, however, that he may well have had this building erected during one of his earlier terms as prefect. Cf. *PLRE* 1, Flavianus 14.
96. *CJ* 2.15.1: see *PLRE* 1, Flavianus 14; Chastagnol 1962, 243. It is also possible that this law should be dated to 431. In his forthcoming book, Alan Cameron will argue for a radical revision of the accepted chronology of the younger Flavian's urban prefectures, placing the first term *before* the usurpation of Eugenius and eliminating the one commonly believed to have been held in 408.
97. O'Donnell 1978.
98. See Cameron 1985b, 179, and Cameron 1995, 254–255. For this particular instance, see Chastagnol 1962, 243, followed by *PLRE* 1, Flavianus 14, and Cameron 1995, 255.
99. Panciera 1992.
100. The texts are collected in Panciera 1992, 255.
101. Panciera 1992, 254; Panciera collects some literary parallels for this use of *saepius* at n. 19. This position will gain some support from arguments that Alan Cameron will make in his forthcoming book.
102. Panciera 1992, 255 with n. 29.
103. Panciera 1992, 255 n. 29.
104. For the use of *saepius* here, see above all De Rossi 1849, 314–323; Chastagnol 1962, 241–242. Cf. Vera 1983, 33–38.
105. See *PLRE* 2, Caecilianus 1. Caecilianus had previously served in Africa as vicarius and proconsul: see Augustine, *Ep.* 86.
106. As we see in the date of the inscription rehabilitating the elder Flavian. The date of the younger Flavian's term in office is confirmed by *CTh* 11.1.36a and 6.23.3a.
107. See e.g. Oost 1968, 231, for bibliography and discussion.
108. See e.g. *PLRE* 2, Dexter 3. See generally on the problem Pecere 1986, 65–66 with bibliography on 236–237 nn. 263–265.
109. See e.g. Ogilvie 1975, praef., vii n. 1. In late antiquity the word can mean "friend," as does *frater* frequently.
110. O. Seeck, *RE* 6, 2 (1909), Flavianus 15, col. 2511.
111. Or, more prosaically, the meaning of a text depends on its relation to an unstated context. On the relation between meaning and context and, more particularly, the role of context in history, see notably Derrida 1988 and the essays collected in Derrida 1982. There is a convenient summary of the subject in Culler 1982, 121–125 and 128–130.

112. Errington 1992, 442 n. 15.
113. The point can be documented by consulting practically any entry in the *PLRE*. See generally Cameron 1985b, 178–179.

3. UNSPEAKABLE PAGANISM?

1. De Rossi 1849, 293.
2. Grünewald 1992, 474.
3. Gibbon 1897–1900, vol. 3, 180 n.
4. Bloch 1945 and 1964.
5. The general issues and basic bibliography can be accessed through any number of surveys of late antique history. The sourcebook, Croke and Harries 1982, is useful as an introduction to the period and the issues. On the history of religious conflict in the fourth century there is a classic collection of essays, Momigliano 1963a, and a standard narrative, Matthews 1975. More recently see Chuvin 1990. For the historiography of the problem, Momigliano 1963c is a typically excellent summary. It can now be supplemented with the thorough survey of the historiography of the "fall of Rome" provided in Demandt 1989, which discusses the role of religion at 246–273. More recent developments in the discussion of religious conflict in the fourth century will be summarized below.
6. For the early spread of Christianity and its urban context, see e.g. Meeks 1983 or Lane Fox 1987. There is a succinct account with further bibliography in Barnes 1986, 43–46. For the infiltration of Christians into the administration of the empire, see MacMullen 1984.
7. On Constantine the major essays are Barnes 1981 and 1982b; see further Barnes 1986. Barnes has returned to the religious reforms of Constantine many times since: see the essays collected in Barnes 1994, pt. 2. According to Eusebius (*VC* 11.44), Constantine appointed Christians to office by preference: for prosopographical confirmation see Barnes 1989, Barnes 1994a–b, and now especially Barnes 1995, arguing against Haehling 1978.
8. Barnes 1989 and Salzman 1990, 205–209.
9. Bowersock 1978.
10. Bloch 1945, 223–224; Cameron 1968 and Matthews 1975, 203–205.
11. In 357 Constantius had had it removed from the Senate house. It was presumably restored to its traditional place under Julian. See Wytzes 1936 and 1977; Matthews 1975, 205–209; the essays collected in Paschoud 1986. The sources are conveniently collected and translated in Croke 1976.
12. Cameron 1968.
13. Matthews 1975, 173–182. For a popular account, see Williams and Friell 1995, 36–41. As Barnes (1992, 10–11) emphasizes, Theodosius recognized Maximus as a legitimate emperor in 383, so the aristocracy would not have been utterly compromised by its support of him.
14. Bloch 1964, 195. On Valentinian II and his policies toward pagans, cf. Bloch 1945, 214–215, and Cameron 1968.

15. Cf. Bloch 1945, 219–220. The text takes on this status immediately: see Ambrose *Epp.* 18 and 57 and the *Contra Symmachum* of Prudentius.
16. For a classic statement of this idea, see Zosimus 4.59.3–4 with the comments in Paschoud 1971–1989, vol. 2, 470–473 with nn. 213–214.
17. See Matthews 1975, 223–238; Williams and Friell 1995, 61–72.
18. The story of the usurpation of Eugenius has often been told. The primary sources for Flavian's consulship and the revolt are conveniently assembled by Jones 1964, vol. 2, 32 n. 79. For further accounts, see notably Bloch 1945; Bloch 1964; Wytzes 1977; Matthews 1975, 238–247; Szidat 1979.
19. See Barnes 1990.
20. The legislation is thought by many to reflect Theodosius' repentance for the massacre of the people of Thessalonica, and the new ascendancy of Ambrose. It may well be that henceforth the admonitions of Ambrose are more vigorously manifested in the deeds of the emperor. See Bloch 1945, 223–224; Jones 1964, vol. 1, 167–169; Matthews 1975, 231–237.
21. Cf. Livy 5.54.5. See further Seeck 1883, cxviii and n. 590; Guey 1950, 83 n. 5; Hubaux 1958, chs. 2–3. Comparable claims were made almost a century later, during the revolt of Illous and Pamprepius: see Chuvin 1990, 99.
22. See especially Bloch 1945, 199–241. Cf. Bloch 1964, 200–201; Guey 1950, 82–83. The clear reference to Eugenius as a dedicand determines the date. O'Donnell (1978, 140 n. 48) questions the date for no very good reason.
23. For this office see Meiggs 1960, 298–312; Chastagnol 1960, 54–63, 297–300.
24. *PLRE* I, Proiectus. It has been suggested that he may be a relative of the Proiecta known from the Esquiline treasure: cf. Shelton 1985 and Cameron 1985a.
25. Becatti 1939, 37–60; Meiggs 1960, 347–348.
26. The standard publication on the battle at the Frigidus remains Seeck 1913; see further Paschoud 1971–1989, vol. 2, 475–500. For a recent account in English, see Williams and Friell 1995, 134–138.
27. Generally see the "Occultism and Theosophy" chapter in Turcan 1996, 266–290; for the religious symbolism employed at the battle of Frigidus, see p. 288.
28. There is a general discussion of the battle and the gesture in Barnes 1981, 43 and 305–306; see further Barnes 1985. For an attempt to deal with the significance of the gesture, see MacMullen 1968, esp. 87. For the signs used on Roman standards and shields, with particular attention to the signs used by the Roman army in late antiquity, see Berger 1981, 41–57.
29. On the tetrarchy and its association with Zeus and Hercules, see Barnes 1981, 11–12; Barnes 1982b, 24. For the specific allusion here, see Bloch 1945, 236; Guey 1950, 83 n. 9.
30. For the Great Persecution, see Barnes 1981, 15–27; Lane Fox 1987, 592–608.
31. See Cameron 1966b. For the words "nostalgia" and "antiquarianism," see p. 36. For confirmation of his argument, see Panciera 1982.
32. He has developed the argument in Cameron 1977 and 1984. See further his argument with K. Shelton over her interpretation of the Esquiline treasure: Shelton 1981 with Shelton 1985 and Cameron 1985a. He will return to the subject in detail in Cameron

forthcoming. Others, notably James O'Donnell, have followed his lead. See his important series of articles: O'Donnell 1977, 1978, and 1979b. For a discussion of the history of the debate, see Salzman 1990, 193–246.
33. See Salzman 1990, esp. 193–196. The most influential essay on the religious assimilation of the pagan aristocracy is P. R. L. Brown 1961.
34. This argument is made in O'Donnell 1979b.
35. Salzman 1990, 205.
36. O'Donnell 1979b.
37. Salzman 1990, 232–235.
38. Cameron 1977, 29.
39. Cameron 1977, 30.
40. Cf. O'Donnell 1978, esp. 139–140; Honoré 1989b, 9, 17; Grünewald 1992, 462–463.
41. O'Donnell 1978, 143.
42. O'Donnell 1978, 140.
43. Notably O'Donnell 1978.
44. See Averil Cameron 1993, 156–157, where whatever religious content the revolt may have had is regarded as an eccentricity of the elder Flavian. For a recent affirmation of the religious component of the revolt, see Barnes 1990.
45. Cameron 1977, 29.
46. Cameron 1984, 45.
47. Cameron 1984, 58.
48. Averil Cameron 1993, 157.
49. See Markus 1990 or Salzman 1990 for the ways in which the line between these two groups was blurred.
50. I find myself sympathetic to the remarks of Barnes 1990, 165–166.
51. O'Donnell 1979b, 48. See further O'Donnell 1977.
52. Fowden 1991, 119 n. There may also be some ancient precedent for the term, albeit very limited and not to my knowledge in the context of social conflict.
53. See further the introduction to Barnes 1994a, x.
54. This point is a commonplace, and I have discussed it in the context of citizenship in ancient Athens: Hedrick 1994b. For social identity and its relation to "others" in the Greek world there is much good in Hartog 1988 and Cartledge 1993. For the development of individual consciousness, see e.g. Lacan's classic description of the "mirror stage": Lacan 1977.
55. Recent work on "blackface" acting makes this point well: see e.g. Rogin 1994. On the invention of the American Indian, see Berkhofer 1978. For recent discussions and bibliography on the historical construction of Jewish identity, see Silberstein and Cohn 1994.
56. Millar 1992, 105.
57. A general consideration of the complex history and meaning of the dichotomy between Christian and pagan would take me far beyond the scope of this book. A good starting point is Koselleck's essay "The Historical-Political Semantics of Asymmetric Counterconcepts," reprinted in Koselleck 1985a, 159–197, where he considers in detail

the successive oppositions of Hellene and barbarian, Christian and heathen, human and nonhuman.
58. See Demandt 1989.
59. This point is as old as Tacitus. Generally on the political powerlessness and cultural conservatism of the aristocracy vis-à-vis the emperor, see the introductory chapters in Arnheim 1972 or Matthews 1975.
60. For a review of this explanation and arguments against it, see P. R. L. Brown 1961.
61. P. R. L. Brown 1961.
62. Eck 1971.
63. Haehling 1978.
64. Barnes 1989, 1994b and, above all, 1995. His articles will be controversial; they have yet to be fully digested and discussed. The general argument seems unexceptionable to me; if his case is to be disproved, it will have to be at the level of his specific data.
65. Another important problem with von Haehling's count is that he lists Arians as a separate category from Christians: see Barnes 1995, 140.
66. Champlin 1982. For more Christian officeholders under Constantine, see Novak 1979.
67. See generally Barnes 1995, 142–144.
68. For the complexities of this passage and evidence for its development through multiple drafts, see Barnes 1991.
69. P. R. L. Brown 1961; Matthews 1975, 183–222, 362–376. Cf. Matthews 1967, esp. 506–509.
70. See Mayor 1992.
71. For a detailed account of this episode, see Manganaro 1960 and 1961. More generally, Matthews 1975, 290; Cracco-Ruggini 1979, 120–123.
72. Cf. P. R. L. Brown 1967, 299–312, esp. 300–301. The first ten books of the *City of God* were devoted to refuting the pagans. Generally on the history of the "pagan perceptions of Christianity," to which Augustine was responding, see Barnes 1991, 1992, and especially 1982a.
73. On this subject see generally P. R. L. Brown 1961, 6–9; Matthews 1975, 360–376. For the Anicii, Matthews 1981. On the Caeionii, Chastagnol 1956. For the Rufii Festi, Matthews 1967.
74. Cf. Chastagnol 1962, 276–279; P. R. L. Brown 1967, 300–303; P. R. L. Brown 1961, 7–8; *PLRE* 2, Volusianus 7.
75. P. R. L. Brown 1961, 10.
76. For such survivals, see Salzman 1990, 235–246.
77. Markus 1990.
78. On this episode see Markus 1990, 131–135, with whose evaluation I do not entirely agree.
79. Markus 1990, 213–228.
80. On this event see Hadot 1971; Salzman 1990, 224–225.
81. Barnes 1995, 142.
82. Barnes 1982a.
83. The only attempt to provide a catalogue is the chart appended to Bloch 1945. Cf. Matthews 1973.

84. The contorniates are collected and discussed in Alföldi 1976.
85. The classic example is the Esquiline treasure: see Shelton 1981 and her later exchange with Cameron (Shelton 1985 and Cameron 1985a).
86. O'Donnell 1978 and 1979b.
87. Cf. the summary of his career in O'Donnell 1979b.
88. See P. R. L. Brown 1961, 6–7; Holum 1982; Salzman 1989; Cooper 1992.
89. The basic text remains that presented by Mommsen (1870), who discusses earlier editions at pp. 352–353. For more recent bibliography on the text of the poem, see Cracco-Ruggini 1979, 75–76 and n. 215. Essential bibliography includes Manganaro 1961, Matthews 1970, Wytzes 1977, Cracco-Ruggini 1979, and Grünewald 1992. For an English translation of the poem, see Croke and Harries 1982, 80–83. Other, comparable poems exist: see Cracco-Ruggini 1979, 124–130. The most notable example was found attached to a manuscript of Cyprian: it, too, evidently dates to the end of the fourth century. This poem is a Christian polemic against a unnamed senator who shaved his head and put on papyrus clothing and a dog-faced mask to participate in religious ceremonies: for the text see *CSEL* 3.302f. and 23.227ff.
90. Mommsen 1870; Bloch 1945, 230 with n. 69 and appended chart. The prominent supporter of this identification in recent years is J. F. Matthews. See Matthews 1970; Matthews 1975, 242; and, for his most recent confirmation of the position, Matthews 1989a.
91. Manganaro 1960 and 1961.
92. Matthews 1970.
93. Grünewald 1992, 474–481. Grünewald describes this amalgam, after the model of Terence's adaptation and combination of various Greek originals to form a new Roman play, as *contaminatio*.
94. Shanzer 1986 and, more recently, 1994. Shanzer's argument is controversial: see Matthews 1992 and Green 1995.
95. Cracco-Ruggini 1979, repeating an identification made in Ellis 1868 which was rejected by Mommsen. This identification has been accepted by Barnes (1990, 167–168), who provides a concise summary of Cracco-Ruggini's arguments. Cameron forthcoming will also argue for the same identification. O'Donnell came to the same conclusion independently: O'Donnell 1978.
96. See Dolbeau 1981. Yet it is unlikely that Bishop Damasus, who was a competent poet, wrote something as inept as the *Carmen*.
97. Matthews 1970, 466.
98. As Mommsen long ago noted, the word *sacratus* is used to describe the initiation into various pagan cults in the inscriptions of Praetextatus and his wife: *CIL* 6.1779 = *ILS* 1259; *CIL* 6.1780 = *ILS* 1260; cf. Mommsen 1870, 358 with n. 1. The related word *sacer* commonly has both of the senses I ascribe to *sacratus* here. Recently on the significance of *sacratus* and its meaning in the poem, see Cracco-Ruggini 1979, 79–80 and n. 230.
99. For the emendation in this line, see Matthews 1970, 472–473.
100. Cameron 1966b; O'Donnell 1979b.
101. The discrimination was first argued in Robinson 1915. The classic statement of it has

been provided by Bloch in his two famous articles: Bloch 1945 and 1964. More recently, see Turcan 1996, 1–12. Turcan is also a good resource for introductory information and bibliography on these various cults. For the devotion of the late Roman aristocracy to these religions, Matthews 1973.
102. There is a general account of the Phrygianum in Richardson 1992, s.v. and *Carta archeologica*.
103. For one attempt to provide an overview of senatorial religious sympathies in this period, see the chart appended to Bloch 1945; cf. Matthews 1973.
104. The most influential statement of the argument is Matthews 1973 (reprinted with some additional notes in the 1985 collection of articles by the same author).
105. Matthews 1973, 191–194.
106. A common though probably mistaken point: see Bloch 1964, 211. Croke 1976 reviews the scholarship and argues that there was no such editing.
107. Bloch 1945, 211–213 and the attached chart; cf. Matthews 1973.
108. References in these letters to the *pontifices* are conveniently collected and summarized in Robinson 1915. Generally for the board of *pontifices* one must consult the two major handbooks on Roman religion: Latte 1960, 400–402; Wissowa 1902, 501–523. More recently see G. J. Szemler, *RE* suppl. 15 (1978), *pontifex*, cols. 331–396. For the *pontifices maiores* in the late fourth century, see Cracco-Ruggini 1979, 63–69; Chastagnol 1960, 96–97 and 140–141.
109. Further references to the cult of Vesta in Symmachus' correspondence are collected in Robinson 1915, 96–97.
110. Bloch 1945, 213.
111. On the connection between the college of *pontifices* and *prodigia*, see Wissowa 1902, 514–515; Latte 1960, 204. On *prodigia*, see Wissowa 1902, 538–549.
112. For *prodigia* and religion in Livy, see Levene 1993; cf. E. Rawson, "Prodigy Lists and the *Annales Maximi*," in Rawson 1991, 1–15.
113. Robinson 1915, 93–94 for references and summary.
114. For the *commentarii* and consular lists kept by the college and their relation to Roman historiography, see Gentili and Cerri 1988, 87–95, with bibliography cited at 87–88 n. 2. Recent important essays include Frier 1979 and Bucher 1987 [1995].
115. Cf. Tacitus, *Hist.* 2.50. For Tacitus' attitude toward *prodigia* see Syme 1958, 522–523, 312; Walker 1960, 244–254.
116. See e.g. Livy 3.20.5, 10.40.10, 43.13.1–2. Cf. Levene 1993, 21–33; Ogilvie 1975, 403–404.
117. Schmidt 1968; cf. the remarks in Cameron 1977, 10, with Schmidt's rejoinder, pp. 38–39.
118. Cf. Momigliano 1963c, 99. On Orosius' use of Livy, see the introduction to Arnaud-Lindet 1990, xxv–xxvi and annexe 4. For Augustine's use of Livy in the first ten books of the *City of God*, see Angus 1906.
119. I am seconding the conclusion of Barnes 1990, 168; see further Barnes 1982a, 69–70.
120. See also Bloch 1945, 239 n. 90.
121. *Vit. Ambr.* 31.4. Most support the later date, but cf. Lamirande 1981 and McLynn 1994, 370 n. 40.

122. See Holum 1982, 50–51.
123. On the diptychs, Delbrück 1929; Volbach 1976; Weitzmann 1979, 186–188. Cf. Cameron 1982. Cameron will be co-editor of a new corpus of these.
124. For an account of the history of the diptych and of how the panels came to be split, see Kinney 1994.
125. For the connections between the families of Symmachus and Flavian, see Seeck 1883, lii; id., *RE* 6, 2 (1909), Flavianus 15, col. 2511; *PLRE* 1, Symmachus 10, 1046–1047.
126. Simon 1992, which I follow here. For other discussions of the diptych, see Volbach and Hirmer 1958; Wytzes 1977, 367–370 with pls. vi–vii. Kinney 1994 provides a thorough review of the bibliography. His interpretation is in general outline comparable to that of Simon.
127. Simon 1992, 58.
128. Simon 1992, 64 n. 15.
129. Simon 1992, 59, with bibliography cited.
130. For bibliography on this inscription, see Cracco-Ruggini 1979, 17–19 and n. 39. See particularly "Initiée par l'époux," in Festugière 1967, 322–323; Polara 1967; and Cooper 1996, 97–103.
131. See della Corte 1980, 205–209.
132. Head 1967, 137; Poole 1963, 58 with drawing. The coins of Enna have recently been treated by Jenkins (1975, 78–83).
133. Simon 1992, 59 and 64 n. 24.
134. Simon 1992, 61 and 64 n. 28.
135. Simon 1992, 61–63.
136. Shelton 1981.
137. Matthews 1973.
138. For a summary of this scholarship, see Paolis 1986–1987, 113–125.
139. For nomenclature and life, see Cameron 1966b; Marinone 1977, intro.; and Panciera 1982.
140. Cameron 1966b, 38.
141. Cameron 1977 and 1984. The general implications of his arguments are well summarized in Averil Cameron 1993, 153–163.
142. The classic statements are Bloch 1945 and 1964; cf. Levine 1966.
143. Cameron 1984, 46. Cf. Cameron 1977, 16: an "idealized portrayal, inspired by nostalgia for what was no more." See too his often quoted representation of it as a "tendentious and idealized portrayal . . . composed almost half a century after the death of its leading representative" (Cameron 1966b, 38).
144. Cameron 1966b, 36; cf. p. 35 and Cameron 1984, 46.
145. Cameron 1977.
146. Cameron 1966b, 36.
147. Cameron 1966b, 38.
148. Matthews 1967, 507.
149. Cameron 1966b, 38.
150. Cameron 1966b, 35.

151. The idea of nostalgia is a major historiographical theme. For general discussion and bibliography, see Davis 1979 and Loewenthal 1985, 4–13, 194–200 et pass.
152. Cameron 1966b, 28–29.
153. As a general rule, there tends to be a connection between status, literacy, and the high culture of learning: see e.g. Harris 1989. For nuanced discussion of this connection in late antiquity, see Kaster 1988 and Cameron 1966b.
154. Cameron 1966b, 34, attributes the first nine chapters to Flavian, for reasons that are unclear to me.
155. On augury, augural law, and the sources for it, see Wissowa 1902, 523–534; Latte 1960, 397.
156. Cf. Türk 1963, 336–337; Cameron 1977, 23–24; Cameron 1968, 101–102.
157. Cameron 1966b, 35–36.
158. Already from the early case history of Dora and many times thereafter. Cf. Rieff 1959, 37–44 et pass. For the persistence of memory, see further Terdiman 1993, which deals with the history of memory over the past two hundred years.

4. REMEMBERING TO FORGET: THE *DAMNATIO MEMORIAE*

1. See Benjamin 1968. The implications of this article for history and writing have been drawn out by many scholars: it is already at the heart of Collingwood's influential notion of "history as re-enactment" (Collingwood 1946 [new ed. 1994]). See more generally Loewenthal 1985, 290–323.
2. On *honor* and *dignitas* see Chapter 2 above.
3. Vittinghoff 1936, which does not even completely supersede Zedler 1885. Among the other scattered essays devoted to particular aspects of these procedures, Mommsen 1899, 987–990, and *Inscr. Ital.* 13.1, 19–20, are particularly useful. There have been books and essays devoted to various aspects of the *damnatio memoriae*, especially to the notion of the public enemy and capital punishment: see e.g. Hinard 1985, Cantarella 1991 and, most recently, Mustakallio 1994. There have been few attempts to analyze the functioning of the *damnatio memoriae* within the political structures of the principate. I note that Le Goff 1992, 67–68, basing himself on Veyne 1990, suggests that public memory was "confiscated" by the Roman emperors, and that the Roman senate retaliated through the *damnatio memoriae;* cf. pp. 98–99. The idea is interesting but inadequate to the evidence. H. I. Flower is now working on a book about the *damnatio memoriae*.
4. See generally Jaworski 1993 and Valesio 1986; for memory and forgetting, Terdiman 1993.
5. For an introductory account of Freud's thought on repression and negation, see e.g. Wollheim 1971, 137–173. Freud himself attempted to apply his ideas to social groups in various essays, principally in his *Group Psychology and the Analysis of the Ego* (Freud SE 18.67–143), and through particular studies. Many historians have tried to transfer psychoanalytical ideas into history: see (a rather pedestrian survey) Gay 1985. For the relationship beween history, memory, and Freudian repression, see N. O. Brown 1985,

esp. the chapter "Neurosis and History"; Marcuse 1955; Certeau 1986 and 1988; and Terdiman 1993.
6. Halbwachs 1980; Nora 1984–1986. For a succinct review of this tradition of writing about memory and society, see Zerubavel 1994; Le Goff 1992.
7. Cf. Bindeman 1981; Coward and Foshay 1992.
8. See the essay in Cage 1961.
9. Friedländer 1992 and Young 1993.
10. Notably Kundera 1980 and Havel 1991.
11. Loewenthal 1985, 66–69 and 263–362.
12. Pamela Johnson draws my attention to a case involving Armand Hammer, reported in the *New Yorker* (23 September 1996, p. 44). After Hammer's death, Occidental Petroleum moved immediately to disassociate itself from his image. "The photographs and statues of Hammer were removed from company headquarters. No photographs or obituaries or homages to him appeared in the annual report."
13. Frequently under the rubric of "taboo": see e.g. Douglas 1966.
14. For a recent and interesting comparative discussion with good bibliography, see Darnton 1995.
15. Esbenshade 1995 along with the other essays collected in that volume of *Representations*; Tumarkin 1983; Smith 1996; Ferretti 1993; Watson 1994. King (1997) pulls together and evaluates a great deal of the physical evidence for the various ways in which the Soviet government has attempted to expunge the memory of a person.
16. As I think does Rudich (1993 and 1997).
17. So Vittinghoff 1936, 12 and 64–74, arguing against Mommsen and others.
18. See Levick 1976, 180–200 with bibliography.
19. Eck and Fernández 1996. For a brief account of the inscription, see Eck 1995.
20. Bloch 1945, 227 and n. 62.
21. See Chapter 2 above and Bloch 1945, 229 and n. 65. For the inscriptions, see Bagnall 1987, 322–323, comment ad ann. 394.
22. Generally on the juridical response to the usurpation of Eugenius and the purge of participants in it, see Vera 1983, 52; Errington 1992, 439–441.
23. So Honoré 1989b.
24. The habit of defacing coins evidently begins with Sulla, who restruck coins of Marius, and carries on down into the empire: see Harl 1996, 35.
25. See Vittinghoff 1936, 13–18, giving many examples from all periods of Roman history.
26. Pollini 1984; Blanck 1969; Bergmann and Zanker 1981; Jucker 1981; Rollin 1979.
27. For this statue, see e.g. Kleiner 1992, 36–37. These busts are probably not wax *imagines*: see Flower 1996, 5–6, with further bibliography.
28. See the commentary in Courtney 1980 ad loc.
29. The fall of the Dzerzhinsky statue was one of the most frequently reproduced images from the coup of August 1991. It can be seen in any newsmagazine dating to late August or September of that year: see e.g. the numbers of *Newsweek* issued during the first half of September. See further the interesting note by J. Gambrell (1991) along with Aulich and Wilcox 1993 and Boym 1994, 215–282. The fallen statues now lying in the "totalitarian art park" can perhaps best be viewed in the James Bond movie *Golden Eye*.

30. Generally on Eutropius see *PLRE* 2, Eutropius 1.
31. See Vittinghoff 1936, 16.
32. Cf. Vittinghoff 1936, 13 n. 28.
33. For Messalina's disgrace and purge, see e.g. Levick 1976, 53–69 with bibliography cited; see also the comments of Koestermann 1963–1968 ad loc. For surviving images of Messalina, see Wood 1992.
34. Many examples are cited by Vittinghoff 1936, 15–17. On family portraits, see Courtney 1980, commentary to Juvenal *Sat.* 8.1–9; Walbank 1957–1979, commentary to Polybius 6.53; and, above all, Flower 1996.
35. There is a convenient short account of the Roman funeral and the practice of parading ancestral busts in it in Toynbee 1971. For more detail, see now Flower 1996, 91–127.
36. The ban clearly was not rigorously enforced. The younger Pliny famously remarks that "it is remarkable with what devotion and diligence the busts of the Brutuses and Cassiuses are kept at home, where it is possible" (Pliny *Ep.* 1.17.3). This allowance should not necessarily be treated as a juristic inconsistency or as an example of disobedience: cf. Furneaux 1896–1897 and Koestermann 1963–1968, commentary on Tacitus *Ann.* 3.76; Levick 1976, 283 n. 50. Rather, it should be kept in mind that there was no established procedure of *damnatio memoriae,* and that any combination of the conventional methods of attack on memory might be used.
37. For the trial of the elder Silius, see Tacitus *Ann.* 4.18–20.
38. Cf. Vittinghoff 1936, 14 n. 37, 16 n. 44, 17 n. 50.
39. See Vittinghoff 1936, 21–43, including many examples.
40. Vittinghoff 1936, 21–43. The evidence for erasure and nonerasure of the names of disgraced emperors and members of their families has been collected in Cagnat 1914, 169–174 and Calabi-Limentani 1973, 467–480. Erasures of consuls' names in the official lists, or *fasti,* are discussed in Degrassi 1952 and *Inscr. Ital.* 13.1. More evidence for erasures in Roman inscriptions is collected and illustrated in Gordon and Gordon 1958–1965. The indexes in the *ILS* to individual emperors and their households conveniently list erased and unerased instances of names as well.
41. Vittinghoff 1936, 21–24.
42. See Levick 1976, 282 n. 50; *Inscr. Ital.* 13.1. In addition to the *fasti,* the *acta triumphorum* and *acta fratrum Arvalium* were supposed to be exempted from erasure. See Vittinghoff 1936, 33 n. 148, 35–42. On the continuance of names in the consular lists in the later empire, see Cameron 1981 and 1982b, though Cameron seems to be operating on the presumption—mistaken, I believe—that the names of those who have suffered the *damnatio memoriae* should regularly have been excised from the official *fasti.*
43. See Vittinghoff 1936, 21–22, 25–26. The record of Piso's consulship was erased from only one preserved monument, where his name occurred in conjunction with Tiberius' own name: *CIL* 6.385 = *ILS* 95.
44. See Chapter 2 above and Bagnall 1987, 322–323, comment ad ann. 394.
45. Mommsen 1892, 3.525; Degrassi 1952.
46. Vittinghoff 1936, 42–43; generally on the Roman *praenomina,* Salomies 1987.
47. This famous story was repeated by many later authors. Cf. the *periocha* to Livy 6; Cicero *Phil.* 1.13.32; Festus *Epitome* 125 (p. 112 Lindsay), 151 (p. 132 Lindsay); Quintilian *Inst.*

Orator. 3.7.20; Dio frag. 26.1; Plutarch *OR* 91. The *De Viris Illustribus* 224.6, confuses the story, saying that the *cognomen* rather than the *praenomen* was banned. The best discussion of the incident remains that of Mommsen 1864, vol. 2, 182–184. See also F. Münzer, *RE* 14.1 (1928), Manlius 51, col. 1174.

48. A certain M. Manlius is attested by consul or military tribune in 434 B.C. (*RE* Manlius 50). Another (*RE* Manlius 96) is known as military tribune in 420 B.C. Finally, the *Fasti Capitolini* name a P. Manlius M. f. (*RE* Manlius 97) as military tribune in 400 B.C.

49. *RE* Claudius 21, mentioned by Cicero *De haruspic. respons.* 6.12. Cicero addresses the same individual in his speech concerning his house (*de dom.* 127).

50. See Mommsen 1864, vol. 1, 15 n. 13, followed by F. Münzer, *RE* 3, 2 (1899), Claudius 21, col. 2670; cf. Taylor 1942, 390.

51. Plutarch, *Cic.* 49.5; Dio 51.19.

52. *RE* Antonius 32.

53. *RE* Antonius 22; *PIR*^{2}, A 800.

54. *RE* Antonius 24; *PIR*^{2}, A 802.

55. *RE* Calpurnius 70; *PIR*^{2}, C 287. Cf. Syme 1980, 334–341; Raepsaet-Charlier 1981, 685–695.

56. For the son, *RE* Calpurnius 76; *PIR*^{2}, C 293.

57. He did have it obliterated where it occurred in connection with his own name, though. In *CIL* 6.385 + 30751 (= *ILS* 95), a dedication made by Tiberius and Calpurnius during their joint consulship to Jupiter Optimus Maximus for the safe return of Augustus, the name of Calpurnius has been erased. His name may also have been erased from the acts of the Arval Brethren: *CIL* 6.2023 = *ILS* 5026, line 21.

58. There is no statement in the ancient sources that Gnaeus changed his *praenomen* to Lucius. For the consul, see Tacitus *Ann.* 4.62; *Inscr. Ital.* 13.1 no. 24 (*fasti Arv.*) ad ann. A.D. 27; *CIL* 2.2633 = *ILS* 6101; *CIL* 5.4919 = *ILS* 6100; *CIL* 6.251 = *ILS* 6080. Of some interest is *CIL* 4.3340, *tab. cer.* Pomp. II, with n. 5: *praenominis nunc quidem forma ambigua est ut C. potius quam L. esse videatur.* For the stemma of the family, see E. Groag, *RE* 3, 1 (1897), col. 1375, and Raepsaet-Charlier 1981; see also the modifications suggested by Syme 1980.

59. Cf. M. Fluss, *RE* ser. 2, 2, 1 (1921), Scribonius 23, cols. 885–887; Weinrib 1967, 263–264. Weinrib argues that the use of the verb *adsumo* in this passage implies that Libo took the *agnomen* Drusus of his own volition and was not given it by his father.

60. Vittinghoff 1936, 42.

61. *Inscr. Ital.* 13.3 no. 25 *ad* 13 September. These *fasti* were inscribed sometime after A.D. 20.

62. In the dedication of Memmius Symmachus, quoted in Chapter 2 above. For Roman nomenclature in late antiquity, see Cameron 1985b; Eck 1993.

63. The name that an individual used at this late date might be called the *diacritical* name: see Cameron 1985b, 171–178.

64. This is the *Liber de praenominibus*, usually printed at the end of modern editions of Valerius Maximus: see Schanz/Hosius 2^4, 592–593.

65. On the dating of the *periochae* of Livy, see Begbie 1967, 332–338; Schmidt 1968.

66. Cf. R. Leonhard, *RE* ser. 2, 1, 1 (1914), *religiosum*, cols. 583–585.

67. Mommsen 1899, 987–990; Vittinghoff 1936, 43–45.
68. Vittinghoff 1936, 43–49, cites many many examples.
69. Cf. Mommsen 1899, 987–989; Mommsen 1887–1888, vol. 3, 1190.
70. Bibliography cited in Vittinghoff 1936, 46 nn. 210 and 211.
71. See *Inscr. Ital.* 13.3 *ad* 14 January.
72. These are all discussed in Degrassi's comments to the various days, *Inscr. Ital.* 13.3. For M. Antony see the Kalends of August; for M. Scribonius Libo, the Ides of September (cf. *CIL* 1² p. 244, *eid. Sept.*; Tac. *Ann.* 2.32; Vell. 2.130.3); on Sejanus see Dio 58.12.5.
73. Cf. Vittinghoff 1936, 23.
74. See Pollini 1984; Blanck 1969; Bergmann and Zanker 1981; Jucker 1981; Rollin 1979.
75. Cf. Gordon 1983, no. 73 and pp. 158–159.
76. Kundera 1980, 3.
77. See Pryce-Jones 1969, 66–69; King 1997, 184–187.
78. Cf. Boym 1994, 230–231.
79. That it was possible for an object to be removed from public view and stored somewhere, rather than being destroyed, is shown by the removal of the altar of Victory under Constantius and its subsequent return (presumably under Julian), as well as by the continuing senatorial petitions for its restoration. See the discussion of the controversy regarding the altar in Chapter 3 above.
80. On Stilicho, see *PLRE* I s.v. Here too is provided a list of his inscriptions. Those which have been erased are indicated as "name to be restored."
81. On this inscription see Nash 1961–1962, vol. 2, s.v. *statua Stilichonis;* Gordon 1983, nos. 93 and 94.
82. In the Soviet Union, fearful citizens often altered their personal copies of photographs with scissors or ink: see King 1997, 8–13.
83. For many examples see Vittinghoff 1936, 29–33.
84. The boastful inscription of Gallus from Assuan (*CIL* 3.14147 = *ILS* 8995) is quoted in part and discussed with bibliography in Gordon 1983, no. 22, pp. 110–111. The bibliography for Gallus' career and subsequent disgrace is conveniently summarized in R. D. Anderson et al. 1979, 151–155, and Kaster 1995, 184–186. There is a substantial discussion about whether or not Gallus actually suffered a *damnatio memoriae*—a discussion that is founded on the mistaken presumption that the *damnatio memoriae* was a formal, juridical procedure rather than a loose set of measures that might be imposed more or less informally: see Boucher 1966, 56–57; Daly 1979.
85. Compare, for example, the inscriptions in which the names of the emperors Domitian or Commodus have been erased with those in which the name has been left, listed in the indexes of the *ILS* under the category "emperors and their households."
86. Other examples are cited in Vittinghoff 1936, 29–32.
87. On the art of memory see Yates 1966 and Blum 1969.
88. The enduring power of what is forgotten, the necessity of a continuing effort to repress certain things from consciousness, is the linchpin of Freudian theorizing about the unconscious: see the beginning of *The Psychopathology of Everyday Life* (Freud *SE* 6) and Wollheim 1971, 81–84, 137–173.

89. The best discussion of this issue is Luce 1991; see further Suerbaum 1971.
90. Eco 1979, 6–7: "Semiotics is in principle the discipline studying everything which can be used in order to lie. If something cannot be used to tell a lie, conversely it cannot be used to tell the truth: it cannot in fact be used 'to tell' at all."
91. This is the traditional linguistic distinction between signifier and signified (representation and idea) and between sign (union of signifier and signified) and referent (the "real world out there"), as explained e.g. by Saussure 1959, 65–70.
92. The diagram I am using here was described by Aristotle at the end of the first book of his *Prior Analytics* (esp. 1.46). Among modern critics, the form is displayed and exploited to best advantage in the "semiotic square" of Greimas: see Greimas 1987.
93. By dissimulation I mean to evoke the idea of an absence of representation, or a silence, which stands in front of something true and real. If one dissimulates fear, for example, one is trying not to give representation to a psychological truth. On this subject see the various books by Jean Baudrillard, especially Baudrillard 1983. For a general introduction to Baudrillard's thought and the role of simulation in it, see Kellner 1989.
94. The issue between these two conceptions is clearest in the writings of Benjamin Whorf. On the famous example of the Eskimo vocabulary for snow, see the eponymous essay in Pullum 1991.
95. See Baudrillard 1983.
96. See the amusing note in Fowler 1927 s.v. euphemism, and the less amusing comments in Enright 1985.
97. In order to do so, it was necessary for Freud to imagine a topography that split the mind between conscious and unconscious: this split is analogous to the representation/reality dichotomy. So consciousness corresponds to representation, and the unconscious to reality. What is forgotten, then, is repressed to the unconscious and fails of its representation in consciousness. On Freud's insistence on the unconscious and its role in forgetting, see e.g. Wollheim 1971, 175–199. For the correlation between the Freudian unconscious and conventional notions of reality, see above all Ricoeur 1970, 431–439.
98. See Hedrick 1994a and 1995.
99. Note the discussion of the "counter-monument" (*Gegen-Denkmal*) of Jochen and Esther Gerz, erected (or should I say un-erected?) in Hamburg, and of other "counter-monuments" in Young 1993, 27–48.
100. For mysticism and silence in late antiquity, Turcan 1996, 266–290. See further Coward 1992 for discussion of silence and Neoplatonism.
101. See Watson 1994.
102. See the last chapter of Larina 1993.
103. Conquest 1990, 488.
104. Kundera 1980, 3.
105. Reprinted many times: see Havel 1991, 125–214.
106. Havel 1991, 136.
107. Cf. the anecdotes of the beer brewer and greengrocer in Havel 1991, 172–179.
108. Lang 1992.
109. A convenient text of the *Res Gestae* with English translation and commentary is provided in Brunt and Moore 1977.

110. It is not clear why Augustus so ostentatiously refuses to mention Lepidus; there is no reason to think that his memory was purged. Note, however, that after Actium his homonymous son was charged with conspiring to kill Octavian. He was apprehended and executed by Maecenas in 30 B.C.: see Syme 1952, 298.
111. See Corcoran 1993. Many examples can be found in book 15, sec. 14, of the Theodosian Code.
112. On silence as a sign, see Jacobson 1987b.
113. I allude to speech-act theory: the classic development of this argument is Austin 1962. For a survey and elaboration of Austin's ideas, see Petrey 1990.
114. Cf. Cheung 1993, 1–26.
115. For Tiberius' attitudes toward funerals, see Flower 1996, 246–253.
116. See Vittinghoff 1936, 15 and 92; Crook 1995, 64, citing Ulpian *Dig.* 4.5.15.3.
117. The measure was not universally appreciated and applauded: see Dio 64.8.
118. There is a convenient collection of the material in the *PLRE* 1, Tatianus 5.
119. For a discussion of these inscriptions, see Robert 1948, 47–53, as well as the more recent list in *PLRE* 1, Tatianus 5. The name of his son Proculus was also erased, notably from the obelisk of Theodosius in Constantinople: see *CIL* 3.737 (= *ILS* 821); cf. Cameron 1966a, 33–34.
120. Of the various sources for his *damnatio memoriae* and rehabilitation listed in the *PLRE*, see particularly Asterius *Hom.* 4 (= *PG* 40, 224–225).
121. Robert 1948, 23, 42, 47–53. Cf. Erim et al. 1989, no. 30 with nos. 25–27; Scharf 1991. A couple of alternatives to Robert's text have been proposed. Merkelbach 1970 suggests ποίνα, "punishment," for πείνα "hunger," in the eighth hexameter; Peek proposed ὥπασ' ἐπεῖναι, and I follow him here. Peek also suggested ἐελδομένοισι, "for men in their longing," for ἔθ' ἀδομένοισιν, "for men yet grateful," in the ninth hexameter: see *Bull. ép.* 1971, 616.
122. As Robert (1948) remarks, it is necessary to understand στήλαις for στήλης. This is a general reference to the restoration of Tatianus' monuments; more specifically, it alludes to the inscribed statue base on which Tatianus' statue stands. It is this statue, personified, that addresses the reader in the inscription.
123. Robert 1948, 49.
124. Robert (1948) collects parallels for the phrase πανδαμάτωρ χρόνος at 49 n. 1. The notion reflects a traditional attitude toward time.

5. SILENCE, TRUTH, AND DEATH: THE COMMEMORATIVE FUNCTION OF HISTORY

1. On the proem, see Hedrick 1993.
2. See Barthes 1987.
3. See Koselleck 1985b.
4. Cf. e.g. the commentaries of Gomme and Hornblower ad loc. It should be emphasized that the passage does not have the strong ethical connotations that are to be found in Roman historians like Livy and Tacitus.
5. For an early and classic statement, see Lévi-Strauss 1966, 245–269.

6. MARHO 1976, ix.
7. "Comment ne pas parler," mistranslated (for fear of the split infinitive?) as "How to Avoid Speaking: Denials" in Burdick and Iser 1989 and Coward and Foshay 1992.
8. See further Burdick and Iser 1989.
9. Vidal-Naquet 1992, 57–58.
10. See "The Politics of Historical Interpretation: Discipline and Desublimation," reprinted in White 1987, 58–82. That essay is also the centerpiece of discussion for the essays in Friedländer 1992.
11. On beginnings see Kermode 1967 and Said 1975.
12. In distinguishing between these two functions of the beginning, I am following Said's basic distinction between the transitive and intransitive beginning: Said 1975, 50–51, 72–78.
13. The classic statement of speech-act theory is by Austin 1962. For a more recent statement of the theory and its implications, see Petrey 1990.
14. See Kermode 1967; cf. Said 1975, 40–42.
15. So Said, 1975, 50–51.
16. Generally on Greco-Roman beginnings, see Wijkstrøm 1936 and, more recently, the various essays in Dunn and Cole 1992.
17. I take the term "phatic" from Jacobson, who in turn took it from Malinowski: see Jacobson 1987c, 68–69.
18. See Wijkstrøm 1936.
19. More generally see Said 1975, 22–24.
20. For this fragment, see Schröder 1971, 52–53, and Chassignet 1986, 57.
21. See Testard 1973, 221–222.
22. For ancient biography, see Momigliano 1971 and Gentili and Cerri 1988. For the *laudatio funebris,* see Kierdorf 1980, comparing the commentary in Walbank 1957–1979 to Polybius 6.53–55.
23. For the similarity between this fragment and the beginning of the *Origines,* see e.g. Ogilvie and Richmond 1967, 126. Cato's statement here gave rise to a substantial (and unfounded) nineteenth-century literature on "the lays of ancient Rome": see esp. Badian 1966. On early Roman historiography, see now Oakley 1997.
24. See further Wijkstrøm 1936, 158–68; Ogilvie and Richmond 1967, 126; Alfonsi 1963, 116; Kierdorf 1978; Cole 1992.
25. Generally on the *Agricola,* see Ogilvie and Richmond 1967 and Ogilvie 1991, discussing the similarities between this work and the funeral oration at 1715–1718.
26. Ogilvie 1980, 257, notes that Tacitus is rarely quoted, except at the end of the fourth century. For Tacitus and later tradition, see the short summary in Benario 1975, ch. 10, "Survival and Popularity," 159–165. For more elaborate treatments of Tacitus' later history, with full quotation of sources, see the old volume by Mendell (1957, 225–238). One of the best sections of Mellor 1993 is that on "Tacitism," 137–162; he has now produced a book on the subject: Mellor 1995.
27. For a similar punning play on his name, see the later *Historia Augusta, Vit. Aurelian* 2, and Sidonius Apollinaris, *Ep.* 4.22.2.

28. Citations are thoroughly collected and quoted in Mendell 1957, 232–234.
29. Syme (1958, 503 n. 8) is overstating the case when he says that "the heir of Tacitus, in every sense, is Ammianus Marcellinus." For bibliography on the attempts to find Tacitean influence in Ammianus, see Matthews 1989b, 482–483 n. 45. Matthews would not deny that Ammianus knows Tacitus, but maintains that the relationship between them "can be little more than formal"; see further pp. 456, 468.
30. Most regard this story as apocryphal, as they do the entire account of the emperor Tacitus' life. Generally see Syme 1971, 237–247, esp. 239–241. Nevertheless, it shows something of the attitude toward the historian and his notoriety during the fourth century.
31. E.g. Tertullian and Orosius: see Mellor 1993, 138.
32. See Grünewald 1992, 471–473. For a summary of nineteenth-century notions about these *Annales,* see Seeck, *RE* Flavianus 14 col. 2508. More recently, see Festy 1997.
33. *Ordo generis Cassiodorum,* in *MGHAA* 12 (Cassiodorus, ed. Mommsen), p. v. For bibliography on this imitation, see Matthews 1975, 231 n. 3.
34. See the remarks of Hartke 1940, 74ff., 163f., etc. cf. further Demandt 1989, 427.
35. So argued in Bleckmann 1992. See further Bleckmann 1995.
36. Ratti 1997.
37. Cf. Matthews 1973, 188 and n. 80; Barnes 1976, 268.
38. Cf. Matthews 1973, 188 and n. 80; Schlumberger 1985, 305–329.
39. Bloch 1945, 220, makes too much of this translation when he says that "this translation may be compared—*mutatis mutandis*—to St. Jerome's translation of the Bible. It is a deliberate act of pagan propaganda: the life of the miracle worker of Tyana was intended to supersede the life of Christ in the Gospels." Further on this work, see *HA Vit. Aurelian* 24.9, 27.6, referring to a Nicomachus who is noted for his translations from the Syrian. Honoré 1989b, 15, would identify this Nicomachus with Flavian the elder. Cf. Cameron 1977, 13 n. 1; Zetzel 1980, 48 n. 32; Courcelle 1969, 16, 258. More generally on translations from Greek to Latin (and vice versa) in late antiquity, see Courcelle 1969, Brock 1979, and Fischer 1982. Cameron forthcoming will argue that Flavian made no such translation at all. For a more detailed discussion of this passage, see Chapter 6 below.
40. Cf. Cameron 1977, 20.
41. Honoré 1989b, 13–17 and appendixes. Given that the imperial rescripts were edited before their inclusion in the Code, it seems to me that this general project should be regarded with some skepticism.
42. Honoré 1989b, 16; Honoré 1987, 156–176.
43. Honoré 1989b, 16.
44. There is a convenient photograph in Barthes 1987, 86.
45. See the development of this line of argument in Ricoeur 1967.
46. I draw this opposition from Ricoeur 1970, 28–36, speaking of a "hermeneutic as recollection of meaning" versus a "hermeneutic as exercise of suspicion."
47. See e.g. the introduction to White 1973.
48. The relationship beween truth and being (*Dasein*) is a central subject in Heidegger's

philosophy, as is the relation of "un-covering" to being; they can be approached through any introduction to his work, such as Steiner 1992. For the famous discussion of *aletheia,* see Seidel 1964.

49. For the "trace," see Ricoeur 1984–1988, vol. 3, 119–126.
50. Cf. Loewenthal 1985, 148–182, 238–243.
51. The classic example is Shelley's poem, "Ozymandias." Cf. e.g. Loewenthal 1985, 245–246.
52. For brief remarks on archaeology and the logic of production, see Hedrick 1995.
53. See e.g. the introduction to MARHO 1976.
54. Thus the slogan "Act up," for the significance of which see Gamson 1989. The association of silence and death appears to be practically universal and primeval. The explicit critical equation of the pair goes back at least to Freud's famous 1913 essay on Lear, "The Theme of the Three Caskets" (Freud *SE* 12.291–301).
55. One wonders whether there is any relation between the prominence of the motif of silence in the histories and the name of the author. For a brilliant analysis of just such a connection, see Barthes' essay on Balzac's short story "Sarrasine": Barthes 1974, esp. 17, 106–107.
56. Generally on the *Agricola,* see Ogilvie and Richmond 1967 and Ogilvie 1991.
57. Cf. Ogilvie and Richmond 1967, intro. 13–14.
58. Again, these sentiments should be associated with the genre of the funeral oration: see Ogilvie 1991, 1715–1718.
59. See e.g. Ogilvie 1980, 250–257, and Benario 1975, 45, 58; the theme is not emphasized in Tacitus' other two minor works, the *Germania* and *Dialogus.*
60. I note that there is now a book on the semantics of silence in Tacitus: Strocchio 1993 (which I have not seen). See the review by Braund in *CR* 44 (1994), 210. The best way of approaching the immense bibliography on Tacitus and his histories is through the 3,000-odd pages of bibliography and exposition devoted to the subject in the *ANRW* 2.33. The definitive book on Tacitus is still Syme 1958, though this should be supplemented by an essay that is more sensitive to literary aspects of the author: I recommend Walker 1960, antiquated though it is. For a recent, well-written survey with essential bibliography, see Mellor 1993.
61. See Fritz 1957. Recent scholarship has emphasized that silence is an important theme in many Flavian authors: see Rudich 1993; Bartsch 1994; McGuire 1997.
62. See above all Fritz 1957; Allison 1990. Most now seem to agree with Tacitus that the quality of inscrutability is representative of the spirit of the time: cf. e.g. Rudich 1993; Bartsch 1994; McGuire 1997.
63. For the *arcana imperii* see e.g. the brief statement in Mellor 1993, 92–94. Generally on politics and dissimulation, Vidal-Naquet 1992, 13; Faye 1972.
64. For this feature of Tacitean style, cf. e.g. Walker 1960, 66–77, and Mellor 1993, ch. 7, 113–136.
65. See Ogilvie and Richmond 1967, ad loc., p. 299.
66. See Luce 1991 and Woodman 1995. I agree with Luce about the interpretation of the passage; and Woodman's objections, even if correct, would make little difference to my argument.

67. See Mellor 1993, 8–9.
68. Despite the comment in Ogilvie and Richmond 1967, ad loc., this passage is clearly relevant to Tacitus' representation of his own silence under Domitian.
69. For "survivor guilt" (or "survival guilt") and the Vietnam War, see e.g. Glover 1984; more generally, see Porot et al. 1985.
70. On these passages, see the excellent treatment in Luce 1989.
71. The idea looms large in the theory of history of Collingwood (1946 [new ed. 1994]) and in the psychoanalytic theory of therapy (explained in e.g. Wollheim 1971, 166–172).
72. This idea is so familiar that it seems to many to be obvious and unproblematic. For a corrective discussion, see Koselleck 1985b.
73. There is a convenient summary of the history of "functionalist" theorizing about myth in Doty 1986, chs. 2 and 3.
74. The idea that there is a connection between the sense of loss, the feeling of guilt, and the compulsion to speak obviously anticipates a major strand of Freudian theorizing. For the significance of Freud for the philosophy of history (as opposed to the practice of history, or "psychohistory"), see the chapter "The Authority of the Past," in Rieff 1959, 186–219. The first two chapters of N. O. Brown 1985, "The Disease Called Man" and "The Neurosis of History," are very stimulating. In recent years, Certeau has done most to develop the significance of Freudian thought for history: see Certeau 1986 and 1988. On psychohistory, see generally Gay 1985. Freud's major statements regarding the psychological motivations for normative writing, e.g. laws or history, are *Totem and Taboo* and *Moses and Monotheism*.
75. Levi 1988, 83–84.
76. So the theme of Terdiman 1993.
77. See generally Benjamin 1985; cf. Stewart 1993.

6. REHABILITATING THE TEXT: PROOFREADING AND THE PAST

1. For one example of the relation of annotations in books to the practice of reading, see Jardine and Grafton 1990.
2. Alan Cameron informs me that Boethius says in another subscription *conditor operis emendavi*. The subscription is discussed in an obscure dissertation that I have not seen: Stangl 1882, 9–10.
3. See e.g. the *OLD* s.v. *quidam¹*, 3.
4. For the range of meaning of *emendatio* and its more specialized use relating to texts, see e.g. *TLL* s.v.
5. For *interpolare*, see generally the *TLL* s.v.
6. Cf. e.g. Forcellini, s.v.; *TLL* s.v. 4 and 5; Mommsen and Meyer 1905–1913, 2.179ff. Berger 1953, s.v., provides a brief summary and cites bibliography.
7. For the word *praeiudicium*, see generally Quintilian, *Inst. Orator.* 5.2.1; Hackl 1975. For a brief definition, see Berger 1953, s.v.
8. See e.g. Suet. *Caes.* 56. For further examples of this usage, see *OLD* s.v. *suppleo*, 3C.

9. Unless we accept Hartke's questionable hypothesis that Flavian the younger was author of the *Historia Augusta:* see Chapter 5 above.
10. For a convenient general introduction to Livy, see Luce 1977 or Miles 1995. For more detailed discussions, see the essays and bibliographies in *ANRW* 2.30.2.
11. See generally Luce 1977; for the relation between the manuscript tradition and this organization, Billanovich 1981–.
12. There is some "contamination" of the traditions of the third and fourth decades. On the manuscript tradition of Livy, see Billanovich 1981–. For a summary, Reynolds 1983, s.v.
13. See Pecere 1986, 38–39, 59–60.
14. These subscriptions are printed in the various editions of Livy. For a collation, see Zetzel 1980. For discussion of their significance and recent bibliography, Pecere 1986, 59–69.
15. See e.g. *PLRE* 2, Victorianus 2.
16. See Bayet's text of Livy, intro. xciii–xciv. On the relationship of grammarians and members of the Roman elite, Kaster 1980 and 1988.
17. The interpretation goes back to W. B. Anderson 1936–1965, notes to *Ep.* 8.3. See further Pecere 1986, 232–233 n. 230.
18. In late antiquity important Christians, such as Jerome, might occasionally copy entire books of Christian authors. This activity, however, exemplifies a Christian ideology of the morality of labor which has no parallel in paganism: see Pecere 1986, 213–214 n. 29. Some of the upper class had an interest in calligraphy, a different matter than routine scribal copying: see Cameron 1992.
19. So Mommsen in Luetjohann 1887, 420. See further Pecere 1986, 232 n. 228.
20. Pecere 1986, 232–233 n. 230.
21. Traube 1904–1906 [1909], 16.
22. Pecere 1986, 60 and 232 n. 229; Pliny (*Ep.* 7.17) uses *emendo* to mean something much stronger than "proofread."
23. Zetzel, in his edition of the subscriptions, apparently treats *Thermas* here as a variant reading of Enna, rather than as a separate text, for reasons that are unclear to me: Zetzel 1980, 40. On the numbers and reputations of hot springs and spas in Sicily, see e.g. Freeman 1898, vol. 1, 75–77.
24. On the interests of the late Roman aristocracy in Sicily, see Matthews 1975, 25, 27, 374; cf. Pecere 1986, 236 n. 262. A late antique Roman villa is known at Piazza Amerina, which is not at a great distance from Enna: Holloway 1991, 167–178 (listing other known Roman villas in Sicily at 183 n. 4).
25. It should be emphasized yet again that *parens* here does not mean "parent," as it is sometimes mistranslated, but "relative." See Chapter 2 above.
26. See notably the subscription of Statilius Maximus to Cicero's *De lege agraria,* reproduced and discussed at length in Zetzel 1974; cf. Pecere 1986, 65–66. Zetzel 1981 provides a general discussion of the practices of the late antique Latin grammarians.
27. See *PLRE* 2, Symmachus 9.
28. *PLRE* 2, Eudoxius 7.
29. The traditional dividing line for the establishment of a modern textual criticism is Lach–

mann's edition of Lucretius. Cf. e.g. Reynolds and Wilson 1991, 207–241; McGann 1983; McGann 1991.
30. See above all Zetzel 1980; cf. Pecere 1986, 65–69.
31. This point is not certain. The subscriptions do not survive in all medieval texts of Livy's first decade. This should not, however, be taken as a sign that the manuscripts do not share a common ancestry. Furthermore, subscriptions have a notorious tendency to wander. Cf. Zetzel 1980, 40; Housman 1926, xiii–xviii.
32. Zetzel 1980.
33. Zetzel 1980, 43–44. De Rossi 1849, 321, even suggests that subscriptions were written in cursive while titles were in capitals.
34. Zetzel 1980, 39–42.
35. The passages in question are Livy 3.26.9, 4.13.6, 6.13.3, 10.5.13, 10.19.21, and 10.37.15.
36. Cf. Zetzel 1980, 45–46.
37. Cf. Voit 1936, 308–322; Billanovich 1959; Billanovich 1981–, 248; Pecere 1986, 68–69.
38. See HA Sept. Sev. 21; Jerome, Quaest. hebr. 283. Cf. FGrH 257, T 2, 5; frag. 35. See further Zetzel 1980, 48, and Pecere 1986, 238 n. 283. A new translation of Phlegon by William Hansen is forthcoming.
39. Cf. Pecere 1986, 238 n. 282, and Mazzarino 1974–1980, vol. 1, 367 n. 7, 393 n. 51.
40. For these Jahn 1851 remains essential. More recently, Zetzel has re-edited the list of subscriptions to secular works, distinguishing some twenty-seven groups of subscriptions: Zetzel 1981, 206–231. The best available discussion of the subscriptions is now Pecere 1986. See further his more recent essay, Pecere 1989, 342–362. Cameron forthcoming will include a discussion of subscriptions, giving attention to Christian practice.
41. Generally for these, see Pecere 1986, 24–29 with bibliography, 213–215. Pecere provides a review of the bibliography for Christian subscriptions, pp. 210–211 n. 3.
42. Cf. Pecere 1986, 27, with nn. 43–44. Generally on the shift from scroll to codex: Roberts and Skeat 1983; the various essays in Blanchard 1989; Cavallo 1975, 83–86; Petrucci 1986.
43. Pecere 1986, 70–71.
44. Cf. Zetzel 1973; Zetzel 1981, 211 n. 1; Reynolds and Wilson 1991, 252; and esp. Pecere 1986, 29–30.
45. See Pecere 1986, 19–24, 69–81.
46. On the vocabulary of the subscriptions, Zetzel 1981, 228; Pecere 1986, 69–70.
47. See Zetzel 1981, 218 n. 11; Pecere 1986, 225 n. 159.
48. Subscription to [Quint.] Declam. maior. 18, discussed in Zetzel 1981, 225 n. 22. For general discussion, see Pecere 1986, 46–51. For further examples, see Zetzel 1981, 227–228.
49. Zetzel 1981 214 n. 4; Pecere 1986, 51–59.
50. See Zetzel 1981, 217 n. 9. Pecere 1986 discusses this subscription and other metrical subscriptions, p. 22 and n. 8.
51. For the texts of these subscriptions, see now van den Hout 1988, xxxvi–xxxviii, 52. Cf. Zetzel 1980, 50; Zetzel 1981, 223 n. 17.
52. Zetzel 1980, 53.
53. Cf. Suetonius, Gramm. 24.2, on Valerius Probus, with Kaster 1995, 260–263.

54. On the meaning of *antigraphum,* or "copy," see Pecere 1986, 58.
55. Zetzel 1980, 56 and n. 50.
56. For correction (*emendatio*) and punctuation (*distinctio*) as elements of education in late antiquity, see Marrou 1958, 22–23. See further Marrou 1976, 65–68, and Pecere 1986, 31–32, 34, 42–43.
57. On this subscription, Zetzel 1981, 213–214, and Pecere 1986, 30–34.
58. See Zetzel 1981, 223, and Pecere 1986, 40–46.
59. Pecere 1986, 34–40.
60. See Zetzel 1981, 218, and Pecere 1986, 47 and 225 n. 159.
61. Pecere 1986, 46–47.
62. For the subscription, see Zetzel 1981. Pecere (1986, 46–51) discusses the meaning of *frater* here and the identity of Dracontius at p. 49.
63. For the subscription, Zetzel 1981, 214, and Pecere 1986, 51–59.
64. On the places at which subscriptions were written, see Pecere 1986, 43.
65. See Zetzel 1981, 217–218; Pecere 1986, 22 and 211–212 nn. 8–9.
66. See Zetzel 1981, 219; Pecere 1986, 22 and 212 nn. 10–12.
67. See Zetzel 1981, 216.
68. On Theodosius' scribal activities, see Jahn 1851, no. 7, 342–344; Holum 1982, 91–92. Cameron has explored some aspects of the intersection of social prestige and calligraphy in his essay on the famous penman Filocalus: Cameron 1992.
69. Bloch 1964, 240–241.
70. See *PLRE* 2, Cassiodorus 4, for a convenient summary of his career and family.
71. For a summary of the history of thought on Cassiodorus, see e.g. Reynolds and Wilson 1991, 82–83, with the bibliography on 258–259. For a more extended and critical account of this picture, see O'Donnell 1979a and especially Pecere 1986, 25 and n. 20.
72. Cameron 1977 and 1984.
73. Cf. Cameron 1977, 26–27.
74. On Cassiodorus and the Vivarium, Reynolds and Wilson 1991, 82–83, 258–259; O'Donnell 1979a.
75. See Pecere 1986, 24 and n. 20.
76. Cameron 1977, 27.
77. Zetzel 1980, 57; cf. Zetzel 1981, 232–239.
78. Cameron 1977, 2 and cf. 27–28.
79. Jahn 1851, 327–372.
80. See Cameron 1977, 27. The essential bibliography on all aspects of the subscriptions is now to be found in Pecere 1986.
81. See Cameron 1977, 5–6. For the "oriental" cults, see Chapter 3 above. For the religious affinities (Isiac) and tone of Apuleius' text, see e.g. Krabbe 1989, 83–122.
82. Cameron 1984, 53.
83. Cameron 1977, 27.
84. For a survey of approaches to this field, see e.g. Febvre and Martin 1976, Eisenstein 1983 and, most recently, H. J. Martin 1994. For the cultural significance of the practices of writing in late antiquity, one might look at Petrucci 1970 or Cavallo 1975 or, more recently, at the impressive five-volume collection Cavallo et al. 1989.

85. Cf. e.g. McGann 1983 and 1991. For a historical account of the emergence of the philological method, see e.g. Todorov 1982.
86. See Timpanaro 1981. Cf. his book contrasting the Freudian attitude toward the "slip" (*lapsus*) and the textual critic's notion of the scribal error (*lapsus*): Timpanaro 1976.
87. For the correction of inscriptions, see Tracy 1975, 109–114, and Susini 1973, 39–49. For papyri see Turner 1980, 93, and Turner 1987, 15–16.
88. Zetzel 1974.
89. See Devreesse 1954, 83–84, 123–124.
90. Eisenstein 1983, 50.
91. So e.g. Kristeller 1955.
92. The classic essay on this subject is Baron 1955; see further Branca 1961.
93. See Jed 1989, esp. the chapter titled "The Politics of Philology," 18–50.
94. For a brief history of proofreading, see Gaskell 1972, 110–116, 351–354. See further Simpson 1935.
95. Hoffman 1995.
96. So in a letter to his editor, Roger Cotes: "You need not give yourself the trouble of examining all the calculations of the scholium. Such errors as do not depend on wrong reasoning can be of no consequence and may be corrected by the reader" (Hall and Tilling 1975, a letter of 15 June 1709, n. 789). It is instructive to recall that the great philologist Richard Bentley was a friend of Newton, and was involved in the production of the second edition of the *Principia*.
97. For the "book of nature," see e.g. Eisenstein 1983, ch. 7, "The Book of Nature Transformed: Printing and the Rise of Modern Science," 185–252. For some amusing examples of the equation between god and proofreader, see the appendix "Musa Typographica" in Simpson 1935, 219–239, particularly the poem "A Contemplation upon the Mystery of Man's Regeneration in Allusion to the Mystery of Printing," which was published by James Watson in his *History of the Art of Printing* (1713).
98. Dellow 1979, 1. For an edifying tale about the value of proofreading in the world of business, see Carnegie 1940 [1936], 27–29.
99. Stainton 1991, 5.
100. See the essay "Behind the Blue Pencil: Censorship or Creeping Creativity" in Barzun 1986, 103–112.
101. Stainton 1991, 6.
102. See generally Todorov 1982. Philology developed in the nineteenth century in reaction to patristic interpretation as an attempt to control interpretive meaning. True meaning was associated with a monolithic "historical" context, most commonly identified with author's intent. Lachmann makes some remarkable statements to this effect. The association with authorial intent remained common through most of the twentieth century. For more recent manifestations of the attitude, see e.g. Peradotto 1983, reprinted and updated in the introduction to Peradotto 1990. Contemporary trends toward opening up texts to multiple interpretations have been paralleled by historical practice, which has moved away from unified grand narratives toward an idea of multiple, competing histories: see Berkhofer 1995.
103. Elaborated by Kaster 1988, esp. 11–95 and 201–230; cf. Pecere 1986, 21.

104. Kaster 1980 is particularly good on this relationship.
105. It is a great virtue of Pecere's discussion to have made this point: Pecere 1986, 21, 36–39, 59–61.
106. This is a common and commonsense point: see e.g. ch. 1, "Defining the Initial Shift," in Eisenstein 1983, 12–40.
107. For a good general treatment of the symbolic aspects of texts, see Clanchy 1993. For discussion of the "book as object" in late antiquity, see Cavallo 1975, 122–124. For some earlier Roman examples see Citroni 1989, 69, 110. The ways in which mass production diminishes the symbolic value of the book and leads to its consideration exclusively in terms of its content are both formal and economic: see Benjamin's classic essay (1968). Nevertheless the production of deluxe books and "coffee table books" continues even now.
108. See e.g. Pecere 1986, 21.
109. So Cameron 1984, 16. The basic essay on this subject is also by Cameron: Cameron 1964. See further Matthews 1975, 1–4, and Matthews 1989b, 9 and 414–416.
110. See Pecere 1986, 37–39.
111. On these subscriptions, see Zetzel 1981, 211–212.
112. Zetzel 1981, 227.
113. For general discussion and bibliography on this calendar, see Salzman 1990.
114. For an alternative interpretation of this passage, see Polara 1967, 276–277.
115. The expression *solutis vocibus* here must mean "in prose." Cf. Polara 1967, 45, who translates "in parole sciolte dal metro." I find no parallel for the use of *voces* in this phrase. More commonly Latin authors say *verba soluta* or *oratio soluta:* cf. e.g. *OLD* s.v. *solutus,* 9.
116. For various issues having to do with this inscription, see "Initiée par l'époux," reprinted in Festugière 1967, 322–333; Polara 1967; Cooper 1996, 97–103.
117. It will be recalled that for Renaissance humanists it was also the goal to make texts "pure and chaste": see Jed 1989.
118. So *disseminas:* one more properly disseminates things like words than one disseminates indivisible individuals. See *TLL* s.v. for examples (many notably from Jerome) of the "dissemination" of texts.
119. See Kaster 1988, 16 with n. 7.
120. Pecere 1986, 24–29.
121. See generally Arns 1953.
122. See Eisenstein 1983, 10–11.
123. Hartke 1940, 164–165, and Chastagnol 1962, 242.
124. Cameron 1984, 53.
125. In more general terms, the categories I am working with are metonymy and metaphor. Even literary criticism is founded on an interaction and confounding of the two: a translation and reduction of narrative to analysis (in the modern period we have tended to privilege analysis over narrative). For a classic statement, see Roman Jacobson's essay "The Dominant" in Jacobson 1987b.
126. This is a very common point in historiography: see e.g. Veyne 1984, ch. 3, "Plots,

Not Facts or Geometrical Figures," 31–46, for a survey of older writing on the subject.
127. Jed 1989, 32–33; cf. Branca 1961.
128. Freud 1939, 52.

7. SILENCE AND AUTHORITY: POLITICS AND REHABILITATION

1. Cf. e.g. Collingwood 1946 [new ed. 1994], 249–253; Veyne 1984, 4–5.
2. See Ricoeur 1984–1988, 3.116–126.
3. See Veyne 1984, 16–18, 153–155.
4. Collingwood 1946 [new ed. 1994], 249–282; for the quotes, see pp. 257, 269–270, 275.
5. See Collingwood 1946 [new ed. 1994], "The Historical Imagination," 231–249. One of the best ways of thinking about these limits is to attempt to define the difference between history and fiction: see e.g. "The Fictions of Factual Representation," in White 1978, 121–134. Barthes attempted to collapse the distinction by treating realism as a rhetorical effect; history, he said, is fiction that "pretends to be true" (see "The Discourse of History," "The Reality Effect," and "Writing the Event," collected in Barthes 1986, 127–154).
6. Roland Barthes is most often cited for this position: see e.g. Barthes 1974 or Barthes 1975.
7. "Perspective and Temporality: A Contribution to the Historiographical Exposure of the Historical World," in Koselleck 1985a, 130–155. The quote is on p. 132.
8. Barthes makes a different but consistent point in his discussion of the authorial persona of the historian in "The Discourse of History," in Barthes 1986, 127–140. As he remarks (on p. 138), "Hence we arrive at that paradox which governs the entire pertinence of historical discourse [in relation to other types of discourse]: fact never has any but a linguistic existence, yet everything happens as if this linguistic existence were merely a pure and simple 'copy' of *another* existence, situated in an extra-structural field, the 'real.'"
9. Arendt makes this point well in her article "What Is Authority?" in Arendt 1968, 91–141.
10. For the function of the Muse in Greek epic a good essay is Murray 1981.
11. Appeal to experience is not the same thing as merely saying "It is so because I say so," any more than it should be regarded as a privileged source of knowledge (as many naive activists would make it): see especially Joan Scott's often reprinted article "The Evidence of Experience" (Scott 1991), or refer to Elaine Scarry's important work on the evidentiary and epistemic value of torture and suffering (Scarry 1985 and 1994). As the title of the 1994 work suggests, there is again a correlation between truth and what is "beyond representation."
12. For god as an authority, who is sometimes represented as giving dictation to the author who takes on the role of scribe, see the interesting account of the history of represen-

tations of Jerome as translator in Rice 1985, 188–195. On some occasions, Jerome is shown as taking dictation from an angel.

13. See H. Arendt, "What Is Authority?" in Arendt 1968, 91–141; R. Barthes, "The Death of the Author," in Barthes 1986, 49–55; M. Foucault, "What Is an Author?" in e.g. Rabinow 1984, 101–120.
14. See e.g. Eisenstein 1983, 192–193. Grafton et al. 1992, 197–256, provides a popular and interesting narrative.
15. Collingwood 1946 [new ed. 1994], 257–261.
16. See Hedrick 1993 and 1995. J. J. Winkler was able to show that some ancient texts (particularly Apuleius) play with the ideas of author and narrator in a very "modern" fashion: see Winkler 1985.
17. This point has been common since Vico: see e.g. Breisach 1994, 205–207.
18. For the large literature on this subject, see the chapter in Eagleton 1983 titled "Phenomenology, Hermeneutics, Reception Theory," 54–90.
19. See e.g. Hirsch 1967; recently *contra* see McGann 1983.
20. Cf. Holum 1982, 7–47.
21. I suspect that there is some special force to this phrase that I have been unable to decipher. Symmachus uses a comparable phrase in discussing the restoration of the younger Flavian to imperial favor, after the debacle of the battle at the Frigidus (Symm. *Ep.* 4.4). More generally, see Ernout 1949, esp. 114–115. For the later history of the phrase, see Michaud-Quantin 1967. See further *TLL* s.v., III 2, cols. 131–132. The phrase has negative connotations. Cf. Cicero *Tusc. disp.* 3.59: *itaque dicuntur nonnulli in maerore, cum de hac communi hominum condicione audivissent, ea lege nos natos ut nemo in perpetuum esse posset expers mali, gravius etiam tulisse.* The phrase may also be used to describe specific disasters that may afflict the lives of men (e.g. civil war). Cf. Cicero *Fam.* 6.6.12: *commemorarem non solum veterum sed horum etiam recentium vel ducum vel comitum tuorum gravissimos casus; etiam externos multos claros viros nominarem. levat enim dolorem communis quasi legis et humanae condicionis recordatio.* The juxtaposition of the words *claros viros, casus,* and *recordatio* in this last quotation is interesting. For a contemporary example, see Augustine *Civ. Dei* 14.4: *si vero condicionem cogitans casusque communes quae accidere possunt.*
22. This has been a basic point in the critical practice known as "narratology." The watershed work on narratology is Genette 1980. For a concise statement of the distinction between narrator and author, see Barthes, "The Death of the Author," in Barthes 1986, 49–55. An exemplary application of narratological ideas to an ancient text might be Winkler 1985 or Peradotto 1990.
23. Generally on Theodosius II, see e.g. *PLRE* 2, Theodosius 6.
24. See *RE* suppl. 13, col. 967; Oost 1968; Holum 1982, 92.
25. On Valentinian III, see e.g. *PLRE* 2, Valentinian 4.
26. *Parentes* in Latin need not mean "parents," but is more commonly used for "relatives," as here. Valentinian's "parents" (i.e. his mother and father) were Galla Placidia and Constantius III (*PLRE* 2, Constantius 17).
27. On Galla Placidia see e.g. *PLRE* 2, Placidia 4; Oost 1968.
28. Oost 1968, 231.

29. Oost 1968, 231 n. 77, cites bibliography. Generally on Aëtius see *PLRE* 2, Aëtius 7. For a general account of "Aëtius' struggle for power," see O'Flynn 1983, 74–87.
30. See Oost 1968, 238 n. 108. More generally on Merobaudes see Clover 1971.
31. See generally Millar 1977, 213–228; Harries 1988.
32. Cf. Harries 1988; Honoré 1993 and 1994.
33. Honoré 1994.
34. Cf. Honoré 1993 and *PLRE* 2, 1259.
35. The inscription does not make this point explicitly, but other statues in the Forum of Trajan were erected at the behest of the senate in this period.
36. Cf. Calabi-Limentani 1973, 171–172.
37. The essential publication on the Roman calendar is *Inscr. Ital.* 13.3; see further Michels 1967 and Salzman 1990.
38. Michels 1967, 167. In detail, Dulabahn 1986.
39. See Salzman 1990, 14–16.
40. Gaius had earlier attempted to rename a month, choosing, like Domitian, the name Germanicus: see Suet. *Cal.* 15.2. There are some further literary *testimonia* for this incident of Domitian's reign: Martial *Ep.* 9.1.4, Suet. *Domit.* 13.3, Eusebius *a. Abr.* 2102, and Jerome *a. Abr.* 2103. The month Germanicus is known from an inscription and from a papyrus: see Bischoff *RE* 7, 1 (1910), 1257–1258 s.v. Germanikeios.
41. See Tacitus, *Ann.* 2.27–32; Dio 57.15.4; Suet. *Tib.* 25.3; Seneca *Ep.* 70.10. For a full account, see *Inscr. Ital.* 13.3, with Degrassi's commentary *ad diem*.
42. For the etymology of the word, see e.g. Ernout and Meillet 1967 s.v.
43. This association is a commonplace: see e.g. Michels 1967, 19–21.
44. See *Inscr. Ital.* 13.3, wth Degrassi's commentary *ad diem;* cf. the popular account in Scullard 1981, 186–187.
45. See particularly Plut. *Popl.* 14 and Livy 2.8. Cf. R. Bloch 1961; Nash 1961–1962 s.v.
46. Cf. especially Mart. *Ep.* 12.48.12 and Gell. 12.8.2. Mommsen 1864, 2.45.4, argued that the *epulum Iovi* was an invention of the empire and that, during the republic, only Minerva had received a feast on the Ides of September. Most subsequent scholars have disagreed, feeling that the practice must date to the early republic. For a review of the argument, see e.g. Scullard 1981, 254 n. 243.
47. See Serv. auct. *ad* Verg. *Ecl.* 8.82. For the making of the *mola salsa* and its uses throughout the year, see e.g. Scullard 1981, 22, 77, 103, 149–150, 187.
48. This practice may have had to do with recordkeeping or apotropaic magic, or with something else. I will content myself with citing here only Bucher 1987 [1995].
49. In the following discussion, I will not make a point of citing the basic resources for the topography of ancient Rome at every turn, though obviously they include brief summary descriptions and bibliography. In general, the reader might consult Platner 1929 or Lugli 1952 (old, but good for literary and epigraphical *testimonia*); Nash 1961–1962 or the *Carta archeologica* or Coarelli 1984 (esp. for the remains); Richardson 1992 and Steinby 1993–. Generally on the development on the imperial fora, see Martin 1972, 912–922.

50. For the Forum of Caesar see Coarelli 1984, vol. 2, 233ff.; C. Morselli in Steinby 1993–, s.v. Forum Iulium.
51. For the Forum of Augustus, see Zanker 1968; V. Kockel in Steinby 1993–, s.v. Forum Augustum.
52. Cf. Anderson 1982; H. Bauer and C. Morselli in Steinby 1993–, s.v. Forum Nervae.
53. It was dedicated in 112. See briefly Boatwright 1987, 77–98; Packer in Steinby 1993–, s.v. Forum Traiani. At more length, see now Packer 1996.
54. For the function of the forum, see R. Martin 1972.
55. The general discussion in Lanciani 1979, 304–307, remains useful. See now, however, Zanker 1990, 210–215.
56. On Bassaeus Rufus see Pflaum 1960–1961, no. 162 + add.; Pflaum 1982. For the inscription and its restorations, see the *CIL*, which compares Dio 71.3.
57. Cf. Platner 1929, 239.
58. Lanciani 1979, 312; cf. Lugli 1952 16 (1969), 47–73.
59. Matthews 1989b, 23–24, citing Chastagnol 1962, 232–233, says that this statue was erected in the Forum of Trajan. I know of no evidence to support this statement. There is a dedication from the Forum by Victor to Theodosius, "who surpassed the kindness and holiness and generosity of earlier emperors" (*veterum principum clementiam sanctitudinem munificentiam supergresso*) (*CIL* 6.1186 = *ILS* 2945), but this clearly is not the statue mentioned by Ammianus. Victor became an eminent bureaucrat later on, but as Ammianus emphasizes, the honor he receives here is owing to his skill as a writer. On Victor, see generally *PLRE* 1, Victor 13; Bird 1984. Nixon 1991 argues against Ammianus that Julian did not favor Victor here because of his literary activity, but for reasons that must remain obscure.
60. See *PLRE* 1, Paulinus 14.
61. Augustine mistakenly locates the statue in the Roman Forum. The error may be owing to Augustine himself or to the manuscript tradition. See Marrou 1976, 79 n. 3. Generally on Victorinus, see *PLRE* 1, Victorinus 11. He is doubtless most famous for his late conversion to Christianity (probably in the 350's) which made a great impression among the elite of Rome. Some scholars would argue that Victorinus converted at some time soon before 354 and that the statue was erected because he had become a Christian: see Courcelle 1962. On the conversion see Hadot (1971, 28–33), who dates it later than the dedication of the statue, ca. 355–357. More recently, see Salzman 1990, 224–225.
62. Further on this inscription see *IGUR* no. 63, pp. 56–58. Cameron 1970 gives only sporadic attention to the statue base: see pp. 1, 361, 390, 415, and 490. Generally on Claudian see *PLRE* 2, Claudianus 5; Cameron 1970.
63. Generally on Merobaudes see Clover 1971. More recently for the career, see *PLRE* 2, Merobaudes. For the dedication of the statue, Clover 1971, 39–40.
64. For Sidonius see *PLRE* 2, s.v. Apollinaris 6; Harries 1994. For the statue, see Harries 1994, 5, 73. For an explicit discussion of the date of the dedication of the statue, see W. B. Anderson 1936–1965, 37.
65. Sidonius here speaks of "the writers of the two libraries" (*inter auctores utriusque fixam bybliothecae,* line 28), and Marrou consequently understood this passage to mean that

the statue was erected within the library proper, not in the Forum of Trajan itself: Marrou 1976, 79 n. 4. On the other hand, Sidonius might here be using the library as a (very appropriate in this context) metonym for the forum in which it was located. In another poem, Sidonius appears to suggest that it was instead situated in front of the library, in a portico of the Forum of Trajan (Sid. *Carm.* 8.7–10).

66. There may be a few more scraps of evidence. For example, a fragment of an inscription found in the Forum of Trajan seems to honor a man of some literary accomplishment. On it the word [*e*]*rudito* can yet be deciphered: *NdSc* ser. 6, 9 (1933), 495 no. 174, line 3.
67. Marrou 1976, 65–80 (revised version of Marrou 1932).
68. See Pecere 1986, 34–40; cf. Marrou 1976, 67–68.
69. Jordan 1871, vol. 2, 472; cf. Steinby 1993–, s.v. Forum Martis.
70. Generally on this subscription, see Pecere 1986, 30–34.
71. Marrou 1976, 65–66.
72. Cf. Pecere 1986, 46–51; Marrou 1976, 68–69.
73. Cf. Kaster 1988, 249; Marrou 1976, 70–71.
74. Marrou 1976, 72–74, 77–78.
75. Kaster 1988, 217; Marrou 1976, 77–78.
76. Marrou 1976, 75–77. For a brief definition and a list of other known *scholae* in Rome, see Richardson 1992 s.v. For the hemicycles in the Forum of Trajan, see Packer in Steinby 1993–, s.v. Forum Traiani, and his new book on the Forum of Trajan (Packer 1996).
77. See e.g. MacKendrick 1980, 221–226; Besnier 1899; Cagnat 1913, vol. 2, 474–497.
78. On Fortunatus and his poetry, see e.g. *PLRE* 3a, Fortunatus 2.
79. For libraries in antiquity and in Rome, see Callmer 1944.
80. See Marrou 1976, 72–73.
81. The word *antiquarius* has a range of meanings, ranging from "copyist," or "scribe," to "master of a group of scribes" or even "bookseller": see especially the assessment on *librarii* and *antiquarii* in Diocletian's price edict, in the edition of Lauffer 1971, 7.69, with Lauffer's discussion at pp. 241–242: *librario sibe antiquario in singulis discipulis menstruos*. For the differentiation of various kinds of scribes in the edict, see 7.39–41.
82. *PLRE* 2, Helpidius 1; cf. *PLRE* 1, Helpidius 10.
83. Kaster 1988.
84. On the "look" of age, see Loewenthal 1985, 125–182.
85. Thomas 1989, 51–59.
86. Copyright law and state censorship are in their origins closely linked: for a brief account, see Gaskell 1972, 183–185. On the connection between the nation and printers, see B. Anderson 1991, 37–46; more generally, see the excellent book Rose 1993 as well as the old standard Putnam 1962 [1898].
87. There is interesting discussion of American attitudes toward "patina" in Loewenthal 1985, 148–182.
88. In terms of semantics, it makes no difference whether damage is accidental (wear and tear) or purposeful (erasure).
89. Zetzel 1980, 44.
90. There is a brief account of the development of textual criticism in Reynolds and Wilson

1991, 207–241. For a more lengthy discussion, see Timpanaro 1981. For an outline of the history of modern textual criticism, see McGann 1983, 16–22.
91. Certeau 1986, 77–82.
92. Tanselle acknowledges this point while minimizing its importance. See Tanselle 1989, particularly the chapter "Reproducing the Texts of Documents," 39–66.
93. For a critique of the actuality of the archetype, and of the availability of "authorial intentions," see McGann 1983.
94. The standard essay on the inscription and the paintings is Panofsky 1963 [1936], discussing the implications of the mistranslation.
95. For themes in pastoral literature, see now Damiani and Mujica 1990.
96. See the chapter "Mourning, Dissimulation and Celebration," in Petrucci 1993, 43–51.
97. For literacy see generally Harris 1989, Humphrey 1991, and Kaster 1988.
98. Hedrick 1995.
99. See Furet and Ozouf 1982, 311–312, and, above all, Certeau 1988, 86–102.

APPENDIX: CONCERNING THE TEXT OF *CIL* 6.1783

1. Chastagnol 1976, 107–109; Grünewald 1992, 465–467.
2. See Matranga 269: "Construendosi un condotto sotterraneo attorno il Foro Trajano, quando i lavoranti giunsero alla parte occidentale del medesimo Foro s'imbatterono in due marmi scritti; il di sequente (22. agosto p. p.) appena n'ebbimo sentore, ci recammo sul luogo e vi leggemmo tra l'acqua marcida la bella iscrizione." Further excavations were undertaken here by L. Canina: see now Packer 1996, 47–48.
3. So they note: "Descripsit De Rossi; locos difficiliores et Brunnius et ego una cum eo (i.e. De Rossi, in 1849), nuper (i.e. for the *CIL* edition of 1882) ego et Bormannus denuo contulimus."
4. All early editors say that the date is located on the *right* side of the base. Barbieri notes that the inscription is on the *left* side.
5. On the prose of the imperial bureaucracy, see Honoré 1994; MacMullen 1962; Millar 1977, 93–94, 226–228.
6. Generally on imperial correspondence, Millar 1977, 203–228, 240–259.
7. See Millar 1977, 327–328.
8. Millar 1977, 206, 277–278.
9. Generally on Roman epigraphical letter forms, see Gordon and Gordon 1957. For the relationship between epigraphical letter forms and those of contemporary manuscripts, see Gordon and Gordon 1957, 65–74, and especially the work of J. Mallon (e.g. Mallon 1961, 564–573). For the terms used to describe various scripts, see Bischoff 1990, 54–63.
10. Gordon and Gordon 1957, 160–166.
11. See generally Gordon and Gordon 1957, 186–205.
12. See Mommsen and Meyer 1905 [repr. 1962], vol. 1 pars prior, prolegomena, cxlix–clii.
13. De Rossi 287. For the characteristics of the orthography of the Theodosian Code, see Mommsen and Meyer 1905 [repr. 1962], vol. 1 pars prior, prolegomena, cxlii–cxlix.
14. See generally Gordon 1948.

15. See generally Gordon and Gordon 1957, 159–160.
16. See De Rossi, 316 n. Use of the genitive is not uncommon: see the *TLL* s.v. *praeficio* II B g, with the general comments at II A; cf. E. Sachers, *RE* 22, 2 (1954), s.v., col. 2503.
17. Grünewald 1992, 465 n. 9, compares lines 34–35 (*redditam . . . eius memoriam et dignitatem*) and suggests that the word "restored" (*reddita*) in line 4 refers to the same qualities. He is certainly wrong. In Roman honorary inscriptions, the thing dedicated is commonly omitted: so, for example, at the end of the inscription we hear that "Dexter supervised the erection (of the statue)" (*Dexter . . . statuendam curavi*, line 37–38). The ellipse is so common that most handbooks treat it as a regularity. The omission may be seen, for example, in the inscription from Lepcis Magna in honor of Flavian: Guey 1950, 79 and n. 5, referring to *TLL* s.v. *colloco*, col. 1639. Borghesi pointed out already in 1849 that the statue itself had to be understood with the adjective *reddita* (*apud* De Rossi, 357). What is unusual about the dedicatory formula is its passive formation. Most commonly, dedications are framed in the active voice, so that we would have *statuam* (i.e. in the accusative, rather than in the nominative as here), and the dedicators in the nominative. See further Chapters 2 and 7 above.
18. So argued by De Rossi, 315 n. 1; Borghesi *apud* De Rossi, 357. Matranga understood lines 29–33 to refer to Appius, not to the younger Flavian.
19. So De Rossi, 315 n. 1, and Borghesi *apud* De Rossi, 357. As Borghesi noted, at this time Romans were called by their *cognomen* or *agnomen*, never by their *praenomen*. See Chapter 2 above.
20. De Rossi, 315 n. 1.
21. Panciera 1992, 254–257.
22. So De Rossi, 348 n. *a*.
23. R. Kaster informs me per litt. that he would favor this interpretation. For the honorific form of address, in which "the honor of Flavian" stands for "the honorable Flavian" (as some mayors are called "hizzoner"), see Kaster 1988, 272.

LIST OF ABBREVIATIONS

FOR ANCIENT AUTHORS, SEE INDEX OF PASSAGES CITED.

AE	L'Année épigraphique, published in the Revue archéologique and separately. 1888–.
AJA	American Journal of Archaeology.
AJAH	American Journal of Ancient History.
AJP	American Journal of Philology.
ANRW	W. Haas and H. Temporini, eds. Aufstieg und Niedergang der römischen Welt. Berlin. 1972–.
Ant. Class.	L'Antiquité classique.
BICS	Bulletin of the Institute of Classical Studies.
Bull. ép.	Bulletin épigraphique, published in the Revue des études grècques and separately.
Carta archeologica	Carta archeologica di Roma. Florence. 1962–.
CIL	Corpus Inscriptionum Latinarum. Berlin. 1863–.
CLA	E. A. Lowe, ed. Codices Latini Antiquiores. 1934–1966. Suppl. 1971; 2nd ed. of vol. 1 1972.
CP	Classical Philology.
CQ	Classical Quarterly.

CR   *Classical Review.*

CSEL   *Corpus Scriptorum Ecclesiasticorum Latinorum.* Editum consilio et impensis Academiae Litterarum Caesareae Vindobonensis. Vindobonae. 1866–.

FGrH   F. Jacoby, ed. *Die Fragmente der griechischen Historiker.* Berlin. 1923–.

Forcellini   J. Facciolati, A. Forcellini, J. Furlanetto. *Lexicon Totius Latinitatis.* Padua. 1859–1878.

Freud SE   S. Freud. *The Standard Edition of the Complete Psychological works of Sigmund Freud.* New York. 1953–1974.

GRBS   *Greek, Roman and Byzantine Studies.*

HSCP   *Harvard Studies in Classical Philology.*

ICUR   G. B. De Rossi, ed. *Inscriptiones Christianae Urbis Romae Septimo Saeculo Antiquiores.* Rome. 1857–. N.s. ed. A. Silvagni. Rome. 1922–.

IGUR   Moretti, L., ed. *Inscriptiones Graecae Urbis Romae.* Rome. 1968–.

ILCV   E. Diehl, ed. *Inscriptiones Latinae Christianae Veteres.* Berlin. 1925–1931.

ILS   H. Dessau, *Inscriptiones Latinae Selectae.* Berlin. 1892–1916.

IMU   *Italia medioevale e umanistica.*

Inscr. Ital. *Inscriptiones Italiae.* 1931/32–.

IRT   J. Reynolds and J. B. Ward Perkins, eds. *The Inscriptions of Roman Tripolitania.* Rome. 1952.

JDAI   *Jahrbuch des [kaiserlich] deutschen archäologischen Instituts.*

JHS   *Journal of Hellenic Studies.*

JRA   *Journal of Roman Archaeology.*

Lindsay   Sexti Pompei Festi, *De Verborum Significatu Quae Supersunt cum Pauli Epitome.* Thewrewkianis copiis usus edidit Wallace M. Lindsay. Bibliotheca Scriptorum Graecorum et Romanorum Teubneriana. Leipzig. 1913.

MAAR   *Memoirs of the American Academy in Rome.*

MAL   *Memorie: Atti della Academia Nazionale dei Lincei, Classe di scienze morali, storiche e filogiche.*

MEFR   *Mélanges d'archéologie et d'histoire de l'École française de Rome.*

MGHAA   *Monumenta Germaniae Historica, Auctores Antiquissimi.* 1877–1919.

NdSc   *Notizie degli scavi di antichità.*

OLD   P. G. W. Glare, ed. *The Oxford Latin Dictionary.* Oxford. 1968–1982.

Orelli   J. C. Orelli and G. Henzen, eds. *Inscriptionum Latinarum Selectarum Amplissima Collectio ad Illustrandum Romanae Antiquitatis Disciplinam Accomadata.* Zurich. 1828–1856.

Peter   H. Peter. *Historicorum Romanorum Reliquiae.* 2nd ed. of vol. 1 1916, vol. 2 1906.

PG   J. P. Migne. *Patrologiae Cursus Completus.* Series Graeca. Paris. 1857–.

PIR^2 E. Groag, A. Stein, et al. *Prosopographia Imperii Romani Saeculi I, II, III.* 2nd ed. 1933–.

PLRE   A. H. M. Jones et al., eds. *The Prosopography of the Later Roman Empire.* Cambridge. 1971–.

RE   A. Pauly, G. Wissowa, and W. Kroll, eds. *Real-Encyclopädie der klassischen Altertumswissenschaft.* Stuttgart. 1893–.

REA   *Revue des études anciennes.*

REAug. *Revue des études augustiniennes.*

REL   *Revue des études latines.*

Schanz/Hosius   Martin von Schanz, *Geschichte der romischen Literatur bis zum Gesetzgebungswerk des Kaisers Justinian.* 4. neubearb. Aufl. von Carl Hosius. Handbuch der Altertumswissenschaft, 8. Abt. Munich. 1927–.

TAPA   *Transactions of the American Philological Association.*

TLL   *Thesaurus Linguae Latinae.* Leipzig. 1900–.

YCS   *Yale Classical Studies.*

ZPE   *Zeitschrift für Papyrologie und Epigraphik.*

SECONDARY WORKS CITED

Alföldi, A. 1976. *Die Kontorniat-Medaillons.* Antike Munzen und geschnittene Steine. Berlin.
Alfonsi, L. 1963. "Nota all'Agricola di Tacito." *Aevum* 37: 116.
Allison, J. 1990. "Dissimulatio: Tiberius or Tacitus?" In *Conflict, Antithesis and the Ancient Historian,* ed. J. Allison, pp. 133–155. Columbus, Oh.
Anderson, B. 1991. *Imagined Communities: Reflections on the Origin and Spread of Nationalism.* London.
Anderson, J. C. Jr. 1982. "Domitian, the Argiletum and the Temple of Peace." *AJA* 86: 101–110.
Anderson, R. D., P. J. Parsons, and R. G. M. Nisbet. 1979. "Elegiacs by Gallus from Qasr Ibrîm." *JRS* 69: 125–155.
Anderson, W. B., trans. 1936–1965. Introduction. In Sidonius, *Poems and Letters.* Loeb Classical Library. Cambridge, Mass.
Angus, S. 1906. "The Sources of the First Ten Books of Augustine's *De Civitate Dei.*" Thesis, Princeton.
Arendt, H. 1968. *Between Past and Future.* New York.
Arnaud-Lindet, M.-P., ed. 1990. Introduction. In Orose, *Histoires (contre les païens).* Paris.
Arnheim, M. T. W. 1972. *The Senatorial Aristocracy in the Later Roman Empire.* Oxford.
Arns, P. E. 1953. *La technique du livre d'après saint Jérome.* Paris.
Aulich, J., and T. Wilcox, eds. 1993. *Europe without Walls: Art, Posters and Revolution 1989–93.* Manchester, Eng.
Austin, J. L. 1962. *How to Do Things with Words.* The William James Lectures. Cambridge, Mass.
Badian, E. 1966. "The Early Historians." In *Latin Historians,* ed. T. A. Dorey, pp. 1–38. London.
———. 1971. "Archons and Strategoi." *Antichthon* 5: 1–34.
Bagnall, R. S., et al. 1987. *Consuls of the Later Roman Empire.* Philological Monographs, no. 36. Atlanta.
Barbieri, G. 1969. "Revisioni di epigrafi." *Rendiconti della Pontificia Accademia Romana di Archeologia* ser. 3, 42: 73–80.
Barnes, T. D. 1976. "The *Epitome de Caesaribus* and Its Sources." *CP* 71: 258–268.
———. 1981. *Constantine and Eusebius.* Cambridge, Mass.

———. 1982a. "Aspects of the Background of the *City of God*." *Revue de l'Université d'Ottowa/University of Ottawa Quarterly* 52: 4–80.
———. 1982b. *The New Empire of Diocletian and Constantine*. Cambridge, Mass.
———. 1985. "The Conversion of Constantine." *Échos du monde classique/Classical Views* n.s. 4: 371–391.
———. 1986. "The Constantinian Reformation." In *The Crake Lectures 1984*, pp. 39–57. Sackville, N.B.
———. 1989. "Christians and Pagans in the Reign of Constantius." In *L'Église et l'empire au I^{Ve} siècle*, pp. 322–337. Entretiens sur l'antiquité classique, 34. Vandoeuvres-Genève.
———. 1990. "Religion and Society in the Reign of Theodosius." In *Grace, Politics and Desire: Essays on Augustine*, ed. H. Meynell, pp. 157–175. Calgary, Alta.
———. 1991. "Pagan Perceptions of Christianity." In *Early Christianity: Origins and Evolution to A.D. 600. In Honour of W. H. C. Frend*, ed. I. Hazlett, pp. 231–243. London.
———. 1992. "Augustine, Symmachus and Ambrose." In *Augustine: From Rhetor to Theologian*, ed. J. McWilliam et al., pp. 7–13. Waterloo, Ont.
———. 1994a. *From Eusebius to Augustine: Selected Papers 1982–1993*. Variorum Collected Studies. London.
———. 1994b. "The Religious Affiliations of Consuls and Prefects, 317–361." In *From Eusebius to Augustine: Selected Papers 1982–1993*, sec. VII, pp. 1–11. Variorum Collected Studies. London.
———. 1995. "Statistics and the Conversion of the Roman Aristocracy." *JRS* 85: 135–147.
Barnes, T. D., and R. W. Westall. 1991. "The Conversion of the Roman Aristocracy in Prudentius' *Contra Symmachum*." *Phoenix* 45: 50–61.
Baron, H. 1955. *The Crisis of the Early Italian Renaissance: Civic Humanism and Republican Liberty in an Age of Classicism and Tyranny*. Princeton.
Barthes, R. 1974. *S/Z*. New York.
———. 1975. *The Pleasure of the Text*. New York.
———. 1986. *The Rustle of Language*. Berkeley and Los Angeles.
———. 1987. *Michelet*. New York.
Bartsch, S. 1994. *Actors in the Audience*. Cambridge, Mass.
Barzun, J. 1986. *On Writing, Editing and Publishing: Essays Explicative and Hortatory*. Chicago.
Baudrillard, J. 1983, *Simulations*. New York.
Becatti, G. 1939. "Il culto di Ercole ad Ostia ed un nuovo rilievo votivo." *Bulletino della Commissione Archeologica Communale in Roma* 47: 37–60.
Begbie, C. M. 1967. "The Epitome of Livy." *CQ* 61: 332–338.
Benario, H. 1975. *An Introduction to Tacitus*. Athens, Ga.
Benjamin, W. 1968. "The Work of Art in the Age of Mechanical Reproduction." In *Illuminations*, pp. 217–251. New York.
———. 1985. *The Origin of German Tragic Drama*. London.
Berger, A. 1953. *An Encyclopedic Dictionary of Roman Law*. Philadelphia.

Berger, P. C. 1981. *The Insignia of the "Notitia Dignitatum."* New York.

Bergmann, M., and P. Zanker. 1981. "'Damnatio Memoriae.' Umgearbeitet Nero- und Domitiansporträts. Zur Ikonographie der flavischen Kaiser und des Nerva." *JDAI* 96: 317–412.

Berkhofer, R. F. 1978. *The White Man's Indian: Images of the American Indian from Columbus to the Present.* New York.

———. 1995. *Beyond the Great Story: History as Text and Discourse.* Cambridge, Mass.

Besnier, M. 1899. "Les *scholae* des sous-officiers dans le camp romain de Lambèse." *MEFR* 19: 199–258.

Billanovich, G. 1959. "Dal Livio di Raterio (Laur. 63.19) al Livio del Petrarca (B. M. Harl. 2493)." *IMU* 2: 103–178.

———. 1981–. *La tradizione del testo di Livio e le origini dell'umanesimo.* Studi sul Petrarca. Padua.

Bindeman, S. L. 1981. *Heidegger and Wittgenstein. The Poetics of Silence.* Lanham, Md.

Bird, H. W. 1984. *Sextus Aurelius Victor: A Historiographical Study.* ARCA. Francis Cairns.

Bischoff, B. 1990. *Latin Paleography: Antiquity and the Middle Ages.* Cambridge.

Blanchard, A., ed. 1989. *Les débuts du codex. Actes de la journée d'étude organisée à Paris le 3e et 4e juillet 1985.* Turnhout.

Blanck, H. 1969. *Wiederverwendung alter Statuen als Ehrendenkmäler bei Griechen und Römern.* 2nd ed. Studia Archaeologica. Rome.

Bleckmann, B. 1992. *Die Reichskrise des III. Jahrhunderts in der spätantiken und byzantinischen Geschichtsschreibung: Untersuchungen zu den nachdionischen Quellen der Chronik des Johannes Zonaras.* Quellen und Forschungen zur antiken Welt, Bd. 11. Munich.

———. 1995. "Bemerkungen zu den *Annales* des Nicomachus Flavianus." *Historia* 44: 83–99.

Bloch, H. 1945. "A New Document in the Last Pagan Revival in the West, 393–394 A.D." *Harvard Theological Review* 38: 199–244.

———. 1964. "The Pagan Revival in the West." In *The Conflict between Paganism and Christianity in the Fourth Century: Essays,* ed. A. Momigliano, pp. 193–218. Oxford.

Bloch, R. 1961. "Le départ des Étrusques de Rome selon l'annalistique et la dédicace du temple du Jupiter Capitolin." *Revue de l'histoire des religions* 159: 141–156.

Blum, H. 1969. *Die antike Mnemotechnik.* Spudasmata 15. Hildesheim.

Boatwright, Mary Taliaferro. 1987. *Hadrian and the City of Rome.* Princeton.

Boucher, J.-P. 1966. *Caius Cornelius Gallus.* Paris.

Bowersock, G. W. 1978. *Julian the Apostate.* Cambridge, Mass.

Boym, S. 1994. *Common Places: Mythologies of Everyday Life in Russia.* Cambridge, Mass.

Branca, V. 1961. *Copisti per passione, tradizione caratterizzante, tradizione di memoria.* Studi e problemi di critica testuale. Bologna.

Breisach, E. 1994. *Historiography: Ancient, Medieval & Modern.* Chicago.

Brock, S. 1979. "Aspects of Translation Technique in Antiquity." *GRBS* 20: 69–87.

Brown, N. O. 1985. *Life against Death.* Middletown, Conn.

Brown, P. R. L. 1961. "Aspects of the Christianization of the Roman Aristocracy." *JRS* 51: 1–11.

———. 1967. *Augustine of Hippo: A Biography.* Berkeley.
Brunt, P. A., and J. M. Moore. 1977. *Res Gestae Divi Augusti; The Achievements of the Divine Augustus.* Oxford.
Bucher, G. S. 1987 [1995]. "The *Annales Maximi* in Light of Roman Methods of Record Keeping." *AJAH* 12: 2–61.
Burdick, S., and W. Iser, eds. 1989. *Languages of the Unsayable: The Play of Negativity in Literature and Literary Theory.* New York.
Cage, J. 1961. *Silence: Lectures and Writings.* Middletown, Conn.
Cagnat, R. 1913. *L'Armée romaine d'Afrique et l'occupation militaire de l'Afrique sous les empereurs.* Paris.
———. 1914. *Cours d'épigraphie latine.* Paris.
Calabi-Limentani, I. 1973. *Epigrafia latina.* Milan.
Callmer, C. 1944. "Antiken Bibliotheken." *Opuscula Archaeologica* 3: 145–193.
Callu, J.-P. 1974. "Les préfectures de Nicomaque Flavien." In *Mélanges d'histoire ancien offertes á Will. W. Seston,* pp. 73–78. Publications de la Sorbonne. Série "Études," 9. Paris.
Cameron, Alan. 1964. "The Roman Friends of Ammianus." *JRS* 54: 15–28.
———. 1966a. "A Biographical Note on Claudian." *Athenaeum* 44: 32–40.
———. 1966b. "The Date and Identity of Macrobius." *JRS* 56: 25–38.
———. 1968. "Gratian's Repudiation of the Pontifical Robe." *JRS* 58: 96–102.
———. 1970. *Poetry and Propaganda at the Court of Honorius.* Oxford.
———. 1977. "Paganism and Literature in Late Fourth Century Rome." In *Christianisme et formes littéraires de l'antiquité tardive en occident,* pp. 1–40. Entretiens sur l'antiquité classique, 23. Geneva.
———. 1981. "The Consuls of A.D. 411–412 Again." *Bulletin of the American Society of Papyrologists* 18: 69–72.
———. 1982a. "The Death of Vitalian (520 A.D.)." *ZPE* 48: 93–94.
———. 1982b. "A Note on Ivory Carving in Fourth Century Constantinople." *AJA* 86: 126–129.
———. 1984. "The Latin Revival of the Fourth Century." In *Renaissances before the Renaissance: Cultural Revivals of Late Antiquity and the Middle Ages,* ed. W. Treadgold, pp. 42–58. Stanford.
———. 1985a. "The Date and Owners of the Esquiline Treasure." *AJA* 89: 135–145.
———. 1985b. "Polyonomy in the Late Roman Aristocracy: The Case of Petronius Probus." *JRS* 75: 164–182.
———. 1992. "Filocalus and Melania." *CP* 87: 140–144.
———. 1995. "Avienus or Avienius." *ZPE* 108: 252–262.
———. Forthcoming. *The Last Pagans of Rome.*
Cameron, Averil. 1993. *The Later Roman Empire, A.D. 284–430.* Cambridge, Mass.
Cantarella, E. 1991. *I supplizi capitali in Grecia e a Roma.* Collana storica Rizzoli. Milan.
Carnegie, D. 1940 [1936]. *How to Win Friends and Influence People.* New York.
Cartledge, P. 1993. *The Greeks: A Portrait of Self and Others.* Oxford.
Cavallo, G. 1975. "Libro e pubblico alla fine del mondo antico." In *Libri editori e pubblico*

nel mondo antico. Guida storica e critica, ed. G. Cavallo. Universale Laterza, 315. Rome.

———. 1989. "Testo, libro, lettura." In *Lo spazio letterario di Roma antica,* ed. G. Cavallo et al., pp. 307–341. Rome.

Cavallo, G., et al., eds. 1989. *Lo spazio letterario di Roma antica.* Rome.

Cavedoni, C. 1850. "Annotazioni al tomo XXI. degli Annali." *Bolletino dell'Istituto di Corrispondenza Archeologica,* pp. 156–160.

Certeau, M. de. 1986. *Heterologies: Discourse on the Other.* Minneapolis.

———. 1988. *The Writing of History.* New York.

Champlin, E. J. 1982. "Saint Gallicanus." *Phoenix* 36: 70–76.

Chassignet, M., ed. 1986. Introduction and commentary. In Caton, *Les origines.* Paris.

Chastagnol, A. 1956. "Le sénateur Volusien." *REA* 58: 241–253.

———. 1958. "Observations sur le consulat suffect et la préture du bas empire." *Revue historique* 219: 221–253.

———. 1960. *La préfecture urbaine à Rome sous le bas empire.* Paris.

———. 1962. *Les fastes de la préfecture de Rome au bas-empire.* Paris.

———. 1963. "L'Administration du diocèse italien au bas-empire." *Historia* 12: 348–379.

———. 1976. *La fin du monde antique.* Paris.

Cheung, K.-K. 1993. *Articulate Silences: Hisaye Yamamoto, Maxine Hong Kingston, Joy Kogawa.* Reading Women Writing. Ithaca, N.Y.

Chuvin, P. 1990. *A Chronicle of the Last Pagans.* Revealing Antiquity. Cambridge, Mass.

Citroni, M. 1989. "I destinatari contemporanei." In *Lo spazio letterario di Roma antica,* ed. G. Cavallo et al., pp. 53–116. Rome.

Clanchy, M. T. 1993. *From Memory to Written Record: England 1066–1307.* Oxford.

Clover, F. 1971. *Flavius Merobaudes: A Translation and Historical Commentary.* Transactions of the American Philosophical Society n.s. 61.1. Philadelphia.

Coarelli, F. 1984. *Il foro romano.* Rome.

Cole, T. 1992. "Initium mihi operis Servius Galba iterum T. Vinius consules . . ." In *Beginnings in Classical Literature,* ed. F. M. Dunn and T. Cole, pp. 231–245. YCS 29. Cambridge.

Collingwood, R. G. 1946 [new ed. 1994]. *The Idea of History.* Oxford.

Collini, A. M. 1944. *Storia e topografia del Celio nell'antichità.* Atti della Pontifica Accademia romana di archeologia. Memorie, ser. 3, vol. 7. Rome.

Conquest, R. 1990. *The Great Terror: A Reassessment.* New York.

Conway, R. W. 1897. *The Italic Dialects.* Cambridge.

Cooper, K. 1992. "Insinuations of Womanly Influence: An Aspect of the Christianization of the Roman Aristocracy." *JRS* 82: 150–164.

———. 1966. *The Virgin and the Bride: Idealized Womanhood in Late Antiquity.* Cambridge, Mass.

Corcoran, S. 1993. "Hidden from History: The Legislation of Licinius." In *The Theodosian Code: Studies in the Imperial Law of Late Antiquity,* ed. J. Harries and I. Wood, pp. 97–119. London.

Courcelle, P. 1962. "Éducation et culture à l'époque précarolingienne." *REA* 64: 127–135.
———. 1969. *Late Latin Writers and Their Greek Sources.* Cambridge, Mass.
Courtney, E. 1980. *A Commentary on the Satires of Juvenal.* London.
Coward, H., and T. Foshay, eds. 1992. *Derrida and Negative Theology; with a Conclusion by Jacques Derrida.* Albany.
Cracco-Ruggini, L. 1979. "Il paganesimo romano tra religione e politica (383–394 d.C.): per un reinterpretazione del 'carmen contra paganos.'" *MAL* ser. 8, 23.
Croke, B. 1976. "The Editing of Symmachus' Letters to Eugenius and Arbogast." *Latomus* 35: 533–549.
Croke, B., and J. Harries, eds. 1982. *Religious Conflict in Fourth Century Rome: a Documentary Study.* Sydney.
Crook, J. A. 1995. *Legal Advocacy in the Roman World.* London.
Culler, J. 1982. *On Deconstruction.* Ithaca, N.Y.
D'Arms, J. H. 1970. *Romans on the Bay of Naples: A Social and Cultural Study of the Villas and Their Owners from 150 B.C. to A.D. 400.* Loeb Classical Monographs. Cambridge, Mass.
Daly, L. J. 1979. "The Gallus Affair and Augustus' *Lex Iulia Maiestatis:* A Study in Historical Chronology and Causality." *Studies in Latin Literature and Roman History* 1: 289–311.
Damiani, Bruno, and Barbara Mujica. 1990. *Et in Arcadia Ego: Essays on Death in the Pastoral Novel.* Lanham, Md.
Darnton, R. 1995. "Censorship, a Comparative View: France, 1789–East Germany 1989." *Representations* 49: 40–60.
Davis, F. 1979. *Yearning for Yesterday: A Sociology of Nostalgia.* New York.
De Rossi, G. B. 1849. "Iscrizione di Nicomacho Flaviano." *Annali dell'Istituto di Corrispondenza Archeologica* n.s. 6: 283–356.
Degrassi, A. 1952. *I fasti consolari dell'Impero dal 30 avanti Cristo al 613 dopo Cristo.* Sussidi eruditi, 3. Rome.
Delbrück, R. 1929. *Die Consulardiptychen und verwändte Denkmäler.* Berlin and Leipzig.
della Corte, F. 1980. "Conflitto di culto in Sicilia." *Ciceroniana* n.s. 4: 205–209.
Dellow, E. L. 1979. *A First Course in Proof Correcting.* London.
Demandt, A. 1989. *Die Spätantike. Römische Geschichte von Diocletian bis Justinian 284–565 n. Chr.* Handbuch der Altertumswissenschaft, 3.6. Munich.
Derrida, J. 1982a. *Margins of Philosophy.* Chicago.
———. 1982b. "Signature Event Context." In *Margins of Philosophy,* pp. 307–330. Chicago.
———. 1988. *Limited Inc.* Evanston, Ill.
Devreesse, R. 1954. *Introduction a l'étude des manuscrits grecs.* Paris.
Dolbeau, F. 1981. "Damase, le *Carmen contra paganos* et Hériger de Lobbes." *REAug* 27: 38–43.
Doty, W. G. 1986. *Mythography: The Study of Myths and Rituals.* Tuscaloosa, Ala.
Douglas, M. 1966. *Purity and Danger: An Analysis of the Concepts of Pollution and Taboo.* New York.

Dulabahn, E. 1986. "The *Laterculus* of Polemius Silvius." Thesis, Bryn Mawr.
Dunn, F. M., and T. Cole, eds. 1992. *Beginnings in Classical Literature*. YCS 29. Cambridge.
Eagleton, T. 1983. *Literary Theory: An Introduction*. Minneapolis.
Eck, W. 1971. "Das Eindringen des Christentums in den Senatorenstand bis zu Konstantin d. Gr." *Chiron* 1: 381–406.
———. 1993. *Prosopographie und Sozialgeschichte: Studien zur Methodik und Erkenntnismöglichkeit der kaiserzeitlichen Prosopographie: Kolloquium, Köln, 24.–26. November 1991*. Vienna.
———. 1995. "Plebs und princeps nach dem Tod des Germanicus." In *Leaders and Masses in the Roman world: Studies in Honor of Zwi Yavetz*, ed. I. Malkin and Z. W. Rubinsohn, pp. 1–10. Leiden.
Eck, W., A. Caballos, and Fdo. Fernández. 1996. *Das s.c. de Cn. Pisone patre*. Vestigia. Munich.
Eco, U. 1979. *A Theory of Semiotics*. Advances in Semiotics. Bloomington, Ind.
Eisenstein, E. 1983. *The Printing Revolution in Early Modern Europe*. Cambridge.
Ellis, J. R. 1868. "On a Recently Discovered Latin Poem of the Fourth Century." *Journal of Philology* 1: 66–80.
Enright, D. J., ed. 1985. *Fair of Speech: The Uses of Euphemism*. Oxford.
Erim, K. T., C. Roueché, and J. M. Reynolds. 1989. *Aphrodisias in Late Antiquity: The Late Roman and Byzantine Inscriptions Including Texts from the Excavations at Aphrodisias Conducted by Kenan T. Erim*. JRS Monographs, no. 5. London.
Ernout, A. 1949. "Condicio et conditio." *Revue Philologique* 23: 107–119.
Ernout, A., and Meillet, A. 1967. *Dictionnaire étymologique de la lange latine: histoire des mots*. Paris.
Errington, R. M. 1992. "The Praetorian Prefectures of Virius Nicomachus Flavianus." *Historia* 41: 439–461.
Esbenshade, R. S. 1995. "Remembering to Forget: Memory, History, National Identity in Postwar East-Central Europe." *Representations* 49: 72–96.
Faye, J. P. 1972. *Langages totalitaires*. Paris.
Febvre, L., and H. J. Martin. 1976. *The Coming of the Book: The Impact of Printing, 1450–1800*. London.
Feliciano, F. 1960. *Alphabetum Romanum*. ed. G. Mardersteig. Verona.
Ferretti, M. 1993. *La memoria mutilata: la Russia ricorda*. Milan.
Festugière, A. J. 1967. *Hermétisme et mystique païenne*. Paris.
Festy, M. 1997. "Le début et la fin des Annales de Nicomaque Flavien." *Historia* 46: 465–478.
Fischer, E. 1982. "Greek Translations of Latin Literature in the Fourth Century A.D." *YCS* 27: 173–215.
Flower, H. I. 1996. *Ancestor Masks and Aristocratic Power in Roman Culture*. Oxford.
Fowden, G. 1991. "Constantine's Porphyry Column: The Earliest Literary Allusion." *JRS* 81: 119–131.
Fowler, H. W. 1927. *A Dictionary of Modern English Usage*. Oxford.

Freeman, E. A. 1898. *The History of Sicily from Earliest Times.* Oxford.
Frend, W. H. C. 1985. *The Donatist Church: A Movement of Protest in Roman North Africa.* Oxford.
Freud, S. 1939. *Moses and Monotheism.* New York.
Friedländer, S., ed. 1992. *Probing the Limits of Representation: Nazism and the "Final Solution."* Cambridge, Mass.
Frier, B. 1979. "*Libri Annales Pontificum Maximorum:* The Origins of the Annalistic Tradition." *MAAR* 27: 297–321.
Fritz, K. von. 1957. "Tacitus, Agricola, Domitian, and the Problem of the Principate." *CP* 52: 73–97.
Furet, F., and J. Ozouf. 1982. *Reading and Writing: Literacy in France from Calvin to Jules Ferry.* Cambridge Studies in Oral and Literate Culture, 5. Cambridge.
Furneaux, H. ed. 1896–1897. Introduction and commentary. In *Annalium ab Excessu Divi Augusti Libri: The Annals of Tactitus.* Oxford.
Galsterer, H. 1990. "A Man, a Book and a Method: Sir Ronald Syme's Roman Revolution after Fifty Years." In *Between Republic and Empire: Interpretations of Augustus and His Principate,* ed. K. Raaflaub and M. Toher, pp. 1–20. Berkeley and Los Angeles.
Gambrell, J. 1991. "Moscow's Monuments Come Tumbling Down." *Art in America* 79: 37.
Gamson, J. 1989. "Silence, Death and the Invisible Enemy: AIDS Activism and Social Movement 'Newness.'" *Social Problems* 36: 351–367.
Gaskell, P. 1972. *A New Introduction to Bibliography.* Oxford.
Gay, P. 1985. *Freud for Historians.* Oxford.
Genette, G. 1980. *Narrative Discourse: An Essay in Method.* Ithaca, N.Y.
Gentili, B., and G. Cerri. 1988. *History and Biography in Ancient Thought.* Amsterdam.
Gibbon, E. 1897–1900. *The History of the Decline and Fall of the Roman Empire; Edited in Seven Volumes with Introduction, Notes, Appendices, and Index by J. B. Bury.* London.
Glover, H. 1984. "Survival Guilt and the Vietnam Veteran." *Journal of Nervous & Mental Disease* 172: 393–397.
Gordon, A. E. 1948. *Supralineate Abbreviations in Latin Inscriptions.* University of California Publications in Classical Archaeology, 2.3. Berkeley.
———. 1983. *Illustrated Introduction to Latin Epigraphy.* Berkeley and Los Angeles.
Gordon, A. E., and J. S. Gordon. 1958–1965. *Album of Dated Latin Inscriptions.* Berkeley.
Gordon, J. S., and A. E. Gordon. 1957. *Contributions to the Paleography of Latin Inscriptions.* University of California Publications in Classical Archaeology, 3.3. Berkeley and Los Angeles.
Grafton, A., A. Shelford, and N. Siraisi. 1992. *New Worlds, Ancient Texts: The Power of Tradition and the Shock of Discovery.* Cambridge, Mass.
Green, R. P. H. 1995. "Proba's *Centro:* Its Date, Purpose and Reception." *CQ* 45: 551–563.
Greimas, A. J. 1987. *On Meaning: Selected Writing in Semiotic Theory.* Minneapolis.
Grünewald, T. 1992. "Der letzte Kampf des Heidentums in Rom? Zur postumen Rehabilitation des Virius Nicomachus Flavianus." *Historia* 41: 462–487.
Guey, J. 1950. "Flavien Nicomaque et Leptis Magna." *REA* 52: 77–89.
Hackl, K. 1975. *Praeiudicium in klassischen römischen Recht.* Munich.

Hadot, P. 1971. *Marius Victorinus: recherches sur sa vie et ses œuvres*. Paris.
Haehling, R. von. 1978. *Die Religionszugehörigkeit der hohen Amtsträger des römischen Reiches seit Constantins I. Alleinherrschaft bus zum Ende der Theodosianischen Dynastie*. Antiquas, Reihe 3, Bd. 23. Bonn.
Halbwachs, M. 1980. *The Collective Memory*. New York.
Hall, A. R., and L. Tilling, eds. 1975. *The Correspondence of Isaac Newton*. Cambridge.
Harl, K. W. 1996. *Coinage in the Roman Economy, 300 B.C. to A.D. 700*. Baltimore.
Harries, J. 1988. "The Roman Imperial Quaestor from Constantine to Theodosius II." *JRS* 78: 148–172.
———. 1994. *Sidonius Apollinaris and the Fall of Rome*. Oxford.
Harris, W. V. 1989. *Ancient Literacy*. Cambridge, Mass.
Hartke, W. 1938. "Zwei chronologische Fragen um Nicomachus Flavianus." *Klio* 31: 430–436.
———. 1940. *Geschichte und Politik im spätantiken Rom. Untersuchungen über die Scriptores Historiae Augustae*. Klio Beiheft 45. Leipzig.
Hartog, F. 1988. *The Mirror of Herodotus: The Representation of the Other in the Writing of History*. New Historicism 5. Berkeley.
Hauler, E., and M. van den Hout, eds. 1988. Introduction. In *M. Cornelii Frontonis epistulae schedis tam editis quam ineditis*. Bibliotheca scriptorum Graecorum et Romanorum Teubneriana. Leipzig.
Havel, V. 1991. *Open Letters: Selected Writings 1965–1990*. New York.
Head, B. 1967. *Historia Numorum: A Manual of Greek Numismatics*. Chicago.
Hedrick, C. W. 1993. "The Meaning of Material Culture: Herodotus, Thucydides and Their Sources." In *Nomodeiktes: Greek Studies in Honor of Martin Ostwald*, ed. R. M. Rosen and J. Farrell, pp. 17–38. Ann Arbor.
———. 1994a. "Writing, Reading and Democracy." In *Ritual, Finance, Politics*, ed. R. Osborne and S. Hornblower, pp. 157–174. Oxford.
———. 1994b. "The Zero Degree of Society: Aristotle and the Athenian Citizen." In *Athenian Political Thought and the Reconstruction of American Democracy*, ed. J. P. Euben, J. R. Wallach, and J. Ober, pp. 289–318. Ithaca, N.Y.
———. 1995. "Thucydides and the Beginnings of Archaeology." In *Methods in the Mediterranean: Historical and Archaeological Views on Texts and Archaeology*, ed. D. Small, pp. 45–88. Leiden.
Hinard, F. 1985. *Les proscriptions de la Rome républicaine*. Collection de l'École française de Rome 83. Rome.
Hirsch, E. D. 1967. *Validity in Interpretation*. New Haven.
Hoffman, G. 1995. "Writing without Leisure: Proofreading as Work in the Renaissance." *Journal of Medieval and Renaissance Studies* 25: 17–31.
Holloway, R. R. 1991. *The Archaeology of Ancient Sicily*. London.
Holum, K. G. 1982. *Theodosian Empresses: Women and Imperial Dominion in Late Antiquity*. The Transformation of the Classical Heritage 3. Berkeley.
Honoré, T. 1987. "Scriptor Historiae Augustae." *JRS* 77: 156–176.
———. 1989a. "Some Writings of the Pagan Champion Virius Nicomachus Flavianus." In *Virius Nicomachus Flavianus*, ed. T. Honoré, pp. 9–17. Xenia. Constance.

———, ed. 1989b. *Virius Nicomachus Flavianus*. Xenia. Constance.

———. 1993. "Quaestors in the Reign of Theodosius." In *The Theodosian Code: Studies in the Imperial Law of Late Antiquity*, ed. J. Harries and I. Wood, pp. 68–94. London.

———. 1994. *Emperors and Lawyers*. Oxford.

Housman, A. E., ed. 1926. Introduction. In M. Annaei Lucani, *Belli civilis libri decem; editorum in usum edidit A. E. Housman*. Oxford.

Hubaux, J. 1958. *Rome et Veies, recherches sur la chronologie legendaire du Moyen Âge romain*. Bibliothèque de la Faculté de philosophie et lettres d l'Université de Liège, fasc. 145. Paris.

Humphrey, J., ed. 1991. *Literacy in the Roman World*. JRA suppl. 3. Ann Arbor.

Hunt, L. 1989. *The New Cultural History*. Berkeley and Los Angeles.

Jacobson, R. 1987a. "Is the Film in Decline?" In *Language in Literature*, pp. 458–465. Cambridge, Mass.

———. 1987b. *Language in Literature*. Cambridge, Mass.

———. 1987c. "Linguistics and Poetics." In *Language in Literature*, pp. 62–94. Cambridge, Mass.

Jahn, O. 1851. "Über die Subscriptionen in den Handschriften römischer Classiker." *Berichte über die Verhandlungen der Sächsischen Gesellschaft der Wissenschaften, philologisch-historische Klasse* 3: 327–372.

Jardine, L., and A. Grafton 1990. "Studied for Action: How Gabriel Harvey Read His Livy." *Past and Present* 129: 30–78.

Jaworski, A. 1993. *The Power of Silence: Social and Pragmatic Perspectives*. Language and Language Behaviours. Newbury Park, Calif.

Jed, S. 1989. *Chaste Thinking: The Rape of Lucretia and the Birth of Humanism*. Bloomington, Ind.

Jenkins, G. K. 1975. "The Coinages of Enna, Galeria, Piakos, Imacharia, Kephaloidion and Longane." *Annali dell'Instituto Italiano di Numismatica* 20 (suppl.): 77–103.

Jones, A. H. M. 1964. *The Later Roman Empire, 282–602: A Social, Economic and Administrative Survey*. Oxford.

Jordan, H. 1871. *Topographie der Stadt Rom im Altertum*. Berlin.

Jucker, H. 1981. "Iulisch-claudische Kaiser- und Prinzenporträts als 'Palimpseste.'" *JDAI* 96: 236–316.

Kajanto, I. 1966 [i.e. 1967]. *Supernomina: A Study in Latin Epigraphy*. Commentationes Humanarum Litterarum, vol. 40, no. 1. Helsinki.

Kaster, R. 1980. "Macrobius and Servius: Verecundia and the Grammarian's Function." *HSCP* 84: 219–262.

———. 1988. *Guardians of Language: Grammarian and Society in Late Antiquity*. Berkeley and Los Angeles.

———, ed. 1995. Commentary. In C. Suetonius Tranquillus, *De grammaticis et rhetoribus*. Oxford.

Kellner, D. 1989. *Jean Baudrillard: From Marxism to Postmodernism and Beyond*. Stanford.

Kermode, F. 1967. *The Sense of an Ending: Studies in the Theory of Fiction*. The Mary Flexner Lectures. New York.

Kierdorf, W. 1978. "Die Proömien zu Tacitus' Hauptwerken: Spiegel einer Entwicklung?" *Gymnasium* 85: 20–36.

———. 1980. *Laudatio funebris: Interpretationen und Untersuchungen der römischen Leichenrede.* Beiträge zur klassischen Philologie, Heft 106. Meisenheim am Glan.

King, D. 1997. *The Commissar Vanishes: The Falsification of Photographs and Art in Stalin's Russia.* New York.

Kinney, D. 1994. "A Late Antique Ivory Plaque and Modern Response." *AJA* 98: 457–480.

Kleiner, D. E. E. 1992. *Roman Sculpture.* Yale Publications in the History of Art. New Haven.

Koestermann, E., ed. 1963–1968. Introduction and commentary. In Cornelius Tacitus, *Annalen. Erlautert und mit einer Einleitung versehen.* Wissenschaftliche Kommentare zu griechischen und lateinischen Schriftstellern. Heidelberg.

Koselleck, R. 1985a. *Futures Past: On the Semantics of Historical Time.* Cambridge, Mass.

———. 1985b. "*Historia Magistra Vitae:* The Dissolution of the Topos into the Perspective of a Modernized Historical Process." In *Futures Past: On the Semantics of Historical Time,* pp. 21–38. Cambridge, Mass.

Krabbe, J. 1989. *The Metamorphoses of Apuleius.* American University Studies ser. xvii. Classical Languages and Literature, vol. 9. New York.

Kristeller, P. O. 1955. *Renaissance Thought: The Classic, Scholastic and Humanist Strains.* New York.

Kundera, M. 1980. *The Book of Laughter and Forgetting.* New York.

Lacan, J. 1977. *Écrits.* New York.

Lamirande, E. 1981. "La datation de la 'Vita Ambrosii.'" *REAug* 27: 44–55.

Lanciani, R. 1979. *The Ruins and Excavations of Ancient Rome.* New York.

Lane Fox, R. 1987. *Pagans and Christians.* New York.

Lang, B. 1992. "The Representation of Limits." In *Probing the Limits of Representation: Nazism and the "Final Solution."* ed. S. Friedländer, pp. 300–317. Cambridge, Mass.

Larina, A. 1993. *This I Cannot Forget: The Memoirs of Nikolai Bukharin's Widow.* New York.

Latte, K. 1960. *Römische Religionsgeschichte.* Handbuch der Altertumswissenschaft 5.4. Munich.

Lauffer, S., ed. 1971. *Diokletians Preisedikt.* Texte und Kommentare: eine altertumswissenschaftliche Reihe, Bd. 5. Berlin.

Le Goff, J. 1992. *History and Memory.* European Perspectives. New York.

Lepelley, C. 1979. *Les cités de l'Afrique romaine au bas-empire.* Paris.

Levene, D. S. 1993. *Religion in Livy.* Mnemosyne, bibliotheca classica Batava, Supplementum. Leiden.

Levi, P. 1988. *The Drowned and the Saved.* New York.

Lévi-Strauss, C. 1966. *The Savage Mind.* Chicago.

Levine, Philip. 1966. "The Continuity and Preservation of the Latin Tradition." In *The Transformation of the Roman World: Gibbon's Problem after Two Centuries,* ed. Lynn White Jr. Berkeley.

Levick, B. 1976. *Tiberius the Politician*. London.
Levy, H. L. 1971. *Claudian's "In Rufinum."* Cleveland.
Loewenthal, D. 1985. *The Past Is a Foreign Country*. Cambridge.
Lowry, M. 1979. *The World of Aldus Manutius: Business and Scholarship in Renaissance Venice*. Ithaca, N.Y.
Luce, T. J. 1977. *Livy: The Composition of His History*. Princeton.
———. 1989. "Ancient Views on the Cause of Bias in Historical Writing." *CP* 84: 16–31.
———. 1991. "Tacitus on 'History's Highest Function': *praecipuum munus annalium* (*Ann.* 3.65)." In *ANRW* 2.33.4: 2904–2927.
Luetjohann, C., ed. 1887. Introduction and notes. In Gai Solii Apollinaris Sidonii, *Epistulae et carmina*. Berlin.
Lugli, I. 1952. *Fontes ad topographia Veteris Urbis Romae Pertinentes*. Rome.
MacKendrick, P. 1980. *The North African Stones Speak*. Chapel Hill.
MacMullen, R. 1962. "Roman Bureaucratese." *Traditio* 18: 364–378.
———. 1968. "Constantine and the Miraculous." *GRBS* 9: 81–96.
———. 1984. *Christianizing the Roman Empire: (A.D. 100–400)*. New Haven.
Malcus, B. 1967. "Die Prokonsuln von Asie von Diokletian bis Theodosius II." *Opuscula Atheniensia* 7: 91–160.
Mallon, J. 1961. "Paléographie romaine." In *L'Histoire et ses méthodes*. Encyclopédie de la Pléiade 11, ed. C. Samaran, pp. 564–573. Paris.
Manganaro, G. 1960. "La reazione pagan a Roma nel 408–9 d.c. e il poemetto anonino 'Contra Paganos.'" *Giornale italiano di filologia* 13: 210–224.
———. 1961. "Il poemetto anonimo contra paganos: testo tradizione e commento." *Nuovo Didaskaleion* 11: 23–45.
Marcuse, H. 1955. *Eros and Civilization*. Boston.
MARHO, The Radical Historians' Organization, ed. 1976. *Visions of History: Interviews with E. P. Thompson etc.* New York.
Marinone, N. 1977. *I Saturnali di Macrobio Teodosio*. Turin.
Markus, R. A. 1990. *The End of Ancient Christianity*. Cambridge.
Marrou, H.-I. 1932. "La vie intellectuelle au forum de Trajan et au forum d'Auguste." *MEFR* 49: 93–110.
———. 1958. *Saint Augustin et la fin de la culture antique*. Paris.
———. 1976. *Patristique et humanisme: mélanges*. Patristica Sorbonensia. Paris.
Martin, H. J. 1994. *The History and Power of Writing*. Chicago.
Martin, R. 1972. "Agora et Forum." *MEFR* 84: 903–933.
Matranga, P. 1849. "Archelogia." In *Giornale di Roma* no. 63: 269–270.
Matthews, J. F. 1967. "Continuity in a Roman family: the Rufii Festi of Volsinii." *Historia* 16: 484–509.
———. 1970. "The Historical Setting of the 'Carmen contra paganos' (cod. par. lat. 8084)." *Historia* 20: 464–479.
———. 1973. "Symmachus and the Oriental Cults." *JRS* 63: 187–191.
———. 1975. *Western Aristocracies and the Imperial Court, A.D. 363–425*. Oxford.

———. 1981. "Anicius Manlius Severinus Boethius." In *Boethius: His Life, Thought and Influence,* ed. M. Gibson, pp. 15–43. Oxford.
———. 1985. *Political Life and Culture in Late Roman Society.* Variorum Collected Studies. London.
———. 1989a. "Nicomachus Flavianus' Quaestorship: The Historical Evidence." In *Virius Nicomachus Flavianus,* ed. T. Honoré, pp. 18–25. Xenia. Constance.
———. 1989b. *The Roman Empire of Ammianus.* London.
———. 1992. "The Poetess Proba and Fourth Century Rome: Questions of Interpretation." In *Institutions, société et vie politique dans l'empire romain au IVe siecle ap. J.-C (284–423): actes de la table ronde autour de l'uvre d'André Chastagnol, Paris, 20–21 janvier 1989.* Collection de l'École française de Rome 159, ed. M. Christol et al., pp. 275–302. Rome.
———. 1997. "'Codex Theodosianus' 9.40.13 and Nicomachus Flavianus." *Historia* 46: 196–213.
Mayor, A. 1992. "Ambiguous Guardians: The 'Omen of the Wolves' (AD 402) and the 'Choking Doberman' (1980's)." *Journal of Folklore Research* 29: 253–268.
Mazzarino, S. 1974–1980. *Antico, tardoantico ed era constantiniana.* Storia e civiltà 13–14. Bari.
McGann, J. J. 1983. *A Critique of Modern Textual Criticism.* Chicago.
———. 1991. *The Textual Condition.* Princeton Studies in Culture/Power/History. Princeton.
McGuire, D. T. 1997. *Acts of Silence: Civil War, Tyranny and Suicide in the Flavian Epics.* Altertumswissenschaftliche Texte und Studien. Hildesheim.
McLynn, N. B. 1994. *Ambrose of Milan: Church and Court in a Christian Capital.* The Transformation of the Classical Heritage 22. Berkeley.
Meeks, W. A. 1983. *The First Urban Christians.* New Haven.
Meiggs, R. 1960. *Roman Ostia.* Oxford.
Mellor, R. 1993. *Tacitus.* New York.
———. 1995. *Tacitus: The Classical Heritage.* Garland Reference Library of the Humanities, Classical Heritage. New York.
Mendell, C. W. 1957. *Tacitus: The Man and His Work.* New Haven.
Merkelbach, R. 1970. "Epigramm aus Aphrodisias." *ZPE* 6: 132.
Michaud-Quantin, P. 1967. "Condicio-conditio, notes de lexicographie mediévale." In *Mélanges offerts à M. D. Chenu,* pp. 399–417. Bibliothèque Thomiste. Paris.
Michels, A. 1967. *The Calendar of the Roman Republic.* Princeton.
Miles, G. B. 1995. *Livy: Reconstructing Early Rome.* Ithaca, N.Y.
Millar, F. 1977. *The Emperor in the Roman World: 31 B.C.–A.D. 337.* London.
———. 1992. "The Jews of the Graeco-Roman Diaspora between Paganism and Christianity, A.D. 312–438." In *The Jews among Pagans and Christians in the Roman Empire,* ed. J. Lieu, J. North, and T. Rajak, pp. 97–123. London.
Momigliano, A., ed. 1963a. *The Conflict between Paganism and Christianity in the Fourth Century: Essays.* Oxford Warburg Studies. Oxford.
——— 1963b. "Introduction: Christianity and the Decline of the Roman Empire." In

The Conflict between Paganism and Christianity in the Fourth Century: Essays, ed. A. Momigliano, pp. 1–16. Oxford Warburg Studies. Oxford.

———. 1963c. "Pagan and Christian Historiography in the Fourth Century A.D." In *The Conflict between Paganism and Christianity in the Fourth Century: Essays,* ed. A. Momigliano, pp. 79–99. Oxford Warburg Studies. Oxford.

———. 1971. *The Development of Greek Biography.* Cambridge, Mass.

Mommsen, T. 1864. *Römische Forschungen.* Berlin.

———. 1870. "Carmen codicis Parisini 8084." *Hermes* 4: 350–363.

———. 1887–1888. *Römisches Staatsrecht.* Handbuch der römischen Alterthümer. Leipzig.

———, ed. 1892. *Chronica Minora saec. IV. V. VI. VII.* MGHAA 9, 11, 13. Berlin.

———. 1899. *Römisches Strafrecht.* Systematisches Handbuch der deutschen Rechtswissenschaft 1.4. Leipzig.

Mommsen, T., and P. Meyer, eds. 1905 [repr. 1962]. Introduction and commentary. In *Theodosiani libri xvi cum constitutionibus Sirmondianis et leges novellae ad Theodosianum pertinentes.* Berlin.

———. 1905–1913. *Gesammelte Schriften.* Berlin.

Murray, P. 1981. "Poetic Inspiration in Early Greece." *JHS* 101: 87–101.

Mustakallio, K. 1994. *Death and Disgrace: Capital Penalties with Post Mortem Sanctions in Early Roman Historiography.* Annales Academiae Scientiarum Fennicae. Dissertationes Humanarum Litterarum 72. Helsinki.

Nash, E. 1961–1962. *Pictorial Dictionary of Ancient Rome.* New York.

Nixon, C. E. V. 1991. "Aurelius, Victor and Julian." *CP* 86: 113–125.

Nora, P., ed. 1984–1986. *Les lieux de memoire.* Bibliotheque des histoires. Paris.

Novak, D. M. 1979. "Constantine and the Senate: An Early Phase of the Christianization of the Roman Aristocracy." *Ancient Society* 10: 271–310.

O'Donnell, J. J. 1977. "Paganus." *Classical Folia* 31: 163–169.

———. 1978. "The Career of Virius Nicomachus Flavianus." *Phoenix* 32: 129–143.

———. 1979a. *Cassiodorus.* Berkeley.

———. 1979b. "The Demise of Paganism." *Traditio* 35: 45–88.

O'Flynn, J. M. 1983. *Generalissimos of the Western Roman Empire.* Edmonton, Alta.

Oakley, S. P. 1997. *A Commentary on Livy, Books VI–X.* Oxford.

Ogilvie, R. M. 1975. *Livy 1–5.* Oxford.

———. 1980. *Roman Literature and Society.* New York.

———. 1991. "An Interim Report on Tacitus' 'Agricola.'" In *ANRW* 2.33.3: 1714–1740. Berlin.

Ogilvie, R. M., and I. Richmond. 1967. *Cornelii Taciti de Vita Agricolae.* Oxford.

Oost, S. 1968. *Galla Placidia Augusta: A Biographical Essay.* Chicago.

Packer, J. E. 1996. *The Forum of Trajan in Rome: A Study of the Monuments.* California Studies in the History of Art. Berkeley and Los Angeles.

Panciera, S. 1982. "Iscrizioni senatorie de Roma e dintorni 38." In *Epigrafia e ordine senatorio,* pp. 658–660. Atti del Colloquio Internazionale AIEGL. Rome.

———. 1992. "Un prefetto del pretorio di Massenzio, Manilius Rusticianus." In *Institutions, société et vie politique dans l'empire romain au IVe siecle ap. J.-C (284–423): actes de la table ronde autour de l'uvre d'André Chastagnol, Paris, 20−21 janvier 1989*. Collection de l'Ecole française de Rome 159, ed. M. Christol et al., pp. 249−263. Rome.

Panofsky, Erwin. 1963 [1936]. "Et in Arcadia Ego." In *Philosophy and History: Essays Presented to Ernst Cassirer*, ed. R. Klibansky and H. J. Paton, pp. 222−254. New York.

Paolis, P. de. 1986−1987. "Macrobio 1934−1984." *Lustrum* 28−29: 107−254.

Paribeni, R. 1933. "Iscrizioni dei Fori Imperiali." *NdSc* ser. 6, 9: 431−523.

Paschoud, F., ed. 1971−1989. Introduction and notes. In *Histoire nouvelle par Zosime*. Collection des universités de France. Paris.

———. 1986. *Colloque genevois sur Symmaque : à l'occasion du mille six centième anniversaire du conflit de l'autel de la Victoire*. Paris.

Pecere, O. 1986. "La tradizione dei testi latini tra IV e V secolo attraverso i libri sottoscritti." In *Società romana e impero tardoantico*. Istituto Gramsci. Seminario di antichistica, ed. A. Giardini, pp. 19−81, 210−246. Rome and Bari.

———. 1989. "I mecanismi della tradizione testuale." In *Lo spazio letterario di Roma antica* 3, ed. G. Cavallo, P. Fedeli, and A. Giardina, pp. 297−386. Rome.

Peradotto, J. 1983. "Texts and Unrefracted Facts: Philology, Hermeneutics and Semiotics." *Arethusa* 16: 15−33.

———. 1990. *Man in the Middle Voice: Name and Narration in the Odyssey*. Martin Classical Lectures, new ser., vol. 1. Princeton.

Petrey, S. 1990. *Speech Acts and Literary Theory*. New York.

Petrucci, A. 1970. "Scrittura e libro nell'Italia altomedievale. Il sesto secolo." In *A Giuseppe Ermini*. p. 174ff. Studi medievali, ser. 3, 10. Spoleto.

———. 1986. "Dal libro unitario al libro miscellaneo." In *Società romana e impero tardoantico*. Istituto Gramsci. Seminario di antichistica, ed. A. Giardini, pp. 173−187. Rome and Bari.

———. 1993. *Public Lettering: Script, Power and Culture*. Chicago.

Pflaum, H. G. 1960−1961. *Les carrières procuratoriennes equestres sous le haut-empire romain*. Bibliothèque archgéologique et historique, t. 57. Paris.

———. 1982. *Les carrières procuratoriennes equestres sous le haut-empire romain. Supplément*. Bibliothèque archéologique et historique, t. 112. Paris.

Platner, S. B. 1929. *A Topographical Dictionary of Ancient Rome*. London.

Polara, G. 1967. "Le iscrizioni sul cippo tombale di Vezzio Agorio Pretestato." *Vichiana* 4: 264−289.

Pollini, J. 1984. "*Damnatio Memoriae* in Stone: Two Portraits of Nero Recut to Vespasian in American Museums." *AJA* 88: 547−555.

Poole, R. 1963. *Catalogue of Greek Coins: Sicily*. Bologna.

Porot, M., A. Couadau, et al. 1985. "Le syndrome de culpabilité du survivant." *Annales Medico-Psychologiques* 143: 256−262.

Pryce-Jones, D. 1969. *The Hungarian Revolution*. Twentieth Century Histories. London.

Pullum, G. K. 191. *The Great Eskimo Vocabulary Hoax, and Other Irreverent Essays on the Study of Language*. Chicago.

Putnam, G. H. 1962 [1898]. *Books and Their Makers during the Middle Ages: A Study of the Conditions of the Production and Distribution of Literature from the Fall of the Roman Empire to the Close of the Seventeenth Century.* New York.
Raaflaub, K., and M. Toher, eds. 1990. *Between Republic and Empire: Interpretations of Augustus and His Principate.* Berkeley and Los Angeles.
Rabinow, P., ed. 1984. *The Foucault Reader.* New York.
Raepsaet-Charlier, M.-T. 1981. "Cornelia Cet(h)egilla." *Ant. Class.* 50: 685–697.
Ratti, S. 1997. "Jerome et Nicomaque Flavien: sur les sources de la Chronique pour les années 357–364." *Historia* 46: 479–508.
Rawson, E. 1991. *Roman Culture and Society.* Oxford.
Reynolds, L. D., ed. 1983. *Texts and Transmission: A Survey of the Latin Classics.* Oxford.
Reynolds, L. D., and N. G. Wilson. 1991. *Scribes and Scholars: A Guide to the Transmission of Greek and Latin Literature.* Oxford.
Rice, E. F. Jr. 1985. *Saint Jerome in the Renaissance.* The Johns Hopkins symposia in Comparative History, 13. Baltimore.
Richardson, L. Jr. 1992. *A New Topographical Dictionary of Ancient Rome.* Baltimore.
Ricoeur, P. 1967. *The Symbolism of Evil.* Beacon Paperback. Boston.
———. 1970. *Freud and Philosophy: An Essay on Interpretation.* New Haven.
———. 1984–1988. *Time and Narrative.* Chicago.
Rieff, P. 1959. *Freud: The Mind of the Moralist.* New York.
Robert, L. 1948. "II. Épigrammes relatives à des gouverneurs." In *Hellenica: recueil d' épigraphie de numismatique et d'antiquités grecques,* pp. 35–114. Paris.
Roberts, C. H., and T. C. Skeat. 1983. *The Birth of the Codex.* Oxford.
Robinson, D. N. 1915. "An Analysis of the Pagan Revival of the Late Fourth Century, with Especial Reference to Symmachus." *TAPA* 46: 87–101.
Rogin, M. 1994. "Democracy and Burnt Cork: The End of Blackface, the Beginning of Civil Rights." *Representations* 46: 1–34.
Rollin, J. P. 1979. *Untersuchungen zu Rechtsfragen römischer Bildnissen.* Habelts Dissertationsdrucke. Reihe klass. Archäologie H.
Rose, M. 1993. *Authors and Owners: The Invention of Copyright.* Cambridge, Mass.
Rosenstone, R. A., ed. 1995a. *Film and the Construction of a New Past.* Princeton Studies in Culture/Power/History. Princeton.
———. 1995b. *Visions of the Past: The Challenge of Film to Our Idea of History.* Cambridge, Mass.
Rudich, V. 1993. *Political Dissidence under Nero: The Price of Dissimulation.* New York.
———. 1997. *Dissidence and Literature under Nero: The Price of Rhetoricization.* New York.
Said, E. 1975. *Beginnings: Intention and Method.* New York.
Salomies, O. 1987. *Die römischen Vornamen: Studien zur römischen Namengebung.* Commentationes Humanarum Litterarum 82. Helsinki.
Salzman, M. R. 1989. "Aristocratic Women: Conductors of Christianity in the Fourth Century." *Helios* 16: 207–220.
———. 1990. *On Roman Time: The Codex Calendar of 354 and the Rhythms of Urban Life in Late Antiquity.* The Transformation of the Classical Heritage. Berkeley and Los Angeles.

Saussure, F. de. 1959. *Course in General Linguistics*. New York.
Scarry, E. 1985. *The Body in Pain: The Making and Unmaking of the World*. New York.
———. 1994. *Resisting Representation*. New York.
Scharf, R. 1991. "Die Familie des Fl. Eutolmius Tatianus." *ZPE* 85: 223–231.
Schlumberger, J. 1985. "Die verlorenen Annalen des Nicomachus Flavianus: ein Werk über Geschichte des römischen Republik oder Kaiserzeit?" In *Bonner Historia-Augusta-Colloquium 1982/1983*, ed. J. Straub, pp. 305–329. Antiquitas 4. Bonn.
Schmidt, P. L. 1968. *Iulius Obsequens und das Problem der Livius-Epitome*. Abh. Akad. Mainz. Geistes-u. sozialwiss. Kl. Wiesbaden.
Schröder, W. 1971. *M. Porcius Cato, das erste Buch der Origines*. Beiträge zur klass. Philol. 41. Meisenheim.
Scott, J. W. 1991. "The Evidence of Experience." *Critical Inquiry* 17: 773–797.
Scullard, H. H. 1981. *Festivals and Ceremonies of the Roman Republic*. Aspects of Greek and Roman Life. London.
Seeck, O., ed. 1883. Introduction. In *Q. Aurelii Symmachi quae supersunt*. MGHAA 6.1. Berlin.
———. 1919. *Regesten der Kaiser und Päpste für die Jahre 311 bis 476 n. Chr. Vorarbeit einer Prosopographie der christlichen Kaiserzeit*. Stuttgart.
Seeck, O., and G. Vieth. 1913. "Die Schlacht am Frigidus." *Klio* 13: 451–467.
Seidel, G. J. 1964. *Martin Heidegger and the Pre-Socratics: An Introduction to His Thought*. Lincoln, Nebr.
Shanzer, D. 1986. "The Anonymous *Carmen contra paganos* and the Date and Identity of the Centonist Proba." *REAug* 32: 232–248.
———. 1994. "The Date and Identity of the Centonist Proba." *Recherches Augustiniennes* 27: 75–96.
Shelton, K. J. 1981. *The Esquiline Treasure*. London.
———. 1985. "The Esquiline Treasure: The Nature of the Evidence." *AJA* 89: 147–155.
Silberstein, L. J., and R. L. Cohn, eds. 1994. *The Other in Jewish Thought and History: Constructions of Jewish Culture and Identity*. New Perspectives on Jewish Studies. New York.
Simon, E. 1992. "The Diptych of the Symmachi and Nicomachi: An Interpretation." *Greece and Rome* 29: 56–65.
Simpson, P. 1935. *Proof-reading in the Sixteenth, Seventeenth and Eighteenth Centuries*. London.
Smith, K. 1996. *Remembering Stalin's Victims: Popular Memory and the End of the USSR*. Ithaca, N.Y.
Spinazzola, V. 1893. "Napoli: nuove scoperte di antichità." *NdSc*: 520–525.
Stainton, E. M. 1991. *The Fine Art of Copyediting*. New York.
Stangl, T. 1882. "Boethiana." Dissertation, Munich.
Steinby, E. M., ed. 1993–. *Lexicon Topographicum Urbis Romae*. Rome.
Steiner, G. 1992. *Heidegger*. Fontana Modern Masters. London.
Stewart, S. 1993. *On Longing: Narratives of the Miniature, the Gigantic, the Souvenir, the Collection*. Durham.

Strocchio, R. 1993. *I significati del silenzio nell'opera di Tacito*. Memorie dell'Accademia delle Scienze di Torino, Classe di scienze morali, storiche e filologiche, ser. V. 16.1–4. Turin.

Suerbaum, W. 1971. "Der Historiker und die Freiheit des Wortes. Die Rede des Cremutius Cordus bei Tacitus, Ann. 4, 34–35." In *Politik und literarische Kunst in Werke des Tacitus,* ed. G. Radke, pp. 61–99. Der altsprachliche Unterricht, Beiheft 1. Stuttgart.

Susini, G. C. 1973. *The Roman Stonecutter: An Introduction to Latin Epigraphy.* Totowa, N.J.

Syme, R. 1952. *The Roman Revolution.* Oxford.

———. 1958. *Tacitus.* Oxford.

———. 1971. *Emperors and Biography: Studies in the "Historia Augusta."* Oxford.

———. 1980. "The Sons of Piso the Pontifex." *AJP* 101: 333–341.

Szidat, J. 1979. "Die Usurpation des Eugeneius." *Historia* 28: 487–508.

Tanselle, G. T. 1989. *A Rationale of Textual Criticism.* Philadelphia.

Taylor, L. R. 1942. "Caesar's Colleagues in the Pontifical College." *AJP* 63: 385–412.

Terdiman, R. 1993. *Present Past: Modernity and the Memory Crisis.* Ithaca, N.Y.

Testard, M. 1973. "Observations sur la thème de las 'conscientia' dan le *De officiis ministrorum* de saint Ambroise." *REL* 51: 219–261.

Thomas, R. 1989. *Oral Tradition and Written Record in Classical Athens.* Cambridge.

———. 1992. *Literacy and Orality in Ancient Greece.* Cambridge.

Timpanaro, S. 1976. *The Freudian Slip: Psychoanalysis and Textual Criticism.* London.

———. 1981. *La genesi del metodo del Lachman.* Biblioteca di cultura. Sezione letteraria. Padua.

Todorov, T. 1982. *Symbolism and Interpretation.* Ithaca, N.Y.

Toynbee, J. M. C. 1971. *Death and Burial in the Roman World.* London.

Tracy, S. 1975. *The Lettering of an Athenian Mason.* Hesperia, suppl. 15. Princeton.

Traube, L. 1904–1906 [1909]. "Bamberger Fragmente der vierten Dekade des Livius." *Abhandlungen der bayerischen Akademie der Wissenschaften, philosophisch-historische Klasse* 24.

Tumarkin, N. 1983. *Lenin Lives! The Lenin Cult in Soviet Russia.* Cambridge, Mass.

Turcan, R. 1996. *The Cults of the Roman Empire.* The Ancient World. Oxford.

Türk, E. 1963. "Les Saturnales de Macrobe source de Servius Danielis." *REL* 41: 327–349.

Turner, E. G. 1980. *Greek Papyri: An Introduction.* Oxford.

———. 1987. *Greek Manuscripts of the Ancient World.* Bulletin Supplement no. 46. University of London, Institute of Classical Studies. London.

Valesio, P. 1986. *Ascoltare il silenzio: la retorica come teoria.* Bologna.

van den Hout, Michael P. J., ed. 1988. Prolegomena. In M. Cornelii Frontonis, *Epistulae.* Bibliotheca scriptorum Graecorum et Romanorum Teubneriana. Leipzig.

Vera, D. 1983. "La carriera di Virius Nicomachus Flavianus e la prefettura dell'Illirico orientale nel IV secolo d. C." *Athenaeum* 71: 24–64, 390–426.

Veyne, P. 1984. *Writing History: Essay on Epistemology.* Middletown, Conn.

———. 1990. *Bread and Circuses: Historical Sociology and Political Pluralism.* London.

Vidal-Naquet, P. 1987. *Les assasins de la mémoire: "Un Eichmann de papier" et autres essais sur la révisionisme.* Paris.
———. 1992. *Assassins of Memory: Essays on the Denial of the Holocaust.* European Perspectives. New York.
Vittinghoff, F. 1936. *Der Staatsfeind in der römischen Kaiserzeit: Untersuchungen zur "Damnatio Memoriae."* Berlin.
Voit, L. 1936. "Marginalnoten zur 1. Dekade des Livius." *Philologus* 91: 308–322.
Volbach, W. F. 1976. *Elfenbeinarbeiten der Spätantike und des frühen Mittelalters.* Mainz.
Volbach, W. F., and M. Hirmer. 1958. *Frühchristliche Kunst.* Munich.
Voss, W. E. 1982. *Recht und Rhetorik in den Kaisergesetzen der Spätantike: ein Untersuchung zum nachklassischen Kauf- und Übereignungsrecht.* Frankfurt.
Walbank, F. W. 1957–1979. *A Historical Commentary on Polybius.* Oxford.
Walker, B. 1960. *The Annals of Tacitus: A Study in the Writing of History.* Manchester, Eng.
Warmington, B. H. 1956. "The Career of Romanus, Comes Africae." *Byzantinische Zeitschrift* 49: 55–64.
Watson, R., ed. 1994. *Memory, History and Opposition under State Socialism.* Santa Fe, N.M.
Weinrib, E. J. 1967. "The Family Connections of M. Livius Drusus Libo." *HSCP* 72: 247–278.
Weitzmann, K., ed. 1979. *Age of Spirituality: Late Antique and Christian Art.* New York.
White, H. 1973. *Metahistory: The Historical Imagination in Nineteenth Century Europe.* Baltimore.
———. 1978. *Tropics of Discourse: Essays in Cultural Criticism.* Baltimore.
———. 1980. "The Value of Narrativity in the Representation of Reality." *Critical Inquiry* 7: 5–27.
———. 1987. *The Content of Form: Narrative Discourse and Historical Representation.* Baltimore.
Wijkstrøm, B. 1936. "Clarorum Virorum Facta Moresque." In *Apophoreta Gotoburgensia Vilelmo Lundstrøm oblata,* pp. 158–168. Göteborg.
Williams, S., and G. Friell. 1995. *Theodosius: The Empire at Bay.* New Haven.
Wilton-Ely, J. 1972. *Giovanni Battista Piranesi: The Polemical Works.* Farnborough, Eng.
Winkler, J. J. 1985. *Auctor and Actor: A Narratological Reading of Apuleius' "Golden Ass."* Berkeley.
Wissowa, G. 1902. *Religion und Kultus der Römer.* Handbuch der Altertumswissenschaft 5.4. Munich.
Witek, J. 1989. *Comic Books as History: The Narrative Art of Jack Jackson, Art Spiegelman, and Harvey Pekar.* Studies in Popular Culture. Jackson, Miss.
Wollheim, R. 1971. *Sigmund Freud.* Cambridge.
Wood, S. 1992. "Messalina, Wife of Claudius." *JRA* 5: 219–234.
Woodman, A. J. 1995. "*Praecipuum munus annalium:* The Construction, Convention and Context of Tacitus, *Annals* 3.65.1." *Museum Helveticum* 52: 111–126.
Wytzes, J. 1936. *Der Streit um den Altar der Viktoria.* Amsterdam.
———. 1977. *Der letzte Kampf des Heidentums in Rom.* Leiden.
Yates, F. A. 1966. *The Art of Memory.* Chicago.

Young, J. E. 1993. *The Texture of Memory: Holocaust Memorials and Meaning*. New Haven.
Zanker, Paul. 1968. *Forum Augustum. Das Bildprogramm*. Monumenta artis antiqua 2. Tübingen.
———. 1990. *The Power of Images in the Age of Augustus*. Trans. Alan Shapiro. Jerome Lectures ser. 16. Ann Arbor.
Zedler, G. 1885. "De Memoriae Damnatione Quae Dicitur." Thesis, Leipzig.
Zerubavel, Y. 1994. "The Death of Memory and the Memory of Death: Masada and the Holocaust as Historical Metaphors." *Representations* 45: 72–100.
Zetzel, J. E. G. 1973. "Emendavi ad Tironem." *HSCP* 77: 227–245.
———. 1974. "Statilius Maximus and Ciceronian Studies in the Antonine Age." *BICS* 21: 107–123.
———. 1980. "The Subscriptions in the Manuscripts of Livy and Fronto and the Meaning of *Emendatio*." *CP* 75: 38–59.
———. 1981. *Latin Textual Criticism in Antiquity*. Monographs in Classical Studies. Salem, N.H.

GENERAL INDEX

Names from late antiquity are given according to cognomen. Early Roman names are listed by gentilicial. Authors and emperors are listed according to their familiar names.

ab epistulis, 224
absolutus, 257
Abundantius, 94
acta fratrum Arvalium, 275n.42, 276n.57
acta triumphorum, 275n.42
administratio, 260n.14
adnoto, 188
adsero, 11
adsumo, 276n.59
Aelius Sejanus, L.: *damnatio memoriae*, 99, 107–108, 277n.72
Aemilianus, Virius Audentius, 261n.30
Aemilius Lepidus, M., 123, 279n.110
Aëtius, Flavius, 32, 224
Africa, province, 18–19, 23, 176
Agricola. *See* Julius
Agricola. See Tacitus
Alaric, the Visigoth, 56, 60, 110
aliquatenus, 174
altar of Victory, 41–42, 48, 60, 66, 71–72, 266n.11, 277n.79
Ambrose, Bishop of Milan, xiv, 39, 42, 45, 49, 51, 54, 71, 72, 85, 142, 153, 267n.20
Ammianus Marcellinus, 13, 19, 81–82, 144, 198, 204, 230, 281n.29, 292n.59
anathematization. *See damnatio memoriae*
Andromachus, Christian, 58
Andromachus, prefect of Rome, 95
Anicii, 16, 57
annales, 146; *Annales Maximi*, 69–70; *annalium, (libri)*, 256–257. *See also* Flavian the elder, *Annales*
antiquarius, 293n.81
Antonia gens, 104
Antonius, Iullus (son of Triumvir), 102, 104
Antonius, L. (son of Iullus), 104
Antonius, M. (son of Triumvir), 104
Antonius, M., Triumvir, 4, 94, 102, 107, 108, 123, 277n.72
Antonius Primus, M., 127
Aphrodisias, 128–129
Aphrodite, 75, 78
Apollonios of Tyana, 281n.39. *See also* Philostratos
apophatic theology, 120, 134
Appuleius Saturninus, L., 101
Apuleius, author of the *Metamorphoses*, 174, 191, 196, 234
Arbogast, 22, 23, 25, 42, 43, 45, 46, 49, 71, 72, 147, 229
Arcadius, emperor, 23, 26, 44, 94–95, 103, 110, 233
arcana imperii, 122, 160, 282n.63
archetype, 244, 294n.93
Archontius Nilus, Flavius, 16
Argiletum, 230, 236
aristocracy of Rome: christianization of, xv, 51, 54–58, 71, 210; cursus of, 17–18, 182, 261n.42; and imperial court, 41, 42, 48, 49, 54, 56, 92, 110, 224, 266, 269n.59; and learning, xix, 49–50, 57–58, 83, 85–86, 193–194, 203–204, 205, 226, 228, 237; and manuscripts, 70, 171, 179, 183, 192, 203; and paganism, 39, 44, 54, 55, 59, 62, 71, 85, 210, 228, 270–271n.101;

sources for, 81–82, 198; and tradition, xviii, xxi, 54, 57–58, 82, 210, 212, 269n.59
Arulenus Rusticus. *See* Iunius
Asterius, Turcius Rufius Apronianus, 189, 192, 195, 206
atria Traiani, 235
Attis, 63, 64, 75, 76
augury, 64, 69, 83, 86, 146
Augustine, Saint (Aurelius Augustinus), xiv, 19, 39, 49, 57, 59, 70–72, 79, 85, 127, 172, 203, 210, 262n.48, 269n.72, 292n.61
Augustus, emperor, 94, 102, 111, 123, 127, 227, 231, 249, 279n.110
Aulus Gellius. *See* Gellius
Aurelius Cotta, M., 104
Aurelius Victor. *See* Victor
Ausonius, Decimus Magnus, 178, 205, 240
Austoriani, devastate Roman Tripolis, 18, 363
author, xxiii, 73, 138–9, 141, 150, 172, 200–201, 214–246, 283n.2, 293n.66

Basilica Ulpia, 230, 247–248
Bassaeus Rufus, M., 232
beginning, 122, 136–145
Bellona, 63, 64
beneficia, 248–249
Bible, 200, 281n.39
Bobbio, 189, 193
Boethius, Anicius Manlius Severinus, 172, 192, 283n.2
Bonifatius, grammarian, 235
books, 9, 163, 197, 200–206, 236
Brutus. *See* Iunius

caeca insimulatio, 123, 221
Caecilianus, envoy to Africa, 31
Caecilius, advisor of Romanus, 18
Caecilius, corrects Fronto, 189
Caecilius Metellus Pius, Q., 228
Caeionii, 57
Caligula. *See* Gaius
calligraphy, 179, 284n.18
Calpurnius Piso Caesonius, L., 102
Calpurnius Piso, Cn. (son of the foregoing), 104, 276n.58
Calpurnius Piso, Cn., 94, 99, 102, 104–105, 127, 157–158, 276n.57
Campania, 16, 261n.30

Canusium, 16
Capitolium, 68, 228; in Constantinople, 235
Caracalla, emperor, xi
career. *See cursus*
Carmen contra paganos, 60–63, 261n.36, 270n.89
Cassiodorus (Magnus Aurelius Cassiodorus Senator), 145, 193, 195, 248
Cassius Dio, 100, 102
Cassius Longinus, C. (descendant of the tyrannicide), 101, 126
Cassius Longinus, C. (the tyrannicide), 94, 101, 111, 123, 162–163, 275n.36
casus condicionis humanae, 128, 221, 290n.21
Cato. *See* Porcius
censorship, 92, 241–242, 293n.86
Ceres, 77, 78
Christianity, xiv–xviii, 2, 37–88, 144–145, 187, 192–197, 202, 209–210, 214, 266n.7, 268n.57, 284n.18
Cicero. *See* Tullius
clarissimate, 179
clarus, 259n.2
Claudia gens, 103–104
Claudian (Claudius Claudianus), poet, 56, 72, 100, 233
Claudius, emperor, 127, 157
Claudius Atticus Herodes, Ti., 103
Claudius Pulcher, L., 104
Clementianus, 33, 182, 186, 188, 208
codex, 187
Codex Theodosianus, 223, 281n.41
cognomen, 16, 104–105
coins, 91, 98, 273n.24
collation, and correction, 184, 186, 188–189
commemoration, xxi–xxii, 100–101, 110, 131–170
commentarii, 69, 271n.114
Commodus, emperor, *damnatio memoriae*, 277n.85
condicio humana, 127, 221, 290n.21
conscientia bona, 168
consecro, 37
Constans, emperor, 40, 47, 55
Constantine, emperor, 40, 46, 54, 55, 266n.7
Constantinople, 21, 42, 73, 235
Constantius, emperor, 71, 177, 277n.79
Constantius II, emperor, 40, 47, 54
Constantius III (father of Valentinian III), 33, 290n.26

consularis Campaniae, 261n.30
consulship, 23, 74, 96, 102, 104
contorniates, 59
contra legente, 191
controversiam, 191, 234–235
conversion, xv, 71, 78–79, 212, 292n.59
copying of books, 179, 209, 217, 236, 284n.18
copyright, 242, 293n.86
Cora, 75, 78
Cornelius Gallus, C., 111, 277n.84
Cornelius Sulla Felix, L., 45, 274n.24
Corpus Inscriptionum Latinarum, Vol 6, 1783: abbreviations, 1, 250–251; erection of, 1, 11, 225–237, 247, 294n.2; history of publication, 247–248; lettering, 1, 250; letter rehabilitating Virius Nicomachus Flavianus, xiv, 1–5, 35, 36, 66; organization of the text, 248–249; orthography, 1, 250–252; a palimpsest, xxiii, 11, 108, 214; state of text, xix, 252; statue base, xxiii, 109, 249–250; text and translation, 2–5, 247–258
correction of manuscripts, xxi–xxiii, 32, 70, 171–213, 214, 223, 234–237, 239, 243, 259n.5, 286n.56. *See also emendatio*, subscriptions
corrigo, 177, 188
Cremutius Cordus, Aulus, 111, 115, 123, 162–163
Crispus Sallustius, corrects Apuleius, 191
cursus (*honorum*), xix, 6–36, 239, 260
Curtius Montanus, proposes that Calpurnius Piso be rehabilitated, 127
Cybele, 63, 64–65, 75, 76
Cyprian (Thascius Caecilius Cyprianus), 270n.89

damage, xiii–xiv, xxiii, 98–99, 113, 129, 172, 240–243, 293n.88
Damasus I, pope, 59, 60, 270n.96
damnatio memoriae, xi–xiv, xxi, 34, 89–130, 139–141, 155–156, 160, 217–218, 238, 241–242, 274n.12, 275n.36
death, 107, 132, 151–153, 166, 240, 244–245, 282n.54
debito religiosi muneris, 170
declamans, 191, 234–235
Demeter, 75, 77, 78
desemino, 208

destruction, vs. erasure, 107–108, 124
Deuterius, corrects Martianus Capella, 191
Dexter, Appius Claudius Tarronius, 27, 33
Dexter, Nicomachus (son of Flavian the younger), xix, xxii, 17, 27, 32–33, 70, 146, 171–213, 208, 226
diabolica figmenta, 58
dignitas, 90, 260n.14
Dio. *See* Cassius Dio
Diocletian, emperor, 19, 40, 46, 293n.81
Dionysios the Areopagite, 120, 134
diploma, 248–249
diptych: general, 59, 73–74; of Nicomachi and Symmachi, 15, 17, 67, 73–75, 77, 272n.124
disciplina, 208
dissemino, 288n.118
dissimulation, 88, 93–94, 117–119, 120, 122, 124–126, 136, 147, 154–161, 162–164, 217–218, 238–239, 278n.93
distinctio, 286n.56
distinguo, 188
divination, 69, 84
doctus, 208
document, 218, 240–246
Domitian, emperor, 107, 126, 127, 143, 153, 157, 165, 227, 291n.40; *damnatio memoriae* of, 101, 111, 277n.85
Donatists, 19–20, 262n.48
Donatus, Aelius, 172
Dracontius, corrects Quintilian, 188, 191
Drusus. *See* Julius Caesar Drusus

education, 201, 286n.56
Eleusis, 75
emendatio, defined, 171–173, 174, 183–190. *See also* correction, subscriptions
emendation, conjectural, 184, 213
emendo, xxii, 188
emperors, 40, 41, 54, 66, 126, 156–160, 249, 269n.59. *See also specific emperors*
Endelechius, orator, 196, 234–235
Enna, 18, 77, 181, 182, 284n.23, 284n.24
Ennius, Q., text corrected, 172, 198
epistula, 248–249
epulum Iovi, 228, 291n.46
erasure, xii, xxiii, 11, 87, 91, 93, 101–103, 107–108, 113, 117, 120, 124, 130, 136, 150, 152, 213, 217, 241, 242, 246, 249–250, 275n.40, 275n.42, 277n.80

Esquiline treasure, 78
et in arcadia ego, 244–245
Etruscans, 63, 228
Eudoxius, Macrobius Plotinus, 183, 192
Eugenius, Flavius (western usurper), 1, 22, 23, 28, 29, 34, 56, 112–113, 147, 181–182, 210; usurpation of, xiv, 1–2, 38, 39–46, 48–49, 50–51, 59, 64, 67, 71–74, 94–96
Eunapius, historian, 145, 146
Eustathius, and elder Flavian, 83, 146
Eutropius, 100, 101
evanescence, 131–132, 169, 215
evidence, 87–88, 151–152, 215–217
exemplum, 208
experience, and truth, 218–219, 289n.11,
explicit, 188
exscribo, 179–180
exsedrae, 235–236
exsistimatur, 175

familiaris, 44
fasti, 102, 275n.42; *Fasti Amiternini*, 104, 227; *Fasti Capitolini*, 276n.48
Felix, corrects Horace and Martianus Capella, 188, 189, 191
figmenta, diabolica, 58
Filocalus, Furius Dionysius, 206
flamen Dialis, 77
Flavian the elder (Virius Nicomachus Flavianus) *passim*: sources for, xvi, 13–16, 19, 35, 66, 72, 74, 83–85, 145, 147, 179–181
—*cursus*, xix, 7, 10–25, 66, 124, 224, 229, 248; consulship, 14, 23–25, 34, 42–43, 94, 95, 102–103, 113; *pontifex maior*, 17–18, 35, 37, 66, 67, 85, 146, 181, 229; *praetorian prefectures*, 15–16, 20–23, 24, 34, 42, 262nn.52,55, 263n.60; praetorship, 17, 24, 35; proconsul of Sicily, 18; *quaestor sacri palatii*, 21–22, 146–147, 224, 262n.52, 263n.60; quaestorship, 17, 24, 35; *vicarius* in Africa, 15–16, 18–19, 20, 31, 176, 261n.43
—*damnatio memoriae* of, xiv, 1, 94–98; ban of *praenomen*[?], 104–105; ban of representations, 98; erasure of inscriptions, 96, 102–103, 112; persistence of memory of, 73, 102–103, 109, 112, 115–116
—family of, 16; date of birth, 17, 261n.36; death of, 46, 67, 71; father Venustus, 16,

83; homes of, 18, 27, 237; names of, 16–17, 105
—and ideal of aristocratic learning, 85–86, 146, 226; author of *Annals*, 70, 86, 145–147, 171, 177, 181, 211, 215, 225, 234; author of *Historia Augusta*[?], 145; author of imperial legal decisions, 21, 146–147; and Livy, 181, 203; and philosophy, 146; translates from Syrian[?], 281n.39]; translates Philostratos' Life of Apollonios of Tyana, 146, 179–180, 192, 281n.39; as writer, 233–234
—and paganism, xv, 17–18, 37–39, 43–45, 48–49, 59, 60, 61, 64–67, 71–73, 83, 84–87, 146; attitude toward Christians, 19–20, 45, 37; and Donatists, 19–20, 262n.48
—rehabilitation of, xiv, xvi, xviii, 11–12, 32, 108, 123, 126, 166–167, 203, 226–230. See also *Corpus Inscriptionum Latinarum*; and Index Locorum, *CIL* 6.1783
Flavian the younger (Virius Nicomachus Flavianus), 27–28, 33, 44, 74, 110, 127, 193, 223–224, 225; birthdate, 27; marriages of, 27, 33, 74; name of, 17, 26, 105
—as author of *HA*[?], 284n.9; corrects Livy, xxii, 70, 113, 146, 171–213
—and *Carmen contra paganos*, 61; dedication from Naples, 25, 113; statue base from Forum of Caesar, 26
—*cursus*, xix, 11, 25–32, 248; consular of Campania, 27; extraordinary envoy to Africa, 19, 31; *praetorian prefect*, 32, 182, 223; proconsul of Asia, 21, 26, 27, 29–30, 262n.55; rebuilds *secretarium senatus*, 28; urban prefectures, 25, 26–27, 28–29, 30–31, 43, 44, 59, 97, 112–113, 127, 181–182, 225, 264n.77, 265n.96
—and usurpation of Eugenius, xiv–xv, 25, 28, 29; aftermath of the usurpation, 28, 73, 97, 127, 290n.21; conversion to Christianity, xv, 28, 56, 71, 74, 78–79, 196, 210; and rehabilitation of the elder Flavian, xiv, 224–225
forgetting, xv–xviii, 39, 73, 91, 93–94, 99, 100, 114–115, 119–121, 132, 160, 278n.97
forum: of Augustus, 213, 230, 234–236; Boarium, 77; Caesar, 230; functions of, 231; imperial fora, 230–232; Nerva

(Forum Transitorium), 230, 236; Romanum, 110, 230, 236; of Trajan, 1, 224, 230–237
Freud, Sigmund, 91, 132, 134, 150, 212–213, 282n.54, 283n.74; on consciousness and truth, 119, 278n.97; on forgetting, 119; on history, 283n.74; on memory, 87; on repression, 114; on slip, 287n.86; on social groups, 273–274n.5
Frigidus, battle of, xiv, 45–46, 56, 57, 67, 70, 72, 73, 95, 229, 290n.21
Fronto, text corrected, 189
Fufius Geminus, C., 107
funeral rites, and *damnatio memoriae*, 93, 101, 106–107, 143

Gabinius, Aulus, 102
Gaius, emperor, 112, 291n.40
Galba, emperor, 125–127
Galerius, emperor, 46
Galla Placidia. *See* Placidia
Gallicanus, Ovinius, 55, 317
Gallus. *See* Cornelius
Gelasius I, pope, 58
Gellius, Aulus, 103, 172, 198
Genius, 43
Germanicus. *See* Julius Caesar Germanicus
Germanicus, month name, 291n.40
Geta. *See* Septimius Geta
god: as author, 217; and authority, 218, 289–290n.12; as proofreader, 200; and representation, 120; unnameable, 121
grammarians, 191–193, 203–204, 234–237
Gratian, emperor, 19–21, 41, 48, 54–55, 68, 261n.43
guilt, and historiography, 165–166, 169–170, 283n.74

Hadrian, emperor, 186, 230
haruspicy, 43, 45
Hecate, 76
Helpidius, 236–237
Heraclianus, 31
Hercules, 44–46, 51, 72, 78
Herennius Senecio, 123, 163–164
hermeneutic, of revelation and suspicion, 132–134, 149–150, 281n.46
Herodes Atticus. *See* Claudius Atticus Herodes, Ti.
Herodotus, 147, 242

Hesiod, 218
Hesperius, proconsul, 18
Hierius, corrects [Quintilian], 188, 191
Historia Augusta, 144–146, 284n.9
Historikerstreit, 134
historiography, xvi, xvii, xxii, 10, 121, 131–170, 176, 212, 216–220, 239–240, 246, 279n.4, 289n.5
—and *damnatio memoriae*, 123, 129–130, 141, 153; and *emendatio*, xxii, 172–173, 176, 211; and rehabilitation, xiv, xxi, 129–130, 147, 156, 211, 215, 238–239
—and reenactment, 147, 172–173, 217; and obligation, 82, 151–152, 164–170, 172, 243, 246, 273n.151; and silence, 125, 131–170, 238–239; and survival, 164–170
—Roman, xvii, xxi, 70, 131, 143, 162–164, 214; alternative, 132, 153; of Holocaust, 134–135; modernist, 132–133, 150
Holocaust, historiography of, 91–92, 119–120, 134–135
Homer, 218
honor, 11, 90, 124
Honorius, emperor, 23, 31, 33, 56, 94–95, 103, 110, 147, 223
Horace, corrected, 191, 192
Horatius, 107
humanism: liberal, 53; Renaissance, 199, 288n.117

idealist theory of language, 117–118, 218
Ides: etymology of, 228; of September, 226–230
illustris, 259n.2
Illyricum, 23, 263–264n.70
imagines, 58, 231
incipit, 188
infidelis, 45, 51
initiation, 78; and *emendatio*, 208; erotic, 76, 78; religious, 62, 78
Innocentius, pope, gives permission for pagan celebrations, 56, 408
inprobi, 123, 221
insimulatio, 123
instinctu divinitatis, 46
integrum, restitutio ad, 126–127
interpolo, 174
Isidis Navigium, survival in late antiquity, 58
Isis, 64

Italy, 23
iterum, 23, 29–30
iudiciariae, 19
iudicium, 19
Iunia Tertia (Tertulla, wife of Cassius, sister of Brutus), 101, 126
Iunius Brutus, L. (founder of the republic), 199
Iunius Brutus, M.: and *damnatio memoriae,* 111, 123, 162–163; the tyrannicide, 94, 101, 126, 275n.36;
Iunius Rusticus, Q. Arulenus, 123, 163–164
ius augurale, 69
Iuventas, 78

Jerome, Saint (Eusebius Hieronymus), 61–62, 68–69, 79, 144–145, 172, 199, 203, 208–210, 281n.39, 289–290n.12
Jewish antiquities, 144
Julia, daughter of Augustus, 249
Julian, emperor, 40–41, 47–48, 55–56, 58, 59, 232, 261n.30, 277n.79, 292n.59
Julius Agricola, Cn., 115, 143, 153–158, 161
Julius Caesar, C., 94, 101, 227
Julius Caesar Drusus (Caligula's brother), rehabilitated, 127
Julius Caesar Germanicus, and Calpurnius Piso, 99
Julius Caesar Nero (Caligula's brother), rehabilitated, 127
Julius Obsequens, *Liber prodigiorum,* 70
Juno, 68
Jupiter, 45–46, 51, 67–68, 70, 72, 77–78, 228–229, 276n.57, 291n.46
Juvenal, 99; corrected, 191

Kore. *See* Cora
Kundera, Milan, *Book of Laughter and Forgetting,* 109, 121

Lachmann, Karl, 198, 284–285n.29
lacuna, 240–246
Lambaesis, 203, 233, 235
Lampadio, corrects text of Ennius, 172, 198
language, 218; realist and idealist theories of, 117–118, 120–121
lapsus, 177, 287n.86
Lares, 43
laudatio funebris, 143

learning: and aristocracy, 83, 85–86, 203–205; and religion, 210
lego, xxii, 188
Lepcis Magna, 15–16, 18, 19, 112
Lepidus. *See* Aemilius Lepidus
Lerna, 78
Levi, Primo, *The Drowned and the Saved,* 169
Libanius, 128
Liber, 77–78
Libera, 77–78
Libo Drusus. *See* Scribonius
libraries: of aristocracy, 180, 193–194, 195, 204; of Rome, 144, 230, 236, 292–293n.65
librarius, 293n.81
lies, and representation, 116–120, 124–126, 136, 278n.90
limit, 122, 135, 215, 289n.5
literacy, 245–246, 273n.153
literature, Roman, xix, 49–50, 106, 139, 141, 214
livor improborum, 123, 221
Livy, 57–58, 69–70, 94, 106, 279n.4; correction of, xxii, 144–146, 171–213
locutionary act, 137–138; beginning as, 137
Lollianus, L. Egnatius Victor, 30
loss, 166–167, 169–170, 283n.74
lucem, revocare in, 127
Lucretius: edited by Lachmann, 284–285n.29; text corrected by Cicero, 172
Lupercalia, continued observance of in late antiquity, 58, 227
Lupus, Virius, 261n.30

Macrobius, Ambrosius Theodosius, 79–80, 183, 197
Macrobius, *Saturnalia,* xvi–xviii, 13, 35, 47, 59, 64, 70, 73, 77, 79–85, 106, 146, 193, 197, 203–205, 210, 226, 228, 229, 237. *See also* Index Locorum, Macrobius, *Saturnalia*
Maecenas, C., 279n.110
magister, 208
Magna Mater, 64–65, 75
Magnus Maximus, emperor, 21, 41, 95–96, 266n.13
maiestas, 94
Manlia gens, 103, 104
Manlius Capitolinus, M., 94; *damnatio memoriae,* 100, 102, 103, 104, 106, 275n.48

Marius, C., 274n.24
marriage, 60, 68–69, 74–77
Mars Ultor, temple of, 230, 234, 235, 236
Martial, 236; correction of, 191, 206, 234; corrects his own text, 172
Martianus Capella, text corrected, 188, 189, 191
masquerade, 117, 122, 160–161
Mausoleum of Augustus, 127
Mavortius, Vettius Agorius Basilius, 191–192
Maxentius, emperor, 30
Maximianus, bookseller, 236
meaning, 34, 202, 203, 219, 246
melancholy, 152, 169–170
memoria damnata, 93
memory, xv-xvii, 53–54, 82, 87, 90–92, 94, 99, 113–126, 129, 135, 141, 152, 154, 156, 166–170
Merobaudes, Flavius, 224, 233–234
Metellus. *See* Caecilius
metonymy, 8–9; and metaphor, 173–174, 288n.125
Milan, 45, 73, 111
militance, pagan, 47–48, 58–63, 64–65
military, and learning, 231, 233
Milvian Bridge, battle of, 46, 312
Minerva, 68, 230
Minucia, Vestal, 186
Mithra, 63, 64; and Praetextatus, 75
modernist historiography, xvii, 87, 132–133, 150
mola salsa, 228
monasteries, 193
monotheism, vs. polytheism, 51–52
monument, xxiii, 109–110, 119–120, 124, 129, 166–167, 240–246, 278n.99
monumentum, 11, 98

name: and *damnatio memoriae,* 93, 101–106, 113; in late antiquity, 16, 261n.26, 276n.63
Naples, 27, 113
nature, and silence, 120, 132, 217; as book, 200
Neoplatonism, 40, 75, 77, 120
Nero. *See* Julius Caesar
Nero, emperor, 101, 127, 157–158, 160
Niceus, corrects Juvenal, 191
Nicomachi, 16, 26, 67, 73–75, 78–79, 182, 195; correction of Livy, 144–145, 182, 184, 195, 225; library of, 180
Nicomachus, Maecius Faltonius, 147
Nigidius Figulus, on divination, 84
nostalgia, 38, 47–48, 81–82, 86, 152, 169–170, 210, 273n.151
Numa Pompilius, 63

obelisk of Theodosius, Constantinople, 279n.119
objectivity, 8–9, 197, 199, 216, 217
omen, 56, 140
omission, and meaning, 34–35
oriental cults, 47, 63–67, 74–77, 196, 270–271n.101
Origen, translated, 180
Origines. See Cato
Orosius, 72, 144, 203
Ostia, 44
Otho, emperor, 107, 127

paganism, xv–xvii, xxi, 2, 17, 35, 37–88, 144–145, 192–197, 202, 206–209, 210, 229, 268n.57
palimpsest, xi, xxiii, 130, 214
parens, 32–33, 284n.24, 290n.26
past, 132, 210, 212; and present, xvii, 137–138, 177, 211–212
pastoralism, 244–245
patina, 241–243
patronus originalis, 27
Paulina, Fabia Ancona, xv, 61–62, 63, 75–77, 206–211, 270n.98
Paulinus, Anicius Junior, 232
Periochae to Livy, 106
Persephone/Kore, 75
Persius, correction of, 188–192
Petrus Petricius, 145, 146
philology, 199, 287nn.85,102
Philostratos, *Life of Apollonios of Tyana,* 146, 179–180, 192, 205, 281n.39
Phlegon of Tralles, 186–187
Phrygianum, 64–65
piaetas, 37
Piazza Amerina, 284n.24
Piranesi, Giovanni Battista, xi–xiv, 240
Piso, consulship of, 275n.43
Placidia, Galla, 33, 80, 220, 223–224, 290n.26; struggle with Aëtius, 32, 224

Plato, 119, 245, 246
Pliny the elder, *Natural History,* 179, 205
Pliny the younger, on correction of ms., 174
Plotius Tucca, corrects text of Aeneid, 172
"poem against pagans." See *Carmen contra paganos*
polytheism, vs. monotheism, 51–52
Pompeianus, Gabinius Barbarus, 56–57, 60–61
Pompeii, 235
pontifices, 17–18, 41, 64, 66–71, 83, 85, 104, 118, 146, 228–229, 271n.108; *pontifex Vestae,* 68
Poppaea Sabina, 127
Porcius Cato, M. (the censor), 142–143, 280n.23
porticus deorum consentium, dedicated by Praetextatus, 41
portraits, 101, 231
praefectus annonae, 44
praefectus urbi iterum vice sacra iudicans, 29–30
praeiudicium, 175–176
praenomen, 16, 105–106, 242, 255–256; and *damnatio memoriae,* 103–106
Praetextatus, Vettius Agorius, xv–xvi, 41, 55, 59–60, 61–62, 65–69, 75–79, 83–85, 187, 193, 203–210, 226–227, 270n.98
praetorian prefecture, 18, 20, 54, 262n.52
praetorship, 17
present, and past, xvii, 137–138, 211–212
priesthoods, pagan, not mentioned in public inscriptions in late antiquity, 17, 37
priestly colleges, endowments, 41, 43, 48
principate, 122, 160–161
Proba, Faltonia Betitia, *Cento Probae,* 61
proconsuls, 29–30, 54
Procopius, 111
Proculus, son of Flavius Eutolmius Tatianus, 128, 279n.119
prodigies, 56, 68–70, 146, 271n.111
Proiectus, Numerius, *praefectus annonae,* 44–45
proofreading, xix, 171–213
prosopography and *cursus,* 8, 9–10
provincial governorships in late antiquity, 18
Prudentius, 54, 60, 71–72; corrected, 192
purge, Soviet, 92, 100, 110, 121. See also *damnatio memoriae*

quaedam, 173
quaestor aulae divae, 20; *intra palatium,* 20; *sacri palatii,* 20, 224, 262n.52
quaestorship in late antiquity, 17
Quinctilis, renamed July, 227
[Quintilian], Declamations, corrected, 188, 191, 235

reading, 197, 202, 204, 225, 244–246
realist theory of language, 117–118, 120, 121, 218
reality, 116, 121, 131, 136, 147–150, 156, 214, 218–219, 278n.97, 289n.8
recenseo, 188
recension, and textual crticism, 184
recognosco, 174, 188
reddo, 10, 11–12, 90, 98, 108, 211, 295n.17
re-enactment, 168, 170, 273n.1
referent, 117, 119, 278n.91
rehabilitation, xxiii, 34, 73, 89, 126, 129–170, 210–212, 215, 217, 220–226, 238–239
rehabilitation, of Flavian the elder: for the text, see *Index Locorum, CIL* 6.1783
relego, 188
religion, xxi, 37–88. See also paganism; Christianity
religiosi muneris debito, 37, 105, 106, 170
remembering, xviii, 39, 100, 114
Renaissance humanism, 288n.117
renatus, 65
representation, 89, 98–101, 113–126, 129–130, 134–136, 141, 147, 149–151, 156, 168, 278n.97, 289n.8
repression, 91, 109, 113–114, 273–274n.5, 277n.88. See also *damnatio memoriae*
reproduction, 241, 288n.107
rescribo, 188
resistance, xvii, 53, 92, 121–122
restitutio, 10, 11, 90, 105, 108, 126–127
restoration, 10–11, 89–91, 129–130, 238–239
resurrection, and history, 147, 211
reverentia, 37
revocare, 11, 90, 127
rex sacrorum, 104
rhetoric, 9, 58, 84–85
Romanus, 16, 18–19
Rome, 56–58, 60, 73, 182
Rufii Festi, 57

Rufinus, Flavius, 20, 21, 72, 128
ruin, 109, 152

Sabinus, Flavius Iulius Tryphonianus, corrects Persius, 188, 192
sacratus, 62, 270n.98
sacrifice, and Flavian the elder, 40, 43, 47, 68, 69, 71
saepius, 30–31, 34, 113, 252–253
Sallustius, corrects Apuleius' *Metamorphoses* in Forum of Augustus [Mars], 174, 196, 234–235
Sallustius, Flavius, 247
Salutati, Collucio, 199
salutations, and subscriptions, 206
Salvius Coccianus, M., 107
sanctissimae, 37
sarcasm, in Tacitus, 161
Saturnalia. *See* Macrobius
Saturnalia, festival, xvi, 83
schedium, 179–180
scholae, 191, 235–236, 293n.6; *schola Traiani*, 235
science, 136, 149, 198
scribe, 171–172, 199, 217, 289–290n.12
scribo, 188
Scribonia gens, 104
Scribonius Libo Drusus, M., *damnatio memoriae*, 101, 105, 107, 227, 276n.59, 277n.72
scriptura actuaria, 250
secretaries, imperial, 224, 238
Secretarium senatus, 28
secular, creation of, 58
Sedulius, *Carmen paschale*, 192
Sejanus. *See* Aelius
semiotic square, 278n.92
senate, and rehabilitation of the elder Flavian, 73, 115, 140–141, 225–226, 231, 249, 291n.35. *See also* aristocracy, Roman
September, 226–230
Septimius Geta, xi, 108
Septimius Severus, arch of, xi, 108
Serapis, 63
Servius, grammarian, 83, 85, 144, 203–204, 237
Servius, school of, 191
Sestius, L., honors Brutus in home, 111
Sextilis, renamed August, 227
Sibyl, 187
Sicily, 77, 182, 261n.42, 284n.24

Sidonius Apollinaris, 144, 146, 179–180, 203, 205, 233, 292–293n.65
sign and referent, 124–126, 152, 278nn.90,91
signum (nickname), 105, 260n.19
silence, xii, xviii, 87–88, 89, 91, 95, 97, 109, 113–126, 130, 131–170, 173–174, 214–217, 230, 238–239, 242, 282nn.54,60,61
Simonides, 114
simulation, 116, 117–119, 124–126, 135
slave collar, 236–237
Socrates (church historian), on Eugenius, 72
Solinus, 192
Sol Invictus, xvi, 75, 77
solutis vocibus, 288n.115
sors, 259n.5
Sozomen, 72
speech-act, 140, 279n.113
speech: and mind, 137–138, 147, 150; and silence, 137, 156, 164; vs. writing, 246
standards and gods, religious functions of, 45–46, 267n.28
Statilius Maximus, corrects Cicero, 172, 187–188, 198
statues, 1, 11–12, 45, 93, 98–100, 108–111, 127, 145, 249–250, 274n.29, 295n.17
status and learning, 203–204, 205, 273n.153
stemmata, 244
Stilicho, 28, 110, 187; *damnatio memoriae*, 110, 277n.80
subscriptions, xxii, 171–213, 243, 285n.31
Subura, 230, 236
Suetonius, 172
Sulla. *See* Cornelius
supplementum, 176, 255
survival, 87, 152, 164–170, 215
Symmachi, 67, 73–75, 78–79
Symmachus, Aurelius Memmius, 145, 183, 192, 195, 196–197
Symmachus, Q. Aurelius, xv–xvi, 13–15, 21, 27, 28, 33, 41–44, 48–50, 56, 64–70, 74, 79–80, 83–85, 112, 127–128, 142, 146, 177–179, 181, 183, 187, 192–193, 203–208, 226, 237, 290n.21
Symmachus, Q. Fabius Memmius, 13–15
syncretism, 59, 75, 77

Tacitus, xxi–xxii, 70, 92–94, 111, 115, 119, 121–122, 125–126, 132–133, 143–144,

153–170, 211, 218, 238, 242, 279n.4, 280n.26, 281n.29, 282nn.55,60
Tacitus, emperor, 147
Tarquinius Priscus, L., 228
Tatianus, Flavius Eutolmius, 169, 240, 279n.119; *damnatio memoriae* and rehabilitation of, 128–129
Tatianus, grandson of Flavius Eutolmius Tatianus, 128
taurobolium, 65, 75–76
teaching, and *emendatio*, 191–192, 206–209
Tertullian, 144
tetrarchy, 40, 46
textual criticism, modern, 10, 184, 190, 195, 197–198, 238–239, 243–244, 284–285n29
Theodoret, 72
Theodorus, Flavius Mallius, 28
Theodosian Code, 13, 248, 251
Theodosian dynasty, 73
Theodosius I, "the Great," xiv–xv, 20–23, 33, 39, 42–48, 51, 54–57, 64, 71–72, 85, 94–96, 103, 110, 115–116, 127, 145–147, 182, 220–221, 234, 238, 249, 266n.13, 267n.20, 279n.119
Theodosius II, 1, 28, 192, 198, 203, 206, 222–223, 248
Thermae, 181, 284n.23
Thessalonica, 267n.20
Thucydides, 119, 132–133, 218, 219
Tiberius, emperor, 94, 104, 107, 119, 124–126, 157–158, 162, 238, 276n.57
Tibur, 45
time, xiii–xiv, 129, 131–132, 151, 169–170, 240, 279n.124
Tiro. *See* Tullius
Titius, Sex., 101
titulus, 11, 98
Torquatus Gennadius, corrects Martial, 191, 206, 234
trace, xiv, 109, 152, 167, 172, 212–213, 215
Trajan: *atria Traiani*, 235; *schola Traiani*, 191, 235; temple of, 230
Trithemius, Johannes, *De laude scriptorum*, 209
truth, 120–122, 151, 156, 217, 281–282n.48, 289n.11
Tucca. *See* Plotius
Tullius Cicero, M., 84, 142, 180, 203, 206; corrects text of Lucretius, 172; *De lege agraria*, corrected, 172, 187, 188

Tullius Tiro, M. (secretary of Cicero), 172, 187
tyrant, 96–97, 123

urban prefecture, 30, 54
Urban VIII, pope, tomb of, 245
Ursinus, contest with Damasus for papacy, 59
usurpers, not mentioned in late antiquity, 123

Valentinian I, 18
Valentinian II, 22, 41, 42, 147
Valentinian III, 32, 33, 220, 222, 233, 248, 290n.26
Valeria Messalina, *damnatio memoriae*, 101
Valerianus, receives copy of Livy from Symmachus, 178, 205
Valerius Maximus, 276n.64
Varius Rufus, corrects text of *Aeneid*, 172
Vegetius, 190
Venantius Fortunatus, 236
veneratio, 37
Venus Genetrix, temple of, 230
Venustus, Virius Volusius (father of Flavian the elder), 16, 18, 83
Vergil, xvi, 57–58, 83, 84, 85, 195, 236, 245; correction of, 172, 189, 192, 206
Vespasian, 127
Vestals, 41, 43, 68, 186–187, 228
vicarius, 15–16, 18–19, 20
vicem praefectorum praetorio, 18
vice sacra, 18, 29–30
Victor, Sextus Aurelius, 232, 233, 292n.59
Victorianus, Tascius, 178–182, 192, 203
Victorinus, Marius, 58–59, 232, 233, 292n.59
videtur, 173
Vienne, 42
Viria gens, 16, 26–27
virtus, 11
Visigoths, sack Rome, 182
Vivarium, 193, 195
Volusianus, Rufius Antonius Agrypnius, 57

writing, 7, 130, 132, 135, 136, 166–167, 197

Zonaras, uses Flavian's *Annales*, 145
Zosimus, on Eugenius, 72

INDEX LOCORUM

I. AUTHORS

Ambrose
   De obitu Theodosii
      10: 45
   De officiis ministrorum
      1.3.9: 142, 153
   Enarr. Psalm. = Enarratio in psalmum
      36: 72
   Ep. = Epistula
      18: 42, 267n.15
      57: 42, 43, 61, 267n.15
Amm. = Ammianus Marcellinus
   16.10.15: 230
   21.10.6: 232
   22.7.6: 59
   28.6: 16, 18–19
App. B.C. = Appian, Bella civilia
   4.51: 111
Aristotle, Prior Analytics
   1.46: 278n.92
Asterius, Hom. = Homiliae
   4: 279n.120
Aug. = Augustine
   Civ. Dei = De civitate Dei
      5.26: 28, 45, 51, 56, 71, 72, 146
      14.4: 290n.21
      18.53–54: 44
   Conf. = Confessions
      8.2: 58, 232
      8.5: 58
   Ep. = Epistulae
      1A.4: 172
      86: 265n.105
      87.8: 19
      135–138: 57

Augustus, Res Gestae: 123
Aul. Gell. See Gell
Ausonius, Epitaph. = Epitaphia
   6.32: 240

Carmen contra paganos: 60–63, 261n.36
Cassius Dio. See Dio
Cato, Origines
   frg. 2 (Peter): 142
   frg. 118 (Peter): 143
Cic. = Cicero
   ad Att. = Epistulae ad Atticum
      6.1.17: 260n.9
   de dom. = De domo sua
      127: 276n.49
   De finibus
      2.104: 113
   De haruspic. resp. = De haruspicum responso
      6.12: 276n.49
   Fam. = Epistulae ad familiares
      6.6.12: 290n.21
   Phil. = Orationes Philippicae
      1.13.32: 275n.47
      13.11.26: 102
   Pro Planc. = Pro Plancio
      66: 142
   Rab. perd. = Pro Rabirio perduellionis reo
      24: 101
   Sest. = Pro Sestio
      14.33: 102
   Tusc. disp. = Tusculanae disputationes
      3.59: 290n.21
CJ = Codex Justinianus
   1.6.1: 18, 20
   2.15.1: 265n.96

Claudian
   de Bello Gothico
      Praef.: 7–14: 233
   de quarto consulatu Honorii
      87–105: 72
   In Eutrop. = *In Eutropium*
      2.70–83: 100
CTh = *Codex Theodosianus*
   1.1.2: 23
   3.1.6: 23
   3.31.1: 28
   4.4.2: 21
   6.23.3a: 265n.106
   7.4.33: 31
   7.18.8: 263n.64, 263n.70
   7.18.81: 21
   9.29.2: 21, 263n.64, 263n.70
   9.38.9: 128
   9.40.13: 21, 23
   9.40.17: 100
   10.10.20: 23
   11.1.36a: 265n.106
   11.30.61: 28
   11.39.11: 23
   12.1.85: 264n.89
   12.6.18: 27
   13.5.19: 21
   13.5.29: 28
   14.9.3: 235
   14.10.3: 28
   15.1.53: 235
   15.2.9: 28
   15.14: 279n.111
   15.14.6: 95
   15.14.7: 95
   15.14.8: 95, 96
   15.14.9: xii, 23, 95, 123
   15.14.11: 23, 96, 123, 265n.90
   15.14.12: 97, 123
   16.2.18: 21
   16.3.1: 21
   16.6.2: 18, 20
   16.7.4–5: 23
   16.10.2: 40
   16.10.6: 40
   16.10.10: 43
   16.10.12: 43
   16.10.19: 56

De Viris Illustribus
   24.6: 104, 276n.47
Dio = Cassius Dio
   51.19.3: 108
   52.32.4: 111
   56.34: 231
   57.15.4: 291n.41
   58.12.5: 277n.72
   62.27: 101
   64.3.4c: 127
   71.3: 292n.56
   frg. 26.1: 102, 276n.47
Donatus, *Vit. Verg.* = *Vita Vergilii*
   39: 172

Epit. de Caes. = *Epitome de Caesaribus*
   48, 11–12: 146
Eusebius
   Chron. = *Chronica*
      ad ann. 94: 172
      ad ann. 2102: 291n.40
   VC = *Vita Constantini*
      11.44: 266n.7

Festus, *Epitome*
   125 (p. 112 Lindsay): 275n.47
   151 (p. 132 Lindsay): 275n.47

Gelasius, *Ep. adversus Andromachum* = *Epistula adversus Andromachum*: 57
Gell. = Aulus Gellius, *Noctes Atticae*
   9.2.11: 103
   12.8.2: 291n.46
   18.5.1: 198
Georgios Monachos
   604.8: 192

HA = *Historia Augusta*
   Aurelian
      2: 144
      24.9: 281n.39
      27.6: 281n.39
   Commodus
      20.5: 101
   Probus
      2: 144
   Tacitus
      6.7: 147
      10.3: 144

Herodotus, proem: 131
Homer, *Il.* = *Iliad*
   9.189: 143

Jerome
  Chron. = *Ab Abraham*
    ad ann. 2103: 291n.40
    ad ann. 2370: 232
  Comm. on Zacchariah = *Commentary on Zacchariah*
    14.1, 2 [3: 914]: 144
  Contra Ioann. Hieros. = *Contra Ioannem Hierosolymitanum*
    8: 60
  Ep. = *Epistulae*
    3.2: 62
    23.2.1: 62
    107.1: 68–69
Julius Obsequens, *Liber prodigiorum*: 70
Juvenal, *Satires*
    8.1–9: 275n.34
    10.58–64: 99

Libanius, *Or.* = *Orationes*
    28.4: 27
Liber de praenominibus: 276n.64
Livy
    1.26.5: 107
    4.13.6: 186
    5.54.5: 267n.21
    6, periocha: 275n.47
    6.20.14: 103
    8.15: 186

Macrob. *Sat.* = Macrobius, *Saturnalia*
    24–25, 47, 64, 79–85
  Book 1
    pref.1–13: 83
    4.4: 83, 204
    5.13: 16, 83, 146
    6.4: 83, 146
    6–2.8: 83
    12–16: 226
    12.1: 226
    12.36–37: 227
    12.37: 101–102
    15.14–15: 228
    15.14–18: 228
    15.16: 228
    15.18: 228
    18: 80
    18.15–18: 77
    22.1: 75
    24: 83
    24.16: 83
    24.21: 83
  Book 2
    2.4: 84
    8.2: 84
  Book 3: 83, 85
    1–12: 83
    2.17: 70
    13.10: 228
  Books 4–7: 84
  Book 7
    6.1–15: 84
Marcell. *Dig.* = Marcellinus, *Digest*
    11.7.35: 107
Mart. *Ep.* = Martial, *Epigrammata*
  Book 1
    117.8–13: 236
    2.5–8: 236
    3.1: 236
  Book 7
    11: 172
  Book 9
    1.4: 291n.40
  Book 12
    48.12: 291n.46
Merobaudes, *Pan.* = *Panegyricus*
    I f. 3A: 2–3: 233
Modest. *Dig.* = Modestinus, *Digest*
    48.19.24: 100

Nep. *Att.* = Nepos, *Atticus*
    18.1–4: 260n.3

Orosius
  Hist. adv. paganos = *Historiae adversus paganos*
  Book 1
    5.1: 144
    10.1: 144
  Book 7
    3.7: 144
    9.7: 144
    10.3: 144
    19.4: 144

27.1: 144
34.5: 144
35: 72

Paul. Dig. = Paulus, *Digest*
  47.12.4: 107
  48.24.3: 107
Paulinus, *Vit. Ambr.* = *Vita S. Ambrosii*
  26: 43
  26–31: 72
  31: 45
  31.4: 271n.121
PG = *Patrologia Graeca*
  40, 224–225: 279n.120
Philostorgius, *HE* = *Historia ecclesiastica*
  11.2: 72
Philostratos, *Life of Apollonius of Tyana*: 179–180
Photios, *Bibl.* = *Bibliotheca*
258: 128
Plato, *Phaedrus*: 119
Pliny the younger
  Ep. = *Epistulae*
  1.17.3: 275n.36
  4.26.1: 174
  7.17: 284n.22
  Paneg. = *Panegyricus*
  52.4: 111
Plut. = Plutarch
  Comp. Brutus and Dio = *Comparison of Brutus and Dio*
    5: 111
  QR = *Quaestiones Romanae*
  91: 276n.47
Polybius
  6.53: 275n.34
  6.53–55: 280n.22
Proba, *Cento Probae*: 61
Procopius, *Hist. arc.* = *Historia arcana*
  8: 111
Prudentius, *Contra Symmachum*: 267n.15
  Book *1*: 72
  1.506–607: 51, 56, 71

Quintilian, *Inst. orator.* = *Institutio oratoria*
  3.7.20: 275–276n.47
  5.2.1: 283n.7
[Quintilian] *Declam. Maior* = *Declamationes maiores*
  18: 285n.48

Rufinus, *HE* = *Historia ecclesiastica*
  11.31: 42
  11.33: 43–44, 71, 72
Seneca, *Ep.* = *Epistulae*
  70.10: 291n.41
Servius, Auct. = Auctus
  In Vergilium commentarius
  ad Aen.: 3.399: 144
  ad Verg. *Ecl.*: 8.82: 291n.47
Sidonius Apollinaris
  Carm. = *Carmina*
  2.190–192: 144
  8.7–10: 292–293n.65
  9.289–295: 233
  9.296–301: 233
  23.153: 144
  Ep. = *Epistulae*
  4.14.1: 144
  4.22.2: 144, 280n.22
  8.3.1: 146, 179, 205
  9.16.2: 180
  21–28: 233
Socrates, *HE* = *Historia ecclesiastica*
  5.25: 72
  7.22.6: 192
Soz. *HE* = Sozomen, *Historia ecclesiastica*
  Praef.: 192
  4.7–8: 192
  4.10–12: 192
  4.18: 192
  7.22–24: 72
  9.6.3: 57
Suet. = Suetonius
  Praef. = *Praefatio*
  2.12: 172
  Aug. = *Augustus*
  31: 231
  Caes. = *Julius Caesar*
  56: 283n.8
  Cal. = *Caligula*
  15.2: 291n.40
  Claud. = *Claudius*
  9: 126–127
  Dom. = *Domitianus*
  10.3: 107
  13.3: 291n.40
  23: 101, 111
  Galba
  23: 127

INDEX LACORUM · 335

Nero
37: 101
Tib. = Tiberius
1: 104
25.3: 291n.41
61.2: 107
Gramm. = De grammaticis
24.2: 285n.53
Symm. = Symmachus
Ep. = Epistulae
Book 1
1: 142
24: 178, 205
46: 68, 70
47: 68
49: 69
51: 68
Book 2
13: 21, 23
18: 23
19: 262n.55
20: 23
22: 27, 262n.55
24: 262n.55, 264n.87
27: 18
30: 18
32: 22
33: 22
33A: 22
34: 67
36: 68
41: 22
42: 22
44: 18
53: 226
60: 27
61: 146
66: 22
75: 22
87: 22
88: 33
Book 3
6: 44
12: 14
69: 27
81: 262n.52
88: 14
90: 20, 21, 262n.52
Book 4
4: 28, 127, 128, 129, 290n.21

6: 28
7: 265n.90
14: 15
19: 28, 97, 221
39: 28
51: 28, 33, 97
71: 18, 77, 182
Book 5
6: 28, 127
47: 28, 97
Book 6
1–81: 33
10: 28
12: 28, 97
30: 28
35: 28
36: 28
40: 69
52: 28
56: 28
57: 18
59: 28
63: 28
66: 18
Book 7
18: 14
19: 14
47: 28
50: 28
93: 28, 127, 265n.90
95: 28
96: 28, 127
102: 28
104: 28, 127, 264n.90
Book 8
29: 28, 127
Book 9
13: 178, 205
47: 28
93: 15
104: 15
105: 15
106: 15
107: 15
147: 68, 187
148: 68, 187
Book 11
44: 18
Rel. = Relationes
3: 41, 42, 48, 176, 221

Tac. = Tacitus
  Agr. = Agricola
    1: 143, 153, 154, 164, 165, 168
    1–3: 154
    2: 115, 123, 154, 163–164, 168
    3: 154, 164–165
    6: 158
    22: 161
    40: 154
    41: 153
    42: 122, 154, 157, 166
    43: 154, 161
    44–46: 154
    45: 165–166
    46: xxii, 154, 165, 168
  Ann. = Annales
  Book 1
    1: 167, 216–217
    11: 157
    69: 157
    81: 159
  Book 2
    27–32: 291n.41
    32: 101, 104, 227, 277n.72
    36: 160
    76: 275n.36
  Book 3
    11–18: 94
    15: 157
    17: 104
    18: 102
    65: 164
    76: 101, 126
  Book 4
    18–20: 275n.37
    35: 111, 115, 123, 132, 156, 162–163
    38: 119
    62: 276n.58
    69: 158
    71: 158, 238
  Book 6
    1: 124–125
    7: 159
    10.1: 107
  Book 11
    38: 101, 157
  Book 14
    64: 161–162
  Book 15
    67: 160
  Book 16
    5: 157
    7: 101
  Hist. = Historiae
  Book 1
    1: 167
    49: 125
    78: 127
  Book 2
    50: 271n.115
    55: 127
  Book 3
    7: 127
  Book 4
    40: 126, 127
  Book 5: 144
Tertullian, *Apologeticus*
    12: 144
Theodoret, *HE* = *Historia ecclesiastica*
    5.17: 45
    5.24: 45, 72
Thucydides
    1.22: 132
    1.23: 132
    2.43: 119

Ulpian, *Dig.* = *Digest*
    3.2.11: 107
    48.24.1: 106–107

Varro, *De L.L.* = *De lingua latina*
    5.47: 228
Vell. = Velleius
    2.130.3: 277n.72
Venantius Fortunatus, *Carm.* = *Carmina*
    3.18.7–8: 236
    7.8.25–26: 236
Vit. S. Melaniae = *Vita Sanctae Melaniae*
    50–55: 57

Zosimus, *Hist. nova* = *Historia nova*
    4.54–55: 72
    4.59.3–4: 267n.16

II. INSCRIPTIONS

For full bibliographic citation of epigraphical works, see the List of Abbreviations.

AE = *L'Année épigraphique*
1902—244: 30, 253
1934—147: 26–30
1941—66: 44, 49

CIL = *Corpus Inscriptionum Latinarum*
Vol. 2
2633: 276n.58
Vol. 3
737: 279n.119
8472: 112
9832: 112
14147: 277n.84
Vol. 4
3340: 276n.58
Vol. 5
4919: 276n.58
Vol. 6
251: 276n.58
385: 275n.43, 276n.57
510: 65
1033: 108
1186: 292n.59
1599: 231
1683: 232
1699: 14, 66
1710: 233
1718: 265n.95
1724: 233
1729: 247
1730: 110
1731: 110
1777: 66
1779: 62, 75, 76–77, 270n.98
1780: 75, 78, 270n.98
1782: 13, 16, 17, 18, 20, 23, 24, 35, 66, 145
1783: line 1: 16–20; line 2: 20–23; lines 1–2: 220, 224; lines 1–6: 11–12, 6–36, 248; line 3: 224; line 4: 11, 19, 32, 90, 98, 108, 175, 252, 295n.17; lines 4–6: 26–32; line 5: 30–31, 32, 113, 252–253; lines 5–6: 223; lines 7–36: 248; line 9: 131; lines 9–10: 128, 221; lines 9–12: 139–145; line 10: 11, 90; lines 10–11: 12, 127, 140, 173–177, 223; line 11: 253–254; lines 11–12: 173–177; line 12: 223, 254–255; line 13: 225, 255; lines 13–14: 108; lines 13–15: 140; line 14: 104–105, 242, 255–256; lines 14–15: 37, 90, 115; line 15: 37, 221, 256; lines 16–17: 71, 225; line 17: 11, 115; lines 17–18: 98; line 18: 123, 221; lines 18–19: 221; line 19: 221, 225; lines 19–20: 145, 221, 234; lines 19–21: 221; line 20: 37, 224, 256–257; line 21: 37, 123, 220, 221; lines 22: 225; lines 22–24: 19, 175; lines 22–24: 225; line 24: 37; lines 25–26: 73, 115, 140, 150, 225; lines 26–27: 73, 116; lines 27–28: 225; line 28: 12, 90; line 28: 11; line 29: 116; lines 29–31: 12; lines 29–33: 32, 224, 253, 257–258, 295n.18; line 30: 33, 223, 257; line 31: 32, 73; line 31: 11; line 32: 37, 170, 257; lines 33–36: 140, 225; line 34: 140, 223; lines 34–35: 12, 98, 108, 140, 174, 295n.17; line 35: 90, 115, 225; line 36: 37; lines 37–38: 226, 248, 295n.17; left side: 248. *See also* General Index: *CIL* = *Corpus Inscriptionum Latinarum,* for specific attributes
1799: 68
2023: 276n.57
2158: 68
30751: 276n.57
31987: 110
Vol. 8
2554: 235
8481: 203, 233
Vol. 10
831: 235
1479: 264n.84
Vol. 15
7190: 236–7

Erim et al. = *Aphrodisias in Late Antiquity*
30: 279n.121

ICUR = *Inscriptiones Christianae Urbis Romae*
suppl.
1855: 24
n.s. vol. 2
4503: 24
6460: 24

n.s. vol. 3
    8648: 24
n.s. vol. 5
    13361: 24
    13364: 24
    13368: 24
n.s. vol. 7
    19975: 24
IGUR = Inscriptiones Graecae Urbis Romae
    63: 56–58, 292n.62
    ILCV = Inscriptiones Latinae Christianae
        Veteres
    1482: 24
    4321: 24
    3822: 24
ILS = Inscriptiones Latinae Selectae
    95: 275n.43, 276n.57
    425: 108
    802: 203, 233
    818: 220
    821: 279n.119
    1221: 232
    1254: 247
    1258: 66
    1259: 62, 68, 75, 76–77, 206–209, 270n.98
    1260: 75, 78, 270n.98
    1326: 231
    2945: 292n.59
    2946: 14, 66
    2947: 13, 16, 17, 18, 20, 23, 24, 35, 66, 145
    2948: 247
    2949: 233
    2950: 233
    4003: 41
    4152: 65
    4196: 264n.84
    4944: 68
    5026: 276n.57
    5522: 265n.95
    5619: 235
    5948: 112
    5949: 112
    6080: 276n.58
    6100: 276n.58
    6101: 276n.58
    8730: 236–237
    8985: 25
    8995: 277n.84
Inscr. Ital. = Inscriptiones Italiae
    24: 276n.58
IRT = The Inscriptions of Roman Tripolitania
    475: 15–18
    526: 262n.46
    562: 16

www.ingramcontent.com/pod-product-compliance
Lightning Source LLC
Chambersburg PA
CBHW020329240426
43665CB00043B/183